Special
Day
Sermons

Special Day Sermons

Outlines and Messages

Second Edition

Ronald Youngblood

BAKER BOOK HOUSE
Grand Rapids, Michigan 49516

ISBN: 0-8010-9924-2

Printed in the United States of America

Contents

Foreword

"Not another book of sermons," I mused, as my friend and colleague Ronald Youngblood told me of his plans to publish. My experience as pastor and as teacher of preaching in three different seminaries has taught me that the quantity of such volumes is great but that the quality is frequently mediocre. Quite frankly, I hated to see a friend join that host of homiletic bores. Too many preachers have yielded to the kindly pressures of a few well-meaning laymen to "publish those sermons."

To my personal delight, Professor Youngblood had something worth saying and hence worth sharing. Helpful sermons related to holidays are not plentiful. These, however, are thought-provoking exemplars of the preaching art as it is applied to specific highlights of the church calendar. And it isn't "God alone who knows" that there is need for new thoughts on a few of these. It is refreshing, for example, to see a Mother's Day sermon on Mary, the mother of Jesus; we've all had our fill of Hannah, Lois, and Eunice. And when was the last time you heard or read a well-reasoned sermon on the separation of church and state? The sermon on love is a particular favorite of mine.

By my standards, an excellent sermon must meet three criteria: It must be biblical, interesting, and present tense. These sermons genuinely qualify!

I commend this volume to you, both as a devotional

treat and as homiletic examples. May your spirit be rejuvenated and your life be challenged, as mine were.

J. Daniel Baumann

Preface

Although the times may seem out of joint, I want to dedicate this series of sermons for special occasions to the proposition that joy and optimism should be the Christian's stock in trade. If we who profess Christ aren't happy, how can others possibly be?

The book consists of eleven messages, one for each of certain days of special significance in the church calendar. Because the church year begins in September, the series starts with Labor Day and ends with the Fourth of July. I have preached each of the sermons at one time or other, and their style may therefore reveal that they are intended to be heard as well as read. It has not always been possible for me to recall the source of a particular statement or illustration, but I have tried to be faithful to my predecessors by giving them credit when I could.

Nancy Baumann, my secretary, prepared the typescript for this revised edition, and I wish to express my gratitude to her for her unfailing patience and good humor throughout. Special thanks go to her husband, J. Daniel Baumann, my former colleague (Associate Professor of Pastoral Ministries, Bethel Theological Seminary, St. Paul, Minnesota) and pastor (Senior Minister, College Avenue Baptist Church, San Diego, California). He read the original manuscript in its entirety and offered many helpful suggestions that I received gladly and gratefully.

The writing of this book thus became a learning experience for me, and it's in that spirit that I'm delighted to be able to share it with you.

1

The Hands of Jesus

Labor Day

"We are God's fellow workers . . ." (1 Cor. 3:9).

Outline

Introduction

    I. Hands Reveal Divine Craftsmanship and Human Character

        A. Housewife

        B. Office Worker

        C. Pianist

Body

    II. Jesus' Hands Reveal His Character

        A. Helping Hands

            1. Lifting a disciple from Galilee's waters

            2. Leading a blind man from Bethsaida's distractions

            3. Exorcising a spirit from a demon-possessed boy

            4. Teaching us to help

        B. Healing Hands

            1. Cleansing a leper

            2. Driving out a fever

            3. Teaching us to heal

        C. Holy Hands

            1. Dying for our sins

            2. Teaching us to be holy

Conclusion

I. Hands Reveal Divine Craftsmanship and Human Character

Labor Day—in spite of its sinister name—is a lazy holiday for most people. The harried mother, with a long, deep sigh of relief, can relax in the knowledge that her bored kids will be back in school the following morning or soon after. Dad can sleep till noon, play thirty-six holes, or otherwise while away the hours.

By contrast, in many of America's congregations the Labor Day weekend hums with activity, signaling the approach of the new church year. And maybe this is only as it should be, since at the beginning of each new church year we emphasize again the need to roll up our sleeves and go to work for Christ. The fishing season is all but over, the summer's vacation is a thing of the past, and the tasks of autumn beckon us.

The symbols of Labor Day, on which we celebrate the virtues of honest toil, are the powerful, muscular arm and the strong, dexterous hand of the working man. In particular, the hand is an awe-inspiring example of God's creative craftsmanship, and it can be trained to do an infinite variety of tasks. Experts tell us that to create a mechanical hand capable of throwing an uncooked egg into the air to random heights and catching it at random positions and speeds would require a commitment of time, energy and money surpassing that of the Manhat-

tan Project that produced the first atomic bomb—and yet
the human hand routinely performs far more difficult
feats.

But the hand is also one of the most telltale features of
a person's appearance. A man's hands often reflect his
thoughts or words. When public speakers want to drive a
point home, their hands will alternately jab and thrust,
stab and sweep. But when a counselor wishes to calm a
distraught client, he may fold his hands on his lap or rest
them under his chin.

A. Housewife

Indeed, a casual glance at the hands of a man or woman
can reveal something about his or her character or liveli-
hood. For example, every housewife knows what the
phrase "dishpan hands" means. It refers to the red,
rough, chapped condition of hands that spend too much
time in soapy water used when washing dishes or scrub-
bing floors. Certain well-advertised detergents and liquids
and lotions extravagantly claim to be able to relieve this
unsightly condition, of course. But many housewives
have learned not only to view such claims with a
jaundiced eye but also to accept them with a grain of salt.
In any event, a stubborn case of dishpan hands is nothing
to be ashamed of. It's simply one of the occupational
hazards of being a housewife and one of the signs by
which she can be easily identified.

B. Office Worker

Now we should immediately warn the businesswoman
or career girl that she has no cause for smugness at this
point. She will discover, if she looks closely enough, that
a callus is slowly developing on the middle finger of her

writing hand. It will become larger and harder and uglier through the years. But, like dishpan hands, it should be no cause for embarrassment. Everyone will recognize it as the badge of the writer, the office worker, the teacher. It's one of the occupational hazards of being a pencil pusher, no more to be singled out for special mention than the permanently tattooed grease marks in the palms of the automobile mechanic or the suntanned, wind-roughened hands of the outdoorsman.

C. Pianist

As a boy in Chicago I used to sit in a music-hall audience enthralled and fascinated while watching one of my favorite pianists perform. His skill and his size were equally prodigious. His name was Baker, and he was just about as wide as he was tall. "Two-Ton Baker, the Music Maker," we called him. But in spite of the enormous bulk of the rest of his body, his fingers were long and slim and strong because of years of diligent practice on the piano. Anyone could tell, simply by looking at his hands, that he was a fine pianist.

II. Jesus' Hands Reveal His Character

It's quite evident, then, that our hands disclose something about ourselves. Let's turn to a passage from the New Testament that sheds some light on this fact. It refers to the day of Jesus' resurrection:

On the evening of that first day of the week, when the disciples were together, with the doors locked for fear of the Jews, Jesus came and stood among them and said, "Peace be with you!" After he said this, he showed them

his hands and side. The disciples were overjoyed when
they saw the Lord. Again Jesus said, ''Peace be with you!
As the Father has sent me, I am sending you'' (John
20:19-21).

From these three verses I want to glean two thoughts.
One concerns something that Jesus said, the other something that he did. What Jesus spoke was this: ''As the
Father has sent me, I am sending you.'' And what Jesus
did was this: ''He showed them his hands.''

A. *Helping Hands*

What do you think the disciples saw when they looked
at the hands of Jesus? What did his hands reveal to them
about his personality, about his character? There they
were—ten disciples and their Lord on that first Easter
Sunday evening. They had walked with him, they had
talked with him, they had been with him for something
more than three years by that time. They had enjoyed
many opportunities to observe him in many different
contexts. What did they see in his hands?

1. Lifting a disciple from Galilee's waters. Maybe
Peter remembered the time when he had seen Christ
walking on the sea. It was shortly after the feeding of the
five thousand, and Jesus had sent his disciples on ahead of
him, across the Sea of Galilee, so that he could spend
some time alone in prayer. A storm arose on the lake, and
the disciples might have become afraid that the high
waves, fulminating masses of foam, would swamp their
little boat. Jesus, aware of their plight, walked on the
water toward them. But far from calming their fears, the
sight of him scared them half to death because they
thought he was a ghost. Although he called out to them
and assured them that he was indeed Jesus himself, Peter

was not convinced. He shouted, "Lord, if it's you, tell me to come to you on the water." Jesus shouted back, "Come on ahead!" So Peter stepped from the boat and, no doubt to his amazement, began walking across the surface of the waves toward Jesus. But before long the novelty of what he was doing wore off, and his attention was drawn to the whistling wind and the wall of waves. He took his eyes off Jesus, his courage failed him, and he began to sink. At that point in the story Matthew 14:31 tells us that "immediately Jesus reached out his hand and caught him," conducting him back to the safety of the boat.

Peter may very well have thought about that incident as he looked at the hands of Jesus.

2. Leading a blind man from Bethsaida's distractions. Or possibly the disciples remembered the occasion when a blind man approached Jesus in the village of Bethsaida and begged him to touch his eyes. Mark 8:23 tells us that Jesus "took the blind man by the hand and led him outside the village," there to perform a marvelous cure that restored his vision to him.

3. Exorcising a spirit from a demon-possessed boy. Or maybe the disciples recalled the miraculous event that took place right after Jesus' transfiguration. Coming down from the mountain with three of his disciples, he learned that the others had been unable to cast out an evil spirit from a demon-possessed boy. Jesus commanded the spirit to leave. It did so, but not before convulsing the boy and leaving him apparently lifeless. Then, as Mark 9:27 tells us, "Jesus took him by the hand and lifted him to his feet" and restored him to his father alive and well.

Clearly there was strength and tenderness in his touch—and his disciples loved him the more, because the hands of Jesus were *helping hands.*

"As the Father has sent me," said our Lord, "I am sending you"; and "he showed them his hands." And why had the Father sent the Son? Let's let Jesus tells us in his own words: "For even the Son of Man did not come to be served, but to serve" (Mark 10:45).

4. Teaching us to help.   Do *you* have helping hands? People all around you—people everywhere—need your help. The stores where you make your purchases, the shops and offices where you make your living, the schools where you study, the houses where you live—all are full of people who desperately need your help. And the help I'm talking about at the moment is not spiritual but physical. You and I are called upon to serve people in physical as well as spiritual ways. As Billy Graham has reminded us, we have to learn to offer people the Bible with one hand and a cup of cold water with the other. And we must learn not to be offended if they reach for the cup first, even if the cup is *all* they want. Christian love is unconditional and always gives itself with no strings attached. Someone has observed that we don't necessarily love in order to win; we love because we've been won. If people want the water but not the Word, we have a right to feel disappointed or even distressed; but we don't have the right to feel offended. Nor should such a response prevent us from offering water a second time. An offer of mercy, given in Jesus' name, is a valid ministry in and of itself.

Some years ago a little girl was left motherless at the age of eight. There were younger children in the family, and taking care of them became the girl's major task. While the father worked long hours to support his family, she cooked meals and scrubbed floors and mended clothes and wiped tears out of little eyes and did all of the other things that the mother had done before her death. For five long years she worked from early morning till late at night. Finally the back-breaking labor took its toll, and she became seriously ill.

A neighbor, visiting the young girl's sickroom one day, found her crying. ''What's the matter, dear?'' she asked. ''I think I'm going to die, and I'm so ashamed!'' ''Why in the world should you be ashamed?'' ''Since Mother left us,'' the girl replied, ''I haven't had time to do anything for Jesus. When I get to heaven, what can I tell him?''

Taking the girl's hands in hers, and looking at the scars and calluses, the neighbor said, ''Honey, I don't think you'll have to tell Jesus anything. Just show him your hands.''

Whenever I think of that little girl, barely in her teens, who gave everything she had in service to others, I look at my hands and ask myself the question, ''Would you be proud—or even able—to show your hands to Jesus Christ?'' Why do our hands so often dangle uselessly at our sides, reluctant to get involved in human needs and problems? Maybe we should consider again that striking gesture of Jesus when, meeting with his disciples on that first Easter Sunday evening, ''he showed them his hands.''

B. Healing Hands

But what else do you think those ten disciples saw when they looked at the hands of Jesus? What other events did the appearance of his hands recall?

1. Cleansing a leper.   I wonder if they remembered the sequel to the Sermon on the Mount, the occasion when a leper came to him and pleaded, ''Lord, if you are willing, you can make me clean.'' Jesus, willing as always, ''reached out his hand,'' Matthew 8:3 tells us, "and touched the man. 'I am willing,' he said"—and immediately the man's leprosy was cleansed.

Incredible! Jesus Christ, healthy and strong, touching a leper, hopelessly sick! Our Lord actually and physically touched the skin of a man who was required by the laws of his day to keep other people at more than arm's length, to avoid contact with nonleprous people and their possessions, to cry out as he walked through the streets and along the roadsides, "Unclean! Unclean!" But Jesus had compassion, and cared enough to touch, and touched in order to cleanse.

2. Driving out a fever. Possibly the disciples also thought of the visit Jesus made to Peter's house in Capernaum a short time later. When he found Peter's mother-in-law bedridden because of a fever "he touched her hand, and the fever left her, and she got up and began to wait on him" (Matt. 8:15).

Taking care of the needs of the sick constituted a significant aspect of Jesus' ministry. The Gospels tell us that he engaged in such activity everywhere he went. Obviously there was power and health and well-being in his touch—and his disciples loved him the more, because the hands of Jesus were *healing hands.*

"As the Father has sent me," said our Lord, "I am sending you"; and "he showed them his hands." And why had the Father sent the Son? Once again, let's let Jesus tell us in his own words: "He hath sent me to heal the brokenhearted" (Luke 4:18 KJV).

3. Teaching us to heal. Do *you* have healing hands? Perhaps at this point you rebel and say, "No, as a matter of fact I don't have healing hands. I'm not a doctor. I don't have an M.D. after my name. If I tried to remove a person's appendix, the poor fellow would be far worse off after the operation than before it. In fact he'd probably die. No, I don't have healing hands." And of course you'd be perfectly right; most of us don't have healing hands in that technical sense.

But in a spiritual sense every Christian should have healing hands, because people all around us—people everywhere—are sick in mind and heart and soul. You and I can be instrumental in the healing of such people. A gentle hand on a fevered brow, a kind and thoughtful word, a genuine interest in a person's needs—all are qualities that can do a great deal to improve mental and spiritual health. And where a physical malady is functional rather than organic, such qualities can be of significant help in these cases as well.

Some time ago the late Archbishop Mowll, primate of Australia, preached during a Sunday morning chapel service at a leper colony in southeastern Uganda. At the close of the service he stood at the only door to greet all the worshipers. Ignoring the warnings of the doctors, he took each leper, by the hand— whether whole or loosely bandaged or partially eaten away—and asked God's blessing on him.

No leper there today remembers his sermon or recalls his text. But no leper who was in that service will ever forget that an elderly Australian clergyman took hold of his diseased hand and asked God to bless him.

Whenever I think of that archbishop—a man who was willing to take chances in order to encourage others—I look at my hands and ask myself the question, "How would you have used your hands in such a situation?" Perhaps all of us need to consider again the scene in the Garden of Gethsemane where sleepy-eyed, impulsive Peter, doing his best to defend Christ, "reached for his sword, drew it out and struck the servant of the high priest, cutting off his ear'' (Matt. 26:51). (It's a good thing his aim was bad, because he probably intended to split the man in two lengthwise!) But our Lord, after rebuking Peter, ''touched the man's ear and healed him'' (Luke 22:51). What a contrast between the destructive act of the disciple and the healing touch of the Savior!

C. Holy Hands

But what else do you think Jesus' disciples saw when they looked at his hands? There they were—ten men and their Master—together in the house on that first Easter Sunday evening. Of course they couldn't fail to see the nailprints in his hands. They must have thought back to the horrors of Friday, when cruel hands had nailed his hands to a cross. The enemies of Jesus had succeeded in killing him, even if only for a little while. And yet we recall that earlier in his ministry our Lord had set his face steadfastly toward Jerusalem, knowing that there he would die for our sins. He had dedicated his hands to a solemn purpose, and his Father had consecrated those hands to that same solemn purpose. When God bared his arms for our salvation, there was a nail-pierced hand at the end of each arm.

1. Dying for our sins. It is in this, then, that we find the distinguishing characteristic of the hands of Jesus: They were separated to the specific task of saving all people everywhere—of saving you and me—from the power and penalty of sin. Unmistakably there was, and there still is, and there always will be grace and love and mercy in his touch—and his disciples loved him the more, because the hands of Jesus were *holy hands.*

''As the Father has sent me,'' said our Lord, ''I am sending you''; and ''he showed them his hands.'' And why had the Father sent the Son? Once again, and finally, let's let Jesus tell us in his own words: "The Son of Man came to seek and to save what was lost" (Luke 19:10). The apostle John adds a wonderful commentary to this thought when he reminds us that "the Father has sent his Son to be the Savior of the world" (1 John 4:14).

2. *Teaching us to be holy.*   Do *you* have holy hands? Perhaps at this point you rebel once again, and you say, "No, as a matter of fact, I don't have holy hands. I can't save anyone. Only God through Christ can do that." And of course you're perfectly right; none of us has holy hands in that sense.

But, in another sense, every Christian should have holy hands, because people all around us—people everywhere—need more than anything else the touch of God and of grace in their lives. Can we supply that need? Are our hands holy enough, consecrated enough to pray for people and their spiritual needs? Are we able to obey the implied command of 1 Timothy 2:8, which tells us to "lift up holy hands" in prayer? Or do our hands fall into the category of those that Jesus commands to be cut off, because they cause us to sin (Matt. 5:30)? Only as we have pure hands will we have consecrated hands; and only then will our present indifference to the spiritual welfare of unbelieving men and women and boys and girls change to a definite interest, a growing concern, a glowing passion.

III. Our Hands Should Reveal Jesus' Character

A. *Helping Hands, Healing Hands, Holy Hands*

All of us need to consider again that striking gesture of Jesus when, meeting with ten of his disciples on that first

Easter Sunday evening, he said to them, "As the Father has sent me, I am sending you"; and "he showed them his hands"—hands that were *helping,* and *healing,* and *holy.*

B. "I Have No Hands But Yours"

During the closing months of World War II a group of American soldiers set about to rebuild a partially destroyed cathedral in one of the bombed-out towns of southern Europe. They began their task with a generous amount of zeal and zest, and in short order they were able to reconstruct the walls and roof, restore the stained-glass windows, and replace the pews. One soldier had been assigned the job of repairing, as best he could, a life-sized white marble statue of Christ that had stood at the front of the church. Not being able to find the hands of the figure in the rubble, he was about to admit failure and throw the statue on the rubbish heap outside. Then he was struck by a flash of inspiration. He found a white rectangle of cardboard, tied the ends of a length of string to two corners of the rectangle, and hung the cardboard around the neck of the statue. Then he tenderly set the statue in its honored place at the front of the cathedral. On the cardboard he wrote these words: "I HAVE NO HANDS BUT YOURS."

One final question during this Labor Day weekend: Does Jesus Christ have *your* hands?

2

Now Thank We All Our God

Thanksgiving Day

"Give thanks in all circumstances" (1 Thess. 5:18).

Outline

Introduction

    I. The Writer of the Hymn

       A. His Life

       B. His Suffering

Body

    II. The Outline of the Hymn

       A. "Voices": A Flow of Spoken Praise

          1. Singing and praying in public

          2. Illustrations from Scripture

          3. Such thanksgiving is prudent

          4. Transition: Actions speak louder than words

       B. "Hands": A Series of Grateful Actions

          1. Giving and offering

          2. Such thanksgiving is urgent

          3. Illustrations from Scripture

       C. "Heart": A Way of Life

          1. Intending and living

          2. Such thanksgiving is indispensable

Conclusion

III. The Meaning of the Hymn

    A. (Illustration) "Let's Give It Because He Was Spared"

    B. (Summary) Thanksgiving Is Word, Action, Attitude

    C. (Application) Give Thanks in All Circumstances

My Uncle Les was crippled by polio when he was only four years old. From that time until his death over fifty years later, he didn't know what it meant to experience a single day without pain and inconvenience. Leg braces rubbing against his skin often kept open sores from healing properly. Through sheer courage and determination he learned to walk without the use of crutches, but every step was torture.

No one, except his closest friends, knew that Les was in pain much of the time. Always cheerful and happy, he could often be heard humming or whistling a tune in step with his limping gait. One day when I was feeling sorry for myself because of an itchy skin rash that I was nursing, Les hobbled over to offer a little encouragement. After joking with me for a few minutes about my ailment, he said to me with a twinkle in his eye, "Ron, I guess you'd better learn to live with your problem." Coming from him, such advice was worth its weight in gold. My Uncle Les had learned to smile through suffering, and I for one will never forget him.

I. The Writer of the Hymn

I'm sure I'll also long remember a few facts from the experiences of one of my uncle's spiritual predecessors, a man who lived over three hundred years ago. He name was Martin Rinkart.

A. His Life

The son of a poor coppersmith, Martin Rinkart was able somehow to work his way through college. At the age of thirty-one he was offered the position of archdeacon in his native town in Germany. A year later, in 1618, the cruel Thirty Years' War broke out in Europe, and Rinkart died one year after the war ended. His official career in the service of Christ thus coincided closely with the duration of the war itself.

B. His Suffering

The plague of 1637 visited his hometown with great severity, and the plague was followed by a terrible famine. These misfortunes naturally made Rinkart's labors very difficult, and his sacrifices for the Savior's cause affected him and his children pathetically. Like my Uncle Les, Martin Rinkart had learned to smile through suffering. Out of his calamities he breathed an unbounded spirit of faith in God and of readiness to give thanks. He is best known as the composer of the words of one of the greatest of all German hymns, translated into English by Catherine Winkworth more than a century ago:

> Now thank we all our God
>   With heart and hands and voices,
> Who wondrous things hath done,
>   In whom his world rejoices.

This was quite a testimony for a man to write, a man whose career coincided with one of the most ravaging wars in history up to his time. "Now thank we all our God . . . who wondrous things hath done"? "Wondrous things"? What is so wondrous about a war, we might ask. But of course Martin Rinkart knew that God was not the perpetrator of that war. He knew that wars are the results of uncontrolled passions and desires in the hearts of people, as his New Testament taught him (James 4:1-2). No, he was praising God for wondrous things that God himself had wrought—for common and spiritual graces that he saw clearly through the suffering and heartache of his work around his parish.

"Now thank we all our God . . . in whom his world rejoices"? How, we might ask, could a man be so deluded as to think that the world of his day—some of whose most civilized nations were engulfed in war—had any time for rejoicing in God? But of course Martin Rinkart knew that though there would be wars and rumors of wars until the consummation of the age, God's hand was nevertheless ruling over history. He knew also that throughout history there would be people in every sector of the planet rejoicing in the goodness of God who in everything "works for the good of those who love him, who have been called according to his purpose" (Rom. 8:28).

II. The Outline of the Hymn

It would appear, then, that this devout deacon, Martin Rinkart, had learned the real meaning of thanksgiving, for the spiritual benefit of his own heart and life as well as for the sanctifying benediction of others who experiences he touched. And in his beautiful hymn he has left for us a crisp outline of what thanksgiving meant to him.

A. "Voices": A Flow of Spoken Praise

1. Singing and praying in public. "Now thank we all our God with . . . voices." Thanksgiving as a flow of spoken praise is one facet of gratitude with which we're all familiar. Every time we sing a hymn of praise we audibly utter our thanks to God for his many blessings. Every time we pray in public, every time we say grace aloud before eating a meal, every time we share in worship around the family altars in our homes, we offer thanksgiving with our voices. The spoken word is without a doubt the most common method of giving thanks.

2. *Illustrations from Scripture.*   This should not surprise us, because the Bible itself overwhelmingly connects thanksgiving with the oral expression of gratitude to God. Of the dozens of references to thanks and thanksgiving in the Bible, the great majority have this speaking or singing aspect in mind. The psalmists urged the people of Israel for several centuries before Christ to thank the Lord for his goodness and to praise him for his gracious love. And, as we might expect, Jesus himself commends such thanksgiving—when it is sincere! In one case, for example, Jesus had healed ten lepers and told them to report the healing to the priests. One of them, a Samaritan, "when he saw he was healed, came back, praising God in a loud voice. He threw himself at Jesus' feet and thanked him. . . . Then [Jesus] said to him, 'Rise and go; your faith has made you well'" (Luke 17:15-19).

3. *Such thanksgiving is prudent.*   We know of course, on principles of common sense alone, that such thanksgiving, expressed with words of love to our Lord, is an important part of our spiritual worship. As they must, our prayers consist mainly of what we call supplications or, to put it more crudely, "gimmies." We're all human beings, creatures of dust, and consequently our lives are filled with needs of every description. We realize that only our God can fill many of those needs directly, not to mention

the fact that he fills *all* of them indirectly. There is no characteristic more hateful and despicable than that of ungratefulness. And so, if for no other reason than to avoid cutting off our source of supply through sheer ingratitude, we thank God consistently and forcefully for his past goodness to us, hoping to persuade him to continue his bounty. We thank him so he'll continue to be good to us in the future. We don't want him to plug up the pipes or turn off the tap.

Make no mistake about it: This is not a praiseworthy motive for offering thanks to God in prayer. But it is, after all, a very human motive; and since we're all human we all participate in it—consciously, subconsciously, unconsciously—at least to a small degree. God forbid that this should ever be our whole or only motive for thanking him, but we can never discount it completely.

On the other hand, there's a much brighter side to the picture. We Christians are humans, to be sure, but by God's grace we're a special breed of humans. As 2 Peter 1:4 reminds us, we "participate in the divine nature" because of the Holy Spirit who lives in our hearts. This divine guest infuses us with loftier motives as we offer our audible thanks to God. We learn through his help to try to thank God because of pure gratitude, to adore him for what he is in us and to us and through us, to worship him in spirit and truth.

Therefore, as Christians we live in two different worlds. Since we're not yet completely sanctified, our motives are always less than completely pure, however little that "less" may be. But as we do our best daily to imitate Christ, and as we conform ourselves slowly—almost imperceptibly—to his image, we'll learn to precede our supplications with thanksgiving that is ever more pure in attitude. The reason? Because we'll precede our thanksgiving with humble confession of sin to pave the way for deeper communion with our Lord.

4. Transition: Actions speak louder than words. Maybe now we're ready to examine Martin Rinkart's concept of thanksgiving a bit further. As a faithful worker in Christ's church, he was acquainted in the most intimate way with the fact that thanksgiving is expressed by word of mouth. But we can be sure that he would have insisted also that actions speak louder than words, that talk as such is cheap, and that we need to practice what we preach. He knew that it's one thing to thank, or pray, or love "with words or tongue," but that it's an entirely different matter to thank, or pray, or love "with actions and in truth" (1 John 3:18). To use a rather crass expression of our own time, Rinkart would have been the first to put his money where his mouth was, because thanksgiving for him was not only a flow of spoken praise. He made that quite clear in the words of his hymn, so let's hear him out.

B. "Hands": A Series of Grateful Actions

"Now thank we all our God with . . . hands." Thanksgiving as a series of grateful actions is only slightly less familiar to us than our vocal expressions of praise.

1. Giving and offering. Every time we give our money toward the current expenses of the local church or to the building fund offering or to any one of the other worthy causes that come to our attention, we offer thanksgiving with our hands. Because we are grateful to God for what he has done for us, we hasten to share our blessings with others.

2. Such thanksgiving is urgent.   Pogo the possum lives with his friends in a swamp deep in the Florida Everglades. It seems that one day Bun Rabbit decided that the year had too many holidays in it, so he set out on a one-man crusade to squeeze every holiday into one corner of the year and get them all out of the way at once. Beating loudly on his drum, he marched from place to place and from hollow tree to hollow tree, trying to gain supporters for his cause. Needless to say, he failed in his attempt.

That's rather like the way things are with local church appeals for money. We know that we can't legislate our needs into one big pile and get them all out of the way at once any more than Bun Rabbit could group all the holidays together. New needs keep cropping up all the time because the world, by virtue of its basically sinful nature, is a very needy place. As Christians we should always be prepared to give financially to the work of churches and other missions. We should also be ready to lend a helping hand to one who is faltering, a healing hand to one who is sick, a holy hand to one who is spiritually destitute. If we don't express our thanksgiving to God with hands that minister to the needs of others, who will?

Consider the Muslim who went to a dispensary for help after breaking his ankle. When asked if his friends would help him pay for the medical attention necessary for the proper setting of the broken bones, he replied, ''No, sir, we are not like the Christians. We must all pay for our own troubles. We have no one to help us in our difficulties.'' The experience of that Muslim—and I hope it's not unique—had been that Christians were not self-seeking but self-denying. They were willing to help others as best they could. Would each of us find his place in such a group of self-effacing Christians? And would our gifts to others be given not out of a sense of duty or obligation but out of gratitude to our Lord, realizing that but for the grace of God there we would be?

3. *Illustrations from Scripture.*   The Old Testament is not without indications that the people of Israel knew what it meant to thank God with their hands. Mentioned among the many types of sacrifice that they offered up to God are "thank offerings," "fellowship offerings of thanksgiving," and the like. May God help us to take our place beside the saints of every age, offering sacrifices of thanksgiving to the God who has redeemed us and whose will is "good, pleasing, and perfect" (Rom. 12:2)!

C. "Heart": A Way of Life

1. *Intending and living.*   But there is yet another phrase in the hymn that Rinkart wrote that reveals something of the great depths his spiritual understanding plumbed. He knew that thanksgiving consisted not only in a flow of spoken praise and a series of grateful actions; and so it was that he sang, most significantly, "Now thank we all our God with heart. . . ."

2. *Such thanksgiving is indispensable.*   "Now thank we all our God with heart. . . ." For Martin Rinkart, thanksgiving was a way of life. This is an aspect of gratitude that we rarely think about. In fact, it's difficult even to discuss it without waxing philosophical. But this we can say for certain: Thanksgiving is an attitude as well as a word and an action. The very life of the Christian should be a perpetual thanksgiving, a continuous testimony, a never-ending witness to the grace and glory of God.

III. The Meaning of the Hymn

A. *"Let's Give It Because He Was Spared"*

The parents of a young soldier killed in action gave their church a gift of money as a memorial for their son. During the presentation service, the mother of another soldier overseas whispered to her husband, "Let's give the same amount for our son." "What's the matter with you?" he asked. "Our boy hasn't died in battle." "That's just it," the mother replied. "Let's give it because he was spared." In giving that reply she showed that she was sensitive to the truth that thanksgiving is a way of life.

B. *Thanksgiving Is Word, Action, Attitude*

Every generation thinks it's standing on the brink of chaos. Perhaps we who live in an age of multiple independently targetable re-entry vehicles and space defense initiatives and unthinkably horrible weapons capable of mutually assured destruction have more cause for alarm than any preceding generation. But we can be sure that times seemed just as much out of joint—or even more so if that's possible—to Martin Rinkart as he mused on the evils of his day. Yet existence for him provided an opportunity for perpetual thanksgiving in a flow of spoken praise, in a continual series of grateful social actions, and in his heart-life itself. On this Thanksgiving Day, you and I can face our perilous futures with that same calm, confident commitment to Christ.

C. *Give Thanks in All Circumstances*

"Thanks be to God, who always leads us in triumphal procession in Christ and through us spreads everywhere the fragrance of the knowledge of him" (2 Cor. 2:14).

Now thank we all our God
　With heart and hands and voices,
Who wondrous things hath done,
　In whom his world rejoices;
Who, from our mothers' arms,
　Hath blessed us on our way
With countless gifts of love,
　And still is ours today.

All praise and thanks to God
　The Father now be given,
The Son, and him who reigns
　With them in highest heaven,
The one eternal God,
　Whom earth and heaven adore;
For thus it was, is now,
　And shall be evermore.

"Be joyful always; pray continually; give thanks in all circumstances, for this is God's will for you in Christ Jesus" (1 Thess. 5:16-18).

3

Stairways to the Stars

Christmas Eve

"Part your heavens, O LORD, and come down" (Ps. 144:5).

Outline

Introduction

    I. Two Vast Scientific Projects

        A. Attempting to Visit Other Worlds

            1. Unmanned probes

            2. Manned spaceships

            3. Questions

        B. Searching for Life on Other Planets

            1. Statistics

            2. Radio telescopes

            3. Questions

Body

    II. Three Biblical Sites

        A. Babel

            1. Ziggurats and their names

            2. Egotism and pride

            3. "Gateway to God"—but a symbol of confusion

        B. Bethel

            1. Jacob and his uneasiness

            2. Deceit and promise

            3. "House of God"—and a symbol of communion

C. Bethlehem

    1. Magi and the star

    2. Guidance and fulfillment

    3. Nathanael's King—and the stairway between God and man

Conclusion

III. Finding a Stairway to the Stars

    A. (Illustration) Looking Beyond Human, Scientific Accomplishments

    B. (Summary) Comparing Three Stairways

I. Two Vast Scientific Projects

"That's one small step for a man, one giant leap for mankind."

While saying those memorable words, astronaut Neil Armstrong firmly pressed his size $9\frac{1}{2}$ boot into the Sea of Tranquility on the moon's surface on Sunday evening, July 20, 1969.

A. Attempting to Visit Other Worlds

The plans of a decade and the dreams of centuries finally found fulfillment as the first serious attempt of earthlings to stride forth into space met with astonishing success.

1. Unmanned probes. The epic flight of Apollo 11 marked a crucial phase in one of two encompassing scientific projects that are of special significance to all Christians everywhere. One is our government's program to explore the planets and planetoids of our solar system through the use of manned and unmanned spacecraft. The Apollo series was preceded by the Ranger lunar probes, those camera-laden rockets that snapped photos from as close as a thousand feet away. The end result of the Ranger series was to prove that the surface of the moon was safe for a manned landing.

But our scientists wanted to be as sure as possible before committing an astronaut to a spaceship bound for the moon, so they launched a series of unmanned vehicles known as Surveyors to attempt "soft" landings there. The Surveyor experiments were successful and confirmed the opinion that the surface of the moon was relatively hard.

2. *Manned spaceships.* The aborted flight of Apollo 13 caused only minor delays in the program of moon exploration. The Apollo series was soon completed, and the Mariner series of Mars probes had already begun.

3. *Questions.* What should such plans for strolling from satellite to satellite mean to the Christian? Even the wildest visionaries doubted that we would find life on the moon—and they were right. Mariners 6 through 9 seemed to show that Mars was inhospitable to presently-known life forms, but we had to await the results of the first Viking soft-landing probe on July 4, 1976, before we thought we could definitely rule out the possibility of life there. Some American and Russian scientists, however, have still not abandoned hope of finding signs of life deep under the Martian surface.

At any rate, will lunar travel prove to have been the first step to interplanetary travel and eventually to interstellar travel? Will the Soviet desire to send a joint U.S.-Soviet manned mission to Mars by the year 2010 be fulfilled? If not the moon or Mars, will Venus or one of the other planets in our solar system be found to harbor life in some form? These and many other similar questions immediately come to mind, but they are of the kind that only the future can answer.

B. Searching for Life on Other Planets

The second of the two scientific projects of special significance to Christians everywhere has to do with the search for life on planets outside our solar system.

1. Statistics. Scientists tell us that our present telescopes reveal the existence of at least 100 trillion trillion stars in the universe—100 trillion trillion—that's 1 with 26 zeros after it! And conservative estimates of the possible number of planets with atmospheric and other conditions necessary for life or compatible to life hover around 100 million!

2. Radio telescopes. Dedicated researchers are now "listening in" on the universe by means of radio telescopes, colossal pieces of electronic equipment with mammoth dish-shaped antennae. Scientists involved in such projects in places like Green Bank, West Virginia, and Arecibo, Puerto Rico, confidently expect to hear radio signals being beamed from inhabited planets other than our own. They hope to discover at least one new civilization every thirty years, once a careful search has begun.

3. Questions. If we find life on other planets, of what sort will it be? Will it consist of a lower order than human life, or will it be of a higher order? Will the creatures be sinful and in need of redemption, or will they be beyond the pale of Adam's fall? Will God have related himself to them in a covenant bond, or will they be outside his reconciling plans for the universe? These and many other similar questions immediately come to mind, but again they are of the kind that only the future can answer. In any event, however, whatever we may think of programs to travel among the planets, or whatever we may think of researchers who try to eavesdrop on unbelievably remote civilizations, such scientific projects are certainly clear indications that modern men are attempting to construct stairways to the stars.

II. Three Biblical Sites

No less certainly, the Bible also has something to say about staircases with a stellar orientation.

A. Babel

Come with me first of all to the dim and distant past, to the city of Babel in Mesopotamia. Genesis 11:1-9 records a story told about a tower that was built at Babel very early in history.

1. Ziggurats and their names. The land of Mesopotamia was known far and wide in ancient times for the great number of magnificent towers that were constructed there. The towers, of a special kind and known as *ziggurats*, were erected in a peculiar and distinctive stepped form. The purpose of each ziggurat was essentially religious with minor political overtones. At the top of the tower the builders ordinarily set up a small shrine, sometimes painted with blue enamel to blend in with the color of their god's celestial home. They believed that their deity would reside temporarily in the shrine as he came down from his heavenly dwelling to meet with his people. And so it was that the worshiper would climb the stairway of the ziggurat, walking up the face of the tower that was conveniently sloped toward the top. He hoped that the result would be communion and fellowship with the god who had condescended to meet him in the little chapel.

Genesis 11:4 refers to its ziggurat as a "tower that reaches to the heavens." Other Mesopotamian towers were called by similar names and given similar descriptions, indicating that they were supposed to be staircases from earth to heaven. The one at Larsa was called the "House of the Link Between Heaven and Earth," Asshur's tower was called the "House of the Mountain of the Universe," and the people of Borsippa knew theirs as the "House of the Seven Guides of Heaven and Earth." The tower at Babel was referred to by the Babylonians themselves as the "House of the Foundation-Platform of Heaven and Earth." Obviously, these ziggurats were meant to be stairways to the stars.

2. Egotism and pride. The tower of Babel mentioned in Genesis 11 was a stairway dedicated not to the one true God but to egotistical mankind. The words spoken by the settlers in Shinar were clearly self-centered: "Come, let *us* build *ourselves* a city, with a tower that reaches to the heavens, so that *we* may make a name for *ourselves* and not be scattered over the face of the whole earth" (Gen. 11:4, italics added). And quite a tower they planned to build, too. Some time ago, when Hollywood filmed one of its extravaganzas based on the Bible, the producer intended to represent the tower of Babel as a huge brick spiral stairway photographed, artificially, in three segments: in the movie studio, on a cliff in Sicily, and on a pyramid in Egypt. The producer was evidently impressed by the scope of the biblical story and wanted to make the tower as magnificent as possible.

Someone has described the tower of Babel as "the cathedral of antiquity." In a certain sense that's an accurate description, because if its builders were motivated by religious impulses one can hardly deny that the end result was a cathedral. And since ziggurats were typically topped by shrines, there can scarcely be a doubt that the structures were religious in nature.

People in that day could build even a cathedral from wrong motives, just as people today can construct even a church building to glorify the architects rather than God. This was doubtless true in the case of the tower of Babel. "So that we may make a name for *ourselves*," the builders said. Blatant pride was their basic motive. If they had an incidentally religious purpose in mind, it would seem to have been that they might storm the bastions of heaven and compel God to do their bidding. This he could not permit, and so the job was stopped almost before it got off the ground. The Babylonians were seeking to fulfill their own false interpretation of God; they were attempting to manipulate him on their own initiative; they were trying to reach ultimates in their own strength. The result was inevitable: God halted them in midflight.

3. *"Gateway to God"—but a symbol of confusion.* The term *Babel*, which originally meant "Gateway to God," has thus come down to us in the sense of "confusion." God's judgment on the inhabitants of most ancient Babylon was to confuse their speech and to scatter them over the face of the earth. They had had one language; now they would speak many mutually unintelligible dialects. They had been one united people; now they would be dispersed far and wide. At Babel, union became separation, and harmony became confusion.

Their single-minded stairway to the stars arrived at a dead end halfway up. Such is always the result of schemes dedicated to egotism.

B. Bethel

Come with me, next, to the village of Bethel, located about twenty miles north of Jerusalem. An early encounter with Bethel occurs in Genesis 28, the record of a critical episode in the life of Jacob.

1. Jacob and his uneasiness. We are told that Jacob was on his way to Haran, a northern city outside the land of promise. No doubt he had a few misgivings about leaving Canaan, because there was a persistent superstition in those days that the god of a clan would not accompany any member of that clan if he left his native land. Gods were considered to be tribal gods and therefore to be related locally to one tribe. We gather that even before his experience at Bethel Jacob was a worshiper of the one true God, but his lifestyle up to that time demonstrates that he was anything but a sanctified believer. He had taken advantage of his brother Esau's hunger and had tempted him to give up his birthright for a bowl of stew. Then Jacob had deceived his blind father, Isaac, into giving him Esau's blessing. In fact, it was because of these despicable acts that Jacob was forced to flee from Esau's anger.

2. Deceit and promise. And so, as we encounter Jacob along the road to Haran, we note that sanctification is not exactly oozing out of him. He is far away from God, and he thinks he's getting further and further away all the time. But the Lord came to Jacob in a dream with a few plans of his own, plans that were filled with grace and love. At Babel, arrogant men sought their god; at Bethel, God seeks an anxiety-ridden man. And the direction of the search makes all the difference in the world. Our search for God is from down upward; God's search for us is from up downward. In the very nature of the case our search for God can never be completed, because we can never find him by mustering our own resources. But God's search for us is complete and perfect. In Jacob's dream there was a stairway "resting on the earth, with its top reaching to heaven, and the angels of God were ascending and descending on it" (Gen. 28:12). That was truly a stairway to the stars.

At the top of the stairway stood God with all of his promises and blessings. Revealing to Jacob his holy name, he told him he would give him all of Canaan, and that the tally of his descendants would rival that of earth's dust, and that they would richly prosper all people everywhere, and—most incredible of all—that he would stay close by his side wherever he wandered. "Don't be afraid, Jacob! I won't leave you or abandon you. I'm not at all like the false gods of the other tribes, gods who are limited by geographic boundaries. You'll have continual fellowship with me wherever you happen to be because I'm always everywhere, and there's no place on the earth's face where you'll be outside the compass of my loving care. I'll shade you by day and shelter you by night, and if you climb into the heavens I'll be there, and if you clamber into the depths I'll be there, and if you rise on the wings of the dawn or settle on the far side of the sea, even there my hand will guide you, even there my right hand will hold you fast" (*see* Gen. 28:13-14). "I am with you and will watch over you wherever you go, and I will bring you back to this land. I will not leave you until I have done what I have promised you" (v. 15). Jacob's stairway was dedicated to communion with his Lord.

3. *"House of God"—and a symbol of communion.* In recognition of God's gracious provisions for his welfare, Jacob renamed the locale of his dream "Bethel." The original meaning of the word *Babel* was "Gateway to God," but in Scripture it came to mean "confusion"; the earliest connotation of the word *Bethel* was "House of God," and in Christian theology it has come to stand for "communion." Whoever is in God's house with God's people knows the meaning of the word *communion.* If you are far from home on this Christmas Eve, you are nonetheless in God's house. And I hope you can exclaim like Jacob, who was also far from home, ". . . This is none other than the house of God; this is the gate of heaven" (28:17). I hope that today your place of communion with Christ becomes for you a stairway to the stars.

C. Bethlehem

Come with me, finally, to the little town of Bethlehem. Come ye, O come ye to Bethlehem, because there was a star there, too. It may not have been one of the many stars that guided the three intrepid wise men of Apollo 8 to their rendezvous with destiny in lunar orbit on Christmas Eve, 1968.

1. *Magi and the star.* But it was a brilliant star nevertheless, a star that wise men—by tradition also three—followed from the east. Theirs was a much more momentous mission, and it did not end till the star rested above the house in which the young child and his parents were living. Those wise men were the descendants of the early Babylonians who, long ages before, had tried to build a stairway to heaven. The star of Bethlehem became for

the Magi the most precise of navigation instruments, a pointer leading them to the feet of the King of the Jews.

2. *Guidance and fulfillment.* Centuries earlier a prophet had cried out to God, "Oh, that you would rend the heavens and come down!" (Isa. 64:1). The Magi, and multitudes since their time, understood that on Christmas Day God did in fact come down—that Christ Jesus,

> . . . being in very nature God, did not consider equality with God something to be grasped, but made himself nothing, taking the very nature of a servant, being made in human likeness (Phil. 2:5-7)

He it was who would increase in wisdom and in stature, and in favor with God and man. After year upon year of obscurity he would suddenly burst upon the scene in Galilee, calling to himself twelve disciples to be with him and to do his bidding.

3. *Nathanael's King—and the stairway between God and man.* To one of those disciples, Nathanael, he would solemnly declare, as his words are recorded in John 1:51, "I tell you the truth, you shall see heaven open, and the angels of God ascending and descending on the Son of Man." And with that single sweeping statement of self-disclosure he would reveal that he himself was God's own stairway to the stars.

III. Finding a Stairway to the Stars

A. Looking Beyond Human, Scientific Accomplishments

One of my former students designed a unique Christmas card some time ago. At first glance it seems to depict

a person kneeling before a three-stage rocket about to
blast off into the dark, night sky. Viewed in that way, the
card appears to be a striking portrayal of our search for
ultimates through the god of science. But closer inspec-
tion reveals that what looks like a three-stage rocket is
really an outline sketch of Mary, Joseph, and the baby
superimposed on each other, with Joseph standing behind
Mary, and the baby in front. And it turns out that the
man in the card is bowing low in awe before the marvel
of the Christmas event.

The remarkable achievements of a space-conscious age
may make it hard for us to keep our lives in eternal
perspective during this blessed season. And man's brilliant accomplishments, from the tower of Babel to the Sea
of Tranquility, may in their own subtle way prevent us
from concentrating on what God has done for us in
Christ. But it is in Jesus, Jacob's greatest descendant, that
we find true access to and communion with God—not
this time in a dream, as was the case with Jacob, but in
living, vital reality.

B. Comparing Three Stairways

The stairway at Babel remained unfinished, constructed against a backdrop of egotism and spiritual pride;
the stairway at Bethel assured Jacob of fellowship with
God, but a fellowship that was in some respects yet
incomplete, as Jacob's later history testifies. But the
stairway to the stars that is Jesus Christ is the way, and
the truth, and the life; no one comes to the Father, but by
him.

When all is said and done, Babel and Bethel must bow
to Bethlehem.

4

The First Noels

Christmas Day

"Let us come before him with thanksgiving and extol him with music and song" (Ps. 95:2).

Outline

Introduction

I. Christmas Customs

   A. Trees for Trimming

   B. Songs for Hymning

Body

II. Three New Testament Noels

   A. *Magnificat*

      1. Song of wonder

      2. Unnatural pregnancies

      3. The song of the incredible

   B. *Gloria in Excelsis Deo*

      1. Song of praise

      2. Uneasy peace

      3. The song of the inevitable

   C. *Nunc Dimittis*

      1. Song of deliverance

      2. Undeniable prospects

      3. The song of the indisputable

Conclusion

III. Many Songs, One Message

    A. (Summary) The Fullness of Time

    B. (Application) Is the Savior Also Our Sovereign?

When people refer to Hollywood as "Tinsel Town," they're usually not paying it a compliment. The superficial glitter of the world's movie capital has earned it that name. And tinsel in the minds of many symbolizes anything that is tawdry and cheap.

But tinsel in a less commercialized context and seen through less jaded eyes can be a thing of beauty. It can gleam and glisten, shine and sparkle, evoke squeals of delight and sighs of appreciation. It has a way of doing just that in late December when we don our gay apparel and deck the halls with boughs of holly.

I. Christmas Customs

During the Christmas season—the only really legitimate time for tinsel strips and popcorn strings—communities and neighborhoods often vie with one another in friendly contests to see which can out-decorate the other.

A. Trees for Trimming

One particularly notable house on North Snelling Avenue in Saint Paul, Minnesota, sports a forest of front-yard firs strung with colored lights. Philadelphia has a community heavily populated by Roman Catholics of southern and eastern European ancestry who provide a brilliant spectacle by means of their gaily decorated houses. And who can forget the traditional Christmas-tree lane in Altadena, California, on which block after block of stately evergreens are tastefully studded with thousands upon thousands of flickering lights?

The men in our armed forces, when transplanted to bases near and far, tend to carry their holiday customs with them. On one occasion during the Christmas season the post commander of Fort Richardson, Alaska, sponsored an exterior decorating contest in the family quarters area. One disgruntled young lieutenant developed a display that was short-lived but unique. A large spotlighted sign, emblazoned with varicolored lights and properly festooned with evergreen boughs, loudly proclaimed in Old English script:

> Hark! the herald angels shout— Six more months and I'll be out!

B. Songs for Hymning

The lieutenant had made clever use of the twin attractions of Christmas: trees for trimming and songs for hymning. All of us would certainly agree with him that singing is an important part of the season. Whether the song is "Hark, the Herald Angels Sing" or "O Come, All Ye Faithful" or "It Came Upon the Midnight Clear" or "The First Noel," we're all impressed by the fact that at Christmas time—

> There's a song in the air!
>   There's a star in the sky!
> There's a mother's deep prayer,
>   And a baby's low cry!
> And the star rains its fire
>   while the beautiful sing,
> For the manger of Bethlehem
>   cradles a King!
>
> Josiah G. Holland

So true is it that Christmas was meant for singing that two special words are used to refer to songs sung only at Christmas. The term *carol* is one that would seem out of place if applied to songs sung at any other time of year. And likewise the word *noel* means only "Christmas hymn," and when it is used it immediately conjures up scenes of angels singing to shepherds on a Palestinian hillside.

II. Three New Testament Noels

When we turn to the gospel of Luke we discover that its first two chapters contain a number of poetic utterances made by individuals and groups as they responded in one way or other to the birth of Jesus Christ. Many of these poems were later adapted and set to music by composers and arrangers, and they may be conveniently and collectively referred to as "The First Noels."

A. Magnificat

1. Song of wonder. One of these "First Noels" to which we will address ourselves on this Christmas Day was spoken by Mary the mother of Jesus. Perhaps we may best describe it as a song of *wonder* (Luke 1:46-55):

My soul glorifies the Lord
  and my spirit rejoices in God my Savior,
for he has been mindful
  of the humble state of his servant.
From now on all generations will call me blessed,
  for the Mighty One has done great things for me—
  holy is his name.
His mercy extends to those who fear him,
  from generation to generation.

He has performed mighty deeds with his arm;
  he has scattered those who are proud in their inmost
  thoughts.
He has brought down rulers from their thrones
  but has lifted up the humble.
He has filled the hungry with good things
  but has sent the rich away empty.
He has helped his servant Israel,
  remembering to be merciful
to Abraham and his descendants forever,
  even as he said to our fathers.

2. *Unnatural pregnancies.*   Mary's first statement set
the stage for her entire poem: "My soul *glorifies* the
Lord." No other word could have described the feeling of
unique wonder that had captured her. She was visiting
her kinswoman Elizabeth, the wife of Zechariah the
priest. Both Zechariah and Elizabeth were elderly, and
Elizabeth had long since passed through her years of
childbearing. Nevertheless, the angel of the Lord had
interrupted Zechariah's temple activities and had announced to him that he and his wife would soon be
blessed with a son. A miracle—a wonder indeed—that an
aged couple should become parents! But no wonder that
Mary, in such circumstances, should say, "My soul
glorifies the Lord"! "Lord, how great thou art!"

But that was not all, because in the sixth month of
Elizabeth's pregnancy that same angel paid a visit to
Mary herself. He told her that she, too, would soon be
blessed with a son. But what's so unusual about that?
Why shouldn't a young woman, in the prime of life,
become a mother? Ah, this would be no ordinary birth
either. Up to this time Mary had no husband, was a
virgin, and would bear her son while still a virgin. A
miracle—a wonder indeed—an even greater wonder than

in Elizabeth's case, that a virgin maiden should become a mother! But no wonder that Mary, in such circumstances, should say, "My soul glorifies the Lord"! "Lord, how great thou art!"

When the soul of a person bursts forth into lyric poetry, it normally does so in terms that uniquely fit the situation in which that soul finds itself. It's not surprising, then, that Mary should have thought of similar words spoken ten centuries earlier by another godly woman. Hannah, having given birth to Samuel after many long years of barrenness, addressed to God a prayer that began: "My heart rejoices in the LORD" (1 Sam. 2:1). Mary quite naturally voiced her thoughts in poetry strongly reminiscent of Hannah's earlier prayer, because Mary's situation was much like that of Hannah and Elizabeth: All three women were participants in births contrary to nature. No wonder that Mary, in such circumstances, should say, "My soul glorifies the Lord"! "Lord, how great thou art!"

3. *The song of the incredible.*   As Mary continued to develop her insights and to express them beautifully in her poem, her true character unmistakably revealed itself. Her hymn is generously sprinkled throughout with allusions to and quotations from the Old Testament, particularly the Psalms. The ideas that spring naturally to mind during times of emotional and spiritual crisis and exultation are part of the very warp and woof of a person's emotional and spiritual fabric. He who curses God at such times doubtless lives a life that is a continual blasphemy; he who blesses God at such times doubtless lives a life that is a continual benediction. In a beautiful act of self-disclosure, Mary stated her unquestioning faith by saying, "My soul glorifies the Lord." And it is from the

word translated "glorifies" that the Latin Church derived its title for Mary's great hymn, the *Magnificat*. Intoned by Mary before the birth of Jesus, it is the song of the miraculous, the song of wonder, the song of the incredible!

B. *Gloria in Excelsis Deo*

Less than a year after Mary's visit to Elizabeth a second "Noel" was composed, this time not by a single individual but by a multitude of angels.

1. Song of praise.   Perhaps we may best describe it as a song of *praise* (Luke 2:14):

> Glory to God in the highest,
> and on earth peace to men on whom his favor rests.

The virgin Mary had just given birth to Jesus Christ, to him whose very name means "Savior," who would reconcile men and women and boys and girls to God, who would mediate God's peace to turbulent hearts and a troubled world. How appropriate then that the angels should sing, "Glory to God in the highest, and on earth peace"!

2. Uneasy peace.   But wasn't there peace on earth when Jesus was born? Indeed there was—the *Pax Romana*, the Roman peace, a peace enforced by the invincible armies of Rome. All about were external signs of peace and prosperity, signs remarkably like those of our own day: law and culture and education and wealth and pleasure. But the peace was uneasy, and pockets of rebellion were continually threatening to explode into open warfare. The New Testament reflects the tense situation and chronicles the dangerous days of the first

Christian century. A scant seventy years after the birth of
Jesus would witness an insurrection by Palestine's Jews
against Rome's oppression—an insurrection that would
bring the imperial wrath against them and lead to the
destruction of Jerusalem and Herod's temple there. A
scant thirty years after the birth of Jesus would witness a
revolt by Jerusalem's religious leaders against Jesus himself—a revolt that would lead to his crucifixion and
death. A scant two years after the birth of Jesus would
witness rebellion in the heart of Herod the Great against
him who had come to be King of the Jews—rebellion that
would lead to the cruel massacre of all infant boys in
Bethlehem.

It's no wonder, then, as he reminisced about the birth
of Jesus and reflected on the similarity between those
days and his own, that Henry Wadsworth Longfellow
should write:

> I heard the bells on Christmas Day
> Their old familiar carols play,
> And wild and sweet the words repeat
> Of peace on earth, goodwill to men!
>
> And thought how, as the day had come,
> The belfries of all Christendom
> Had rolled along the unbroken song
> Of peace on earth, goodwill to men.
>
> And in despair I bowed my head:
> "There is no peace on earth," I said,
> "For hate is strong, and mocks the song
> Of peace on earth, goodwill to men."

But Longfellow didn't stop there. Man's inhumanity to
man was evident everywhere, but Longfellow's Bible told
him of a future filled with promise; and he continued to
write:

Then pealed the bells more loud and deep:
"God is not dead, nor doth he sleep!
The wrong shall fail, the right prevail,
With peace on earth, goodwill to men."

3. The song of the inevitable. In a similar way the angel host, on that first Christmas night in a world much like Longfellow's and our own, envisioned the eventual rule of Jesus Christ over the hearts of all people and therefore hymned their paean of praise: "Glory to God in the highest, and on earth peace!" It is from the phrase translated "Glory to God in the highest" that the Latin Church derived its title for the angels' great hymn, *Gloria in Excelsis Deo.* Intoned by the heavenly choir on the day of the birth of Jesus, it is the song of hope, the song of praise, the song of the inevitable!

C. Nunc Dimittis

Scarcely a month after Jesus' birth a third "Noel" was spoken, this time once again by an individual, Simeon by name.

1. Song of deliverance. Perhaps we may best describe it as a song of *deliverance.* It was occasioned by a series of circumstances that were commonplace enough. By this time Mary had evidently married Joseph. As dutiful parents were expected to do, she and her husband brought the baby Jesus to the temple forty days after his birth. In an act of dedication and sacrifice they presented their firstborn son to the Lord.

They entered Herod's temple, and by a miracle of timing Simeon was also there. Taking the child in his arms and blessing God, he said (Luke 2:29-32):

> Sovereign Lord, as you have promised,
>   you now dismiss your servant in peace.
> For my eyes have seen your salvation,
>   which you have prepared in the sight of all people,
> a light for revelation to the Gentiles
>   and for glory to your people Israel.

We have no way of knowing how long after this occasion Simeon continued to live, but we can be fairly sure that on his deathbed he was singing the same song.

2. Undeniable prospects.   When the noted agnostic Robert Ingersoll died, the printed funeral notices read: "There will be no singing." No need to search for choruses or anthems, carols or noels, psalms and hymns and spiritual songs on the lips of unbelievers. Without God, without Christ, without hope in the world, what do they have to sing about?

A thought-provoking Christmas card entitled, "If Christ Had Not Come," told the story of a pastor who had fallen asleep in the church study on Christmas morning. In his dream he found himself walking through his home, looking in vain for Christmas bells, holly wreaths, and stockings by the fireplace. He stepped outside, but there was no church with its steeple pointing heavenward. Returning to his library, he noticed that every book about the Savior was missing.

The doorbell rang. A boy asked him to visit his dying mother. He hurried along with the weeping child; when he reached the home he sat by the bedside and whispered, "I have something here that will comfort you." He opened his Bible eagerly, but it ended with Malachi and contained no Gospel, no account of how Jesus had overcome death, no consolation for a dying woman and her despairing son.

A few days later he conducted the funeral service. He could offer no message about a glorious resurrection, no promise of an open heaven, but only "ashes to ashes, dust to dust," and a long, eternal farewell. Able to control himself no longer, he burst into bitter tears.

Suddenly he awoke, aroused from his sorrowful dream by the voices of his choir rehearsing in the room next to his study:

> O come, all ye faithful, joyful and triumphant,
> O come ye, O come ye to Bethlehem!
> Come and behold him, born the King of angels;
> O come, let us adore him, Christ the Lord.

3. The song of the indisputable. Christ *has* come —and Simeon was one of the first to recognize him. His eyes had seen the salvation of God, and he was now ready to leave this life. It is from the phrase translated "you now dismiss" in his poetic blessing that the Latin Church derived its title for Simeon's great hymn, *Nunc Dimittis.* Intoned by a devoted saint shortly after the birth of Jesus, it is the song of deliverance, the song of assurance, the song of the indisputable!

III. Many Songs, One Message

These three "First Noels," and others like them, have been added to through the centuries, so that today there are innumerable Christmas hymns and choruses.

A. *The Fullness of Time*

Whether written by a young mother or an angelic choir or a saintly believer or a professional composer, all have essentially the same message: "When the time had fully come, God sent his Son, born of a woman, born under law, to redeem those under law, that we might receive the full rights of sons" (Gal. 4:4-5). "Here is a trustworthy saying that deserves full acceptance: Christ Jesus came into the world to save sinners" (1 Tim. 1:15).

B. Is the Savior Also Our Sovereign?

But if Jesus came as the Savior of the world, he came also as the sovereign of history. Mary's melody reminds us of how incredible was his first coming, in a virgin-conceived birth that stopped the stars in their tracks. Simeon's song shows us how indisputable is his salvation, reaching with calm conviction deeply into the heart of a lifelong student of Scripture. The angelic anthem assures us of how inevitable is his sovereignty, soon to surround all people everywhere with justice perfected by love. And if the present state of our world is an accurate indicator of our need, the second coming of the Prince of peace must be near indeed.

5

Three Cheers for New Year's!

New Year's Eve

"Rejoice in the Lord always" (Phil. 4:4).

Outline

Introduction

    I. Why Is New Year's Eve a Time for Happiness?

        A. Christmas Is a Recent Memory

        B. The Old Year's Disappointments Are Past

        C. The New Year's Prospects Are Bright

Body

    II. The Secret of Happiness: "Take Heart"

        A. Jesus Says, "Your Sins Are Forgiven"

            1. Deep and abiding joy a Christian concept

            2. Christian joy contrasted with worldly happiness

            3. "I'm so happy, and here's the reason why"

        B. Jesus Says, "I Have Overcome the World"

            1. Victory over problems and difficulties

            2. Victory over temptation and persecution

            3. "I am happy in the service of the King"

        C. Jesus Says, "It Is I!"

Conclusion

III. Sending Up a Cheer on New Year's Eve

    A. (Summary) Forgiveness, Freedom, Fellowship

    B. (Illustration) The Difference Between Happiness and Joy

    C. (Application) Let Jesus Turn Your Sorrow into Joy

When Mark Twain was once asked what his New Year's resolution would be, he answered, "I'm going to live within my income this year even if I have to borrow money to do it." Of course, we would have expected the great humorist to respond with humor to a question like that. But as it turns out, most New Year's resolutions have an air of levity about them. The prospect of a brand new year seems to bring out the comedian hidden inside all of us.

I. Why Is New Year's Eve a Time for Happiness?

A. Christmas Is a Recent Memory

Why do you suppose that's so? Maybe it's because the warm, happy experience of the Christmas season is still a recent memory. Mince pie and mistletoe, toys and tinsel and time off all tend to make us subjectively cheerful if not objectively comical. "'Tis the season to be jolly!" shouts my secular neighbor. Madonnas and Magi, stables and shepherds and starry skies all combine to remind us of an ancient night of singular bliss. "Joy to the world!" sings my fellow Christian. And the afterglow spills over at least to the end of the month.

B. The Old Year's Disappointments Are Past

Or maybe it's because the old year, successful though it might have been in some ways, did have its share of difficulties and disappointments after all. Maybe for every promise kept, two were broken. Perhaps for every project brought to a satisfying conclusion, two remained undone. Possibly for every bad habit conquered, two sprang up to take its place. Maybe we're glad to have the opportunity of turning the page and getting a fresh start. Perhaps it's with a sigh of relief that we say good-bye to auld lang syne.

C. The New Year's Prospects Are Bright

Or maybe it's simply that the new year is, when all is said and done, just that: *new*. To be new is to be filled with excitement. Newness is always freighted with mystery. What's new is attractive and intriguing; what's new is young and fresh and alive. All of these qualities and characteristics cause us to tingle with anticipation. They bring involuntary (if uncertain) smiles to our faces. In the words of C. S. Lewis, they give all of us the potential for being "surprised by joy."

So here we are, teetering on the brink of another new year; and if we're like nearly everyone else we're supposed to be deliriously happy about it. Beckoning, the new year stretches out before us, bright with the promise of happiness. Where will we look for it, though?

For many the pinnacle of happiness nestles securely at the top of a pile of greenbacks. If they're right, people in show business should be happier than almost everyone else because they make more money than almost everyone else. But Art Linkletter, one of the more astute observers of the entertainment scene, isn't so sure about that. Wealthy in his own right, he's still not convinced that money is everything. Several years ago he published in a national magazine an article entitled "How to Be

Happy, Though Successful." Financial success and happiness don't always go hand in hand, says Art Linkletter. The tragic suicide of his daughter, Diane, underscored that belief in his own experience.

Fame fares no better in our search for happiness. The sports pages headline the names of athletes who are famous today but will be forgotten tomorrow. Yesterday's battlefield hero may be today's bum. Even prominent statesmen soon fade from the passing scene. For example, who of us could list, without making a single mistake, the losing major-party vice-presidential candidates in our last five national elections? Fame is a fleeting thing.

And so it goes: The "happiness" derived from power can be snuffed out in an instant by an assassin's bullet; the "happiness" based on friendship can be wiped out by betrayal; the "happiness" found in the love of a man for a woman can be destroyed forever by a single act of infidelity.

II. The Secret of Happiness: "Take Heart"

Where, then, should we look for happiness as the new year dawns? What word do we, as Christian witnesses, have for the person who is overwhelmed by sadness, by frustration, by discontent? Do we have the right to comfort and encourage people with commands like "Be happy! Be courageous! Be of good cheer!"?

You bet we do! The teachings of Jesus Christ contain the biblical prescription for happiness. Billy Graham has shown in his book *The Secret of Happiness* that the beatitudes, for example, are intensely practical for modern living. He has demonstrated that happiness, in its most satisfying form, is the inevitable result of gaining the proper relationships with God and with one another. Let me remind you of three instances from the life of our Lord that illustrate the truth of this approach.

A. Jesus Says, "Your Sins Are Forgiven"

All but one of the Gospel writers relate an incident that took place during Jesus' Galilean ministry. No sooner had he entered the home where he was staying in Capernaum than a group of four men tried to bring their paralyzed friend to him for healing. The curious crowds, hemming Jesus in on all sides, were no match for the resourceful four. After ripping off a few of the roof tiles, they gently lowered the stretcher into the center of the room. To reward the unusual faith of these men, Jesus did something for their companion that up to that time was quite unusual. With words that have deep significance also for you and me, he said to the paralytic, "Take heart!" "Why, sir? Why should I take heart? Why should I be happy, in my hopelessly sad situation?" "Take heart, son; your sins are forgiven!"

And what better reason to be happy? Here is reason for lasting and abundant rejoicing! When our sins are forgiven, we're at peace with our consciences; when our sins are forgiven, we're at peace with our friends and neighbors; when our sins are forgiven, we're at peace with our Lord. We're happy, because Jesus has forgiven our sins!

1. Deep and abiding joy a Christian concept. The quality of joy is a distinctively Christian concept. Nowhere in the Greco-Roman world of New Testament days, much less in any of the civilizations that preceded it, do we find the attribute of Christian joy. Believers in Christ are the only people who have ever experienced

that deep and abiding sense of satisfaction and contentment that finds its source in the realization of sins
forgiven and a right relationship to God. The virtue of joy
is unique with Christianity and has never had a genuine
counterpart in any other ethical system or religious
philosophy.

One of the primary factors in the conversion of Augustine was his observation of the fact that the Christians of
his day were joyful people. Augustine saw in his Christian peers something that he lacked but desperately
wanted. Their joy attracted him to their Lord, who soon
became his Lord also. The winsome warmth of a Christian community did its work in the heart of a brilliant
young man, and he succumbed. Augustine turned his life
over to the living God, and the joy of salvation filled him
with the peace that surpasses all understanding. "Take
heart, because your sins are forgiven!"

The best-selling novels and other entertainment media
of our time often reflect on how hollow and superficial
the joy of the average person is. His fruitless search for
happiness may not end quite so tragically as did Edwin
Arlington Robinson's *Richard Cory* who, after gaining all
the wealth and prestige a man might reasonably expect,
"went home and put a bullet through his head." Nevertheless, he characteristically flits from one source of
pleasure to another, smiles a little, laughs a little, and
more often than not is more despondent after his night of
partying and merriment than he was when the evening
was young. Typical of our current scene is today's drug
user whose happiness is far more temporary and less
enduring than the high or rush he gets from indulging his
addiction. One of Job's friends knew well how shallow
and short-lived pleasure can be: "The mirth of the

wicked is brief, the joy of the godless lasts but a moment''
(20:5). Like a fountain about to run dry, such joy is not
connected to a full reservoir. It bubbles up bravely for a
while, then spurts, then sputters, then stops flowing
altogether.

2. *Christian joy contrasted with worldly happiness.*
Christian joy, on the other hand, is lasting. Hear the
words of Jesus to his disciples: ''I have told you this so
that my joy may be in you and that your joy may be
complete'' (John 15:11). The joy of the Christian is like a
deep, quiet river whose waters are continually replen-
ished from mountain streams. To the woman at the well
in Samaria Jesus said, ''Everyone who drinks this water
will be thirsty again, but whoever drinks the water I give
him will never thirst. Indeed, the water I give him will
become in him a spring of water welling up to eternal
life'' (John 4:13-14). When the Holy Spirit plants salvation in a seeking heart, the joy that grows alongside it is
just as lasting and eternal as is the assurance of sins
forgiven. And such joy, announced initially by an angel
choir on that first Christmas night, already has a two-
thousand-year-long history. It's the indispensable theme
of that ''good news of great joy'' (Luke 2:10) that imparts
salvation to the waiting soul.

The Old Testament has only foregleams of the joy of
sins forgiven. Statements like these of the psalmist are
few and far between:

> Blessed is he
>   whose transgressions are forgiven,
>   whose sins are covered.
> Blessed is the man
>   whose sin the LORD does not count against him
> (Ps. 32:1-2).

But the joy of salvation permeates the New Testament, and expressions like the one found in Romans 5:11 are common: ". . . we also rejoice in God through our Lord Jesus Christ, through whom we have now received reconciliation."

3. *"I'm so happy, and here's the reason why."* As the old year passes into oblivion and the new year dawns, why should we Christians send up a cheer? Let the words of the gospel chorus tell us:

> I'm so happy, and here's the reason why:
>   Jesus took my burdens all away!
> Now I'm singing as the days go by:
>   Jesus took my burdens all away!
> Once my heart was heavy with a load of sin;
>   Jesus took the load and gave me peace within!
> Now I'm singing as the days go by:
>   Jesus took my burdens all away!

"Take heart, because your sins are forgiven!"

B. Jesus Says, "I Have Overcome the World"

John's gospel informs us of another incident that took place during Jesus' ministry. It happened, in fact, during that fearsome final week of Jesus' life. Although he would soon be betrayed into the hands of his enemies, his thoughts were not centered on his own problems. He was very much involved in the task of encouraging his disciples to be brave in the difficult and dangerous days that lay just ahead. He warned them that they would be severely persecuted for professing faith in him, that their lives would be anything but easy after he was gone. Nevertheless, with words that have deep significance also for you and me, he commanded them, "In this world you will have trouble. But take heart!" "Why, Lord? Why should we be lighthearted and courageous, in our precarious position?" "Take heart! I have overcome the world!"

1. Victory over problems and difficulties. And what better reason to be happy? Here is reason for lasting and abundant rejoicing: Jesus has overcome the world! This means that we're free from the oppressive power of the world and its attractions; it means that the world no longer exercises dominion over us; it means that no matter what the world does to us, it can't disturb our inner peace and contentment. We're happy, because Jesus has overcome the world!

2. Victory over temptation and persecution. The devil's fiery darts take many shapes and forms. Temptation can come to us as the lust of the flesh, or the lust of the eyes, or the pride of life. Satan can creep up on us unaware, or he can confront us brazenly and openly. But God hasn't left us without resources to withstand even the most frontal attacks: "No temptation has seized you except what is common to man. And God is faithful; he will not let you be tempted beyond what you can bear. But when you are tempted, he will also provide a way out so that you can stand up under it" (1 Cor. 10:13). Temptation, however subtle and however beguiling, no longer has the upper hand, because Jesus has overcome the world.

Persecution also assumes many shapes. It can take the form of ridicule, or slander, or bodily harm, or torture, or martyrdom. It can come from friend and enemy alike. The history of the church teaches us that Christians have always been persecuted, and there is no reason for us to suppose that things will be much different in our case.

But God hasn't abandoned us to face persecution alone. Jesus declared:

> Blessed are those who are persecuted
>   because of righteousness,
> for theirs is the kingdom of heaven.

> Blessed are you when people insult you,
>   persecute you and falsely say all kinds of evil against
> you because of me.
> Rejoice and be glad, because great is your reward in
> heaven, for in the same way they persecuted the prophets
> who were before you (Matt. 5:10-12).

Persecution of the most horrible kind imaginable overtook prophets, apostles, and Jesus himself. If God should decide that we are to endure similar trials, why should we expect more lenient treatment? The apostle James, who understood something of what it meant to be persecuted, summed up the matter well: "Consider it pure joy, my brothers, whenever you face trials of many kinds, because you know that the testing of your faith develops perseverance. . . . Blessed is the man who perseveres under trial, because when he has stood the test, he will receive the crown of life that God has promised to those who love him" (1:2-3, 12). Persecution, however severe and however threatening, no longer is a cause for dread, because Jesus has overcome the world.

Freedom from bondage to the world allows us to become slaves of Jesus, and his yoke is easy and his burden light. Serving Christ, full-time or part-time or anytime, is the delight of every Christian heart. We can rest in the assurance of victory over the world and rejoice in the resulting opportunities to serve our Lord.

3. *"I am happy in the service of the King."* So then, as the old year passes into oblivion and the new year dawns, why should we Christians send up a cheer? Let the words of the gospel hymn tell us:

> I am happy in the service of the King!
>> I am happy, O so happy!
> I have peace and joy that nothing else can bring,
>> In the service of the King!
> In the service of the King,
>> Every talent I will bring;
> I have peace and joy and blessing
>> In the service of the King!

A. H. Ackley

"Take heart, because I have overcome the world!"

C. Jesus Says, *"It Is I"*

Three of the gospels inform us of a final incident in Jesus' ministry that places the finishing touches on our reasons for rejoicing in him. Twelve disciples were struggling to keep their boat afloat during a storm on Lake Galilee. Suddenly the figure of a man walking on the waves toward them caught their attention. They of course became terrified, thinking it was a ghost. Then came the command of Jesus to them in words that have deep significance also for you and me: "Take courage!" "Why, you phantom? Why shouldn't we be frightened and filled with dread?" "Take courage! It is I. Don't be afraid."

III. Sending Up a Cheer on New Year's Eve

A. Forgiveness, Freedom, Fellowship

And what better reason to be happy? We've seen Jesus! He has come walking toward us, surmounting the problems and dangers and vicissitudes of life; and after hearing his reassuring voice, we've recognized him. We've looked into his face, and we've seen in him the answer to all our questions. We've looked into his face, and we've realized immediately that he's the only one who could possibly free us from the curse of sin and death. We've looked into his face, and we've understood that joyous fellowship and communion with God and with his people is possible through him. And the semi-gleams of his presence that we enjoy now are dim indeed when compared with the supreme delight that we'll experience when we stand before him some day. We'll be happy, because we'll be with Jesus.

B. The Difference Between Happiness and Joy

As a high-school boy I found myself in a pouting, petulant mood one day. Nothing had been turning out well for me. I was too short to make the basketball team and too homely to get a date. A wise pastor friend, observing that I was not exactly in the best of spirits, made a useful distinction when he said to me, "Happiness is found in happenings, but joy is found in Jesus." "Take courage, because it is I!"

C. Let Jesus Turn Your Sorrow into Joy

As the old year passes into oblivion and the new year dawns, why should we Christians send up a cheer? Let the words of the gospel song tell us:

> My heart was sad till I met Jesus;
>   My friends were gone, and life seemed vain;
> I sought for riches and for glory—
>   Each joy had turned to grief and pain.

Then, one day, I met the Savior,
   Met him in the twilight dim;
Joy overwhelmed my soul, and sorrow vanished,
   And I'm happy, since his love came in.

Three cheers for New Year's!

6

The Bible's Love Song

Valentine's Day

"We love because he first loved us" (1 John 4:19).

Outline

Introduction

    I. Love Is a Many-Splendored Thing

        A. Modern Popular Music

        B. Ancient Love Poems

        C. God's Love Letter to Us

Body

    II. A Biblical Ballad in Three Stanzas

        A. Love Is Essential

            1. The inadequacy of eloquence

            2. The ineffectiveness of intelligence and spirituality

            3. The insufficiency of generosity and self-sacrifice

        B. Love Is Ethical

            1. The patience of love

            2. The understanding of love

            3. The selflessness of love

            4. The purity of love

        C. Love Is Eternal

Conclusion

I. Love Is a Many-Splendored Thing

A. Modern Popular Music

Love may not make the world go around, but it certainly keeps the music business solvent. Popular songs attest to the universal appeal of the theme of love. Without it, most of the revolving records and spinning tapes and whirring cassettes played by America's disc jockeys would lapse into eternal silence (which would be hailed as a blessing by many radio listeners). With ballads ranging from "Let Me Call You Sweetheart" to "Love Is a Many-Splendored Thing" to "Endless Love," generations of lovers pay homage to that most powerful of all human emotions.

B. Ancient Love Poems

In fact, "the way of a man with a maiden" (Prov. 30:19) has been a favorite subject for lyrical expression from time immemorial. Ancient Egyptian and Babylonian swains wrote passionate poetry to their lady loves. The Song of Solomon clearly portrays the affectionate delight that a bridegroom and bride take in one another. Greeks and Romans, Persians and Arabs, Frenchmen and Englishmen, and a host of others have added their attempts to do descriptive justice to that complex quality known as *love*.

C. God's Love Letter to Us

Someone has declared the entire Bible to be God's love letter to us, and not without good reason. It is, after all, a book that outlines in great detail God's mercy, his patience, his longsuffering toward his creatures. Above all it depicts his grace, which is neither more nor less than undeserved concern, unmerited favor, aggressive love. It is divided into two covenants, the Old and the New: marriage contracts between God and Israel on the one hand, and Christ and the church on the other. God loves us; and so, among other things, he wrote us a long letter to tell us all about it.

As children of the heavenly Father, in everything we do we want to imitate him to the greatest extent possible. When he shows mercy, we should do the same. Where he demonstrates patience, we should be willing to do likewise. And because he first loved us, we love. Wherever we are, whenever we act, whatever we're doing—our lives mirror his if we're really his children.

II. A Biblical Ballad in Three Stanzas

If we can agree for the sake of the argument that the Bible is a description of how and to what degree Gods loves us, then perhaps we wouldn't be going too far afield by stating that 1 Corinthians 13 describes how and to what degree we should love one another. It is a biblical ballad in three stanzas. Paul's first letter to Corinth addressed itself to competing groups within the church there. The resulting theological debates and personal quarrels threatened to tear the church apart. First Corinthians 13, then, was intended primarily to heal wounds that had already been opened and to keep further battles from getting started.

This whole chapter, however, may legitimately be used in wider contexts as well, because it outlines characteristics of love that should apply to every human situation. Needless to say, it defines the nature of our love for our brothers and sisters in Christ. But we should also use it as a guide for our relationships with people *outside* the household of faith. And last but not least, if every Christian husband would learn to apply its teachings to his relationship with his wife, and if every wife would do the same with respect to her husband, that one program of concern would go a long way toward making our homes the paradises God intended them to be. It's mainly in this latter sense that I want to make a few comments on what has been called "the Bible's love song" on this Valentines' Day.

A. Love Is Essential

> If I speak in the tongues of men and of angels, but have not love, I am only a resounding gong or a clanging cymbal.

> If I have the gift of prophecy and can fathom all mysteries and all knowledge, and if I have a faith that can move mountains, but have not love, I am nothing.

> If I give all I possess to the poor and surrender my body to the flames, but have not love, I gain nothing (vv. 1-3).

Stanza one of the Bible's love song tells us that love is *essential.* The refrain that rings throughout each of these three verses is "but have not love." Whatever else we might be or have or do, if we're not loving we're nothing. Love is the irreducible minimum, the indispensable con-

dition, the fundamental basis of all Christian relationships. In short, love is absolutely essential.

The teachings of Jesus make the same point. Love is
the foundation of God's commandments, which are basically two: "Love the Lord your God with all your heart
and with all your soul and with all your mind and with all
your strength," and "Love your neighbor as yourself"
(Mark 12:30-31). Love for God and love for one another,
says our Lord, are the sum and substance of the divine
commands. Paul's emphasis in 1 Corinthians 13 is on
love for one another—including our mates.

One fine day several years ago I decided that from that
time on I would say "I love you" every day to Carolyn
(she's my wife). I'm happy to be able to report that down
through the years I've kept that promise with only rare
exceptions. I've tried never to use it as a mystical
incantation to guarantee our relationship in a magical sort
of way. When I've said it, I've meant it; and when,
temporarily, I haven't meant it, I've avoided saying it.
Amazingly enough, this verbalizing of my love for Carolyn has been one factor that has deepened and strengthened that love as the years have come and gone. I
constantly remind myself of what a shame it would be if
anger or busyness or fatigue should keep me from saying
those three little words to her on any particular day. This
peculiar habit of mine still hasn't given me the most
even-tempered disposition in the world, but I'm sure it's
at least helped. And I wouldn't hesitate for a moment to
recommend it to you without reservation!

Social scientists also currently stress the idea that a
loving attitude must back up our actions if those actions
are to be more than merely mechanical. Ashley Montagu,
the humanistic philosopher, emphasizes "the awesome

power of human love" in straightening out interpersonal relationships. Hobart Mowrer, one of our leading psychologists, states that our inability to love and be loved, to have friends and be friendly, can cause emotional illness. Erich Fromm, in *The Art of Loving,* agrees with this concept when he insists that loneliness and our failure to love are the underlying causes of emotional and psychic disorders. Paul Tournier, the Swiss psychiatrist, believes that love and honest friendship can promote psychic healing. Carl Rogers, the founder of the nondirective school of counseling, claims that he can quickly train as psychotherapists those who possess love, but that without love no amount of training can produce an effective counselor. Perhaps Karl Menninger, one of the greatest of contemporary psychiatrists, summed it up best by asserting that "love is the medicine for the sickness of the world."

1. The inadequacy of eloquence.   But can't eloquence cover up for a lack of love? Hardly. "If I speak in the tongues of men and of angels, but have not love, I am only a resounding gong or a clanging cymbal." Many a husband has tried to sweet-talk his way out of the doghouse, only to discover that a glib tongue is no substitute for the tender affection his wife needs. Unless your lofty oratory and high-flown sentiments are informed by love, your mate will remain unimpressed. Love is far more important than language. In fact *love is absolutely essential.*

2. The ineffectiveness of intelligence and spirituality. Well, then, how about intelligence and spirituality? Can they carry the day? Almost never. "If I have the gift of prophecy and can fathom all mysteries and all knowledge, and if I have a faith that can move mountains, but have not love, I am nothing." Many a Christian wife has attempted to convert her husband through theological argument and pietistic behavior, but to no avail. In far too many cases she has failed to win him because she hasn't loved him while witnessing to him. Love is far more important than logic and life. In fact *love is absolutely essential.*

3. *The insufficiency of generosity and self-sacrifice.* What if we should try generosity and self-sacrifice? Won't they succeed even if nothing else does? Not at all. "If I give all I possess to the poor and surrender my body to the flames, but have not love, I gain nothing." After your next spat with your wife, slip a signed check or two from your personal account under her locked bedroom door. Even if you've left the amount of money undesignated, your scheme doesn't have a chance of success! Nor does a truckload of explosives driven into an embassy building by a misguided fanatic gain a reaction other than horror from the vast majority of thinking, sensitive men and women. Forgiveness can be bought only with repentance sanctified by love, and wars will cease only when people stop hating each other. Love will always go much further than either liberality or lunacy. In fact *love is absolutely essential.*

The necessity of love is a theme that resounds and reverberates throughout the Bible. But to add to what Paul has already said would be to gild the lily. In any event, there is much more to say about love than simply to assert that it's essential.

B. Love Is Ethical

In fact, Paul himself would remind us that we've barely begun his great ode to love; so let's return to it and consider the ethics of love:

Love is patient, love is kind. It does not envy, it does not boast, it is not proud. It is not rude, it is not self-seeking, it is not easily angered, it keeps no record of wrongs.

Love does not delight in evil but rejoices with the truth.

It always protects, always trusts, always hopes, always perseveres (vv. 4-7).

Stanza two of the Bible's love song tells us that love is *ethical.* Running his finger down a list of qualities and characteristics, Paul informs us what love is not as well as what love is. Love flees in terror from everything that is hateful in God's eyes, but flings its arms around everything that God himself commends. Love is on the side of the true, the good, the beautiful; it avoids association with the false, the wicked, the despicable. In short *love is totally ethical.*

1. The patience of love. "Love is patient, love is kind." And yet how often we commit unloving acts in the name of love! Edward Carnell used to illustrate (in reverse) the patience of love to his theology classes at Fuller Seminary by describing his experiences on California's freeways. One morning, so the story goes, the car in front of his wasn't moving fast enough to suit him. He whipped out into the next lane and shouted across to the other driver, "Hey, you melonhead! Pull that thing off the road if it can't go any faster than that! Can't you see I'm trying to get to Fuller Seminary in time to teach my students all about the law of love?" Carnell's rare ethical sensitivity helped him to tell that anecdote on himself with just the right combination of humor and remorse. He, more than most other Christian statesmen I've known, realized full well that love is patient and kind.

2. *The understanding of love.* "It does not envy, it does not boast, it is not proud." And yet how often are we suspicious of the very ones that we should trust the most! How often we brag, even though we know that the simple, unvarnished truth would gain us far more respect! How often we strive for recognition we don't deserve or insult those we love to feed our own egos! If we really love we're always courteous, even if it means maintaining our status as wallflowers. If we really love we refuse to call attention to ourselves, even if it means that nobody ever notices us. Such love has something to say to those of us who think that living in the best of all possible worlds involves driving the fastest cars and wearing the finest clothes.

3. *The selflessness of love.* "It is not rude, it is not self-seeking, it is not easily angered, it keeps no record of wrongs." And yet how often do we make selfish requests and then lash out with irritation and resentment if those requests are not met! Maybe whenever our children seem to be thinking only of their own needs, it's because we dads and moms have set the pattern for them. Maybe when our students badger their teachers and boycott their classes if their nonnegotiable demands are not met, it's because they've learned something about selfishness from their parents. Maybe deadlocks at the bargaining table in management-labor negotiations can be traced back to a lack of mutual understanding and concern in the home. By contrast, true love always acts in the spirit of him who said, "It is more blessed to give than to receive" (Acts 20:35).

4. *The purity of love.* "Love does not delight in evil but rejoices with the truth. It always protects, always trusts, always hopes, always perseveres." Whenever we

take even the slightest pleasure in misfortunes that befall our mates, we fail to exemplify Christian love. Such love responds with anything but happiness when all is not well. My confidence in Carolyn should be so complete that I should be characterized by loving stability in the face of domestic emergencies, loving trust in the face of vicious rumors, and loving optimism in the face of uncertain prospects for the future. That's quite an order, as all of you married men will quickly agree, but—fortunately for us—our wives share with us the burden of that responsibility.

This central stanza of the Bible's love song contains more hard sayings than most of us can handle. The fact that love is totally ethical means that we're always being called on to make moral decisions, and those are never easy. But our Lord says to us, "Husbands, love your wives, just as Christ loved the church and gave himself up for her" (Eph. 5:25). And we hardly need to stress that Christ's love was completely selfless and thoroughly ethical. In addition to enjoying countless other privileges only dimly understood by unbelievers, a Christian husband and his Christian wife are heirs together of "the gracious gift of life" (1 Peter 3:7). Each for the other and both for Christ—that's the love triangle that guarantees true fulfillment within the gracious limits of God's law. Jesus brings the needed dimension that prevents a potentially loveless marriage from becoming hell on earth. When he becomes a vital partner in a couple's life, he enables them to sing the third stanza of 1 Corinthians 13 fearlessly:

C. Love Is Eternal

Love never fails. But where there are prophecies, they will cease; where there are tongues, they will be stilled; where there is knowledge, it will pass away.

For we know in part and we prophesy in part, but when perfection comes, the imperfect disappears.

When I was a child, I talked like a child, I thought like a child, I reasoned like a child. When I became a man, I put childish ways behind me. Now we see but a poor reflection as in a mirror; then we shall see face to face. Now I know in part; then I shall know fully, even as I am fully known (vv. 8-12).

Stanza three of the Bible's love song tells us that love is *eternal.* And if it's joined to Christ, that's the only way we'd want it. Everything else may be transitory and ephemeral, but love never ends. Everything else may be truncated and fragmented, but love is everlasting. Everything else may be temporary and immature, but love goes on forever. Though nothing else can be, *love is eternal.*

III. Love Is Supreme

A. *You Are the Other One*

For most newlyweds the first anniversary is a special occasion indeed. Sometimes, though, circumstances can separate a couple on that memorable day. And so it was that a bride and her serviceman husband found themselves celebrating their wedding anniversary thousands of miles apart. When the mailman brought no letter to her, the girl felt lonelier than ever. Then in the late afternoon, her heart skipped a beat when the florist delivered a long white box. Removing the red roses from the green tissue, she counted them, almost automatically. There were only eleven, but when she looked at the card she knew there was no mistake. It read: "YOU ARE THE OTHER ONE."

That's love that cares; there's a marriage that got off to a great start. If its continuation was as promising as its beginning, it didn't arrive at a dead end in a divorce court, as half of all first American marriages do. If their love for each other deepens as time goes on, they'll live up to their marriage vows in which they pledged to each other that they would participate in mutual love, honor, and obedience "as long as we both shall live." And if their marriage was made in heaven because they acknowledge themselves to be children of the heavenly Father, who can say that they will not continue to share an essential, ethical, eternal love throughout an interminable future?

B. Where Love Is Concerned, Aim for the Highest

The Bible's love song ends by reminding us that "these three remain: faith, hope, and love. But the greatest of these is love." Faith as a past decisive act and hope as a future glorious promise are bridged by a love that knows no time. It's that kind of love for Carolyn, which at best can be only a pale reflection of God's love for me, that I want to make my aim. An impossible goal? Maybe. But if I can manage a partial attainment of it, that in itself will sanctify even our most common hours.

7

The Cross
in Christian Experience

Good Friday

"I have been crucified with Christ" (Gal. 2:20).

Outline

Introduction

    I. The Symbolism of Crosses

        A. The Swastika of Nazism

        B. The Hammer-and-Sickle of Communism

        C. The Cross of Christianity

            1. Necessary for Jesus

            2. Necessary for us

Body

    II. Bearing the Cross of Jesus

        A. Losing Our Lives for His Sake

            1. Death precedes life

            2. The need to die experientially

        B. Giving Up Everything for One's Life

            1. The value of salvation

            2. The need to sacrifice for the sake of others

        C. Receiving an Eternal Reward

            1. Crosses precede crowns

            2. The need to endure potential ridicule

Conclusion

I. The Symbolism of Crosses

A. The Swastika of Nazism

Seventy years ago, in the summer of 1920, Adolf Hitler decided to provide the Nazi party with an emblem, a symbol that would appeal to the imagination of the people of Germany. After giving the matter some thought, he finally chose a red flag, in the middle of which was a white disc imprinted with a black swastika. And so it was that the twisted cross of Nazism was born—the cross that promised political salvation to the frustrated lower middle classes of Germany but proved so repulsive to most of the rest of the world's people.

B. The Hammer-and-Sickle of Communism

For all practical purposes, Nazism has passed from the world scene—but only to be replaced by another and more deadly enemy: international communism. Like the Nazis, the Communists have chosen a twisted cross as the symbol of their plans and purposes, this time in the form of a hammer intersecting a sickle. "Rally to our banner," they advise the oppressed peoples of the world, "and we will release you from the back-breaking drudgery of your labor and bring you economic salvation." But those who have snatched at the straw of communism's cross have eventually found themselves in a form of slavery far worse than anything they had previously experienced. The result has been that relocation centers

on every hand are becoming increasingly overpopulated
with refugees from so-called "workers' paradises" all over
our world.

C. The Cross of Christianity

The swastika and the hammer-and-sickle are diabolical
caricatures of the cross of Christianity, even though the
resemblance may be purely coincidental. Surely no one
can doubt that just as the swastika is the emblem of
Nazism, and just as the hammer-and-sickle is the insignia
of communism, so also the cross of Christ has always
been the undisputed symbol of Christianity. So much is
this the case that we use replicas of the cross to crown our
church steeples and outlines of the cross to plot the floor
plans of our sanctuaries. We wear little crosses on chains
around our necks or in the lapels of our coats. We
emblazon crosses on the official emblems of our Christian
schools. And all of this is only as it should be, because the
cross of Christendom is emblematic of the death of Jesus
Christ, the Savior of the world.

1. Necessary for Jesus.   The cross of Christ is central
in Christian symbolism because the death of Christ is
central in Christian teaching. All of the gospel writers
focus on the death of Christ with a minuteness of detail
unparalleled in connection with any other New Testament theme. John devotes almost half of his gospel to the
events of the last few days of Jesus' life. Paul says in
1 Corinthians 2:2: "I resolved to know nothing while I
was with you except Jesus Christ and him crucified," and
in Galatians 6:14: "May I never boast except in the cross
of our Lord Jesus Christ, through which the world has
been crucified to me, and I to the world."

Yes, the cross is central in Christian symbolism, and
the cross is pivotal in Christian theology. This the church

rarely forgets, and this the church normally practices. But there is another area in which the cross should be central—another sphere in which the cross ought to be uppermost in our minds. The cross should be central in Christian *experience.* This the church knows also, but sad to say, this the church often fails to practice. The cross in our symbolism? Yea and amen! The cross in our teaching? God forbid that we should ever forget it! But the cross in our personal experience? You and I, personally, to experience what it means to bear a cross? You and I to suffer many things? You and I to die to the world, the flesh, and the devil? That may be fine for monks and ascetics and other fanatics, you say, but not for *me.*

Jesus, as his words are recorded in Matthew 16:13-27, had just told his disciples, for the first time in unmistakable terms, that he had to go to Jerusalem, suffer many things from those in authority there, die, and be glorified through resurrection. Never before had he told his disciples these things, because never before had they been ready to receive them. But just prior to this time Peter had solemnly confessed to Jesus, "You are the Christ, the Son of the living God." What better time could Jesus have chosen to begin to tell his followers that he must suffer and die? Peter, as the self-appointed spokesman of the group, had just proclaimed their absolute trust in the fact that their Lord was supernatural, that he had the breath of heaven about him, that he was the very Son of God himself. If that confession would not steel them for an announcement about the impending crisis, nothing would.

And yet that very announcement seemed quite out of place to Peter. He "took him aside, and began to rebuke him. 'Never, Lord!' he said. 'This shall never happen to

you!'" In other words: "Let's have no more of this talk of
your dying. Suffering and death don't befit your station in
life. Humiliation and ill treatment don't match our
understanding of what a Messiah has a right to expect.
You're going to rule, not die! Never! This shall never
happen!"

But Jesus turned and said to Peter, "Out of my sight,
Satan! You are a stumbling block to me; you do not have
in mind the things of God, but the things of men."

When Peter had said to Jesus, "You are the Christ, the
Son of the living God," our Lord had ascribed that
confession to a divine source: "This was not revealed to
you by man, but by my Father in heaven." But now,
when Peter rebukes Jesus with the words, "Never, Lord!
This shall never happen to you," Jesus ascribes that
statement to satanic agency—a declaration from the devil
himself.

To this very hour, Jesus hears the cry from more than
one quarter, "Come down from the cross, and we'll
believe in you!" It comes from those who are moral
cowards—those who are worldly-minded and pleasure-
bent, those who can't get along without their favorite
sins—who have no idea of their hopeless condition before
a holy and righteous God—who can't understand what
punishment, atonement, and redemption are all about. It
comes also from those who think that all sincere travelers
will get to heaven eventually—those who feel that
stained-glass windows and the muffled tones of an organ
are the sum total of religion— those who want a creed
without a cross—those who prefer an apron of fig leaves
to a garment of skins—those who rebel at the idea of
mingling with Jesus' despised followers and sharing his
reproach—those who don't want to get involved in

Christ's sufferings and the world's problems. These and countless others shout, "Come down from the cross! Eliminate the blood from your religion, and we'll believe in you!" But to all such people the Bible answers quite plainly: "Without the shedding of blood there is no forgiveness" (Heb. 9:22). It is the blood of Jesus Christ, God's Son, that "purifies us from every sin" (1 John 1:7). Indeed, in the words of our Lord to Peter, a statement insisting that it was not necessary for Christ to die can be made only with the help of Satan himself.

2. Necessary for us. "Then Jesus said to his disciples, 'If anyone would come after me, he must deny himself and take up his cross and follow me.'"

What's the key to personal self-realization, to the best of all possible worlds, to all you want out of life? If you had posed that question to the Platonic philosophers of Jesus' day, they would have pointed to the motto engraved above the main doorway leading into Plato's academy: KNOW YOURSELF. The Stoics, on the other hand, proposed a different answer to the problems of life. Success lies in self-discipline, they urged; "Control yourself," they suggested. To all such, and not least to those who would be his followers even today, Jesus proclaims the truth that the only philosophy of life worth embracing is the one that requires, as its basic principle, obedience to his command, "Deny yourself."

Self-denial instead of self-indulgence; self-effacement in lieu of self-assertion; self-crucifixion rather than self-seeking—these are necessary prerequisites to following Jesus. "Christ suffered for you, leaving you an example, that you should follow in his steps" (1 Peter 2:21). And following in the steps of Jesus is synonymous with denying oneself and bearing a cross.

II. Bearing the Cross of Jesus

After pointing to his coming experience of suffering and death as the supreme example of what it means to bear a cross, and after informing his disciples of the absolute necessity of bearing a cross, Jesus went on to list three reasons why it's necessary to bear a cross.

A. Losing Our Lives for His Sake

"If anyone would come after me, he must deny himself and take up his cross and follow me. For whoever wants to save his life will lose it, but whoever loses his life for me will find it." This is the first lesson on the road to self-crucifixion. But what in the world does it mean?

1. Death precedes life.   Let me try to paraphrase it: "Whoever decides that it's the most important thing in the world to pamper and preserve his natural life and well-being, the life lived here on earth, will lose the life that really matters, the blessed life in God's eternal heaven; but whoever is willing to forsake his natural life, for my sake, will find the life that really matters." Christ makes it very plain that we have to lose something, the only question being what we'll lose: temporary happiness, or eternal joy. The lesson is clear: We must bear a cross because death precedes life. Just as the golden stalk of grain is vibrant with life because a few months earlier the seed fell into the ground and died, so also it's possible for us to enjoy spiritual life and vitality only as a result of death to the old nature.

2. The need to die experientially.   If you're a Christian, the New Testament teaches that the old nature in you is dead positionally; but it also teaches that traces of that old nature are not dead experientially. And it goes on to teach that you have to keep trying to root out the sins and habits that reflect the old nature and that scandalize and disgrace the Holy Spirit who lives within you. You must root them out at all costs. And when a well-meaning friend sidles up to you and says, "Never! This shall never happen to you! Live it up! Eat, drink, and be merry! Don't take your religion so seriously! Variety is the spice of life, you know. Why not indulge in a questionable practice now and then? Enjoy yourself; it's later than you think! Never! This shall never happen to you!"—on such occasions you must be willing to respond to him, as our Lord did to Peter: "Out of my sight, Satan! You are a stumbling block to me; you do not have in mind the things of God, but the things of men." This word of Jesus strikes the death blow at sensualism.

B. Giving Up Everything for One's Life

Here, then, is the second reason. "If anyone would come after me, he must deny himself and take up his cross and follow me. . . . What good will it be for a man if he gains the whole world, yet forfeits his soul? Or what can a man give in exchange for his soul?"

1. The value of salvation. The way of the cross will teach you something about values. It will show you how much your own salvation is worth to you; it will show you how much the destinies of unbelievers are worth to Jesus. Your eternal salvation is too high a price to exchange even for the whole world, not to mention for that very small part of it that you can claim as your own.

The ancient Hebrew prophet expressed it well when he said (Micah 6:6-7):

> With what shall I come before the LORD
> and bow down before the exalted God?

Shall I come before him with burnt offerings,
   with calves a year old?
Will the LORD be pleased with thousands of rams,
   with ten thousand rivers of oil?
Shall I offer my firstborn for my transgression,
   the fruit of my body for the sin of my soul?

The only possible answer to that rhetorical question is "No, a thousand times no!" Such fleeting things couldn't pay for the undying soul of one single human being. Death on God's terms is the only thing that can pay for life, and that's why it took the death of God's Son himself to pay for your redemption and mine. So also it's only as you deny yourself, take up your cross, follow your Lord into the valley of death, and learn to die to sin in all of its insidious forms—it's only *then* that your self-sacrifice can bring the person for whom you've been praying to the place where the Holy Spirit can work in his heart. Your death to self can help to bring eternal life to someone else.

2. The need to sacrifice for the sake of others. The next time the Spirit incites you to speak to someone about his or her soul's destiny, you might hear yourself saying to yourself, "Never! This shall never happen to you! You don't have any time for such people! Besides, they might refuse to listen to you, or even ridicule you. At any rate, they're too far gone, or at least they're happy enough the way they're going. Never! This shall never happen to you!" If that's the situation, listen carefully, and you'll hear in the distance the voice of Jesus saying directly to you, "Out of my sight, Satan! You are a stumbling block to me; you do no have in mind the things of God, but the things of men." This word of our Lord strikes the death blow at a careless ranking of priorities.

C. Receiving an Eternal Reward

1. Crosses precede crowns.   Here, then, is the final reason. ''If anyone would come after me, he must deny himself and take up his cross and follow me. . . . For the Son of Man is going to come in his Father's glory with his angels, and then he will reward each person according to what he has done.'' We must bear a cross because crosses always precede crowns. God will reward all of us according to what we've done. The reward that Jesus himself received was the glory that followed his resurrection.

2. The need to endure potential ridicule.   The implication is that the degree of self-denial determines the degree of the reward. He who suffers much for Jesus in this life will receive much from Jesus in the life to come. The very thought of the Master's approval should spur us on to fresh efforts for him, because the magnitude of his ''Well done!'' will depend on the magnitude of our well-doing. Our Lord has told us to rejoice whenever people ridicule us and persecute us and utter all kinds of evil against us falsely on his account, because our reward in such cases is great in heaven. And persecution in some form is inevitable as we learn to crucify our old natures. But let's remember the prospect of the reward that awaits us—a reward that beggars description. Let's remember it especially if a well-meaning friend should ever say, ''Never! This shall never happen to you! You're not actually looking for rewards, are you? It's unseemly for you to seek favors from the Savior. Anyhow, a mediocre showing will bring you just as much fame and glory as an all-out effort will. Besides, virtue is its own reward. Never! This shall never happen to you!'' If that should ever be your situation, be willing to turn sadly to your friend and whisper, ''Out of my sight, Satan! You are a stumbling block to me; you do not have in mind the things of God, but the things of men." This word of Jesus strikes the death blow at false modesty.

III. The Choice Is Yours

A. There's a Cross for Everyone

The first three gospel writers tell us that Simon of Cyrene was pressed into service to carry Jesus' cross for him. It would seem, then, that Simon didn't carry it of his own free will. Maybe it's in this context that we should understand the observation of John that Jesus, "carrying his own cross, . . . went out" (John 19:17). Compulsory service is not the hallmark of whole-soul devotion. Apparently there were no volunteers on the road to Golgotha. Simon bore the cross, that's true, but in a deeper sense Jesus carried it himself. "Must Jesus bear the cross alone, and all the world go free?" Will we remain content with sitting on the sidelines as spectators, members of a faceless crowd in a heartless world, because it would be too risky to do otherwise? Or will we address ourselves to the staggering tasks that lie before us, and will we begin to do so by seizing, each one, his individual cross? Because, you see, there's a cross for every one, and there's a cross for you, and there's one for me as well.

So it was that Jesus told his disciples (his disciples in all ages, not just the twelve who were there at the time): "If anyone proposes, if anyone wishes, if anyone desires to come after me"—and who doesn't, after all?—"he must deny himself"; he must humble himself; he must forget himself; he must lose sight of himself and his own interests; he must begin thinking about the interests of his fellow Christians, and the interests of his neighbors and friends and relatives outside of Christ and the interests of his God; he must seek first the kingdom of God and his righteousness; he must deny himself—"and take up his cross"—take up the symbol of suffering and death, as Jesus did—"and follow me."

B. Will You Bear a Cross, or Simply Wear One?

But how best to follow Christ? We're nearing the close of Holy Week—those last few terrible days of Jesus' earthly life. In Gethsemane, he experienced the extended agony of persevering prayer in wresting from his Father the strength he needed for the next few hours. At Gabbatha, he bore the brunt of physical and spiritual humiliation and suffering at the hands of his enemies. On Golgotha, he demonstrated his willingness to pay the ultimate price, come what may and cost what it might. If you and I would follow him, we have no choice but to prepare ourselves to walk the same way he walked.

> Go to dark Gethsemane,
>   Ye that feel the tempter's power;
> Your Redeemer's conflict see;
>   Watch with him one bitter hour;
> Turn not from his griefs away;
> Learn of Jesus Christ to pray.
>
> Follow to the judgment-hall;
>   View the Lord of life arraigned.
> O the wormwood and the gall!
>   O the pangs his soul sustained!
> Shun not suffering, shame, or loss;
> Learn of him to bear the cross.
>
> Calvary's mournful mountain climb;
>   There, adoring at his feet,

Mark that miracle of time,
   God's own sacrifice complete:
"It is finished!"—hear the cry;
Learn of Jesus Christ to die.

                          James Montgomery

8

Reacting to the Resurrection

Easter Sunday

"Christ was raised from the dead through the glory of the Father" (Rom. 6:4).

Outline

Introduction

    I. The Glory of Sunday

        A. Every Sunday a Glorious Day

        B. Easter Sunday the Most Glorious of All

Body

    II. Possible Responses to the Story of Jesus' Resurrection

        A. The Folly of Derision: "Some of Them Sneered"

            1. Mockery in secular matters

            2. Mockery in spiritual matters

        B. The Danger of Delay: "We Want to Hear You Again"

            1. Procrastination: the thief of time

            2. Examples: the five foolish maidens, Peter, Judas, Felix

        C. The Blessedness of Belief: "A Few Men . . . Believed"

            1. Alternatives: false philosophies

            2. Results: forgiveness, power, eternal life

Conclusion

I. The Glory of Sunday

All of you look great today! And why shouldn't you? It's Sunday, and Sunday seems to bring out the best in all of us.

A. Every Sunday a Glorious Day

In our culture it's the most carefree, work-free day of the week. On it we tend to be less nervous and uptight, more relaxed and friendly. It's Sunday, the day of the sun, the day of light and brightness. In the words of the hymn writer, for the Christian it's the "day of rest and gladness." And we who believe in Christ enjoy other blessings also on this day, as the second stanza of that hymn reminds us:

> On thee, at the creation,
>   The light first had its birth;
> On thee, for our salvation,
>   Christ rose from depths of earth;
> On thee our Lord victorious
>   The Spirit sent from heaven;
> And thus on thee most glorious
>   A triple light was given.
>
> Christopher Wordsworth

Sandwiched between the light of creation's first day and the light of the Holy Spirit's appearance on the day of Pentecost in that stanza is the sunburst of Christ's resurrection from the dead on the inaugural day of the Christian Sabbath. When Jesus rose, our day of rest moved from the seventh of the week all the way back to the first of the week. Because Jesus rose, we look back on the Sabbath rather than forward to it. Since Jesus rose, we begin our week with worship instead of ending it with worship. Every Sunday, then, should be a bright and joyful day, the best day of the week.

B. Easter Sunday the Most Glorious of All

And if Sunday is the best day of the week, Easter Sunday is the best day of the year! It celebrates the most earthshaking fact in history: that Jesus Christ, the third day after dying on a cross and being buried in a tomb, literally rose from the dead. So astounding was that event to his disciples that at first they found it hard to believe. But a series of remarkable post-resurrection appearances by their Lord gradually transformed them from cringing cowards into courageous preachers. The resurrection of Christ—the very possibility of which they had formerly doubted—became their favorite subject of conversation and proclamation.

II. Possible Responses to the Story of Jesus' Resurrection

The New Testament mentions the overall topic of resurrection so often that we can't ignore it or remain indifferent to it. It forces itself on us and compels us to react to it in some way. If we are Christians, we have already responded positively, because Romans 10:9 defines a Christian as a person who believes in Jesus' resurrection: "If you confess with your mouth, 'Jesus is

Lord,' and believe in your heart that God raised him from the dead, you will be saved." But let's assume that you have never consented to receive Jesus as your Savior, and that you are now being confronted with the story of his resurrection for the first time. How might you react to that story?

Acts 17:16-34 records an incident that has a strangely modern ring. Paul was visiting Athens, the intellectual and cultural capital of the Roman empire. While waiting for a couple of friends, he had an opportunity to do a little sightseeing. The farther he walked the clearer it became to him that most of the people of Athens were superstitious idol worshipers. So he decided to share with them his knowledge of a personal and loving God. Especially in the *agora*, the marketplace, he was able to find people who were willing to debate with him. It was the novel and the unusual that seemed to intrigue them most. Like so many Americans today, "All the Athenians and the foreigners who lived there spent their time doing nothing but talking about and listening to the latest ideas" (v. 21).

If it was something new that they wanted to hear, Paul would have no trouble obliging them. What he had to tell the Athenians was very new indeed. It was hot off the presses, as we would say. And it was not only new, it was also good. The gospel, the "good news," Paul called it. His mission on that particular day was to herald "Jesus and the resurrection" (v. 18), the headline story of the ages.

Some of the philosophers who were there considered Paul to be at worst a "babbler" and at best one who was "advocating foreign gods." But as a group they decided that what he had to say might be worth listening to after all. So they ushered him over to the Areopagus, a large outcropping of rock near the marketplace. A flat area near the top became his speaker's platform, but before he began his address he surveyed the surrounding scene.

To the north and below him was the agora itself, a many-avenued complex of shops and stores, stands and stalls. At its western end Paul could see a splendid temple dedicated to Hephaestus, the Greek god of metallurgy. Everywhere throughout the marketplace stone and marble statues of pagan deities were visible. And Paul could hear the cries of the hawkers, peddling their portable images and idols.

To the southeast and above him was the hallowed Acropolis, the highest and holiest section of the city. Even today the visitor can see on its summit much of what Paul saw: the incomparable temple of Athena, known as the Parthenon; the classic Erechtheum, a shrine believed to contain gifts from Poseidon, the watergod; the exquisite little temple of Nike, the deity of victory; and other similar architectural monuments to the pantheon of Greece.

With such sights before his eyes, it is no wonder that Paul started his speech with these words: "Men of Athens! I see that in every way you are very religious." Reminders of the gods of Greece were all around them. But Paul knew that the story of Jesus and the resurrection was worlds away from that totally pagan context, and so in a brilliant series of startling statements he swiftly and deftly took his hearers from where they were to where he wanted them to go. He called their attention to a nearby altar erected to an "unknown god" and used it as a stepping-stone leading to the God that he knew personally. That God is sovereign, omnipotent, and independent; but at the same time he is near, provident, and loving—as even some of their own poets would have admitted. It is only the ignorant, then, who would attempt to portray such a God in images of metal and stone. He wants from his children not artistic proficiency but heartfelt penitence to prepare them for the time when the whole world would be judged by a man whom he had recently raised from the dead.

Back now to our earlier question: If you were not a Christian, how might you react to the story of the resurrection of Jesus after hearing it for the first time? There would be several options open to you, of course. In fact, they would be much the same choices that the Athenians made on the occasion we're considering. Let's take a look at what those reactions were.

A. The Folly of Derision: "Some of Them Sneered"

"When they heard about the resurrection of the dead, some of them sneered." Now there's a reaction for you! To some of Paul's listeners, immortality in any sense was a preposterous idea. But resurrection? The actual, physical raising to life of a dead man? Ridiculous! When faced with such a thought, they responded with a predictable reaction: They made fun of it, they laughed it to scorn.

1. Mockery in secular matters. Very few of the noblest of our western traditions and institutions are immune from mockery in our time. Perhaps unwittingly, some city workmen in San Antonio, Texas, were mocking modern art when they hauled a thirty-five-thousand-dollar, two-ton abstract sculpture from its exhibition site to the municipal scrapyard. It wasn't missed for months, which may mean that the sculptor had been mocking traditional art when he welded it together in the first place. At any rate, when the donor finally discovered it was gone, he soon located it in a serious state of disrepair. Fortunately the San Antonio city manager was sure that the pieces could be recreated as art for about seven thousand dollars—unless the welders in that area decided to strike for higher wages. And so it goes: Certain workmen mock some modern art; certain art dealers mock some wealthy patrons; certain modern artists mock some traditional art; and certain welders mock some city managers.

If that were the end of the matter, we could all have a good laugh over it. But the fact is that many concerned people in our country are beginning to see that much of what passes for "modern poetry" and "modern music" and "modern art" is making a mockery of what the mandate of history has been pleased to call "the true, the good, and the beautiful." Every time a witness in a court trial evades his responsibility by hiding behind the Fifth Amendment he mocks our federal Constitution. Whenever our laws are too lenient with drug dealers and pornography publishers they make a mockery of justice. By paroling criminals who have proven by the viciousness of their actions that they are not fit for even a contingent freedom, our policing officials mock law enforcement. And some of our children—of whatever age—are ridiculing our educational system by vandalizing and destroying school property, for whatever cause.

To speak with a mocking attitude is to scoff and scorn, and to act out mockery is to make a laughingstock of the products of our culture and the institutions of our civilization. The products of our culture are for our edification and enjoyment; how foolish it is to mock them! The institutions of our civilization are for our protection and welfare; how unpardonable it is to mock them! Yet there seems to be a demonic spirit of mockery on every hand.

2. *Mockery in spiritual matters.* Regrettably, that spirit extends also into the realm of religion. Gone are the days when characters in novels and actors on stage and screen refrained from taking the name of the Lord in vain in their role playing. All branches of Christendom are openly ridiculed in current theatrical productions. No longer are even the most revered teachings of our faith or the most saintly figures in the Bible considered sacrosanct by the public media. High living and moral failure on the part of respected Christian leaders adds to the problem. And worst of all, even the resurrection of Jesus Christ is often made the butt of jokes today, just as it was in ancient Athens.

All of this is to the everlasting sorrow of God, who does not want "anyone to perish, but everyone to come to repentance" (2 Peter 3:9). But when we mock God and his righteous demands and his purposes and his Son, irreversible spiritual laws take over. "Do not be deceived: God cannot be mocked. A man reaps what he sows" (Gal. 6:7). People may ridicule certain things and get away with it for the most part, but nothing is ever gained by laughing at God. "The One enthroned in heaven laughs; the Lord scoffs at them" (Ps. 2:4).

B. The Danger of Delay: "We Want to Hear You Again"

The real and present danger for most people, when confronted by the resurrection of Christ, however, is not that they mock it. Very few are as blatant in their negative reaction to it as were some of the Athenian philosophers on the Areopagus. The folly of derision doesn't characterize the vast majority. Much more widespread, because much more subtle, is the reaction of postponement. We observe that others of Paul's listeners said, ''We want to hear you again on this subject.'' ''We're interested, but we're pretty busy right now. What you're saying, Paul, sounds good; but we've got to have a little more time to consider the pros and cons of believing in Jesus. Rome wasn't built in a day, you know. Look before you leap, haste makes waste; business before pleasure——and all that. We want to hear you again on this subject.''

1. Procrastination: the thief of time. No doubt the second group of listeners made those and many similar comments to Paul that day. They hauled out all the excuses they could think of to avoid committing themselves to the Savior. But unhappily for them, Scripture is transparently clear in pointing out the dangers of that kind of behavior. ''I tell you, now is the time of God's favor, now is the day of salvation'' (2 Cor. 6:2). The Bible reminds us that procrastination is the thief of time, that it is dangerous in the extreme to play around with and linger over God's gracious invitations.

2. Examples: the five foolish maidens, Peter, Judas, Felix. In the parable of the foolish and wise maidens, the five who were foolish waited too long to buy enough oil for their lamps and as a result missed out on the marriage feast. Peter, loitering in a courtyard during the trial of Jesus, remembered his vow to the Master only after a rooster had already crowed. Judas, too late, repented of his betrayal of Christ, and his feeble attempt to right a wrong ended in suicide.

One of the most pitiful characters in all of Scripture is Felix, a Roman governor of Palestine, as he is pictured in Acts 24:25: ''As Paul discoursed on righteousness, self-control and the judgment to come, Felix was afraid and said, 'That's enough for now! You may leave. When I find it convenient, I will send for you.'" God said *today,* but Felix said *tomorrow.* God said *now,* but Felix said *later on.* God recommended *the present,* but Felix preferred to wait for a more *convenient* time. During the next two years Felix often sent for Paul, but apparently only to try to bribe Paul to buy his way out of jail. He must have continued to postpone his spiritual decision making because at the end of the two-year period he left both his post in Palestine and Paul in prison. Scripture is silent as to whether Felix ever found a more "convenient" time to confess faith in the resurrected Jesus.

Those of us who believe need desperately to recapture some of the urgency of Paul's gospel witness. We need to remind our unbelieving friends of the perils of procrastination, of the madness of waiting for a tomorrow that never comes. We must point out to them that today is neither more nor less than yesterday's tomorrow. We have to declare as firmly and lovingly as we can that every moment they delay in taking their stand for Christ is at best a wasted moment. It's just as important to denounce the agnosticism of delay as it is to condemn the atheism of mockery.

C. The Blessedness of Belief: "A Few Men . . . Believed"

But scoffers and procrastinators didn't comprise Paul's entire audience on the Areopagus. Illumined by the light of Easter faith, these words glow forth from the page: "A few men became followers of Paul and believed."

1. Alternatives: false philosophies. There they were, a small group of cultured Athenians on that never-to-be-forgotten day when Paul gave the invitation at the close of his Mars' Hill sermon. Having been exposed to the Epicurean and Stoic philosophies of their day, having studied the teachings of Socrates and Plato and Aristotle and found them spiritually sterile, having examined the ceremonial rites and ethical precepts of the oriental mystery cults prevalent in the Near East during the apostolic age, having looked for God in vain, "a few men became followers of Paul and believed." A few allowed God to find them. A few suddenly discovered the very reason for which they had been created. A few opened themselves up to the saving power of the living Christ. "A few men . . . believed."

2. *Results: forgiveness, power, eternal life.* With that belief came eternal life. With that belief came freedom from condemnation and judgment. With that belief came forgiveness of sins and justification in God's eyes. With that belief came the power to become God's children and Christ's fellow heirs. With that belief came several new entries in the Lamb's book of life: "Dionysius, a member of the Areopagus, also a woman named Damaris, and a number of others."

III. Our Reactions Always Have Eternal Consequences

A. *Laughing It Off, Putting It Off, Taking It In*

So to laugh it off, or to put it off, or to take it in—these are a few of the options available to us when faced by the story of Jesus' resurrection. But Biblical faith excludes the first two and embraces only the third. And when all is said and done, the presence of the living Lord working through the record of his resurrection produces its own miracle in the experience of the sympathetic listener.

B. "I Felt My Heart Strangely Warmed"

Along the road to Emmaus on that first Easter Sunday, two of Jesus' disciples had confessed to each other, "Were not our hearts burning within us while he talked with us on the road and opened the Scriptures to us?" The way of the resurrected Christ is always the way of the believing, burning heart. As John Wesley, the founder of Methodism, put it as he later reflected on the day of his conversion: "I felt my heart strangely warmed."

Does what you know about the resurrection of Jesus affect you like that today?

used from 5-12-96

9

The Crises in Mary's Life

Mother's Day

"A woman who fears the LORD is to be praised" (Prov. 31:30).

Outline

Introduction

    I. The Battle of the Sexes

        A. A Woman's World Today

        B. Not a Woman's World in Ancient Times

        C. The Position of Women Elevated by Jesus

        D. Resulting Clashes and Crises Between Women and Men

Body

    II. Crises in the Life and Experiences of Mary

        A. The Crisis of the Miraculous Birth

            1. Every birth a crisis

            2. How to treat an unexpected—or unwanted—baby

            3. Mary's response to Jesus' birth

            4. Suggested responses for modern mothers

        B. The Crisis of the Growing Child

            1. The generation gap

            2. How to handle an unpredictable teenager

            3. Mary's response to Jesus' boyhood days

I. The Battle of the Sexes

A. A Woman's World Today

Let's face it, fellows: It's a woman's world. I make all the important decisions around our house, of course, like how to ward off nuclear disaster, stop the pollution of our environment, and end the Middle East crisis. Carolyn determines only minor matters like the kind of food we'll eat, the style of clothes we'll wear, and the way our rooms will be furnished. But it's a woman's world for all that. After all, when a man is born, the question on everyone's lips is: "How is the mother?" When a man is married, everybody exclaims, "Isn't the bride lovely?" And when a man dies, people ask, "How much did he leave her?"

B. Not a Woman's World in Ancient Times

But the world at the beginning of the first Christian century was anything *but* a woman's world. According to Jewish law, a man could divorce his wife but the woman didn't have the same privilege. Daughters were considered less desirable than sons, and fathers heavily in debt were permitted to sell their daughters as slaves. In general, the role of the woman was largely one of subordination to her husband or father. And in short, the inferior status of ancient women would have given our modern feminist organizations an awful lot to do.

C. The Position of Women Elevated by Jesus

Inevitably, the teachings of Jesus elevated the position of women during the New Testament period. Maintaining her subordinate role, the woman was still admonished to be subject to her husband, but "as to the Lord" (Eph. 5:22). The husband still enjoyed his superior status, but only as interpreted by love (5:23-25). The early church demanded mutual respect as the governing principle in marital as well as in all other relationships (5:21). So although the woman was expected to continue to exhibit the domestic virtues of modesty and submission, her influence and leadership soon began to make their mark on the wider Christian community, for better or for worse.

D. Resulting Clashes and Crises Between Women and Men

The New Testament, then, displays a prominence for women that was in many respects unique for that time. Although they were not yet living in a woman's world, women in the early church participated in many of its activities and performed many of its services. They often also shared in making decisions at home and in the marketplace. In so doing it was only natural that they occasionally came into conflict with their male counterparts. And it was perhaps unavoidable that now and then those conflicts erupted into crises.

Crises are not necessarily always to be shunned of course. Sometimes, in fact, a series of good, healthy crises can strengthen us. In the spring of 1965 the twin cities of St. Paul and Minneapolis were treated to a paralyzing snowstorm. At about the same time, rivers swollen by the melting snows of the previous winter began to invade homes in several low-lying neighborhoods. As if that were not enough, a wave of tornados almost leveled an entire suburban community. Then, adding insult to injury, the local authorities couldn't agree on the date for switching over from central standard time to daylight saving time. During that critical period someone defined a Twin Cities resident as a person who had snow in his driveway, water in his basement, no roof over his head, and who didn't know the time of day.

But such crises, though severe, can usually be overcome. When that happens we often realize how much they have taught us about life and how greatly they have helped to develop our character. G. Campbell Morgan in *The Crises of the Christ* discusses seven pivotal events in the life of Jesus, describing the wholesome effect they had on Jesus himself as well as on his friends and loved ones.

II. Crises in the Life and Experiences of Mary

In much the same way I wish to isolate a few of the crises in the life of Mary, the mother of our Lord. Doing this will help to clarify her relationship to Jesus, illumine her remarkable personal strength, and spotlight her difficulties in making her way through what was anything but a woman's world.

A. The Crisis of the Miraculous Birth

While still a young girl, Mary was summoned to endure the crisis of the miraculous birth. The account of the annunciation in Luke 1:26-38 is enveloped in the atmosphere of the extraordinary. Rarely does an angel visit a young woman and tell her she's about to become pregnant, but that's what happened in Mary's case. Never before had a virgin conceived a child while remaining a virgin, but Mary did. At no time had a promised infant been called "the Son of the Most High" or "the Son of God," but the one Mary expected was. Countless questions surged through her mind. She summed them all up by asking the most logical one: "How will this be, since I am a virgin?"

The angel assured her that the Holy Spirit himself would perform the miracle in her body. He added that her aged kinswoman, Elizabeth, had also conceived a son after a lifetime of barrenness. Though faced with those two improbabilities, Mary responded with the submissive loyalty expected of her: "I am the Lord's servant. May it be to me as you have said."

1. Every birth a crisis. In a way, every birth is a crisis. A new baby is not always a welcome guest. Through the use of various techniques the modern wife often tries to prevent the conception of an undesired baby. If she fails and doesn't want to bear the child, in her desperation she may yield her body to the instruments of the abortionist. The medical, legal, ethical, and spiritual implications of all types of birth control and prevention continue to rank among the most hotly debated issues of our time. But if the pregnancy is allowed to continue to its full term and the baby in fact arrives on the scene, the crisis becomes full-blown.

2. How to treat an unexpected—or unwanted—baby. How will you treat that unexpected and perhaps unwanted new baby, Mom? If you wish, you can meet the crisis with spitefulness and frustration. In that case the baby will double your sorrows by adding to the already enormous problems in your home, your neighborhood, your church, and your world. Or, if you wish, you can meet the crisis with excitement and gratitude. In that case the baby will double the joys of your home, your neighborhood, your church, and your world by brightening your life and the lives of your family and friends. Your reaction to the crisis of birth will test your mettle and set the pattern for your role as a mother.

3. *Mary's response to Jesus' birth.*   Take a page from the life of Mary! No sooner had she confirmed the fact of her pregnancy than she rushed out to tell Elizabeth all about it. Abortion—even had she known what it was——would have held no attraction for her. As the time of the birth drew near, Mary and Joseph, whom she had married in the meantime, busied themselves in preparation for the arrival of their son. No matter that they had to make a long and grueling journey just before the baby was born; their anticipation of his coming lifted their spirits! A manger became his crib and swaddling clothes his layette, but never mind; his birth was good news to "all the people," but especially to Mary and Joseph.

4. *Suggested responses for modern mothers.*   New parents know that new babies bring a generous supply of problems along with them. At one level, they learn to appreciate the deeper meaning of the sign on the nursery door in a local church: "WE SHALL NOT ALL SLEEP, BUT WE SHALL ALL BE CHANGED." At a much higher level they learn something of the delightful combination of privilege and responsibility bound up in the mystery and ministry of parenthood. Their best efforts will never be quite good enough, of course. But if it's true that well begun is half done, the first few years of a child's life are

well worth the most intense concentration that any parent is able to give them. The onset of one teachable mother's experience is described like this by Luke: "Mary treasured up all these things and pondered them in her heart" (2:19). What a great start for Jesus' life!

B. The Crisis of the Growing Child

But our Lord, like all other baby boys, became a teenager before Mary realized what was happening—and she was soon faced with the crisis of the growing child. The only glimpse we have into the boyhood days of Jesus is the one found in Luke 2:40-51. At the age of twelve he was obviously a normal, healthy, strong- willed lad. He and his family visited Jerusalem to celebrate a typical Passover festival. Always wanting to be where the action was, he stayed behind in the temple while his parents were beginning the long trip back to Nazareth. Soon missing him they returned to the city, where it took them three days to locate him. Understandably annoyed, Mary said to him, "Son, why have you treated us like this? Your father and I have been anxiously searching for you."

1. The generation gap   To say the least, Jesus' answer was a bit cryptic; and his parents' response to it was one of bewilderment. The answer and its response are excellent examples of what is sometimes called "the generation gap." Jesus said, "Why were you searching for me? Didn't you know I had to be in my Father's house?" He expressed surprise that they had been looking for him, and then he went on to use the word *father* in a different way than Mary had used it. His motives were doubtless pure, but the end result was lack of communication. Mary and Joseph didn't understand him.

A number of years ago Robert Paul Smith wrote a book entitled *"Where Did you Go?" "Out." "What Did You*

Do?" "Nothing." Those two brief questions and their even briefer answers summarize—humorously on the one hand but tragically on the other—parent-child conversations in all too many homes. Because the interests of a female adult and a male child often differ radically from each other, statements exchanged between mother and son often become shorter and more meaningless as time marches on. The mother, hopefully being the more mature of the two, should make the first moves toward clarity and comprehension. If she and her son remain on different wavelengths, communication will become impossible and the crisis will become unmanageable.

2. *How to handle an unpredictable teenager.*   How will you handle that unpredictable young man of yours, Mom? No longer a child but not yet an adult, he demands the privileges of the former and denies the responsibilities of the latter. He'll try your patience and tease you into forgiving him; he'll break your heart and expect your love. If you always react in anger, he'll soon withdraw into a shell and you may lose him forever. But if you respond with affectionate concern, you have a better-than-even chance of winning him back. Commend him for the good things he does, and overlook the things that annoy you if they are otherwise harmless. Paul's words to fathers in Ephesians 6:4 apply to mothers too: "Do not exasperate your children; instead, bring them up in the training and instruction of the Lord."

3. *Mary's response to Jesus' boyhood days.*   Take a page from the life of Mary! After Jesus, always obedient to his parents, accompanied them back to Nazareth, "his mother treasured all these things in her heart" (Luke 2:51). Happily for Jesus, she was as teachable now as she had been twelve years earlier. As "Jesus grew in wisdom

and stature, and in favor with God and men," Mary tried her best to keep up with him. Even when she didn't fully understand him, she maintained her confidence in him, knowing that his sense of divine vocation would be his guide. Mary's womanly intuition, guided by God himself, must have smoothed out many a rough road for Jesus while he was passing along the way from boyhood to manhood.

C. The Crisis of the Successful Career

But the mother of our Lord watched with growing uneasiness as her son slipped from her maternal grasp. The apron strings to which Jesus was tied became longer and longer, and before she knew it he was so far away she could hardly see him. He had won his wings and now wanted to make his own way, and Mary was confronted with the crisis of the successful career.

It all began during a wedding at Cana in Galilee (John 2:1-11). Among the guests were Jesus and Mary, who was understandably quite proud of her son's growing popularity. The solicitous nature of a Jewish mother's relationship to her son is legendary. Depending on his profession, she will introduce him as "my son, the doctor" or "my son, the lawyer" or the like. An apocryphal story has it that one such mother, whose son had entered the Catholic priesthood, introduced him as "my son, the father." On this particular occasion, Mary would soon be able to introduce Jesus as "my son, the miracle-worker"—but of course she didn't realize that at first.

1. "Please, Mom, I'd rather do it myself!" When she discovered that the master of the wedding banquet had run out of wine, she told Jesus about it. Apparently she felt that he would somehow be able to handle the emergency. His response sounds harsher in translation than the writer originally intended: "Dear woman, why do you involve me? My time has not yet come." He was simply warning his mother, gently but firmly, not to interfere in his affairs. His rebuke was the ancient reflex of another mild (if more modern) word of reproach: "Please, Mom, I'd rather do it myself!"

Jesus was indicating to Mary that he neither needed nor desired her help. He was a grown man now, and he wanted to establish his independence in no uncertain terms. Whatever deeper theological significance one might seek in his answer, he surely meant to suggest at the very least that his vocational concerns were now solely his own and that he wouldn't be willing to share his burdens or be able to share his triumphs with his mother—or with anyone else, for that matter. For the rest of his life the loneliness of his prophetic office would force him to alter his previous relationship with her. The apron strings had now been cut, and the separation created a crisis.

2. How to handle a mature, self-sufficient son. How will you fill the aching emptiness left behind when that completely self-sufficient son leaves the nest forever, Mom? If you wish, you can tag along after him, dogging his steps and hampering his progress. In that case he'll shudder every time he sees you coming and suffer inward agony until you leave. On the other hand, you can send him on his way with your prayers and God's promises, telling him that if he ever needs you, you'll come at a moment's notice. In that case he'll be your friend as well as your son, and you'll be like the mother the wise man described: "Her children arise and call her blessed" (Prov. 31:28).

3. *Mary's response to Jesus' fame and popularity.*
Take a page from the life of Mary! As soon as Jesus made
it clear to her that she was meddling, however harmlessly,
she retreated into the shadows. When she spoke again it
was to some servants rather than to her son. After Jesus
had changed the water into wine, she became only one
member (the most important member, to be sure) of the
group that accompanied him back to Capernaum. By
agreeing to his increase while accepting her own decrease,
Mary once again proved that she was teachable and had
Jesus' best interests at heart.

III. Spiritual Relationships and Family Ties

A. Mary and John Beneath the Cross

Needless to say, no mother is perfect—not even the
mother of our Lord. At one particularly crucial time in his
career when Mary came asking for him, Jesus had to
remind her once again that spiritual relationships must
sometimes take precedence over family ties (Mark 3:31-
35). This is not to say that Christ lacked understanding of
how close such ties could be, even though he himself
never had a wife or children. When he healed the sick and
raised the dead he usually restored them to their families
as an integral part of his gracious ministry in their lives.
Even while nailed to the cross he demonstrated how
genuine was his concern for Mary by assigning her to the
care of one of his favorite disciples. In his most critical
hour, Jesus found time for a mundane detail of domestic
life. And his remarkable mother, with him to the end,
shared that unforgettable moment.

B. The Infant, The Adolescent, the Adult

As an infant, as an adolescent, and as an adult Jesus was blessed with a mother who cared. Mary transformed all her crises into opportunities for growth in herself and in her family. In the midst of birth pangs and growing pains, reluctant good-byes and final farewells, she helped to change potential alienation into loving reconciliation. By her son's cradle on the day he was born and beneath his cross on the day he died, she demonstrated a maternal loyalty seldom equaled before or since. In so doing she left a record of devotion that, in its own small way, shows today's Christian mother how much it can cost to close the generation gap—even in a woman's world.

10

Thanks, Dad!

Father's Day

"Be perfect, therefore, as your heavenly Father is perfect" (Matt. 5:48).

Outline

Introduction

    I. Fathers Good and Bad

        A. The Modern Father in Our Confused Society

        B. The Jewish Father in New Testament Times

        C. God as Father

Body

    II. Divine and Human Fathers and Children

        A. A Father's Duty: Provision

            1. Awareness of children's needs

            2. Impartiality toward children

            3. Giving good gifts to children

        B. A Child's Response: Praise

            1. Giving glory and respect to one's father

            2. Hallowing the name of one's father

            3. Obeying one's father

Conclusion

I. Fathers Good and Bad

When my son Glenn was a small boy, he used to tell me that he wanted to be "just like daddy" when he grew up. Since my home (like so many others) had its share of problems as well as joys, Glenn made statements like that only in his more unguarded moments. But the father image in the average stable household is an attractive one for many a child. He sees in his father an example of generosity and authority and strength worth imitating. By the same token a bad father's image can affect his children adversely—often for life.

A. The Modern Father in Our Confused Society

The pressures and confusions of the modern world often strain that father-son relationship. A man often finds himself trapped by practices and habits from which he would very much like to spare his boy. Some time ago an American Cancer Society television commercial showed a father engaged in a number of commendable activities, such as washing the family car. His young son, tagging along after his dad, dutifully imitated each of the man's actions as best he could. In the last scene the father sat down under a tree, lit a cigarette, and laid the package on the grass beside him. As the commercial ended, the little boy—unnoticed by his father—picked up the package in anticipation of imitating his father's latest act. In similar if less obvious ways we as Christian fathers often cause our little ones to stumble.

When a father—Christian or otherwise—provides a bad example for his son, the father image itself loses its appeal. We can't expect a boy who lives in a broken or fatherless home to have very much respect for his father. A boy whose father is always drunk will probably either detest him or become a drunkard himself. In such cases we can hardly be surprised if the boy should be turned off by the biblical references to God as "Father." We shouldn't be shocked to learn that more and more boys are saying, "If God is like my father, I don't want anything to do with him."

B. The Jewish Father in New Testament Times

I hope that when our children refer to God as their heavenly Father they're able to do so with no regrets. I hope that our conduct at home doesn't give our sons a negative picture of what God is like. Since Jesus' favorite name for God was "Father," I trust that our homelife doesn't distort large sections of Jesus' teachings in the eyes of our daughters. I'm praying that our Lord's words mean as much to our sons today as they did to Jewish boys in first-century Palestine, in a time and place and culture that recognized the authority of human fathers and offered them respect and obedience.

C. God as Father

One of the most delightfully informative expositions of the fatherhood of God to be found anywhere in the teachings of Jesus is the Sermon on the Mount as recorded in Matthew 5-7. In those three chapters Jesus uses the word *God* only five times but calls God *Father* seventeen times. The frequency of his references to God as *Father* reflects his understanding of his own relationship as Son in the mystery of the Trinity. His willingness to use the term so often underscores his confidence that it would be properly understood by people for whom the word *father* had positive and pleasant connotations. And his description of the qualities of our Father God in such glowing terms can teach all of us who are human fathers lessons that we need to learn.

What does God the Father do for his children? In his masterful volume entitled *The Work of the Holy Spirit,* Abraham Kuyper states that the Father is the source of all that the Son arranges and the Spirit kindles. This emphasis also characterizes Jesus' portrait of God in the Sermon on the Mount. God as Father is the source of provision for all the needs of every one of his children. We who are fathers should be the same if we want to emulate him.

II. Divine and Human Fathers and Children

A. A Father's Duty: Provision

It's a father's duty to provide for his children.

1. Awareness of children's needs. At the outset, the good father is one who is aware of what his children need. It isn't necessary for us to heap up empty phrases in our prayers to our heavenly Father, to pray loudly and long to him as the heathen do, because, Jesus tells us, "your Father knows what you need before you ask him" (Matt. 6:8). His omniscience keeps him well informed about every problem that his children face. Nothing in the world is beyond the scope of his loving care. As the gospel folk song puts it, "He's got the little bitsy baby in his hands."

During the first few years of a child's life, it's imperative that his needs are supplied promptly and sufficiently.
If there's carelessness or indifference in this area, the
child will become thin and sickly. He will fall an easy
prey to disease and, if the neglect continues, he will
eventually die. Because the young child is too helpless to
do anything about his situation himself, it's vitally
important that his father be aware of the child's needs.
How grateful we who were fortunate enough to have
good fathers should be to them for having anticipated our
needs in advance!

We all enjoy kidding the doting father who in pajamas
and bathrobe gropes his way to the kitchen at two o'clock
in the morning to get his baby some milk. He's a funny
sight, no doubt about that—but I'm sure his little son or
daughter doesn't think so! Have you ever wondered what
goes on inside the mind of a baby? It doesn't take much
of an imagination to guess what the hungry little rascal is
thinking about at feeding time. But as he snuggles down
in the warm protection of his father's arm, I can't help
thinking that mingled with those pleasant thoughts of his
nourishment there's also the assurance that someone
cares. God our heavenly Father knows what his children
need before we ask him, and on the human level the good
father does likewise.

2. Impartiality toward children.   If he has more than
one child and if he wants to follow the example of the
One who is not a respecter of persons, the good father will
always strive to be impartial toward his children. "Love
your enemies and pray for those who persecute you, that
you may be sons of your Father in heaven. He causes his
sun to rise on the evil and the good, and sends rain on the
righteous and the unrighteous. If you love those who love

you, what reward will you get?'' (Matt. 5:44-46). God the Father sends the common graces of life—those things that we need for our sustenance and growth and enjoyment—to saint and sinner alike. Sunshine and rainfall, except in special providential cases, do not depend on faithfulness or antagonism toward God, nor do they fall on the beautiful, the rich, and the healthy more often than they do on the ugly, the poor, and the sick. Our heavenly Father meets us at the point of our need whether we are riding the crests of spiritual joy or whether our lives are at ebb tide. If his grace comes to us as unmerited favor, so also does his love come to us as undeserved affection.

The good father, if he is a man after God's own heart, will likewise be impartial toward his children. This fact should be so obvious as not to need further comment; yet all of us can think of homes in which one child is favored over the others. Such partiality can easily destroy not only the children who are comparatively neglected but the pampered one as well. There is nothing quite so ugly in the Christian home as parental favoritism. Its consequences are painfully evident in the well-known case of Rebekah-plus-Jacob versus Isaac-plus-Esau. Rivalry, jealousy and bitterness are the inevitable results, now as well as then. While it's certainly true that some children are more lovable than others, the beauty of the less lovable child will never be brought forth or nurtured by neglecting him. The temptation to be partial will sternly test a man's character, but if he is sincerely trying to emulate the qualities of his heavenly Father, he will dispense his paternal bounty without fear or favor. The result then can only be that every child in the family will have the opportunity to develop his capacities and abilities to the fullest.

3. *Giving good gifts to children.* Having disposed of every temptation to play favorites, the good father is one who gives good gifts to his children. "Which of you, if his son asks for bread, will give him a stone? Or if he asks for a fish, will give him a snake? If you, then, though you are evil, know how to give good gifts to your children, how much more will your Father in heaven give good gifts to those who ask him!" (Matt. 7:9-11). God is the source of everything worthwhile: "Every good and perfect gift is from above, coming down from the Father of the heavenly lights, who does not change like shifting shadows" (James 1:17). Because God is always good, his gifts are always good.

And here again we are confronted with what appears to be a self-evident fact: The conscientious father shouldn't have to be reminded to give good things to his children. But the problem arises when we try to figure out just what's meant by a "good gift." Any particular item might well be a good gift for one child but the worst thing in the world if given to another child.

Most of us, I suppose, would agree that a college education is a worthy goal and that the father who puts his son through college has given him a good gift. But an all-expenses-paid college education has ruined more than one young person by robbing him of incentives toward self-reliance, thrift, and the profitable use of leisure time. In many cases the father who pays only that part of his son's college expenses that the boy is unable to earn for himself gives to that son a finer gift than does the well-meaning father who foots the whole bill and so deprives his son of the chance to develop the qualities he'll need when he's out on his own.

In the final analysis, whether a gift is good is determined not by the *value* of the gift but rather *by what that gift will do to the one who receives it.* If the results are good results, then the gift, no matter how humble, is a good gift. Such are the gifts that God bestows on us; they always eventuate in our good. So if the human father wants to be like the heavenly Father, he must determine the need, put aside all pretense of partiality, and carefully evaluate each of the gifts that he offers his children, doing everything in his power to make sure that they will result in their good.

B. A Child's Response: Praise

1. Giving glory and respect to one's father.   Now I'd like to say a word or two also to children on this Father's Day. And of course by "children" I mean children of all ages! If the Sermon on the Mount suggests to us that it's the duty and privilege of the good father to provide, it suggests also that it's the duty and privilege of the good son or daughter to praise.

"Let your light shine before men," says Jesus, "that they may see your good deeds and praise your Father in heaven" (Matt 5:16). We find much the same sort of emphasis in 1 Corinthians 4:7: "What do you have that you did not receive? And if you did receive it, why do you boast as though you did not?" Both Jesus and Paul tell us that all the credit for spiritual success in our Christian lives is to be given to God the Father who has made it possible. Because the Father gives good gifts to us, our gratitude should compel us to give the glory to him. The very idea of a self-made Christian is a contradiction in terms.

If this is true in the spiritual realm, it applies also to the relationship between the child and his human father.

I'd be the first to admit that the situations portrayed on such television programs as the "Father Knows Best" reruns are somewhat idealized. But the general attitude of affection and respect that Betty and Bud and Kathy Anderson display toward their television father is, sad to say, more Christlike than the way in which many of us treat our fathers. If God should be given the glory for our good works, so also do our fathers deserve the plaudits that we often deny them. In most cases it's their help and encouragement that have made us what we are today.

2. Hallowing the name of one's father.   In much the same way, the good son should respect and protect his father's good name. The opening words of the Lord's Prayer are familiar to all of us: "Our Father in heaven, hallowed be your name" (Matt. 6:9). In the thought life of ancient Israel, "name" was equivalent to "character" or "personality." Maybe that's why the average Israelite treated the name of God with more honor and reverence than the average Christian does today. Contrary to what many people think, God is not an amiable namby-pamby, permissive in attitude and undeserving of our respect. All of us need to call ourselves back to the conviction that the name of God the Father is to be hallowed.

In ancient Israel people understood that disrespect for the Father's name could easily lead to disrespect for the Father's person. Similarly, the reference of a modern American to his earthly father as "my old man" is sometimes symptomatic of a deeper indifference. Whether that expression was originally a term of endearment I'm not sure, but I do know that it's often used today as a term of condescension or contempt. Even if only to avoid inheriting a name and reputation that we ourselves have helped to degrade, each of us should always honor and respect and revere the name of his or her father. To do less is the height of ingratitude, and the son or daughter who has no respect for his or her father's name is just one short step away from rebellion against all of society.

3. Obeying one's father.   These latter remarks are just another way of saying that the best way to praise our fathers is to obey them, because in so doing we demonstrate our confidence in them. Jesus states in Matthew 7:21: "Not everyone who says to me, 'Lord, Lord,' will enter the kingdom of heaven, but only he who does the will of my Father who is in heaven." We may solemnly swear our allegiance to Christ Sunday after Sunday in song and testimony and prayer, but if we refuse to do his Father's will he just as solemnly, if sadly, states that he has no time for us. Just so, we may give lip service to our respect for our earthly fathers—but if our actions belie our claims to obedience, all our pious statements are worthless.

The juvenile crime rate in Italy is among the lowest in the world because the Italian father, however poor or lowly, is respected and obeyed by his children and soundly thrashes them whenever they get into the slightest mischief. A juvenile court judge in New York City some time ago made the statement that in his thirty years on the bench he had scarcely to examine a single child of Chinese parentage because every Chinese-American father impresses his children with the shame involved in dishonoring the family name.

III. Our Christian Homes and Our Heavenly Home

As a miniature reflection of the kingdom of heaven, each Christian home should be a place where the good father enjoys the loyalty and obedience of the good sons and daughters for whom he provides the good things of life.

A. Mutual Respect Produces Children of Good Character

The foundation of such a household is built of many stones with the word *love* stamped prominently on each. Where love fills the heart of the father, there you'll find the good father: one who provides for his children's requirements, who is aware of their needs before they ask him, who is impartial to them, and who gives them good gifts. And where love fills the heart of the son, there you'll find the good son: one who praises his father continually and in numberless ways, who respects his father, who hallows his father's name, and who unfailingly obeys his every command.

B. Unstinting Provision Begets Unceasing Praise

Show me a home where every fatherly and filial relationship is based on love, and I'll show you a home where unstinting provision calls forth unceasing praise.

11

Freedom in Christ

Independence Day

"Proclaim liberty throughout the land to all its inhabitants" (Lev. 25:10).

Outline

Introduction

    I. Freedom Is a Universal Longing

        A. Freedom Variously Defined

        B. Freedom in America's Historic Documents

        C. Eternal Vigilance the Price of Freedom

Body

    II. Implications of Paul's "Charter of Christian Freedom"

        A. A Free Church in a Free State

            1. "Give to Caesar what is Caesar's and to God what is God's"

            2. Separation of church and state

        B. Autonomy of the Local Church

            1. China's "Three-self" movement

            2. Expediency of interchurch affiliation

        C. Freedom of Individual Conscience Before God

            1. Each believer his own priest

            2. Minimum of spiritual red tape

Conclusion

I. Freedom Is a Universal Longing

"Uhuru!" "Libertad!" "Freedom now!" Whether in Swahili or Spanish or Stateside English, whether in Africa or in Latin America or in our own country, the cry goes up all over the world: "I want to be free!" People everywhere demand the elimination of colonialism, totalitarianism, and other forms of oppression. They want immediate release from the chains of slavery—real or imagined—that bind them.

A. Freedom Variously Defined

Not everyone, of course, defines freedom in the same way. Feminist movements use the word in one sense, terrorist organizations in another. Freedom may be economic or political or social. If it's the right to have, freedom may be restricted by discrimination. If it's the right to belong, freedom may be curtailed by segregation. If it's the right to be, freedom may be destroyed by stereotyping. But however defined, the flight from bondage to liberty is the almost universal dream of our time.

B. Freedom in America's Historic Documents

America calls herself the "land of the free," and we who live here sometimes pride ourselves on having a corner on freedom. Our most cherished historic documents fervently insist that every human being should be free. Each Fourth of July we celebrate our national emancipation. The Declaration of Independence describes its foundations like this:

> We hold these truths to be self-evident, that all men are created equal; that they are endowed by their Creator with certain unalienable rights; that among these, are life, *liberty*, and the pursuit of happiness (italics added).

The framers of our federal Constitution said much the same thing in its Preamble:

> We, the people of the United States, in order to form a more perfect Union, establish justice, insure domestic tranquility, provide for the common defence, promote the general welfare, and secure the blessings of *liberty* to ourselves and our posterity, do ordain and establish this Constitution for the United States of America (italics added).

Many years later Abraham Lincoln recalled the first Independence Day in his Gettysburg Address:

> Fourscore and seven years ago our fathers brought forth upon this continent a new nation, conceived in *liberty*, and dedicated to the proposition that all men are created equal (italics added).

C. Eternal Vigilance the Price of Freedom

Further quotations from our important state papers would only strengthen our contention that the word *liberty* looms large in our national life. But there are untold numbers of people, here and abroad, who are whittling away at our freedoms with a success that many find alarming. All of us know about the communist and other transparent threats to our liberties. One wag has pointed out that the Communists have just as much freedom as we Americans have, because we can stand in front of the White House and denounce the president of the United States and they can stand in front of the Kremlin and denounce the president of the United States.

But not all of us, of whatever political persuasion, have thought carefully enough about the fact that every time we permit local, state, or federal agencies of the government to provide us with an additional service that with a little effort we could provide for ourselves, we're a bit less free than we were before. Too few of us, for example, pay attention to the fact that often the biggest item in the average family budget is taxes. Our freedoms decrease in proportion to increases in the size and cost of government.

The picture isn't all dark, of course. Gradually, if grudgingly, civil rights have been extended to black Americans and other minority groups in our society. Most of our people are reacting with revulsion to acts of arson, bombing, and looting by disenchanted radicals throughout the world who call themselves libertarians but who are really anarchists. And there are other encouraging signs that personal liberties are either holding their own or being augmented in certain areas. But if we want to preserve the progress we've already made, we can't forget that eternal vigilance is the price of freedom.

II. Implications of Paul's ''Charter of Christian Freedom''

Liberty is a worthy subject for examination in the spiritual realm also. Paul's letter to the Galatian church is often called "The Charter of Christian Freedom" because of how intensely it crusades for an unencumbered and unfettered faith. The prerequisites for trusting Christ, Paul insists, don't include belonging to a certain race or sex or occupying a certain station in life. Believing Greeks, slaves, and women are equally members of the body of Christ with believing Jews and freemen. All are "one in Christ Jesus" (Gal. 3:28). The apostle sums up his argument in 5:1: "It is for freedom that Christ has set us free. Stand firm, then, and do not let yourselves be burdened again by a yoke of slavery."

Early European settlers on our shores didn't hesitate to make striking modern applications of that general principle. As Paul argued that Gentiles didn't have to submit to circumcision to be saved, so the Puritans and others insisted that it was about time to eliminate some of their own nonbiblical requirements for salvation. When religious and political oppression resulted, they fled their homelands. Names of cities like Providence, Rhode Island, and New Canaan, Connecticut, testify to the spiritual aspirations of their founders. In particular the vitality of the many denominations in our country is directly traceable to their fervency in proclaiming the implications of Paul's Magna Charta for Christian life today. In the light of current trends in our society, those implications are still well worth a word or two of emphasis.

A. A Free Church in a Free State

"It is for freedom that Christ has set us free. Stand firm, then, and do not let yourselves be burdened again by a yoke of slavery." With regard to spiritual freedom, Christians in our tradition stand first of all for a free church in a free state.

1. "Give to Caesar what is Caesar's and to God what is God's." In other words, we believe in the "separation of church and state." By that phrase we don't mean that Christians as individual citizens shouldn't speak out against political evils that may arise, or that they shouldn't write to their congressmen, or that they shouldn't exercise the right to vote. We do mean that the state must never control the church and the church must never control the state. Church is church and state is state, and neither shall ever dominate. The classic statement of this principle is, of course, that of Jesus himself: "Give to Caesar what is Caesar's and to God what is God's" (Mark 12:17). Whenever we give Caesar control of the things that are God's, we get into trouble.

2. Separation of church and state. Many years ago it became clear to a few concerned Protestant churchmen that the wall of separation between church and state in America was being battered with increasing intensity by powerful religious minorities. State legislatures were beginning to do things like passing bills to provide bus transportation for children attending parochial schools. It's very difficult not to conclude that using public tax money for such purposes violates those portions of the federal and state constitutions that forbid the government to aid in the establishment of religion. In short these leaders foresaw a dangerous trend in our political life. Acting on their convictions, they founded the organization originally known as Protestants and Other Americans United for the Separation of Church and State.

Probably no one has calculated how many millions of tax dollars Americans United has kept from flowing into the treasuries of religious and other pressure groups since the date of its founding. But all of us owe its members a debt of gratitude for the work they've done to protect religious freedom by being fearless in clarifying church-state issues before our state and federal legislatures. Several denominations in our country have officially endorsed and approved of the work that Americans United is doing, and they have voted to support it financially. By such action they have demonstrated their conviction that Americans United is performing a crucial function in our society.

It would be difficult to overemphasize the importance of the principle of the separation of church and state to the development of America as we know it today. Without that principle woven into the fabric of our country's life, we would be a far weaker nation politically, materially, morally, and spiritually. The relatively impotent state churches of Europe and Latin America illustrate the fact that when the church depends on the state for its strength and influence, it shows just how weak it really is. By contrast, "the weapons we fight with are not the weapons of the world. On the contrary, they have divine power to demolish strongholds" (2 Cor. 10:4).

We believe, then, that the church is the visible body of professed believers in Christ, free alike from state control and state support. And we are convinced that any other view may lead to government pressures that inevitably result in the destruction of religious freedom and tolerance.

B. Autonomy of the Local Church

"It is for freedom that Christ has set us free. Stand firm, then, and do not let yourselves be burdened again by a yoke of slavery." With regard to spiritual freedom,

Christians in some traditions also insist on the autonomy of the local church. In this form of church government each local house of worship is a self-governing unit, not responsible to any larger organization for the conduct of its internal affairs.

1. China's "Three-self" movement.   News coming to the outside world from the heart of mainland China during the Mao Zedong era indicated that the church there was holding its own in the face of fearful persecution. Local churches in China had loosely banded together to form what they called the "Three-self" movement. To survive in a hostile environment, each church determined to be self-supporting, self-governing, and self-propagating. By so doing they managed to maintain their ministry in spite of almost insurmountable odds.

As church bureaucracies and hierarchies continue to grow and extend their tentacles over the religious scene, the courageous example of Chinese Christians should serve as a warning to us. They found out quite by accident that adopting local church autonomy strengthened their work, but their experience is nonetheless instructive for the church throughout the world. Churches that exhibit the most spiritual vitality are usually churches that display the most independent self-confidence.

2. Expediency of interchurch affiliation.   Many independent churches have decided to affiliate themselves with other like-minded independent churches into wider associations. In so doing they've been able to undertake large-scale projects such as missionary enterprises and the publication of Christian education materials, any one of which would be too expensive and cumbersome for the resources of a small congregation. With such endeavors we heartily agree, and to such endeavors we joyfully contribute.

C. Freedom of Individual Conscience Before God

"It is for freedom that Christ has set us free. Stand firm, then, and do not let yourselves be burdened again by a yoke of slavery."

1. Each believer his own priest.   With regard to spiritual freedom, most Christians stand, finally, for the freedom of the individual conscience before God. In other words, we believe in the competence of the individual to find his or her way to God as he is revealed in his Son, Jesus Christ. We hold to the clearly presented Scriptural teaching that each believer is his own priest. We assert that it's possible to approach God only through Christ without the intervention of a human mediator. Needing no mortal authority to relay our confessions to God for us, we take our sins and shortcomings directly to him in prayer. We teach that the final court of appeal for the Christian conscience is found in the Bible alone, not in the decisions of councils or clergymen.

2. Minimum of spiritual red tape.   In short, we believe in a minimum of red tape where spiritual issues are at stake. We're convinced that all you have to do to become a Christian is to sincerely mean it when you say, "God, be merciful to me, a sinner, and give me the eternal life that Jesus provides!" We know this is true because "if you confess with your mouth, 'Jesus is Lord,' and believe in your heart that God raised him from the dead, you will be saved" (Rom. 10:9).

III. Freedom Is a Precious Commodity

A. *Freedom Nationally, Locally, Individually*

The principle of a free church in a free state could be taken away from us without much advance warning. Millions of people in the world believe that such a principle should be abolished, and they're working very hard to do just that. If they're successful, the second privilege—that of the autonomy of the local church—will be denied to us also. There can be no question of local autonomy where the church is state controlled or where freedom of worship is forbidden.

But even if these two bulwarks of spiritual freedom should be torn down, the third, by its very nature, can never be destroyed. The freedom of the individual conscience is one of those unalienable rights with which our Creator has endowed us. Through the centuries of church history countless Christians have frustrated their executioners by facing death with happy hearts and serene consciences. They have been persuaded, as we also should be, "that neither death nor life, neither angels nor demons, neither the present nor the future, nor any powers, neither height nor depth, nor anything else in all creation, will be able to separate us from the love of God that is in Christ Jesus our Lord" (Rom. 8:38-39).

B. *Choosing Our Slavery*

Such a persuasion reminds us that there is no such thing as absolute freedom. The other side of the coin marked "separated from" reads "enslaved to." Each of us must choose his form of bondage. If you're a Christian, Paul beautifully describes the choice you've made: "Though you used to be slaves to sin, you wholeheartedly obeyed the form of teaching to which you were entrusted. You have been set free from sin and have become slaves to righteousness" (6:17-18). But to be a slave of righteousness is the only way to enjoy freedom in Christ. And "if the Son sets you free, you will be free indeed" (John 8:36)!

C. Express Gratitude to All Who Grant Us Our Freedoms

The Fourth of July provides us with a natural interlude during which to ponder our freedoms. In fact, someone has referred to Independence Day as a "summertime Thanksgiving." It should grant all of us an opportunity to be grateful to our government, which has so far granted us the freedom to worship as we please. It should remind us to be thankful for every denomination that has not restricted in any way the freedoms of local churches. Most of all, it should give us yet another occasion on which to express our gratitude to Jesus Christ, who freely gave his life to provide us with free access to his Father and our God.

BELGIQUE

Rhin

LUXEMBOURG

ALLEMAGNE

•Reims

CHAMPAGNE

LORRAINE

VOSGES

ALSACE

•Strasbourg

Rhin

Dijon

FRANCHE-COMTÉ

JURA

BOURGOGNE

Saône

AIS

Loire

SUISSE

A   L   P   E   S

LYONNAIS   •Lyon

Rhône

SAVOIE

•Saint-Etienne

Grenoble•

DOC

Rhône

DAUPHINÉ

ITALIE

COMTAT

Avignon•

PROVENCE

NICE

Nice•   •MONACO

•Cannes

•Marseille

Mer Méditerranée

CORSE

SANDERSON

S0-EGS-476

FRANC-PARLER

Simone Renaud Dietiker

SAN JOSÉ STATE UNIVERSITY

FRANC-PARLER

D. C. Heath and Company

Lexington, Massachusetts   Toronto

PHOTOGRAPH   ACKNOWLEDGMENTS

Gamma: Olivier Villeneuve, pp. 36 and 194; Daniel Simon, pg. 224.
Institut Pedagogique National: Pierre Allard, pg. 22.
French Consulate, San Francisco: pp. 44, 98, 165, 176, 217, 283.
Rapho Guillumette Pictures: pg. 46; YAN, pg. 62; Niépce, pp. 81, 131, 232, 256, 265, 275, 279, 288, 303; S. Fourier, pg. 137; Louis Goldman, pg. 345.
French Embassy Press and Information Division, pp. 58, 66, 159, 173, 200, 204, 208, 237, 246, 247, 270, 337.
Peter Menzel, pp. 78, 88, 114, 119, 149, 161, 186, 228, 325, 330, 335.
Jacques Verroust, pp. 95, 261, 299.
National Council of French Industries, pg. 135.
Clemens Kalischer, pg. 154.
Edward Jones, pp. 180, 185, 191, 211, 215, 341.
Institut National de Recherche, pg. 198.
Cheri Brownton, pg. 242; also, front matter photograph of author.
French Cultural Services, pg. 290.
Wes Kemp, pg. 295.
Black Star: AGIP, pp. 313 and 320; Dominique Berretty, pg. 318.

The writing of a textbook is a demanding task—one worth undertaking only if it will improve significantly upon those already on the market. The challenges are many: how to deal with simplified constructions and limited vocabulary and yet avoid repetition and boredom; whether to use English for clear, concise directions and explanations or to approach directly the target language itself; how to provide a practical vocabulary—parts of the body, the weather, time, clothing—and yet appeal to contemporary student interests (money, love, travel, youth and old age, women's lib); how to present French culture in a manner which is interesting and which offers insights into the behavior of another people; how to give the students flexible, practical "formulas" for expressing themselves, yet not crowd the book (or the mind) with complex, unnecessary, grammar — *l'imparfait du subjonctif,* for example. And finally, but certainly no less important, the writer must confront the problem of conveying the importance of the sound of French, the spoken language, while dealing with the other skills. In *Franc-Parler* all of these problems have been carefully addressed, and the result is what we hope will be a refreshing, practical, well-balanced, and flexible approach to the teaching of French.

I have tried most of the approaches to the teaching of French, from the completely Direct Method (at the Alliance Française in Paris, in classes of foreigners from fifteen or more different countries) to the old-fashioned method of translation (in extension classes for adults and in classes of two to five-year old children in a Montessori school). Each method has its merits, and each has served me well, although proving to be restrictive when practiced too rigidly. Rest assured, *Franc-Parler* does not offer a new method. Efficiency and practicality—what works best at the moment to help students understand, speak, and write French—were the guiding forces in its preparation. The program has been developed according to three general principles: The belief that the spoken language should be taught first, with a strong emphasis on correct pronunciation; the conviction that French grammar, at times so complex and confusing, is fairly logical and reasonable, and can be simplified, clarified, and made palatable; and the confidence that all this can be attained while making the study of French fun and enjoyable to both teacher and student.

What features of *Franc-Parler* make it distinctive? How does it differ from other beginning French texts? One difference is that *Franc-Parler* has been developed to meet more accurately the frequently diverse needs of both the student and teacher. The textbook itself has been designed to satisfy the needs of the student, and each explanation of grammar is thus followed immediately by exercises which allow the students to proceed through the material at their own pace, and with frequent reinforcement. In addition, the unnatural question-answer-question-answer format and the frequently artificial dialogue formats have been shunned in favor of a more realistic monologue (dialogues in the first two chapters) which serves the student, once out of the classroom, as an authentic model of French in a realistic context. The Instructor's Manual completes the dual function of the program by providing suggestions for introducing the new vocabulary and grammar of each chapter around the theme of the Presentation, and for developing increasingly more meaningful situations which help the student progress systematically from the more mechanistic exercises to the generation of real language.

With this separation of roles in view, I have not hesitated, especially in early chapters, to incorporate English explanations into the textbook. If an explanation can be made in precise, simple French I do so, but at times a clear statement in English will save considerable time and can avoid misleading mimicry. We can differentiate between exposure to the French language, which we all favor, and explaining problems of usage. In any case, it is the teacher who determines the amount of English to be used in the classroom, and that implies not an absolute, but a judicious ban of the student's language.

Similarly, I have included in the review chapters and the tape program translation exercises which emphasize the pitfalls the students will encounter in moving from one language to another. In these translations are emphasized what I call "contrastive translation," a preventive translation. For example, students must be reminded of the difference between "Look at the flower" and **"Regarde la fleur"**; they need to practice the occasions when "to be" is translated by **"avoir"** (**avoir faim** and so forth)—not because translation is good or bad, but because behind every direct perception in a second language lurks a translation, implicit or explicit.

And finally, since I believe that French phonetics should be taught before anything else, *Franc-Parler* contains two brief units of pronunciation preliminary to the succession of body chapters. Each unit should take no more than one or two class periods, and will pay dividends throughout the rest of the semester in correct spellings, better pronunciation, and a more self-assured student. The Instructor's Manual contains a variety of suggestions for presenting the phonetic material in a stimulating manner.

Franc-Parler itself is a pun; it means to speak French, and to speak frankly. I have spoken frankly about what is good and perhaps not so good about France. And I have tried to teach students to speak a French that is equally forceful and clear, personal yet direct. If this book lives up to its title, the credit must be shared with a number of people. Most of the credit for developing the exercises and more creative games in the workbook goes to Gérard Burger. He is also responsible for the workbook being more than a simple repetition of the material in the text and for integrating the text, workbook and tape. Credit must be shared too with Stanley Galek, Modern Language Editor, for his most reasonable direction in the development of *Franc-Parler*. I am also grateful to Kathy and Nancy, who typed, typed, typed, and to my children, who "liberated" me of household chores while I was at my desk.

Simone Renaud Dietiker was born in the western part of France, near La Rochelle. She was raised in Morocco, where her parents taught until 1946. She studied in Paris and took her degrees at the Sorbonne. These include a License in Classic Languages, a CAPES in Modern Languages, a Diplôme in Teaching French to Foreign Students. She taught successively in French Schools in Paris, in Geneva, Switzerland (Smith College Junior Year Abroad), at the ESPPPFE at the Sorbonne, at the Institut de Phonétique, Alliance Française, Cours de Civilisation Française, all in Paris. She came to the US in 1959 and has lived here since. She has taught at the University of Oregon in Eugene and, since 1964, at San José State University. Professor Dietiker is also the author of *En Bonne Forme*, Révision de grammaire française, published by D. C. Heath in 1973.

TABLE DES MATIÈRES

Structures: **Fuir** ■ Les verbes **entendre dire** et **entendre parler** ■ L'expression **il s'agit de** ■ La contradiction **quand même, malgré, avoir beau** ■ Le subjonctif ■ Le sub-jonctif passé ■ Les pronoms relatifs **dont, lequel** ■ Le discours indirect

Lecture: Un voyage à Paris

INTRODUCTION

Franc-Parler is divided into two pronunciation units, twenty body chapters, and a comprehensive section of review exercises (in the Appendix). Each body chapter centers on a subject and a practical vocabulary—weather, family, clothes, among others; later chapters include subjects that are more challenging such as money, travel, and women's rights. Throughout the book I have tried to give a realistic picture of French culture—what the problems are for the inhabitants as well as what remains attractive to tourists who visit the "city of light." For instance, as early as Chapter 5 a paragraph on the characteristics of French feast days, saints' days, and holidays appears. The reading selection in Chapter 8 is a dialogue between a French woman and an American woman—a humorous comparison of shopping practices. Similarly, a later dialogue between two boys—one French, one American—compares habits of dress and ways of spending a Sunday. As soon as the student's vocabulary and proficiency allow, the cultural matter becomes more challenging. The last chapters consider the state of French medicine and social security; French vacation habits—the August holiday, the flight to the Mediterranean; the division of labor in French society—who gets paid for what; and finally, the social problems that plague the French today—low pay, foreign workers, defense cost, political corruption, pollution of landscape, sea, air, and so

LESSON STRUCTURE

forth. That chapter is appropriately called "Rien ne va!" and grammatically deals with negative forms.

Chansons

Each of the twenty chapters follows a similar format, beginning with a song which is related to the theme of the chapter. These songs are not meant to be treated as grammar exercises, though they have been selected because of their consistency with the contents of each chapter (e.g., "Mon père m'a donné un mari"—la famille; "Alouette je te plumerai"—les parties du corps). I have chosen old French tunes because they are an important part of French culture. Some have real historical interest (Orleáns, Beaugency); others convey both historical and emotional interest ("Le roi a fait battre tambour"). Texts for a number of these songs appear in the Appendix, and historical explanations are made available to the instructor in the Instructor's Manual.

Présentation

The "présentation"—a dialogue or monologue—presents the lexical and grammatical problems of the chapter. The theme of the chapter, appropriate vocabulary and idioms, irregular verbs (if any are treated), and grammar problems are all drawn together in this initial section. I have made these presentations as humorous or entertaining as possible to highlight the problems for students and to make the forms and the problems more memorable.

I have chosen to present this material in the form of a monologue or dialogue for several reasons: 1) a monologue or simple dialogue serves as an authentic model of language; 2) the theme of a monologue lends itself well to the oral presentation of vocabulary and grammar to the class; 3) the monologue or dialogue provides students with an excellent model for speaking or writing about themselves or for communicating to others. Using the theme of each chapter as a point of departure for presenting the grammar and vocabulary, the instructor should "reconstruct" each *Présentation* to adapt it to his or her own situation, and should apply it whenever possible to the personality and situation of the class, or of individual students. This exercise also provides students with a model for altering the *Présentation* to suit individual circumstances for both conversation and composition.

Prononciation

In addition to the two preliminary units, a brief section dealing with specific sounds and pronunciation problems appears in each chapter.

Verbes Irréguliers

Beginning in Chapter 4, and then in numerous chapters throughout, irregular verbs and orthographic changes in verbs are presented. Corresponding exercises are provided for both written and oral development.

Constructions à retenir

Also beginning in Chapter 4 and continuing throughout the text is the presentation of practical idiomatic expressions, together with numerous exercises designed to promote both comprehension and retention.

Structures

The grammar section is central to each chapter. Wherever possible I have unified related grammar points to avoid teaching in bits and pieces. For instance, all the material on adjectives appears in Chapters 2–5. This arises logically from the treatment of gender in Chapter 2. In Chapter 10, the material on direct and indirect objects and pronominal verbs has been brought together. I progress as logically as possible from one problem to another. The use of **avoir** *positif* (**j'ai une auto**) calls for the negative: **je n'ai pas d'auto, il n'y a pas d'auto.** This in turn suggests the use of **pas de** with other types of verbs: **je ne mange pas d'escargots** and then **beaucoup d'escargots,** since the construction is similar (disappearance of the indefinite or partitive article). I explain the pronominal verbs, **"je me regarde,"** in relation to **"il me regarde,"** the direct object pronoun.

Franc-Parler does not attempt to present all of French grammar at the first-year level. Many books still include the *passé simple, passé antérieur,* and *plus-que-parfait du subjonctif* in their last chapters. These tenses are not very useful to a first-year student. Complexities tend to confuse rather than to clarify a problem. Therefore, a number of grammatical points which are premature to the study of French at the first-year level have been eliminated; the students will not find the forms of the tenses mentioned except for the *passé simple* which is presented in the Appendix.

Exercises

Each grammatical point is followed by an exercise so that the students can immediately practice what they have learned. These exercises do not test so much as reinforce. They are meant to involve the student actively in the lesson before moving on to new material.

I have not provided "conversation," "question-and-answer," or "creative" exercises in the textbook. Conversation is spontaneous and oral. Such exercises are neither. I cannot imagine students sitting down at home and asking themselves such questions as: **"Que fait ton père?" "Mon père est mécanicien." "A quelle heure est-ce que tu te lèves?" "Je me lève à 6 h." "Comment vas-tu?" "Je vais bien."** When studying outside the classroom the students are better served by an authentic language model than by questions and answers.

Creative exercises are very important, but they should remain oral. Therefore, I have included them in the Instructor's Manual only, and I suggest that the teacher use the presentation or lecture as a point of departure and that meaningful exercises be developed around these topics. Moreover, I have offered suggestions for personalizing each grammar exercise in order to put the grammar into action. Within a short time, the students should be in control of sufficient vocabulary and grammar patterns to carry on real conversations with a variety of vocabulary and spontaneity. In addition, the laboratory program also provides for the personal questioning of the student.

Lectures

Following the grammar discussions are "lectures" in the form of cultural readings and poems which relate to the subject of the chapter. These are meant to be read and commented on in class. A wide variety of subjects are included, such as the travel habits and vacation preferences of the French people, the French MLF, and the reluctance of some French women to be liberated.

Most of the poems have not appeared in other textbooks before. "Chant Song" and "Familiale" by Prévert, "Conversation" by Jean Tardieu, and "Si tu t'imagines" by R. Queneau are some of the poems included.

Composition

Each chapter ends with a "composition" which can be done orally in class and then written. At the beginning of the book, such compositions are *"dirigées"* by questions, suggestions, and sentences that are half-finished in order to guide the students and encourage them to make use of the material learned. The instructor should discourage the use of a dictionary, since the book supplies sufficient questions, vocabulary, and syntactical models for a dialogue or short informal essay in French.

It is difficult to provide a book for all academic situations: quarters, trimesters, semesters, three and five-day schedules. Some books with thirty to forty chapters contain enough material for two years. The twenty chapters of *Franc-Parler* provide the right amount of material for a full-year course. The grammar has been streamlined to the needs of the first-year student. The twenty body chapters can be divided into two semesters of ten chapters; three trimesters of seven, seven and six; or four quarters of five. The review material in the Appendix is progressive in nature, which allows the instructor to assign review exercises at any period break, for example, the fifth, seventh, tenth, or fourteenth chapters. The exercises in the review section often combine problems of two or three chapters. Tests covering the appropriate materials are provided in the Instructor's Manual.

Cahier de travail et de laboratoire

The laboratory manual/workbook is closely integrated with the textbook and the tape program; it has been designed to reinforce the textbook material by providing original and stimulating readings, pronunciation drills, exercises, *dictées*, crossword puzzles, and numerous other activities.

Throughout the textbook are slogans, illustrations, and photos with captions that can be used for comments or conversations. The slogans are explained in the Instructor's Manual; they are in the form of sayings, mottos, or colloquial sentences that will hopefully give students a feeling for the language and an insight into French culture. **"Métro, Boulot, Dodo," "Faut l'faire"** are part of French life and culture, as much as Versailles and the RER; these, I believe, will enable the students to learn not only French, but more about France.

Chapitre Préliminaire

I

1

Phonetic Alphabet

vowels

[i]	il, livre, stylo
[e]	bébé, aller, papier, les, allez
[ɛ]	fenêtre, père, lait, hôtel
[a]	madame, patte
[ɑ]	pâte, classe
[ɔ]	porte, homme, donne
[o]	pot, eau, pauvre
[u]	ou, vous
[y]	du, tu, une
[ø]	deux
[œ]	professeur, fleur
[ə]	le, de
[ɛ̃]	vin, main, bien
[ɑ̃]	France, content
[ɔ̃]	mon, non, oncle
[œ̃]	un, lundi

semivowels

[j]	papier, crayon, fille
[w]	oui, soir
[ɥ]	huit, nuit

consonants

[p]	porte, soupe
[t]	table, thé
[k]	comment, quatre, coin
[b]	bonjour, bonne
[d]	du, de
[g]	garçon, bague
[f]	femme, photo
[s]	sa, classe, ça, nation, ce
[ʃ]	chambre, chez
[v]	voir, venir, wagon
[z]	zéro, chaise, deuxième
[ʒ]	Georges, gym, jeune
[l]	la, aller, livre
[ʀ]	rouler, roue, vivre
[m]	manger, maman
[n]	nous, tonne
[ɲ]	magnifique, vigne
[ŋ]	camping

Basic French Vowel Sounds

/a/   the letter **a**

    ma   ta   la   sac
    papa   bla-bla-bla

/i/   the letters **i** or **y**

    mi   si   ni   il   if   midi
    stylo   Guy   lys

/o/   the letter **o** + **se**

    rosé   dosé*

/ɔ/   the letter **o** + another consonant

    coq   sol   bol

/e/   the letters **é** (called **e** accent aigu) or **éé**

    dé   cité   été   alléé

/y/   the letter **u** (a new sound). If you know German, you may compare it with *ü*. If not, try to say *ou* (you), then try to say French /i/, keeping your lips in the same position.

    du   lu   su   tu

French Consonant Sounds

Many consonants are similar in French and in English.

The sound	*The letter*	*Example*
/b/	b	bal
/d/	d	detté
/f/	f, ph	féé, photo
/g/	g + a	gaz
	g + o	gogo
	g + u	Gustavé
/k/	c + a	cavé
	c + o	coca
	c + u	cuí
	k	kilo
/l/	l	listé

*Letters crossed out in the text are not pronounced.

The sound	The letter	Example
/m/	m	madamé
/n/	n	noté
/p/	p	pipé
/s/	s	sac
	c + i	cité
	c + e	Cécilé
	ss	classé
/t/	t	tablé
/v/	v	vesté
/z/	z	zoné
	s between vowels	pausé

Some English consonants are pronounced differently in French.

r /R/ arc

If you know Spanish, you may compare the French **r** with the *j* as in *baja*. If you know German, you may compare it with the *ch* in *Bach*. If you don't know either, produce a strong *h* or imitate the tape or your teacher. In any case, do not keep the English /R/, and do not use a trilled /R/. Repeat:

arc	parc	arcadé
turc	Turquié	cirqué
circulé	orchidéé	orchestré

ch is pronounced /ʃ/ as in *shoe*. Never /tʃ/ as in *church*. Repeat:

chair   Charléé   charté   choc

It is sometimes pronounced /k/. Repeat:

choléra   écho   orchestré   orchidéé

g with *e* and *i*, and *j* with any vowel are sounded /ʒ/ as in *pleasure* and not /dʒ/ as in *judge*. Repeat:

général	géologié	Genèvé
journal	Jérusalem	Juda

EXCEPTIONS: Some very commonly used "Franglais" words:

job   jazz   jet /dʒ/

qu is not usually sounded /kw/ as in *queen*. It is /k/. Repeat:

qui   que   quel

There are exceptions: équateur /kwa/.

gn   is not usually sounded /gn/ but /ɲ/ as in *canyon*. Repeat:

magnifiqu~~e~~   Agnès   ignor~~e~~

Some English sounds do not exist in French.

h   does not represent a sound in French. Repeat:

~~h~~alt~~e~~   ~~h~~orreur   ~~h~~orribl~~e~~   ~~h~~ôpital

th   therefore is not sounded as in English. It is always /t/. Repeat:

t~~h~~éâtr~~e~~   T~~h~~éodor~~e~~   at~~h~~é~~e~~

Indicate the correct sound of the group of letters.   *Exercise I*

EXAMPLE: *Charl~~es~~*   /ʃ/

a*th*é~~e~~	géogra*phi*~~e~~	Jordani~~e~~	quêt~~e~~
*ch*ar	magnétiqu~~e~~	*ch*éri~~e~~	hord~~e~~
*th*éologi~~e~~	jad~~e~~	ga*gn*~~e~~	quar~~t~~

When you begin to read French aloud, you will notice that most written final consonants are not pronounced.

po~~t~~   por~~t~~   pa~~s~~   cou~~p~~   ni~~d~~

The consonants you occasionally hear are **c-r-f-l** as in the word **careful**. Repeat:

sac	or	bref	bol
bloc	car	bif	journal

But there are exceptions. Two of them are in the title of this book, *Fran~~c~~-Parle~~r~~,* and the final **r** in all verbs ending in **-er** is silent.

Do not pronounce an unaccented final **e**. What you sound, and hear, is the preceding consonant.

EXAMPLE: madam~~e~~   class~~e~~   tabl~~e~~   pip~~e~~

Repeat and compare: ca~~s~~   cas~~e~~
pa~~s~~   pass~~e~~
cou~~p~~   coup~~e~~
por~~t~~   port~~e~~

Cross out final **e**, or unpronounced final consonants.   *Exercise II*

EXAMPLE: garde   gard~~e~~   tas   ta~~s~~

Circle the last sound, vowel or consonant, you hear and pronounce.

EXAMPLE: gard~~e~~   gar ⓓ ~~e~~   ta~~s~~   t ⓐ ~~s~~

Paris	canif	passe	cave	salut
bac	sport	dame	truc	lilas
sel	parler	groupe	table	pot

Syllabification

If you divide words into syllables, it will help you to pronounce French distinctly and correctly.

1. A syllable is made of a consonant and a vowel.

    la   pa / pa   ca / na / pé

2. If the word begins with a vowel, this vowel is pronounced alone.

    a / ni / mal

3. A double consonant counts for one.

    i / mma / cu / lé   a / tti / tu / dé   sy / llabé

4. If a word has two different consonants, they are separated; the first one belongs to the preceding syllable, the second belongs to the following syllable.

    sec / teur   al / ti / tudé

5. Some groups of consonants are inseparable: **bl, dr, pr, tr** (usually any consonant plus **-r** or **-l**).

    ta / blé   a / droit   pra / tiqué   maî / tré

Exercise III   Cut into syllables. Cross out the final **e**'s and unpronounced consonants.

EXAMPLE: mi / ra / clé

joli	ami	diplôme	copie
crocodile	vital	Italie	palissade
stylo	police	animal	cabane
hérétique	anarchiste	atomique	attitude
syllabe	garage	rapide	potable
canari	solitude	amical	Canada
général	résultat	spectacle	journal

Stress Accent

In French, there is no stress on the first or second syllable of a long word. Only the last syllable has a light stress. All other syllables are equivalent. Compare:

ENGLISH	FRENCH
general	géné**ral**
de**part**ment	départe**ment**
uni**ver**sity	universi**té**

Poem

Repeat the poem.

JOLI CROCODILE

Salut, joli crocodile
Sur l'île du lac, à Genève
A midi
Spectacle unique: le pyjama lilas
De l'animal vital, qui lit le journal,
Le stylo à la patte,
Fume sa pipe, ignore le trafic,
Pique une rose sur la statue de Théologie.
Sur la palissade, il crie:
 "A bas le général
 A mort le maréchal!
 Nice à l'Italie. . .bla, bla, bla"
La police arrive:
 "Sale type! Hérétique! Anarchiste!"
Résultat: A la cabane, le crocodile amical!

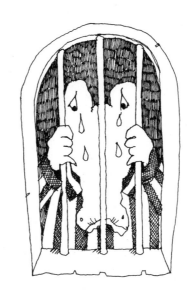

● PRONUNCIATION:

Other Vowel Sounds: A. The sounds /o/, /u/, /wa/, /ø/, /œ/
B. The sounds /ɛ/, /e/, /a/
C. Nasal vowels
D. The sound /j/

● POEM: «Chant Song» JACQUES PRÉVERT

Chapitre Préliminaire **II**

PRONUNCIATION   Other Vowel Sounds

French has no diphthongs. All vowel sounds are clear and undivided.

A. The sounds /o/, /u/, /wa/, /ø/, /œ/

/o/   is also represented by the spelling **au,** or **eau.** Remember to keep the lips rounded; *no diphthong.* Repeat:

au   autre   pause   cause   auto
eau   veau (*veal*)   beau   bureau

/u/   is spelled **ou,** and is close to the English *oo,* although tighter. Repeat:

poule   foule   boule   rouge   mousse

/wa/   is represented by the spelling **oi.** Repeat:

moi   toi   loi   quoi   fois   trois

/ø/   (close to /y/) is spelled **eu.** It is usually the final sound of the word (lips rounded, tighter than for /o/). Repeat:

peu   bleu   deux

/œ/   (close to /ɔ/) is also spelled **eu.** It is followed by a sounded consonant **r, l, f, n** (lips opened). Repeat:

seul   neuf   jeune   peur

Exercise I   Dictation. Write the following words as your teacher says them.

poule   neuf   autre
paume   rouge   foi(s)
moi   bleu   deux
feu   beau   seul

B. The sounds /ɛ/, /e/, /ə/

/ɛ/   can be spelled: **e** + *double consonant:* belle, cigarette, caresse

     e + *one consonant* inside a word: veste, verte

     NOTE: (**er** inside a word is always /ɛR/)

     è (called **e** accent grave): Genève, crème

     ê (called **e** accent circonflexe): tête, fête, rêve

     ei: Seine, beige

     ai: Français, Anglais

     et: ballet, ticket

/e/   can be spelled: **é** (as previously seen)

     ée: allée, arrivée (as previously seen)

ez (a frequent verb ending): alle~~z~~, répéte~~z~~, ne~~z~~ (*nose*)

er (final in verb endings, nouns, adjectives): alle~~r~~, parle~~r~~, danse~~r~~, bouche~~r~~, premie~~r~~

EXCEPTIONS: mer, enfer, cancer /ɛR/

es (final): le~~s~~, de~~s~~, me~~s~~, ce~~s~~

/ə/ is spelled: **e** without accent and is final in a group (see *Syllabification,* Chapitre Préliminaire I.): me/sur~~e~~, re/gre~~t~~, se/cre~~t~~, je, le, me

It is called *mute* **e,** and it presents problems that will be studied later on in the book. (It is often omitted as in **Mademoisell~~e~~; Mad′moisell~~e~~.)**

Cross out unpronounced **e** and consonants; divide the words into syllables. Also indicate if the group with an **e** is: /ɛ/, /e/, or /ə/.   *Exercise II*

EXAMPLE: regret   re + gre~~t~~   /ə/ + /ɛ/

tête	allée	passer	les	me
mai	Seine	Mexicaine	secret	objet
beauté	cancer	merci	regret	régime
père	renne	Renée	vélo	poète
belle	ballet	défilé	assez	raquette
léger	mer	bébé	liberté	le
mes	fraternité	fer	premier	crevette
affecté	cherche	parler	sujet	

C. Nasal vowels

French has four nasal vowel sounds: /ã/, /õ/, /ɛ̃/, /œ̃/. The nasal vowels are: **a, o, i, e, u + n,** or **m,** but the **n** or **m** are not sounded.

/ã/ is commonly spelled **an, am,** or **en, em.** Repeat:

dan~~s~~   fran~~c~~   blan~~c~~   gran~~d~~   lam~~pe~~
len~~t~~   den~~t~~   en~~semble~~   trem~~ble~~

/õ/ is spelled **on, om.** Repeat:

bon~~~~   ton~~~~   son~~~~   don~~~~   fon~~t~~   plom~~b~~

/ɛ̃/ is spelled **in, im; ain, aim; yn, ym.** Repeat:

vin~~~~   pin~~~~   fin~~~~   sim~~ple~~
vain~~~~   pain~~~~   sain~~t~~   faim~~~~
syn~~dicat~~   sym~~phonie~~   thym~~~~

/œ̃/ is spelled **un, um.** Repeat:

parfum~~~~   un~~~~

Exercise III   Dictation. Write the words you hear. (Most of them are cognates.)

an	humble	dentiste	bon
vin (vain)	blanc	lampe	pompon
pin (pain)	franc	Adam	blond
un	parent	grand	enfant
impossible	symphonie	simple	syndicat

When you read French the problem will be to decide when there is a nasal vowel and when there is none. Syllabification helps. If you divide words into syllables, you will see that, for example: **a / ni / mal,** has no nasal vowel, but: **pan / ta / lon** contains two!

Repeat the following words:

Sounds		*with nasal vowels*	*with no nasal vowels*
/ɑ̃/	/an/	an	A / nne
	/am/	dans	da / me
		plan	pla / ne
/ɔ̃/	/ɔn/	don	do / nne
		bon	bo / nne
		ton	to / nne
/ɛ̃/	/ɛn/	vain	vai / ne
	/in/	divin	divi / ne
	/im/	impossible	i / mmense
/œ̃/	/yn/	un	u / ne
		l'un	lu / ne
		parfum	parfu / me

Exercise IV   Divide the following words into syllables. Circle each nasal vowel, and write its phonetic symbol. Indicate the absence of a nasal with the letters 'n.n.'

EXAMPLE: u / ni / té   n.n.

par / f (um) / œ̃ /

un	immense	unité	parfum	plante
pont	impossible	dame	année	maman
enfant	parfume	bonne	brun	renne
bon	plane	lunatique	animal	immaculé
parent	fini	ballon	lundi	bain
fume	pain	bonnet	brunir	passion
vin	donne	intéressant	an	dentiste

D. The sound /j/

The sound /j/ (as in English *yes*) is represented by the letter **i** + *a vowel,* for example:

/je/   **ier**   papier, premier, familier

/jo/	**iot**	idiot
/jã/	**iant**	étudiant
/jõ/	**ion**	réunion, question
/sjõ/	**tion**	nation, conversation

It is also represented by the letter **i** + **lle: fille, gentille.** Note the pronunciation of **bien** /bjɛ̃/.

Poem

Read the poem aloud with another student. One can say the English words, the other the French words. Exchange parts.

CHANT SONG

Moon lune
chant song
rivière river
garden rêveur
petite house
little maison

Chant song
chant song
et oiseau bleu
blood sang
et bird oiseau
chant song
chant song

Moon lune
chant song
rivière rêveur
garden river
rêve dream
mer sea

Thank you
moon lune
thank you
mer sea

Moon lune
chant song
rivière river
garden rêveur
children enfant
mer sea
time temps

Chant song
chant song
blue song
et oiseau bleu
blood sang
blue song red song

Oh girl fille
oh yes je t'aime
oh oui love you
oh girl fille
oh flower girl
je t'aime tant

Oh girl fille
oh oui love you

Oh flower girl
children enfant
oh yes je t'aime
je t'aime tant
t'aime tant
t'aime tant
time temps
time temps
time temps
et tant et tant
et tant et tant
et tant
et temps

JACQUES PRÉVERT
Spectacle, p. 194

Tongue Twisters

Pour délier la langue.

La pipe au papa du pape Pie pue.

Ton thé t'a-t-il ôté ta toux?

Les chaussettes de l'archiduchesse sont-elles sèches, archisèches?

Ces six saucissons-ci sont six sous les six?

Didon dîna, dit-on, du dos d'un dodu dindon.

- **PRÉSENTATION:** La classe de français. Salutations.
- **PRONONCIATION:** l'alphabet français
  les lettres **c** et **ç**
  la prononciation de **comment**
- **STRUCTURES:** les nombres de 1 à 10
  masculin et féminin
  l'article indéfini: **un, une**
  l'article défini: **le, la, l'**
  le genre
  le verbe **être**
- **LECTURE:** Adieu!

- **PROVERBE:** Jamais deux sans trois

Orléans, Beaugency

Mes a — mis que res — te — til à ce

dau — phin si gen — til Or — lé — ans Beau — gen — cy No — tre

Da — me de Clé — ry Ven — dô — me Ven — dô — me

PRÉSENTATION   La classe de français.   Salutations.

(*C'est le commencement de la classe.*)

LE PROFESSEUR: Bonjour, M.
Bonjour, Madame.
Bonjour, Mademoiselle.
Comment‿allez-vous?*
UN ÉTUDIANT: Très bien, merci, et vous?
LE PROFESSEUR: Très bien, merci.
Moi, je suis le professeur.
Je m'appelle M. _____ (Madame _____ , Mademoiselle
_____). Et vous?
UN ÉTUDIANT: Je m'appelle Paul.
UNE ÉTUDIANTE: Moi, je m'appelle Suzanne.

LE PREMIER ÉTUDIANT: Salut!
L'AUTRE ÉTUDIANT: Salut, ça va?
LE PREMIER ÉTUDIANT: Oui, pas mal. Et toi?
L'AUTRE ÉTUDIANT: Comme ci, comme ça.
Je m'appelle Tom. Et toi?
LE PREMIER ÉTUDIANT: Je m'appelle Paul.
L'AUTRE ÉTUDIANT: Tu es un‿étudiant?
LE PREMIER ÉTUDIANT: Oui, toi aussi?
L'AUTRE ÉTUDIANT: Oui. C'est la classe de français?
LE PREMIER ÉTUDIANT: Oui. C'est ça.

(*C'est la fin de la classe.*)

LE PROFESSEUR: La classe est finie. Comment est la classe de français?
Difficile?
UN ÉTUDIANT: Oui, difficile.
LE PROFESSEUR: Au revoir. A demain.
UN ÉTUDIANT: Au revoir, M. _____ , Madame _____ , Mademoiselle
_____ . A demain. (*A l'autre étudiant*)
Tchao. Adieu. A demain, d'accord? (d'ac)

Vocabulaire

à demain see you tomorrow
adieu, au revoir good-bye (**Adieu** literally means: Good-bye forever!)
autre other; **un autre:** another; **l'autre:** the other
aussi too

ça va? how are you (*familiar*)
c'est ça! that's right!
comme ci, comme ça so-so
comment allez-vous? how are you?
d'accord o.k.
difficile difficult; **facile:** easy
fin, (*f.*) end

*The sign ‿ indicates a "liaison"; here, the last consonant of **comment, t,** is sounded with the beginning vowel of **allez, a: /ta/.**

je m'appelle   my name is
pas mal   not bad
(le) premier   the first
salut!   hi!
tchao!   (*Italian,* 'ciao' frequently used
        among young people)

L'alphabet français

The French alphabet is the same as the English alphabet, but it is pronounced differently. Repeat:

a	a	**h**	aché	**o**	o	**v**	vé
b	bé	**i**	i	**p**	pé	**w**	double vé
c	cé	**j**	ji	**q**	ku	**x**	iks
d	dé	**k**	ka	**r**	erré	**y**	i grec
e	e	**l**	ellé	**s**	essé	**z**	zèdé
f	effé	**m**	emmé	**t**	té		
g	gé	**n**	enné	**u**	u		

Epelez chaque mot.

Exercice I

conversation   appartement   journal
crocodile   spectacle   pyjama
zombi   psychologie   gouvernement
prononciation

Epelez votre nom.

Les lettres **c** et **ç**

La lettre **c** est prononcée /s/ avec **i** ou **e: ce, cité**
                                /k/ avec **a, o, u: car, coq, culture**

ç (cé cédille) est prononcée /s/ avec **a, o, u: ça, çon, çu**

Comparez et répétez:

comme ci	comme ça
car	ça va
continuez	leçon
comment	garçon

Indiquez l'orthographe correcte, **c** ou **ç**. Répétez:

Exercice II

gar __ on	__ urieux	pla __ ez
__ ommen __ ez	__ ommen __ ement	fran __ ais
__ arte	ré __ eption	le __ on

La prononciation de **comment**

Comment_allez-vous?   (**t** est prononcé.)
Comment est la classe? (**t** n'est pas prononcé.)

STRUCTURES   ## Les nombres

Comptez de 1 à 10.

1	un	/œ̃/	**6**	six	/sis/
2	deux	/dø/	**7**	sept	/sɛt/
3	trois	/trwa/	**8**	huit	/ɥit/
4	quatre	/katr/, /kat/	**9**	neuf	/nœf/
5	cinq	/sɛ̃k/	**10**	dix	/dis/

Exercice I   Répétez les mots avec le nombre.

Chapitre 1   ligne 2   page 3   paragraphe 4   exercice 5
Chapitre 6   ligne 7   page 8   paragraphe 9   exercice 10

Masculin et féminin

In French, even things have a gender. A noun is either masculine or feminine: **la classe, le commencement, une classe, un commencement. Classe** is a feminine noun. **Commencement** is a masculine noun. A noun is almost always accompanied by an article. The article may be indefinite, **article indéfini,** or definite, **article défini,** and the article reflects or indicates the gender of the noun: **la, une** are feminine; **le, un** are masculine.

L'article indéfini: **un, une** (*a, an*)

Un est masculin: **un tableau**
Une est féminin: **une classe**

Un: prononcez /œ̃/ (the **n** is not sounded when the noun starts with a consonant).

un tableau   un crayon
un garçon   un livre

Prononcez /œ̃n/ (**n** is sounded and linked with the first vowel when the noun starts with a vowel).

un_animal   un_étudiant
un_exercice   un_appartement

Répétez les mots avec l'article masculin **un**. (Prononcez /œ̃/ ou /œ̃n/.) Écrivez *Exercice II*
l'exercice. (*Write the exercise.*)

| garage | département | anarchiste | tableau | oiseau |
| ami | gouvernement | journal | crocodile | autre |

Une: prononcez /yn/.

    une fille   une page
    une leçon   une table

Prononcez /yne/, /yno/, etc. (**e** is not pronounced; **n** is pronounced with the first
vowel of the noun).

    un͜e étudiante   un͜e adresse
    un͜e opération   un͜e université

Répétez les mots avec l'article féminin: **une** /yn/. Écrivez l'exercice.   *Exercice III*

bicyclette	liberté	auto	invention
composition	absence	unité	cigarette
prononciation	explication		

L'article défini: **le, la, l'** (*the*)

> **le** est masculin: **le tableau**
> **la** est féminin: **la classe**
> **l'** est masculin et féminin: **l'étudiant, l'étudiante**

Both **le** and **la** are reduced to **l'** in front of a noun that begins with a vowel. This is
called "élision."

le, prononcez /lə/	**l',** prononcez /la/, /le/, /lɛ/, /lwa/
le tableau	l'animal
le crayon	l'étudiant
le garçon	l'exercice
le livre	l'oiseau

Répétez les mots de l'exercice II avec **le** ou **l'**.   *Exercice IV*

la, prononcez /la/	**l',** prononcez /le/, /la/, /lo/, /ly/
la fille	l'étudiante
la page	l'adresse
la leçon	l'opération
la table	l'université

Répétez les mots de l'exercice III avec **la** ou **l'**.   *Exercice V*

Le genre

For many words, the ending is a possible indication of the gender of the word. Study these endings.

Masculin		*Féminin*	
al	un journal	**-ance**	une importance
-ant	un restaurant	**-ence**	une préférence
-ent	un parent	**-ée**	une allée
-eau	un tableau	**-ette**	une cigarette
-et	un ballet	**-esse**	une adresse
-ès	un succès	**-ie**	une démocratie
-isme	un socialisme	**-té**	une liberté
-ment	un gouvernement	**-ice**	une police
		-tion	une conversation
		-tude	une attitude
		-ure	une nature

This general rule has some important exceptions:

1. Words ending in **-age** or **-aire** are usually masculine, but several are not:

	Masculin	*Féminin*
-age	un gar**age**	une p**age**, une c**age** (*f.*)
-aire	un dictionn**aire**	la gramm**aire** (*f.*)

2. Words ending in **-eur** that are male agents are masculine:

   un dans**eur**   un doct**eur**

   Abstract nouns ending in **-eur** are feminine:

   une horr**eur**   une pâl**eur**

3. Some words are always masculine, even when they refer to women:

   un professeur   un auteur

   Some are always feminine, even when they refer to men:

   une vedette   une victime

4. For many words, the gender has nothing to do with endings, and it should be memorized with each word:

   un laboratoire   une histoire
   un problème   une leçon
   un théâtre   une maison

Indiquez le genre des mots avec l'article **un**, masculin, ou **une**, féminin.   *Exercice VI*

différence	évolution	instrument	armée
département	permanence	tourisme	invention
ordonnance	terreur *fem*	accident	nation
entrée	couvent	assistant	science
despotisme	opération	appartement	restaurant
passage *masc.*	parent	patience	certitude
latitude	raquette	carnage	obscurité
barrette	finesse	mirage	beauté
unité	possibilité	alphabet	ciseau
bicyclette	courage *masc*	vitalité	béret
animal	récital	laboratoire	leçon *fem.*
théâtre *masc*	maison *fem.*	problème *masc.*	omelette
justice	énergie	progrès	culture

Répétez l'exercice avec l'article **le, la, l'**.   *Exercice VII*

Un ou **le? Une** ou **la?**

Use **un** or **une** when the object is indefinite and single:

   C'est **un** tableau.   C'est **une** classe.

Use **le, la, l'** when the object is single and definite, and is determined by an owner.
De indicates the ownership.

   C'est **le** sac **de** Catherine.

Indiquez la forme correcte: **un, une, le, la, l'**.   *Exercice VIII*

C'est _un_ crayon.   C'est _une_ adresse.
C'est _le_ crayon de Bernard.   C'est _la_ adresse d'Elizabeth.
C'est _une_ classe.   C'est _un_ appartement.
C'est _la_ classe de M. Dupont.   C'est _le_ appartement de Philippe.
C'est _un_ lac.   C'est _une_ bicyclette.
C'est _le_ lac de Genève.   C'est _la_ bicyclette de Patricia.

Le verbe **être** (*to be*)

   Je **suis** le professeur.   Vous **êtes** M. Smith.
   Tu **es** un étudiant.   C'**est** la classe.

> je **suis**   *I am*
> tu **es**   *You are* (familier)
> vous **êtes**   *You are* (forme polie du singulier ou forme du pluriel)*
> **c'est**   *This is*

Exercice IX   Donnez la forme correcte du verbe **être.**

EXEMPLE: Je _____ le professeur.   Je suis le professeur.

1. Je _____ un étudiant.
2. Vous _____ le professeur?
3. C'_____ le crayon de Gérard.
4. Tu _____ pâle.
5. C'_____ une explication.
6. Tu _____ un étudiant.
7. C'_____ un tableau.
8. Vous _____ la secrétaire?
9. Tu _____ une vedette.
10. Je _____ une victime.

*In French, one says **vous** to an unknown person, a superior, an adult, or to a group of persons. One says **tu** to a child, an animal, a relative, or a close friend. Students say **tu** to one another.

Adieu

UN ÉTUDIANT: Bonjour!

UN AUTRE ÉTUDIANT: Salut!

LE PREMIER ÉTUDIANT: Vous êtes le professeur?

L'AUTRE ÉTUDIANT: Non, je suis un étudiant. Toi aussi?

LE PREMIER ÉTUDIANT: Oui. C'est la classe de français?

L'AUTRE ÉTUDIANT: Oui, c'est ça.

LE PREMIER ÉTUDIANT: Bien. (*Silence*)

L'AUTRE ÉTUDIANT: Ça va?

LE PREMIER ÉTUDIANT: Pas mal, merci. Et toi?

L'AUTRE ÉTUDIANT: Moi, comme ci, comme ça.

LE PREMIER ÉTUDIANT: ?   ?   ?   ?

L'AUTRE ÉTUDIANT: Eh, oui! La classe, le professeur, l'université...

LE PROFESSEUR: (*Très dramatique*) Bonjour! Répétez: la conversation, la prononciation, l'organisation, le commencement et la fin, la destruction et la désolation.

LE PREMIER ÉTUDIANT: (*A l'autre étudiant*) Ça va? Tu es pâle!

L'AUTRE ÉTUDIANT: Non, ça va très mal, au revoir.

LE PREMIER ÉTUDIANT: A demain?

L'AUTRE ÉTUDIANT: Non, adieu! (*Exit l'autre étudiant*)

C'est un jour d'examen.

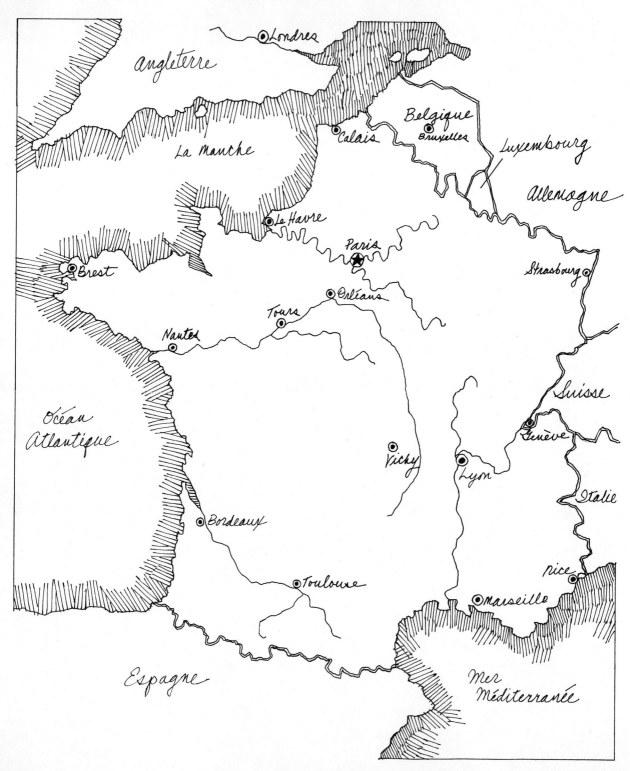

Londres

Angleterre

Belgique

Bruxelles

Luxembourg

Allemagne

Calais

La Manche

Le Havre

Paris

Strasbourg

Brest

Orléans

Tours

Nantes

Suisse

Océan
Atlantique

Genève

Vichy

Lyon

Italie

Bordeaux

nice

Toulouse

Marseille

Espagne

Mer
Méditerranée

Chapitre 2

Au clair de la lune

Au clair de la lu — ne, mon a — mi Pier — rot,

pre — te — moi ta plu — me, pour é — crire un mot.

Ma chan — delle est mor — te, je n'ai plus de feu:

ou — vre moi ta por — te, pour l'a mour de Dieu.

PRÉSENTATION   Une description simple de l'univers

Où est la classe?
>   Elle est à l'université, sur le campus.

Où sommes-nous?
>   Je suis dans la classe. Nous sommes dans la classe.

Où est l'université? Où sont l'université et le campus?
>   Ils sont dans la ville. Il y a une université dans la ville.

Et la ville?
>   Elle est dans l'état.

Où est l'état?
>   Il est dans le pays, aux États-Unis.

Les États-Unis, c'est un pays?
>   Oui, et la France, le Mexique, c'est aussi des pays. Mais nous ne sommes
>   pas en France, nous ne sommes pas au Mexique.

Les pays, les continents, les océans, les mers sont sur la terre?
>   Oui, ils sont sur la terre. Sur la terre il y a des pays, des continents, des mers.
>   La terre est une planète.

Et la lune, c'est aussi une planète?
>   Non, Vénus, Mars, Jupiter sont des planètes. La lune est un satellite. Les
>   planètes, les satellites, le soleil sont dans l'espace et forment le système
>   solaire, une partie de l'univers.

Vous allez en voyage dans l'espace?
>   Non, je vais seulement à l'université, sur une bicyclette. Les astronautes
>   vont dans l'espace. Ils vont sur la lune, dans une fusée. Ils explorent le
>   firmament, ils marchent et probablement dansent sur la lune.

Ici, c'est la terre, là, c'est la lune. C'est extraordinaire! C'est immense.
>   Ici, c'est la classe de français, c'est ordinaire, c'est moche!

Vocabulaire

à at, to, on
aller to go
dans in
en in, to
état, (*m.*) state
fusée, (*f.*) rocket
ici here
ils dansent they dance
ils explorent they explore
ils forment they form
ils marchent they walk
il y a there is, there are

là there
mais but
moche crummy, ugly (*familiar*)
partie, (*f.*) part
pays, (*m.*) country
probablement probably
seulement only
soleil, (*m.*) sun
sur on
terre, (*f.*) earth
ville, (*f.*) city

L'accent tonique dans un groupe

PRONONCIATION

EXEMPLE: Elle est à l'univer<u>si</u>té.
Pierre est dans une fu<u>sée</u>.

In a group of words, stress only the last syllable of the last word.

Répétez avec l'accent correct:

Exercice I

1. Je vais à l'université.
2. Le soleil est dans l'espace.
3. Nous ne sommes pas en France.
4. C'est une partie de l'univers.

L'intonation

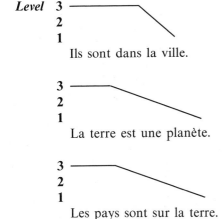

Level **3**
2
1
            Ils sont dans la ville.

3
2
1
            La terre est une planète.

3
2
1
            Les pays sont sur la terre.

In a statement, the voice falls.

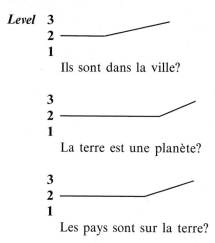

Level 3
2
1
    Ils sont dans la ville?

3
2
1
    La terre est une planète?

3
2
1
    Les pays sont sur la terre?

Make a simple statement into a question by raising your voice.

Exercice II   Répétez les phrases avec l'intonation correcte.

1. Vous_allez à l'université.   Vous_allez à l'université?
2. La lune est_un satellite.   La lune est_un satellite?
3. Les_astronautes sont sur la lune.   Les_astronautes sont sur la lune?
4. C'est la classe de français.   C'est la classe de français?
5. Nous sommes au Mexique.   Nous sommes au Mexique?

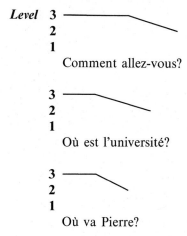

Level 3
2
1
    Comment allez-vous?

3
2
1
    Où est l'université?

3
2
1
    Où va Pierre?

In a question starting with **où, comment,** the voice is up on the word **où** or **comment,** then falls, and rises just a bit on the last word.

Exercice III   Répétez avec l'intonation correcte.

1. Où est la classe?
2. Comment est la classe?
3. Où sommes-nous?
4. Comment va la lune?
5. Où sont les planètes et le soleil?
6. Où sont les astronautes?

La terminaison *-ent*

-ent as a verb ending is not pronounced. You pronounce and hear the preceding consonant:

> les astronautes march(ent)
> ils dans(ent)
> ils explor(ent)

-ent in nouns and adverbs represents the sound /ã/:

> continent   firmament   seulement   probablement

RÉPÉTEZ: ils march(ent) doucement sur le continent
            ils dans(ent) probablement dans le firmament
            ils visit(ent) seulement l'appartement
            ils form(ent) simplement le gouvernement

Exercice IV

Le pluriel

STRUCTURES

> un garçon, deux, trois, quatre garçons
> une fille, deux, trois, quatre filles

Garçons et **filles** sont pluriels; la prononciation est identique au singulier et au pluriel. **S** n'est pas prononcé.

Le pluriel des articles

L'article indéfini: **un, une, des**

> Dans la classe, il y a quatre, cinq, **des** garçons.
> Dans la classe, il y a quatre, cinq, **des** filles.

L'article **des** indique le pluriel indéfini. Prononcez /de/. (In English one says: *There are boys, some boys. . . .*)

Répétez au pluriel. Ecrivez.

Exercice I

un camarade	un satellite	une planète
une classe	un continent	un voyage
un système	une bicyclette	

> **un** étudiant   **des** étudiants
> **une** étudiante   **des** étudiantes

Quand le mot commence par une voyelle, prononcez /dez/. C'est une liaison.

Exercice II   Répétez au pluriel.

une adresse	un état	un océan
un espace	un astronaute	une université
un instrument	un exercice	

L'article défini: **le, la, l', les**

le professeur   **les** professeurs
la classe   **les** classes

L'article **les** /le/ indique le pluriel défini. En anglais l'article défini (*the*) est identique au singulier et au pluriel.

Exercice III   Répétez au pluriel. Ecrivez.

le camarade	le satellite	la planète
la classe	le continent	le voyage
le système	la bicyclette	

l'étudiant   **les** étudiants
l'étudiante   **les** étudiantes

Quand le mot commence par une voyelle, prononcez /lez/. C'est une liaison.

Exercice IV   Répétez au pluriel. Ecrivez.

l'adresse	l'état
l'océan	l'espace
l'astronaute	l'université
l'instrument	l'exercice

Exercice V   Répétez avec: (*a.*) **un, une, des;** (*b.*) **le, la, l', les.**

portes	oranges	infinités	conversations
table	tomates	auto	addition
lampes	crocodile	anarchistes	opérations
ami	aventures	protestant	mer

Le pluriel des noms

EXEMPLE 1:   un professeur   des professeur**s**
             une description   des description**s**
             le camarade   les camarade**s**
             la mer   les mer**s**

Ajoutez (*Add*) **s** pour indiquer le pluriel de la majorité des noms. Le **s** n'est pas prononcé.

EXEMPLE 2:   un campus   des campus
             le pays   les pays

La terminaison est **s?** Un autre **s** n'est pas nécessaire. Le pluriel est identique.

EXAMPLE 3:   un oiseau   des oiseau**x**
                un tableau   des tableau**x**

Le nom est en **-eau?** Le pluriel est en **-eaux** /o/. Le **x** n'est pas prononcé.

EXAMPLE 4:   un journal   des journ**aux**
                un général   des génér**aux**

Le nom est en **-al?** Le pluriel est en **-aux** /o/. Le **x** n'est pas prononcé. Notez les exceptions: un bal, des bals; un récital, des récitals.

Répétez au pluriel. Ecrivez.   *Exercice VI*

une consonne	un groupe	la liberté	une fois
une voyelle	l'animal	un stylo	le premier
un bureau	un pyjama	l'eau	le récital
une statue	un ciseau	un pays	le maréchal
une pipe			

Le verbe **être** complet

Maurice **est** dans la maison, il **est** dans la maison.
Suzanne **est** dans le jardin, elle **est** dans le jardin.
Nous **sommes** à l'université.
Les‿astronautes **sont** sur la lune, ils **sont** sur la lune.
Les‿étudiantes **sont** dans la classe, elles **sont** dans la classe.

être   *to be*

Singulier	*Pluriel*
je **suis**	nous **sommes**
tu **es**	vous **êtes**
vous **êtes***	
il ⎫ **est**	ils ⎫ **sont**
elle ⎭	elles ⎭

Mettez la forme correcte du verbe **être.**   *Exercice VII*

1. je _____   4. vous _____   7. ils _____
2. il _____   5. tu _____   8. elles _____ .
3. nous _____   6. elle _____

La forme négative

Je suis le professeur de français.
     Je **ne** suis **pas** le professeur de maths.
    Vous‿êtes un‿étudiant.
     Vous **n'**êtes **pas** le chauffeur.

*Attention à la liaison.

Tu es dans la classe.

Tu **n'**es **pas** dans un restaurant.

Jacques est pâle. Il est pâle.

Il **n'**est **pas** rouge.

Suzanne est dans la classe. Elle est dans la classe.

Elle **n'**est **pas** dans le jardin.

Nous sommes sur la terre.

Nous **ne** sommes **pas** sur Jupiter.

Les étudiants sont ici. Ils sont ici.

Ils **ne** sont **pas** là.

Les étudiantes sont à l'université. Elles sont à l'université.

Elles **ne** sont **pas** au cinéma.

La négation est en deux mots: **ne ... pas** ou **n' ... pas**. **Ne** est élidé devant (*in front of*) **es, est, êtes.** Comparez avec l'élision de l'article dans **l'étudiant.**

$$\boxed{\textbf{ne} + \text{verbe} + \textbf{pas}}$$

Non, je **ne** suis **pas.**   Nous **ne** sommes **pas.**

Tu **n'**es **pas.**   Vous **n'**êtes **pas.**

Il **n'**est **pas.**   Ils **ne** sont **pas.**

Elle **n'**est **pas.**   Elles **ne** sont **pas.**

Exercice VIII   Répétez à la forme négative.

1. Je suis le professeur.
2. Vous êtes pâle.
3. Tu es dans la classe.
4. Ils sont sur la terre.
5. Elle est à l'université.
6. Elles sont à la mer.
7. Nous sommes sur la lune.

Les expressions **c'est, il est, elle est** (*it is*)

Où est le tableau?   **Il est** dans la classe.

Le nom **tableau** est masculin singulier. Le pronom est **il.**

Où est la classe?   **Elle est** à l'université.

Le nom **classe** est féminin singulier. Le pronom est **elle.**

Où sont les journaux?   **Ils sont** sur la table.

Journaux est masculin pluriel. Le pronom est **ils.**

Où sont les fleurs?   **Elles sont** dans le vase.

Fleurs est féminin pluriel. Le pronom est **elles.**

C'est un tableau?	Oui, **c'est** un tableau.
	Non, **ce n'est pas** une table.
C'est des journaux?	Oui, **c'est** des journaux.
	Non, **ce n'est pas** des cartes.

C'est une identification, on répète **c'est, ce n'est pas.***

Répondez aux questions par **c'est** ou **il est, elle est, ils sont, elles sont.**   *Exercice IX*

1. C'est un crayon? Oui, _____ un crayon.
2. Où est le crayon? _____ sur la table.
3. Où sont les bonbons? _____ dans le sac.
4. C'est une table? Oui, _____ une table.
5. Où sont les planètes? _____ dans l'espace.
6. Où est la bicyclette? _____ dans le jardin.
7. Mars, c'est une planète? Oui, _____ une planète.
8. Et la lune, c'est un satellite? Oui, _____ un satellite.
9. Où est la France? _____ en Europe.
10. Les États-Unis, où sont-ils? _____ en Amérique.

Répondez aux questions par: **Il n'est pas, elle n'est pas . . .; Ils ne sont pas, elles ne**   *Exercice X*
sont pas . . .; Ce n'est pas.

1. C'est un crayon? Non, ce _____ un crayon.
2. Le crayon est sur la table? Non, il _____ .
3. C'est des fleurs? Non, _____ .
4. Le Canada, le Mexique, ils sont en Europe? Non, _____ .
5. C'est un éléphant? Non, _____ .
6. La fusée est dans la classe? Non, _____ .
7. La lune, c'est une planète? Non, _____ .
8. Les étudiants sont à la mer? Non, _____ .

Le verbe **aller**

Comment allez-vous?	Ça va?

You have already encountered these forms of the verb **aller** which mean: "How are you?"

Vous **allez** à l'université?	Il **va** à la mer.

More often, the verb **aller** means *to go.*

EXEMPLES: Je **vais** à la mer.
        Tu **vas** à la poste. Vous **allez** à l'université.

*Dans la langue élégante, on a: **Ce sont** des journaux. **Ce ne sont pas** des cartes.

Il **va** à la maison. Elle **va** à la maison.
Nous **allons*** à l'opéra.
Les garçons **vont** à la mer. Ils **vont** à la mer.
Les jeunes filles **vont** à la banque. Elles **vont** à la banque.

La forme positive:

aller

je **vais**	nous **allons***
tu **vas**	vous **allez***
il **va**	ils **vont**
elle **va**	elles **vont**

La forme négative:

non, je **ne vais pas**	nous **n'allons pas****
tu **ne vas pas**	vous **n'allez pas****
il **ne va pas**	ils **ne vont pas**

Exercice XI   Mettez la forme correcte du verbe **aller.**

1. Il _____ à l'université.
2. Ils _____ à la maison.
3. Tu _____ à l'opéra?
4. Je _____ à la poste.
5. Elles _____ à la mer?
6. Vous _____ à l'université.
7. Nous _____ à la maison.

Exercice XII   Répétez l'exercice XI à la forme négative.

La localisation

Les principales prépositions de localisation sont: **à** (*at or to*), **en** (*in or to*), **dans** (*into, inside of*).

Nous sommes **à** Chicago.
Il va **à** Paris.

Utilisez **à** devant un nom de ville.

Je suis **à** la maison.
Il va **à** l'université.
Elles vont **à** l'opéra.

Ajoutez **à** à l'article **la, l'.**

Nous allons **au** cinéma?

À~~le~~ est impossible; utilisez l'article contracté, **au.**

Il va **en** France, **au** Canada, ou **aux** États-Unis.

*Attention à la liaison.   **Avec élision de **ne = n'.**

Utilisez **en, au, aux** devant un nom de pays. Il y a des noms de pays avec **en: en France, en Italie, en Espagne,** et il y a des noms de pays avec **au, aux: au Canada, au Japon, au Mexique, aux États-Unis.** (For a more detailed rule, see Chapitre 12.)

> Il est **dans** le jardin.
> Nous allons **dans** la classe.

Utilisez **dans** avec un nom commun et un article.

EXCEPTIONS: en classe   *in class* (avec **en,** l'article est absent)
  dans la classe   *in the classroom*
  en ville   *downtown*
  dans la ville   *in the city*

à Paris			
à la maison	**au** cinéma		
à l'université	**au** Mexique	**en** France	**dans** le jardin
à l'opéra	**aux** États-Unis	**en** classe	

Mettez **à, en** ou **dans.**   *Exercice XIII*

1. Les étudiants sont _____ la classe.
2. Vous allez _____ France.
3. Oui, il va _____ Paris.
4. New York est _____ Mexique.
5. Idiot, New York est _____ États-Unis.
6. _____ le jardin, il y a des fleurs.
7. Nous allons _____ Italie et _____ Espagne.
8. La banque est _____ ville.

Mettez la forme correcte: **à, à l', à la, au.**   *Exercice XIV*

1. Nous allons _____ université. 2. Elle est _____ cafétéria. (*f.*) 3. Les dollars sont _____ banque. (*f.*) 4. Les pingouins sont _____ pôle Sud. (*m.*) 5. Le programme est _____ télévision. 6. Je suis _____ Paris. 7. L'auto est _____ garage. 8. Il va _____ laboratoire. 9. Jacques va _____ cinéma. 10. Vous allez _____ New York.

Des étudiants sur un campus.

LECTURE   Une évasion

Pierre est en voyage. Il est dans une fusée. Il va sur Vénus, à une autre université. Une autre université, pas dans un pays, pas dans une ville, mais sur une autre planète, avec des jardins, des fleurs, des plantes, des oiseaux, des étudiants, et des bicyclettes. Les autos, les professeurs? Ils ne sont pas sur le campus. Vénus est une planète extraordinaire. Les villes, les états, les présidents et les généraux, les problèmes et les difficultés, les catastrophes, les calamités et les accidents sont sur la terre, en France, aux États-Unis, en Italie, ou au Mexique. Sur Vénus, il y a la mer, les fleurs, le soleil, les oiseaux; c'est un univers de rêve. Oui, c'est un rêve. Ce n'est pas une réalité. C'est une évasion. Pierre n'est pas en voyage; il est dans la classe, avec les autres étudiants et le professeur. Mais la réalité, c'est moche, alors Pierre n'est pas sur la terre, il est dans la lune,* il est dans un rêve.

Un dialogue entre deux étudiants: une description simple de l'univers, de l'université.

Composition dirigée

Je m'appelle _____. Je suis un étudiant (une étudiante) à l'université de _____. Et toi? Où es-tu? Où sommes-nous? Où est la terre? Où sont les autres planètes? La ville, c'est. . . Où est-elle? Elle est dans l'état de. . . Il y a des fleurs sur la terre? Il y a des fleurs sur le campus? Où sont les étudiants et les professeurs?

*Il est dans la lune = il rêve.

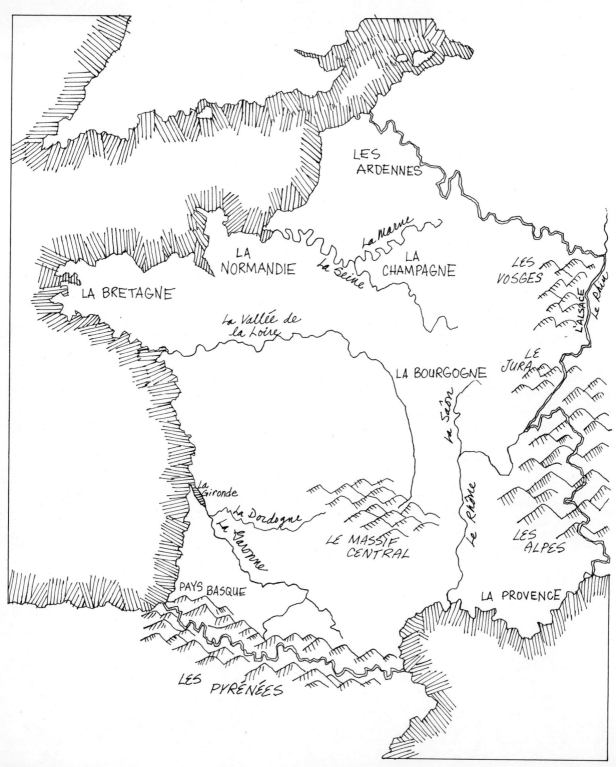

LES ARDENNES

La Marne

LA NORMANDIE

LA BRETAGNE

La Seine

LA CHAMPAGNE

LES VOSGES

L'ALSACE

Le Rhin

La Vallée de la Loire

LA BOURGOGNE

LE JURA

La Saône

Le Rhône

La Gironde

La Dordogne

LE MASSIF CENTRAL

LES ALPES

La Garonne

PAYS BASQUE

LA PROVENCE

LES PYRÉNÉES

- ● PRÉSENTATION: La famille
- ● PRONONCIATION: la liaison
- ● STRUCTURES: le mot interrogatif **est-ce que**
  le verbe **avoir;** la forme négative de **avoir**
  les verbes du premier groupe
  la possession avec **de (du, des)**
  l'adjectif possessif
  les adjectifs en **–e**
- ● LECTURE: Un père formidable

- ● PROVERBE: Tel père tel fils

Chapitre 3

Mon père m'a donné un mari

Mon pèr' m'a don — né un ma — ri, Mon Dieu! quel

homm', quel pe — tit hom —me. Mon pèr' m'a don — né un ma —

ri Mon Dieu! quel homm', qu'il est pe — tit!

PRÉSENTATION La famille

Un homme plus une femme, c'est un couple. Ils sont mariés, ils ont des enfants, c'est une famille. J'ai une famille. Vous avez aussi une famille. Tout le monde a une famille. Quelquefois les parents sont divorcés, alors le père est absent (généralement le père; la mère garde les enfants).

Ma famille, c'est mon mari et mes enfants, un garçon, mon fils* et une fille, ma fille. Je suis la mère de mes enfants, leur mère. Mon mari est le père. C'est leur père. Je suis sa femme.**

Et vous, dans votre famille, vous avez un père, une mère, un frère, une sœur? Vous êtes un adulte, alors vous êtes marié, vous avez un mari ou une femme et des enfants, un bébé peut-être, deux, trois bébés. Non, non. Une grande famille, ce n'est pas économique.

La famille, c'est aussi les grands-parents: le grand-père, la grand-mère, les oncles et les tantes, les cousins et les cousines. Ils n'habitent pas dans votre maison; ils habitent dans une autre ville, dans un autre état peut-être. Est-ce que vous avez des oncles et des tantes, des neveux et des nièces***? J'ai des neveux, mais je n'ai pas de nièces. Ma sœur et mon frère n'ont pas de filles. Une grande famille, c'est agréable, quand elle arrive pour une réunion. C'est agréable un jour de fête, pour Noël, ou pour une cérémonie magnifique, un baptême, un mariage. Les membres de la famille organisent un dîner immense; ils parlent, ils chantent, ils dansent. Mais une famille simple, avec les parents et deux enfants au maximum, c'est préférable, n'est-ce pas?

*/fis/   **/fam/   ***/njes/

Vocabulaire

alors then, therefore
baptême, (*m.*) baptism
cousine, (*f.*) cousin
divorcé divorced
enfant, (*m.*) or (*f.*) child
famille, (*f.*) family, relatives
femme, (*f.*) woman, wife
fille, (*f.*) *here:* daughter
fils, (*m.*) son
frère, (*m.*) brother
garder to keep, to guard
généralement generally
grand-mère, (*f.*) grandmother
grand-père, (*m.*) grandfather
habiter to live

homme, (*m.*) man
maison, (*f.*) house
mari, (*m.*) husband
marié married
mère, (*f.*) mother
neveu, (*m.*) nephew
oncle, (*m.*) uncle
père, (*m.*) father
peut-être maybe
pour for
quand when
quelquefois sometimes
sœur, (*f.*) sister
tante, (*f.*) aunt
tout le monde everybody

PRONONCIATION

La liaison

Linking between words is an important phenomenon in French speech. You connect the sound of the last consonant of some words (consonants that are usually unsounded) with the first vowel of the following word. "Liaison" usually occurs between a rather short word, for example an article or a pronoun, and a more important word, a noun or a verb. Here are some words you should link.

les, des, mes, ses, tes
ils, elles, nous, vous   le son est /z/
leurs, vos
dans

un,
mon, ton, son   le son est /n/

Exercice I

RÉPÉTEZ:

les‿amis	les / parents
des‿amis	des / parents
leurs‿amis	leurs / parents
mes‿amis	mes / parents
ils‿ont	ils / marchent
nous‿avons	nous / dansons
elles‿ont	elles / parlent
vous‿avez	vous / chantez
dans‿une fusée	dans / le jardin
un‿enfant	un / lac
mon‿enfant	mon / lac
son‿enfant	son / lac
ton‿enfant	ton / lac

REMARQUES: 1. **h** is not pronounced. The liaison is made with the first vowel of the word.*

un h̸omme   des h̸ommes
ils h̸abitent   vous h̸abitez
c'est h̸orrible

2. Do not link after **et.**

RÉPÉTEZ:

et / alors   et / Adèle
et / elle est   et / Annie
et / il arrive   et / André

3. Link between a pronoun subject and a verb: **ils‿arrivent.** Do not link between a noun subject and the following word:

Les astronautes / explorent l'univers.
L'univers / est‿immense.
Jean / arrive.

Exercice II   Est-ce qu'il y a une liaison? Indiquez **oui:‿non:/**

1. elles aiment
2. vous êtes
3. dans une maison
4. et elle va à l'université
5. comment allez-vous
6. des animaux
7. dans un train
8. des horizons
9. mon énergie
10. c'est héroique
11. et il a
12. des hommes
13. ses habitudes
14. Manon aime Gérard
15. nous allons
16. les professeurs expliquent la leçon
17. ils parlent
18. vous habitez ici
19. c'est horrible

Liaison avec les nombres. RÉPÉTEZ:

un̸ / camarade   un‿étudiant, un̸ étudiante

deux̸ / camarades   deux‿étudiants

trois̸ / camarades   trois‿étudiants

quatr̸e / camarades   quatr̸e‿étudiants

cinq̸ / camarades   cinq étudiants

six̸ / camarades   six‿étudiants

sept̸ / camarades   sept‿étudiants

huit̸ / camarades   huit‿étudiants

neuf / camarades   neuf‿étudiants

dix̸ / camarades   dix‿étudiants

*For other words with **h** see Chapitre 12.

Some numbers are pronounced differently.

a. If they are at the end of a group: **chapitre six** /sis/
b. In front of a noun beginning with a consonant: **si̶x̶ chapitres** /si/
c. In front of a noun beginning with a vowel: **six exercices** /siz/

Prononcez les nombres avec les mots.

Exercice III

6 bicyclettes	10 gouvernements	1 proposition
la proposition 5	l'exercice 3	4 exercices
2 garages	2 astronautes	5 enfants
8 tableaux	3 adresses	8 oiseaux
9 étudiants	l'exercice 10	le chapitre 7
6 exercices	le chapitre 6	10 enfants

Le mot interrogatif **est-ce que**

STRUCTURES

A. 1. Vous habitez ici.
    2. Vous habitez ici?
    3. **Est-ce que** vous habitez ici?

La phrase 1 est une phrase énonciative. La phrase 2 est une question avec l'intonation. La phrase 3 est une question avec **est-ce que.**

> **Est-ce que** + une phrase énonciative = **une question**

La phrase 2 et la phrase 3 ont la même signification, mais l'intonation est différente. Dans la phrase avec **est-ce que,** la voix descend et remonte sur la dernière (*last*) syllabe. Comparez:

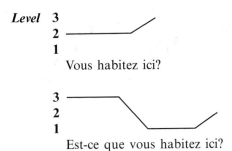

Level **3**
    2
    1
      Vous habitez ici?

    3
    2
    1
      Est-ce que vous habitez ici?

B. Vous habitez ici.
    Vous habitez **où?** (la voix monte sur **où**)
    Où est-ce que vous habitez? (la voix descend et monte sur **habitez**)
    Elle arrive pour Noël.

Elle arrive **quand?** (la voix monte sur **quand**)
Quand est-ce qu'elle arrive? (la voix descend et monte sur **arrive**)
Ils parlent bien.
Ils parlent **comment?** (la voix monte sur **comment**)
Comment est-ce qu'ils parlent? (la voix descend et monte sur **parlent**)

Ajoutez **est-ce que** au mot de question: **où, quand, comment.**

Où est-ce que...?
Quand est-ce que...?
Comment est-ce que...?

Exercice I   (*a.*) Répétez en questions avec l'intonation montante (*rising*).
Répétez avec **est-ce que** et l'intonation descendante (*falling*).

1. Vous êtes un adulte.
2. Tu es dans le jardin.
3. Nous avons des exercices.
4. Les astronautes vont sur la lune.

5. Il a des enfants.
6. C'est tranquille.
7. Vous êtes marié.
8. Ils explorent le firmament.

La famille du Président.

(*b.*) Répétez les phrases en questions avec: **où? Où est-ce que? quand? Quand est-ce que? comment? Comment est-ce que?**

1. La voix monte. **(quand)**
2. Les astronautes marchent. **(où)**
3. Le professeur explique. **(comment)**

Le verbe **avoir**

J'ai un mari.   **Vous avez** des enfants.

avoir

Singulier	*Pluriel*
j'**ai***	nous **avons****
tu **as**	vous **avez****
il, elle **a**	ils, elles **ont****

Prononciation des formes similaires de **avoir, être, aller.**

RÉPÉTEZ: J'ai   Tu es   Il est
           Il a   Il y a
           Tu as, Tu es Elle a   Elle est
           Il a   Il va   Ils sont   Ils ont   Ils vont

           Il est étudiant.   Vous êtes étudiant.

Mettez la forme correcte du verbe **avoir.**   *Exercice II*

1. Elle _____ un bébé.   4. Vous _____ une maison.
2. J'_____ un appartement.   5. Ils _____ un grand-père et une grand-mère.
3. Elles _____ des parents.   6. Nous _____ une classe à l'université.

Mettez la forme correcte du verbe **être** ou du verbe **avoir.**   *Exercice III*

1. Vous _____ étudiant.   6. Tu _____ deux frères.
2. C'_____ un appartement.   7. Vous _____ une maison.
3. La ville _____ en France.   8. Il _____ à l'université.
4. Elles _____ une famille.   9. La ville _____ une cathédrale.
5. Tu _____ dans le jardin.   10. Nous _____ en Europe.

Mettez la forme correcte du verbe **avoir** ou du verbe **aller.**   *Exercice IV*

1. Elle _____ en Italie.   5. Nous _____ en voyage.
2. Vous _____ des frères.   6. Tu _____ un camarade de chambre?
3. Vous _____ à Paris.   7. Vous _____ une maison.
4. Ils _____ en France.   8. Ils _____ des enfants.

*****Je** in front of a vowel always becomes **j'**. It is an "élision." Compare with **l'acteur.**
******Attention à la liaison.

A demain? D'accord!

La forme négative:

La négation de $\begin{cases} \textbf{j'ai un} \\ \textbf{j'ai une} \\ \textbf{j'ai des} \end{cases}$ est: **je n'ai pas de. . .** **pas d'. . .**

je n'ai **pas***   nous n'avons **pas**
tu n'as **pas**   vous n'avez **pas**
il, elle n'a **pas**   ils, elles n'ont **pas**

Il a des sœurs. Il **n'a pas** de sœurs.
J'ai une amie. Je **n'ai pas** d'amie.
J'ai un frère. Je **n'ai pas** de frère.

Exercice V Répétez à la forme négative.

1. Tu a une sœur?
2. Nous avons des cousins.
3. Ils ont une grand-mère.
4. Elles ont une famille.
5. Ils ont une auto.
6. Vous avez un enfant.
7. Elle a un chat.
8. J'ai une famille.

***Ne** est élidé en **n'** devant les voyelles **a** et **o:** n~e~ ai; n~e~ ont.

Les verbes du premier groupe

The French verbs other than **être** and **avoir** are organized into three groups of regular verbs, plus a quantity of irregular verbs. The three regular groups are easily recognizable.

The first group (*premier groupe*)	ends in **-er:**	**danser, adorer**
The second group (*deuxième groupe*)	ends in **-ir:**	**finir, obéir**
The third group (*troisième groupe*)	ends in **-dre:**	**vendre, entendre**

Danser, finir, and **entendre** are infinitives. An infinitive in French is characterized by its ending: **-er, -ir, -re.** There is no preposition *to* as in English. Compare: *to dance* — **danser;** *to finish* — **finir.** The irregular verbs do not belong to any group.

danser	*Terminaison*	*Prononciation*
je dans~~e~~	**-e**	
tu dans~~es~~	**-es**	/s/ **s** est la consonne prononcée
il, elle dans~~e~~	**-e**	
ils, elles dans~~ent~~	**-ent**	
nous dansons	**-ons**	/sõ/
vous dansez	**-ez**	/se/

Exercice VI

Donnez les formes des verbes.

Je (chanter)	Tu (visiter)	Il (former)
Nous (passer)	Vous (regarder)	Elles (travailler)
Je (détester)	Tu (préparer)	Elle (respecter)
Vous (consulter)	Il (cultiver)	Ils (parler)

La forme négative du verbe est:

Je **ne danse pas.** Tu **ne visites pas.**

Exercice VII

Répétez l'exercice VI à la forme négative.

adorer (voyelle initiale)	*Prononciation*
j'ador~~e~~*	
tu ador~~es~~	/R/ **r** est la consonne prononcée
il, elle ador~~e~~	
ils, elles‿ador~~ent~~**	
nous‿ador**ons****	/Rõ/
vous‿ador**ez****	/Re/

Exercice VIII

Donnez les formes des verbes et écrivez.

Je (accuser)	Tu (admirer)	Elle (observer)
Il (abandonner)	Nous (inventer)	Vous (arriver)
Ils (accepter)	Nous (entrer)	Vous (imiter)
Il (imaginer)	Tu (expliquer)	Je (organiser)

*Il y a une élision. **Il y a une liaison.

La forme négative est:

> Je **n'arrive pas.**   Tu **n'imagines pas.**

Il y a une élision de **ne** avec la voyelle du verbe: **n'... pas**

Exercice IX   Répétez l'exercice VIII à la forme négative.

La possession

La préposition **de** indique la possession, la dépendance.

> Bernard a une maison: la maison **de B**ernard.
> Paris a des charmes: les charmes **de P**aris.
> André a un livre: le livre **d'A**ndré.

Il n'y a pas d'article entre **de, d'** et un nom propre.

> La classe a un professeur: le professeur **de la** classe.
> L'étudiant a une table: la table **de l'**étudiant.
> L'étudiante a un sac: le sac **de l'**étudiante.

Ajoutez **de** à l'article **la, l'** avec un nom commun.

> Le professeur a une auto: l'auto **du** professeur.
> Les étudiants ont des livres: les livres **des** étudiants.

~~De le~~ et ~~de les~~ sont impossibles. Utilisez les articles contractés **du** et **des.**

```
de + le  = du
de + les = des
```

de Bernard	de la classe	du professeur
	de l'étudiante	des étudiants
	de l'oncle	

Exercice X   Donnez la forme correcte de l'article avec la préposition **de, de la, de l', du,** ou **des.**

1. Le mari _____ sœur _____ Jeanne.
2. Le cousin _____ Jules et _____ Joséphine.
3. Le fils _____ oncle _____ Claire.
4. Le père _____ parents _____ Paul.
5. Le bébé _____ femme _____ cousin _____ Gertrude.
6. Le jardin _____ campus et _____ université.
7. La décision _____ président.
8. Les avantages _____ pilule.
9. L'enfant _____ Marie.

L'adjectif possessif

Les adjectifs possessifs de la troisième personne **il** ou **elle** sont: **son, sa, ses.**

le livre de Jacques: **son livre**
le livre de Catherine: **son livre**
l'appartement de Jacques: **son appartement**
l'appartement de Catherine: **son appartement**
l'adresse de Jacques: **son adresse**
l'adresse de Catherine: **son adresse**

Le possessif est **son** si l'article est **le, l'.**

la famille de Jacques: **sa famille**
la famille de Catherine: **sa famille**

Le possessif est **sa** si l'article est **la.**

REMARQUEZ: En français il n'y a pas de différence entre *his* et *her*.

les livres de Jacques: **ses livres**
les livres de Catherine: **ses livres**
les idées de Jacques: **ses idées**
les idées de Catherine: **ses idées**

Le possessif est **ses** si le nom est pluriel.

Mettez l'adjectif possessif correct. *Exercice XI*

Voilà Gilles, un garçon. Voilà _____ bicyclette, _____ auto, _____ appartement,
_____ fiancée, _____ adresse, _____ camarades, _____ rêve, _____ oncle,
_____ tante, _____ professeur, _____ animal favori, _____ livres.

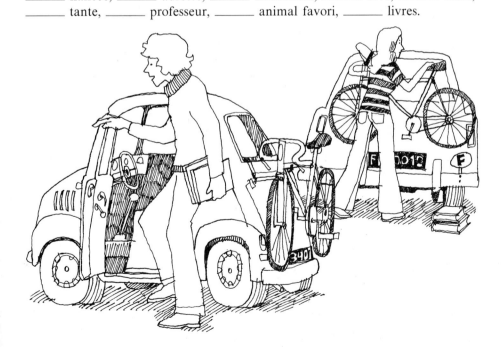

Voilà Marie, une fille: _____ auto, _____ appartement, _____ fiancé, _____ classes, _____ cousins, _____ adresse, _____ rêves, _____ grand-père, _____ grand-mère, _____ parents, _____ maison.

> le charme de Paris: **son** charme
> l'intérêt de Paris: **son** intérêt
> l'université de Paris: **son** université
> la population de Paris: **sa** population
> les musées de Paris: **ses** musées

Son, sa, et **ses** sont aussi la traduction de *its.*

Exercice XII   Mettez l'adjectif possessif.

Visitez New York: _____ monuments, _____ système d'autobus, _____ cathédrale St. Patrick, _____ université Columbia, _____ musées.

J'adore ma ville: _____ jardins, _____ parcs _____ atmosphère, _____ situation, _____ université, _____ calme, _____ habitants.

Les adjectifs possessifs des autres personnes:

Moi, j'ai **mon** livre, **mon** appartement, **mon** université

> **ma** famille   **mes** classes

Toi, tu as **ton** livre, **ton** appartement, **ton** université

> **ta** famille   **tes** classes

Nous, nous avons **notre** livre, **notre** appartement, **notre** université

> **notre** famille   **nos** classes

Vous, vous avez **votre** livre, **votre** appartement, **votre** université

> **votre** famille   **vos** classes

Mes cousins, **ils** ont **leur** livre, **leur** appartement, **leur** université

> **leur** famille   **leurs** classes

You will note that where the English say *our books* (speaking of one book owned by each person) the French say **notre livre** using the singular.

(Moi)	je	mon	ma	mes
(Toi)	tu	ton	ta	tes
(Roger)	il	son	sa	ses
(Odette)	elle	son	sa	ses
(Nous)	nous	notre	notre	nos
(Vous)	vous	votre	votre	vos
(Les garçons)	ils	leur	leur	leurs
(Les jeunes filles)	elles	leur	leur	leurs

Mettez l'adjectif possessif correct.

Nous avons _____ auto au garage. Ils vont à _____ maison. Vous avez _____ livres? Moi, j'ai _____ adresse sur un papier. Elle a _____ oncle et _____ tante en France. Toi, tu as _____ livres dans _____ auto?

Mettez le possesseur correct et la forme du verbe **avoir**.

EXEMPLE: _____ mon stylo: **j'ai** mon stylo.

_____ ton livre. _____ votre adresse. _____ ses parents.
_____ leurs habitudes. _____ ma famille en France. _____ nos problèmes.
_____ tes livres. _____ son adresse.

Les adjectifs en -e (masculin-féminin)

> Le professeur est **extraordinaire.**
> La classe est **fantastique.**

Une quantité d'adjectifs avec un **e** final sont identiques au masculin et au féminin.

> Les explications sont logiqu**es.**

L'adjectif en **e** a aussi son pluriel avec un **s,** comme le nom.

> C'est une description **simple.**

L'adjectif est après (*after*) le nom.

Mettez l'adjectif au pluriel.

riche	Mes oncles sont _____.
féroce	Les professeurs sont _____.
chauviniste	Ce sont des étudiants _____.
tranquille	Les enfants ne sont pas _____.
grave	Il y a des accidents _____.
féministe	Les jeunes filles sont _____.
obligatoire	Les exercices ne sont pas _____.
démocratique	Les gouvernements sont _____.
comique	Elles ont des idées _____.

Liste d'adjectifs "*cognates.*"

-able: agréable, confortable, désagréable, durable, désirable, habitable, préférable, responsable, respectable

-ique: (anglais *–ic, –ical*) comique, dramatique, économique, exotique, énergique, fantastique, identique, logique, magnifique, organique, pacifique, pratique

-ible: horrible, possible, impossible, terrible

-iste: féministe, optimiste, pessimiste, socialiste, communiste, impérialiste

Une idée est absurde, bizarre, étrange, juste, vague.

Une maison est calme, moderne, robuste, solide, tranquille, immense.

Une personne est célèbre, sincère, sobre, brave, féroce, simple, timide, riche, honnête.

Une chose est obligatoire, difficile, énorme, grave, rare, ridicule.

LECTURE   Un père formidable

Deux étudiants habitent dans une maison avec deux étudiantes. Maris et femmes? Non, c'est simplement une cohabitation économique et pratique. Les garçons détestent le ménage et adorent la cuisine organique. Les jeunes filles sont féministes, et elles ne sont pas riches. Elles préparent la cuisine, elles décorent la maison, elles cultivent le jardin, elles vont aussi à l'université, quelquefois.

Les parents des deux garçons arrivent pour une visite. Scandale! La maman n'est pas moderne, et elle est féroce.

LA MÈRE: Mes enfants! La situation n'est pas respectable. Vite, un juge! Un temple! Une bénédiction!

LES ETUDIANTS: Mais maman, le mariage, c'est grave. Une décision rapide n'est pas obligatoire.

LES JEUNES FILLES: (*Silence*)

LA MÈRE: Impossible! C'est tragique. C'est horrible!

LES JEUNES FILLES: (*Silence*)

LES ÉTUDIANTS: Tu exagères, Maman, ce n'est pas dramatique. Nous sommes pacifistes. Nous détestons les batailles.

LE PÈRE: Allons, allons. Ma femme! Mes enfants! Voici un compromis raisonnable: un million de dollars à la banque, à votre nom, mes enfants?

LES JEUNES FILLES: Oui, oui! Nous ne sommes pas féministes. Nous préférons une famille, une maison immense, une quantité de bébés. Vos parents sont formidables. Vite, un juge, un temple, une bénédiction. Une cérémonie magnifique n'est pas nécessaire.

Vocabulaire

bataille, (*f.*) battle
formidable terrific

ménage, (*m.*) house cleaning
vite quickly

Composition dirigée   Est-ce que vous avez une famille? Oui, _____. Dans ma famille il y a _____. J'ai _____ sœurs, _____ frères. Est-ce que vous avez aussi des oncles, des tantes, etc? Des cousins, des cousines? Combien? Est-ce qu'ils habitent avec vous? Si non, où est-ce qu'ils habitent? Est-ce que vous avez des grand-parents? Où est-ce qu'ils habitent? Est-ce que vous avez un ami ou une amie? Où est-ce qu'il (ou elle) habite? Avec ses parents?

- PRÉSENTATION: La maison
- PRONONCIATION: le son /j/: **ille, euil,** etc.
  changement d'accent dans les verbes du type **préférer**
  le **e** sans accent: /ɛ/et/ə/
- Structures:

  Constructions à retenir: les nombres ordinaux
  les adverbes de temps: **d'abord, ensuite, enfin**
  les expressions **voici, il y a**
  la préposition **chez**
  le pronom **on**

  Points de grammaire: l'impératif
  la forme interrogative des verbes
  l'adjectif (suite)

- LECTURE: Une querelle classique

- SLOGAN: Allez, France!

Cadet Rousselle

Ca — det Rous — selle a trois mai — sons, Ca — det Rous —
selle a trois mai — sons, qui n'ont ni pou — tres ni che —
vrons, qui n'ont ni pou — tres ni che — vrons. C'est pour lo —
ger les hi — ron — del — les. Que di — rez — vous d'Ca — det Rous — sel — le? Ah!
Ah! Ah! oui vrai — ment! Ca — det Rous — selle est bon en — fant!

PRÉSENTATION   La maison

Regardez. Voici ma maison. Elle est située dans une petite rue tranquille. Elle a un balcon, un porche... Quoi? Elle n'a pas de porte? Très juste. Alors, voilà, je dessine une porte. Quoi? Comment? Elle n'a pas de fenêtres? Bon, d'accord, je dessine les fenêtres. Quoi encore? Elle n'a pas de toit? Alors, voilà le toit; il est rouge, bien sûr. Voilà aussi la cheminée et l'antenne de télévision. Vous constatez une chose intéressante: ma maison a un étage. D'abord regardez bien: devant ma maison, il y a un jardin avec une pelouse verte, des arbres, des fleurs—des roses rouges, des géraniums roses, des tulipes blanches, jaunes, bleues, et violettes. A côté de ma maison, il y a un garage pour les autos. (Oui, nous avons deux autos. Nous sommes une famille américaine typique et traditionnelle.) Derrière la maison? Il y a un autre jardin, il est invisible sur mon dessin; hélas, non! il n'y a pas de piscine.

Maintenant, entrez dans ma maison et regardez: au rez-de-chaussée, à droite, il y a un salon, avec un divan rouge, des fauteuils gris, une télévision, trois petites tables, un piano, des plantes vertes, une cheminée, et des tableaux sur les murs; c'est la pièce principale de la maison; elle est spacieuse et agréable. A gauche, il y a la salle à manger avec une table ronde, six chaises, un buffet. Ensuite passons dans la cuisine: elle n'est pas spéciale; les murs sont jaunes; il y a un frigidaire blanc, une cuisinière électrique blanche, une table et des chaises jaunes, et une quantité de placards pratiques. Il y a une autre pièce, entre la cuisine et le garage: c'est mon bureau, ma pièce personnelle: il y a une grande table, des étagères avec des quantités de livres, et une machine à écrire.

Enfin, allons au premier étage et visitons les chambres. Il y a trois chambres dans ma maison: la chambre bleue pour les parents, la chambre rose pour notre fille, et la chambre violette pour notre fils. Dans chaque chambre il y a un lit, une commode, des petites tables pour les lampes, la radio, et des placards. Il y a aussi deux salles de bains. Non, il n'y a pas de deuxième étage. Chez ma sœur, il y a deux

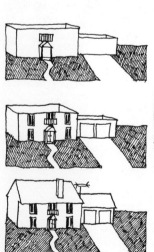

étages, quatre chambres et une quantité de meubles élégants. Ma maison n'est pas immense, mais elle est suffisante pour ma famille.

Vocabulaire

Adjectifs de couleur: **blanc** white   **bleu** blue   **gris** grey
                       jaune yellow   **noir** black   **rouge** red
                       vert green   **violet** purple

à côté de next to	**fenêtre**, (_f._) window
à droite to the right	**fauteuil**, (_m._) armchair
à gauche to the left	**lit**, (_m._) bed
chaise, (_f._) chair	**machine à écrire**, (_f._) typewriter
chambre, (_f._) bedroom	**maintenant** now
chaque each	**meuble**, (_m._) piece of furniture
cheminée, (_f._) chimney and fireplace	**mur**, (_m._) wall
chez at the house of	**pelouse**, (_f._) lawn
commode, (_f._) chest of drawers	**pièce**, (_f._) room
cuisine, (_f._) kitchen (also: cooking, food)	**piscine**, (_f._) swimming pool
cuisinière, (_f._) stove	**placard**, (_m._) cupboard, closet
d'abord first	**porte**, (_f._) door
derrière behind	**rez-de-chaussée**, (_m._) first floor /redʃose/
dessin, (_m._) drawing	**rue**, (_f._) street
dessiner to draw	**salle à manger**, (_f._) dining room
devant in front (of)	**salle de bain**, (_f._) bathroom
enfin finally	**salon**, (_m._) living room
ensuite then (second)	**tableau**, (_m._) painting (blackboard)
étage, (_m._) floor	**toit**, (_m._) roof
étagère, (_f._) shelf	**très juste** (you are) so right

PRONONCIATION

Le son /j/

Prononcez		
-ille	/ij/	f**ille**, fam**ille**
	/il/	v**ille**, tranqu**ille**, m**ille**
-eil	/ɛj/	par**eil**, sol**eil**
-euil	/œj/	faut**euil**, f**euille**
-ia	/ja/	p**ia**no, spéc**ia**l
-ier	/je/	prem**ier**
-iè	/jɛ/	p**iè**ce, cuis**iniè**re, derr**iè**re, deux**iè**me, tro**isiè**me
-ion	/jɔ̃/	télévi**sion**, tradi**tion**
-ieu	/jø/	spac**ieu**se, ad**ieu**
-io	/jo/	rad**io**, id**io**t

Changement d'accent dans les verbes **préférer, espérer, exagérer, pénétrer, répéter, précéder, révéler**

préf $\boxed{é}$ rer   préf $\boxed{é}$ rons   préf $\boxed{é}$ rez

A l'infinitif et aux personnes **nous** et **vous**, la finale est **-er, -ons, -ez**. Ce ne sont pas des sons muets: /e/, /õ/, /e/. L'accent sur $\boxed{é}$ est aigu (´), et la prononciation est /e/:

préf $\boxed{é}$ rer   je préf $\boxed{è}$ re

Aux autres personnes **(je, tu, il, elle, ils, elles)**, la finale est **-e, -es, -ent**. C'est un **e** muet. L'accent sur $\boxed{è}$ est grave (`), et la prononciation est /ɛ/.

Le **e** sans accent: le son /ɛ/ et le son /ə/

e + double consonne est prononcé /ɛ/:   de**ss**ine de**ss**in
intér**ess**ante traditionn**e**lle
ant**enne** violet**t**es

e + une consonne est prononcé /ə/:   r**e**gardez d**e**vant
pr**e**mier f**e**nêtre
p**e**louse ch**e**minée
p**e**tite

In some cases this **e** can be omitted: ch/eminée, maint/enant, f/enêtre. (Voir Chapitre 8 pour les détails.)

Exercice I   Une révision sur les **e** et les accents (voir Chapitre Préliminaire 2, p. 10). Mettez l'accent correct.

la piece	je dessine	la fenetre	agreable
tu exageres	derriere	interessante	j'espere
electrique	television	premiere	nous repetons
personnelle	etagere	elle prefere	regardez

STRUCTURES   CONSTRUCTIONS A RETENIR

Les nombres ordinaux

le premier (féminin: **la première**)
le, la deuxième
le, la troisième
le, la quatrième (il n'y a pas le **e** de **quatre**)
le, la cinquième (ajoutez **u** à **cinq**)
le, la sixième
le, la septième

le, la huitième
le, la neuvième (il y a **v** à la place de **f** du nombre **neuf**)
le, la dixième

Répétez avec le nombre ordinal.   *Exercice I*

EXEMPLE: page 8   la huitième page

chapitre 2   paragraphe 10   ligne 7
exercice 5   page 3

Les adverbes de temps: **d'abord, ensuite, enfin**

> **D'abord,** regardez mon jardin; **ensuite,** entrons dans le salon; **enfin,** allons au premier étage.

Dans une histoire, une énumération, utilisez les adverbes: **d'abord** — *first;* **ensuite** — *next, then;* **enfin** — *finally.*

Répétez avec les adverbes.   *Exercice II*

1. Je regarde dans le frigidaire, je prépare le dîner, je dîne.
2. Il visite Paris, il va en Italie, il retourne aux U.S.A.
3. Nous écoutons le professeur, nous répétons les modèles, nous préparons une composition.

Les expressions **voici, voilà; il y a** (*there is, there are*)

> **Voici** ma maison.   **Voilà** le professeur.

Vous montrez un objet, une personne.

> **Il y a** un jardin devant ma maison. **Il y a** des étudiants dans la classe.

Vous constatez l'existence d'un objet, d'une personne.

REMARQUE: Il y a généralement un groupe prépositionnel après le nom: **devant ma maison, dans la classe.**

Exercice III   Répétez avec **voici, voilà,** ou **il y a.**

1. _____ une souris dans le salon.
2. _____ des fleurs sur le piano.
3. _____ mon jardin.
4. _____ une piscine dans votre jardin.
5. _____ une jolie chambre.
6. _____ une quantité de livres dans le bureau.
7. _____ la salle de bains.

La préposition **chez**

Vous dînez **chez** vos cousins?

La préposition **chez** est l'équivalent de **dans la maison de** ou **à la maison de.**

Exercice IV   Répétez avec **chez.**

1. Il habite dans la maison de ses parents.
2. A la maison de mon oncle, il y a des plantes vertes.
3. Nous dînons à la maison de Gérard.
4. Il y a une partie à la maison de ma grand-mère.

Un château? Non, une ferme.

Le pronom **on**

> En été **on** est en vacances, **on** va à la plage.
> En France, **on** ne travaille pas le premier mai.
> **On** va au cinéma dimanche?

Le pronom indéfini **on** est très populaire en français. Il a trois significations importantes. Il signifie:

a. Une personne indéfinie (en anglais *one*):

> En été **on** va à la plage.

b. Un groupe de personnes indéfinies (en anglais *they, people*):

> En France **on** ne travaille pas le premier mai.

c. **Nous** (dans une langue familière correcte):

> **On** va au cinéma dimanche?

Le verbe est toujours au singulier.

Répétez avec **on** comme sujet. Changez le verbe, si c'est nécessaire.   ***Exercice V***

1. Les Français célèbrent le 11 novembre par des défilés.
2. Quand une personne est riche, elle n'habite pas sous la tente.
3. Nous organisons une partie?
4. En France les Français adorent le soleil du Midi.
5. Une personne brunit au soleil.
6. Nous voyageons en été.

POINTS DE GRAMMAIRE

L'impératif

C'est le mode (*mood*) de l'ordre, du commandement.

Come in!	**Entrez!**	**Entre!**
Look!	**Regardez!**	**Regarde!**

Comme en anglais, le sujet n'est pas exprimé (*expressed*). **Entrez! Regardez!** C'est la forme du pluriel ou la forme polie du singulier. **Entre! Regarde!** C'est la forme familière du singulier (vous parlez à un ami). La forme de **Entre!** et **Regarde!** est identique à la première personne du singulier:

J'entre.	**Entre!**
Je regarde.	**Regarde!**

En français il y a aussi une forme de l'impératif pour la personne **nous** (le sujet est absent).

Entrons!	*Let's come in!*	**Regardons!**	*Let's look.*

Vous invitez une personne ou des personnes à entrer, à regarder, et vous entrez et vous regardez aussi.

La forme négative de l'impératif (*Do not come in!*) est:

N'entre **pas!**	Ne regarde **pas!**
N'entrez **pas!**	Ne regardez **pas!**
N'entrons **pas!**	Ne regardons **pas!**

REMARQUE: Le verbe **aller** a un impératif irrégulier pour la forme familière: **Va.** Les autres formes sont: **Allez! Allons!**

L'intonation de la phrase impérative:

La voix descend, comme dans ce schéma.

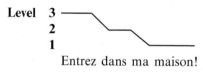

Level 3
2
1
Entrez dans ma maison!

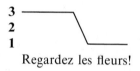

3
2
1
Regardez les fleurs!

3
2
1
Allons au premier étage!

Exercice VI Répétez (*a.*) à l'impératif positif; (*b.*) à l'impératif négatif.

1. Vous (aller) à la mer?
2. Tu (respecter) tes parents.
3. Nous (visiter) la ville.
4. Tu (imiter) le professeur.
5. Vous (identifier) les adjectifs.
6. Tu (entrer) dans la maison.
7. Nous (gouverner) avec justice.
8. Vous (arriver) à l'heure.
9. Tu (aller) à la cuisine.
10. Vous (répéter) les exercices.

La forme interrogative des verbes

Sommes-nous dans la classe?
Avez-vous un appartement?
Habitez-vous avec vos parents?

Placez le pronom sujet après le verbe. Pour les verbes **être** et **avoir** la construction est identique en anglais et en français:

Are you? **Êtes-vous?**   *Are we?* **Sommes-nous?**
Have you? **Avez-vous?**   *Have we?* **Avons-nous?**

Mais en français ajoutez un tiret (-) (*hyphen*).

Il y a un problème à la troisième personne du singulier — **il, elle.**

COMPAREZ: Est-il? Est-elle?
Sont-ils? Sont-elles?   **A-t-il?**
Ont-ils? Ont-elles?   **A-t-elle?**

On ajoute un **t** entre (*between*) **a** et **il, a** et **elle** pour la symétrie des sons (*to match the sounds*). C'est le même phénomène pour les verbes du premier groupe:

Habite-t-il?   Préfère-t-il?
Habite-t-elle?   Préfère-t-elle?

Pour la première personne du singulier **(je)** la construction avec **est-ce que** est obligatoire pour un verbe autre que **être** ou **avoir.**

Suis-je?   **Est-ce que** j'étudie mes verbes?
Ai-je?   mais   **Est-ce que** je danse bien?

Pour les autres personnes, la construction avec **est-ce que** est toujours possible, pratique, et facile.

Répétez à la forme interrogative, avec inversion du sujet.   *Exercice VII*

1. Nous avons une composition.
2. Ils gouvernent bien.
3. Vous préférez une piscine?
4. Elle a des enfants.
5. Ils sont dans le jardin.
6. Elle prépare un grand dîner.
7. J'exagère.
8. Je suis calme.
9. Tu as une cigarette.
10. Il a un appartement confortable.

L'adjectif (suite)

Le genre:

Une quantité d'adjectifs en français ont un changement dans l'orthographe. Au féminin il y a **-e**; au masculin il n'y a pas **-e.** La prononciation est identique.

Féminin		*Masculin*	
-ale	une femme norm**ale**	**-al**	un homme normal
-elle	une femme sensationn**elle**	**-el**	un homme sensationnel
-ure	une idée p**ure**	**-ur**	un vin pur
-eure	supérie**ure**	**-eur**	supérieur
-ée	une fille obstin**ée**	**-é**	un garçon obstiné

C'est la maison de vos rêves?

D'autres adjectifs ont une prononciation différente au masculin et au féminin. Au masculin il n'y a pas **e**, et la consonne finale n'est pas prononcée.

–de	Suzanne est gran**de**,	**–d̸**	Paul est gran**d̸**,
–te	intelligen**te**.	**–t̸**	intelligen**t̸**.
–aise	une cuisine fran**çaise**,	**–ai̸s**	un camembert fran**çai̸s**,
–euse	délici**euse**	**–eu̸x**	délici**eu̸x**
–ère	la premi**ère** leçon	**–er̸**	le premi**er̸** exercice

-aine /ɛn/	la démocratie améric**aine**	**-ain** /ɛ̃/	le peuple améric**ain**	
-onne /ɔn/	une **bonne** place	**-on** /õ/	un **bon** film	
-une /yn/	une jeune fille br**une**	**-un** /œ̃/	un garçon br**un**	

Pour les trois types **-aine, -ain; -onne, -on; -une, -un,** on a une voyelle orale au féminin; **n** est prononcé. On a une voyelle nasale au masculin; **n** n'est pas prononcé.

Le pluriel:

L'adjectif aussi a un pluriel.

EXEMPLE: une étudiante intelligente   un étudiant intelligent
            des étudiantes intelligente**s**   des étudiants intelligent**s**

Pour certains adjectifs on ajoute **s,** mais la prononciation est identique au pluriel et au singulier.

EXEMPLE: des femmes française**s**   des journaux françai**s**
            des fleurs mystérieuse**s**   des jardins mystérieu**x**

On ajoute **s** au féminin, et on garde **s** ou **x** au pluriel.

EXEMPLE: un enfant norm**al**   des enfants norm**aux**

L'adjectif en **-al** a son pluriel en **-aux** /o/. Le féminin pluriel est **-ales** (au singulier **-ale**):

    une cuisine norm**ale**   des cuisines norm**ales**

Notez les exceptions au masculin:

    un examen fin**al**   des examens fin**als**
    un accident fat**al**   des accidents fat**als**

Accordez l'adjectif avec le nom ou le pronom.   *Exercice VIII*

1. (normal) Ils ont un enfant _____. C'est une maison _____.
2. (sensationnel) C'est une fille _____. Son frère est _____.
3. (pur) L'air (*m.*) des villes n'est pas _____. La rivière est _____.
4. (supérieur) C'est une situation _____. C'est un officier _____.
5. (intelligent) Les étudiants sont _____. Les étudiantes sont _____ aussi.
6. (furieux) Ma mère est _____. Mon professeur est _____.
7. (anglais) Ses parents sont _____. Sa grand-mère est _____.
8. (spécial) Son attitude est _____. Son courage est _____.
9. (obstiné) Mademoiselle, vous êtes _____. M., vous êtes _____.
10. (délicieux) Les bonbons sont _____. La cuisine est _____.
11. (américain) Nous sommes _____. Elle est _____.
12. (canadien) La frontière _____ est une ligne sur la carte. Mon ami est _____.

Exercice IX Mettez les phrases au pluriel.

1. C'est un pays mystérieux.
2. L'enfant est curieux.
3. Tu vas a un bal important.
4. La leçon est spéciale.
5. C'est l'examen final.
6. Le journal provincial est intéressant.
7. La jeune fille est joyeuse.
8. L'exercice n'est pas sensationnel.

Attention: La grammaire française est sexiste!

Pierre et Jacques sont intelligen**ts**.

Si le sujet est masculin pluriel, l'adjectif est masculin pluriel.

Pierrette et Jacqueline sont intelligen**tes**.

Si le sujet est féminin pluriel, l'adjectif est féminin pluriel.

Pierre et Jacqueline sont intelligen**ts**.

Mais si le sujet est masculin et féminin, l'adjectif est masculin pluriel!

Les adjectifs de couleur

Voici les principaux adjectifs de couleur:

Masc. *Sing.*	*Masc.* *Pluriel*	*Fém.* *Sing.*	*Fém.* *Pluriel*
bleu	bleus	bleue	bleues
jaune	jaunes	jaune	jaunes
rose	roses	rose	roses
rouge	rouges	rouge	rouges
noir	noirs	noire	noires

La prononciation est identique pour le masculin, le féminin, le singulier, et le pluriel.

blanc	blancs	blanche	blanches
brun	bruns	brune	brunes
gris	gris	grise	grises
vert	verts	verte	vertes
violet	violets	violette	violettes

La prononciation change au masculin et au féminin.

orange: un divan orang**e**, des murs orang**e**, une cuisine orang**e**, des fleurs orang**e**

marron: un mur marr**on**, une robe marr**on**, des placards marr**on**, des chaises marr**on**

Les autres adjectifs de couleur sont invariables.

REMARQUE: Un nom de couleur est masculin: **le** bleu, **le** blanc, **le** rouge.

De quelle couleur est la chambre de Marie-Claude? Elle est bleue.
De quelle couleur sont les murs? Ils sont blancs.

La question a la forme suivante:

De quelle couleur est...?
De quelle couleur sont...?

La place des adjectifs:

la maison blanche   les plantes vertes

Les adjectifs de couleur sont placés après le nom.

une maison immense   des étudiants brillants

La majorité des adjectifs sont placés après le nom.

une petite fille   le premier étage
un grand salon   les bons enfants

Certains adjectifs courants sont placés devant le nom. Voici une liste préliminaire:
petit, grand, premier, joli, bon. La liste complète est à la page 79.

une petite maison blanche   un grand salon agréable

Placez un adjectif devant et l'autre après, si c'est nécessaire.

une jolie petite fille

Il y a certaines combinaisons fixes pour les adjectifs placés devant le nom: **joli
petit, bon petit, premier grand,** etc.

Accordez l'adjectif de couleur avec le nom.   *Exercice X*

1. (brun) une maison _____
2. (vert) des livres _____
3. (rouge) des fleurs _____
4. (gris) des toits _____
5. (jaune) des tulipes _____
6. (orange) un fauteuil _____
7. (blanc) une cuisine _____
8. (bleu) des autos _____
9. (noir) des tableaux _____
10. (violet) une fleur _____
11. (gris) une souris _____
12. (marron) une plante _____
13. (rose) des commodes _____

Répétez le nom avec les deux adjectifs.   *Exercice XI*

1. (petit, charmant) une fille
2. (grand, blanc) une maison
3. (premier, intelligent) l'action
4. (joli, japonais) un jardin
5. (grand, noir) les tableaux
6. (petit, bleu) les autos
7. (premier, rouge) les roses
8. (joli, petit) une photo
9. (bon, anglais) un film

Où est le rez-de-chaussée?

LECTURE   Une querelle classique

SUZANNE: Chéri, cherchons une autre maison. Notre appartement est petit, inconfortable. Je n'aime pas la cuisine. Je préfère une grande cuisine. Je n'aime pas nos meubles. Et puis, il n'y a pas de piscine. Il n'y a pas de jardin.

BERNARD: Mais, chérie, une maison avec une piscine, c'est exorbitant!

SUZANNE: Mais nous sommes riches, non? Tu es professeur à l'université, et moi, je suis la secrétaire du président.

BERNARD: Oui, c'est des situations supérieures. Mais il y a l'inflation, la récession. Elles sont terribles. Nous n'avons pas de fortune.

SUZANNE: Mais je n'aime pas notre logement. Une maison immense n'est pas nécessaire, mais regarde: un salon minuscule, un divan vert avec des fauteuils marron, une chambre violette et une salle de bain noire. C'est horrible. Et puis il n'y a pas de chambre pour un bébé.

BERNARD: Mais nous n'avons pas de bébé! Allons, ce n'est pas si terrible et ce n'est pas catastrophique. J'ai une solution à notre problème: organisons une partie de peinture pour changer la décoration de notre appartement: une cuisine blanche, la chambre rose, la salle de bains bleue, le salon gris.

SUZANNE: Non, non! Ce n'est pas suffisant. Ta famille arrive pour une visite à Noël, et notre appartement n'est pas habitable.

BERNARD: Tu exagères et tu n'es pas raisonnable.

SUZANNE: Je suis malheureuse. Tu es tyrannique.

BERNARD: Allons! Allons! Ne crie pas! Ne pleure pas! J'accepte! Je suis d'accord pour un petit changement.

SUZANNE: Chéri! tu es adorable! Vite, allons à une agence de logement.

BERNARD: Non, ce n'est pas nécessaire. Il y a des plantes vertes très économiques dans le jardin de mon oncle. Trois ou quatre plantes vertes dans la maison et voilà... un décor différent et charmant.

SUZANNE: Ouin... Tu es horrible... Je suis furieuse. Je quitte la maison. Adieu.

BERNARD: Où vas-tu?

SUZANNE: Je retourne chez ma mère!

Vocabulaire

crier to shout, to cry out
peinture, (*f.*) painting
pleurer to cry

ouin boohoo!
retourner to go back

1. Où habitez-vous? Comment est votre maison, ou votre appartement (petit, grand, spacieux, agréable, confortable)? Il y a deux, quatre, dix pièces dans votre maison? Comment est la cuisine? Comment est le salon? Dans le salon il y a _____ meubles. Dans ma chambre il y a _____. Il y a un jardin ou il n'y a pas de jardin? Il y a une piscine ou il n'y a pas de piscine?

2. Comment est la maison de vos rêves? (Bien sûr c'est un palais, un château, avec une quantité de pièces, des meubles magnifiques, des piscines, un parc, des animaux en liberté.)

Composition dirigée

- **PRÉSENTATION:** La date, l'heure

- **PRONONCIATION:** les groupes **–ui** et **–uin; oui** et **–oin**
  la lettre **–s** en finale
  l'orthographe **c** ou **ç** dans les verbes en **–cer** (**commencer**)
  les mots en **–bre** et **–tre**
  l'enchaînement avec **quelle heure**

- **STRUCTURES:**
  Constructions à retenir: les nombres de 10 à 31
  l'adjectif **quel**
  l'heure, le jour, la date
  les prépositions **avant, après; devant, derrière**
  les expressions **en avance, tôt** (*early*); **en retard, tard** (*late*)

  Points de grammaire: les verbes du 2ème groupe: **finir**
  les adjectifs irréguliers

- **LECTURES:**
  1. Un jeune homme distrait
  2. Fêtes françaises

- **DICTONS:** Jamais le dimanche • L'heure H

Voici le mois de Mai

Voi–ci le mois de Mai, où les fleurs vol't au

vent, voi – ci le mois de Mai, où les fleurs vol't au vent, où

les fleurs vol't au vent si jo–lies, mi – gnon – nes, où

les fleurs vol't au vent si mi–gnon – ne – ment.

PRÉSENTATION La date, l'heure

Quel jour est-ce que nous sommes, aujourd'hui?

Aujourd'hui, nous sommes lundi, six octobre, le lundi six octobre. C'est lundi, le 6 octobre.

Lundi, c'est un jour?

Oui, et demain, c'est mardi. Les autres jours sont mercredi, jeudi, vendredi, samedi, et dimanche. En France, la semaine commence le lundi — le dernier jour, c'est le dimanche. La semaine finit le dimanche, c'est l'organisation de Dieu. En Amérique, dimanche, c'est le premier jour de la semaine! En France, c'est le dernier. Bizarre!

Bon, nous sommes en octobre. Quels sont les autres mois de l'année?

Les autres mois de l'année sont novembre, décembre, janvier, février, mars, avril, mai, juin, juillet, août,* et septembre.** Il y a 12 mois dans une année.

Je regarde ma montre. Je regarde la pendule; elles indiquent l'heure. Quelle heure est-il?

Il est midi.	Il est minuit.
Il est une heure.	Il est six heures.
Il est une heure cinq.	Il est six heures moins vingt-cinq.
Il est une heure dix.	Il est six heures moins vingt.
Il est une heure et quart.	Il est six heures moins le quart.
Il est une heure vingt.	Il est une heure et demie.

De minuit à midi, il est 1 h, 2 h... 6 h... 11 h du matin: _A.M._
De midi à cinq heures, il est 1 h... 5 h, de l'après-midi: _P.M._
De cinq heures à minuit, il est 5 h, 6 h... 11 h du soir.

Les trains français et les théâtres ont leur horaire fixé sur 24 heures:

2 heures de l'après-midi, c'est 14 00
5 h 30 = 17 h 30
11 heures du soir = 23 00

Vous avez vite l'habitude de cette petite gymnastique mathématique.

*Prononcez /u/ ou /ut/.   **N'employez pas l'article avec le nom de mois.

A quelle heure est-ce que la classe de français commence?
    Elle commence à midi et demi.*
A quelle heure est-ce qu'elle finit?
    Elle finit à une heure vingt.
    La classe commence à midi et demi. C'est tard. J'arrive à une heure moins
    le quart: je suis en retard. Mais si j'arrive à midi vingt, je suis en avance.
Le lundi, où est-ce que vous êtes?
    Le lundi, je suis à l'université, à la bibliothèque, au laboratoire, et à mes
    autres classes, et les autres jours aussi. Le samedi et le dimanche, c'est le
    week-end et je reste à la maison.
Quelles sont vos occupations le week-end?
    Chaque week-end, si j'ai le courage, je travaille, j'étudie mes leçons; le
    samedi matin je vais au supermarché; le soir, quelquefois, je dîne au
    restaurant avec ma petite amie (mon petit ami) et après, nous allons au
    cinéma (si nous sommes riches, bien sûr).

Vocabulaire

an, (*m.*); **année,** (*f.*) year
après after, afterwards
après-midi, (*m.*) ou (*f.*) afternoon
août August
aujourd'hui today
avril April
bibliothèque, (*f.*) library
bien sûr of course
de ... à from ... to
décembre December
demain tomorrow
Dieu God
dimanche Sunday
dernier, (*m.*) last
étudier to study
février February
heure, (*f.*) hour
janvier January
jeudi Thursday
jour, (*m.*) day
juillet July
juin June
lundi Monday
mai May
mardi Tuesday

mars March
mercredi Wednesday
midi noon
minuit midnight
moins minus
mois, (*m.*) month
montre, (*f.*) watch
novembre November
octobre October
pendule, (*f.*) clock
petit ami, (*m.*) boyfriend
petite amie, (*f.*) girl friend
quart, (*m.*) quarter
quel which
rester to stay
samedi Saturday
semaine, (*f.*) week
septembre September
soir, (*m.*) evening
tard late (*for the hour*); **en retard** late
    (*for people*)
tôt early (*for the hour*); **en avance** early
    (*for people*)
travailler to work (to study)
vendredi Friday

*Note the spelling: midi et **demi**, minuit et **demi**, une **demi**-heure (no **e**); une heure et **demie**, deux
heures et **demie**, etc. (with **e**)—no change in pronunciation.

PRONONCIATION   Les groupes **ui** et **uin; oui** et **ouin**

-ui: Prononcez /y/ et /i/ vite (*fast*) en une syllabe.

RÉPÉTEZ: huit   puis   minuit   suis
aujourd'hui   juillet /ʒɥijɛ/

-uin: Prononcez /y/ et /ɛ̃/ ensemble (*together*).

RÉPÉTEZ: juin /ʒɥɛ̃/

-oui: Prononcez /u/ et /i/ vite ensemble.

RÉPÉTEZ: oui   Louis   COMPAREZ: oui   huit
Louis   lui

-oin: Prononcez /w/ et /ɛ̃/ vite ensemble.

RÉPÉTEZ: mois   moins
poids   point
lois   loin
foi   foin

La lettre **s** en finale

S final, généralement, n'est pas prononcé.

RÉPÉTEZ: dans̸   cours̸   univers̸

Mais prononcez /s/ dans les mots:

Vénus   campus   autobus
hélas   fils̸   as (*ace*)
plus (+)   mars   sens

C ou **ç** dans les verbes en **–cer:**
commencer, prononcer, avancer, placer

je commence   nous commençons

C est prononcé /s/ devant un **e** ou un **é**. Une cédille est nécessaire devant un **o:**
commençons, plaçons, avançons.

Exercice I   Répétez et écrivez la forme correcte du verbe.

1. (placer) Je _____ les livres sur une étagère. Vous _____. Nous _____.
2. (commencer) Je _____ l'explication. Elle _____. Nous _____.
3. (prononcer) Elle _____ bien. Tu _____. Nous _____.
4. (avancer) L'auto n'_____ pas. Elles _____ progressivement. Nous _____.

Les mots en **–bre** et **–tre**

–bre et **–tre** sont chuchotés (*whispered*) dans les mots: octo**bre**, novem**bre**, décem**bre**; mon**tre**, au**tre**.

L'enchaînement avec **quelle heure**

A quel $\boxed{l\not{e}\ heu}$ re...?

Prononcez l avec **eu**: /lœ/. C'est un enchaînement. Comparez avec u $\boxed{n\not{e}\ \acute{e}}$ tudiante.

RÉPÉTEZ: Quelle heure /kɛlœr/   Quelle année /kɛlane/
Quel or /kɛlɔr/   Quel autre /kɛlotr/
Quel art /kɛlar/

CONSTRUCTIONS A RETENIR   STRUCTURES

Les nombres de 10 à 31

11 onze (le onze*)	18 dix-huit	25 vingt-cinq
12 douze	19 dix-neuf	26 vingt-six
13 treize	20 vingt	27 vingt-sept
14 quatorze	21 vingt et un	28 vingt-huit
15 quinze	22 vingt-deux	29 vingt-neuf
16 seize	23 vingt-trois	30 trente
17 dix-sept	24 vingt-quatre	31 trente et un

Répétez. Comptez!

Exercice I

EXEMPLE: Deux plus trois? cinq
Cinq moins trois? deux

17 + 3 = _____   13 + 18 = _____   30 + 1 = _____   22 − 7 = _____
30 − 5 = _____   19 − 6 = _____   8 + 12 = _____   29 − 14 = _____

Les ordinaux sont **le onzième, le douzième, le dix-septième, le vingt et unième**, etc.

L'adjectif **quel**

Quelle classe préférez-vous?   **Quels** étudiants aiment le lundi?

Voici les formes de l'adjectif **quel**.

	Singulier	*Pluriel*
Fém.	**quelle**	**quelles**
Masc.	**quel**	**quels**

*Il n'y a pas d'élision. C'est une exception.

Quel est généralement interrogatif.

> Quelle chance! (*How lucky!*)   Quel idiot!
> Quelle barbe! (*What a drag!*)   Quels exercices!

Quel est quelquefois exclamatif.

Exercice II   Mettez la forme correcte de **quel, quelle, quels, quelles.**

1. _____ classes est-ce que vous avez aujourd'hui?
2. _____ exercices est-ce que vous préférez?
3. _____ barbe!
4. _____ jour est-ce que nous sommes?
5. _____ étudiantes sont intelligentes?
6. A _____ université allez-vous?
7. Dans _____ ville habitez-vous?

L'heure, le jour, la date

L'heure:

> Quelle heure est-il?

C'est la question pour demander l'heure.
La réponse est:

> Il est une heure.
> Il est deux heures vingt, etc.
> Il est six heures du matin. (*A.M.*)
> Il est trois heures de l'après-midi. (*P.M.*)
> Il est dix heures du soir. (*P.M. after 5:00*)

Exercice III   Quelle heure est-il?

(2:15)	(11:05)	(12:00 *noon*)	(4:30)	(7:10)
(8:35)	(9:55)	(5:45)	(1:20)	(3:40)
(12:30 A.M.)	(5:00 A.M.)	(10:15 P.M.)	(3:30 P.M.)	(12:45 P.M.)

> A quelle heure est-ce qu'il arrive?
> Il arrive **à** une heure.
> Où est-ce que vous êtes **de** deux heures **à** quatre heures?
> **De** deux heures **à** quatre heures je suis à la bibliothèque.

La traduction de *at* pour l'heure est **à;** *from . . . to* est exprimé par **de . . . à.**

Exercice IV   Mettez la préposition **à, de,** ou rien (*nothing*).

1. Il est _____ trois heures.
2. Il arrive _____ quatre heures.
3. _____ midi _____ une heure je suis à la cafétéria.
4. Il est _____ midi. _____ midi j'ai un rendez-vous avec Bernadette. Elle arrive _____ deux heures.

Le jour, la date:

Quel jour est-ce que nous sommes?
Aujourd'hui **nous sommes** lundi; **c'est** lundi.

Il y a deux formules possibles: **nous sommes, c'est.**

Aujourd'hui c'est **lundi, six** octobre.
Aujourd'hui c'est **lundi le six** octobre.
Aujourd'hui c'est **le lundi six** octobre.

Les trois formules sont possibles.

Aujourd'hui c'est le premier octobre; non, c'est le deux, le trois.

Le nombre est différent: **le premier,** et en suite **le deux, le trois, le trente.**

Il arrive **lundi.**   **Le lundi,** je vais à l'université.

REMARQUEZ: **lundi:**   (*this*) *Monday* (il n'y a pas d'article)
              le lundi: *on Mondays* (il y a un article)

Donnez la date en français. Répétez les dates.   *Exercice V*

EXEMPLE: 6/5   le 6 mai (En français, on donne le jour d'abord, le mois ensuite.)

5/12   24/1   31/12   11/11   25/4
23/3   1/4   4/1   14/7   29/8

Mettez le mot absent.   *Exercice VI*

1. _____ est avant jeudi.
2. _____ est avant dimanche.
3. _____ est après lundi.
4. _____ est après mercredi.
5. _____ est avant septembre et après _____.

Écrivez les réponses.   *Exercice VII*
  1. Noël, c'est quel jour?
  2. Quelle est la date de votre anniversaire? de l'anniversaire de votre petit ami
     (petite amie)? (Noël, c'est l'anniversaire de Jésus.)
  3. L'année commence quel jour?
  4. Quelle est la date de l'indépendance des États-Unis?
  5. Quelle est la date de la fête nationale en France? (14/7)
  6. Quelle est la date de l'anniversaire de Lincoln?
  7. Donnez deux anniversaires: l'assassinat du président Kennedy (22/11) et
     l'arrivée des astronautes sur la lune. (20/7)
  8. Donnez deux anniversaires importants de votre existence ou de votre famille.
  9. Où êtes-vous le mardi à 10 heures et demie? (la bibliothèque?)
 10. Où êtes-vous le jeudi à 3 heures de l'après-midi? (le laboratoire?)

Les prépositions **avant, après; devant, derrière**

EXEMPLES: Décembre est **avant** janvier.
Août est **après** juillet.
Le jardin est **derrière** la maison.
Le professeur est **devant** le tableau.

Employez **avant** et **après** pour le temps, **devant** et **derrière** pour l'espace.

Exercice VIII Mettez le mot correct: **avant, après, devant, derrière.**

1. La classe est à 10 h. Le déjeuner est à 12 h. La classe est _____ le déjeuner.
2. Lundi est _____ dimanche.
3. La piscine est _____ la maison.
4. Mon jeune frère est _____ la télévision.
5. Les livres sont _____ les étudiants.
6. _____ Noël, il y a des préparatifs.
7. _____ un mariage, les deux jeunes mariés vont en voyage de noces.

Les expressions **en avance, tôt; en retard, tard**

EXEMPLES: Une personne est **en avance,** une autre est **en retard** pour un rendez-vous.
Quelle heure est-il? Il est minuit et demi. C'est **tard.**
Elle est à l'université à 7 heures du matin. C'est **tôt.**

Utilisez **en retard** ou **en avance** pour une personne, **tôt** ou **tard** pour l'heure.

Exercice IX Mettez la forme correcte.

1. Le rendez-vous est à 5 h. Jean-Pierre arrive à 6 h. Jean-Pierre est _____.
2. Le film commence à 8 h. Nous arrivons à 7 h½. Nous sommes _____.
3. La classe commence à 6 h du soir. C'est _____.
4. L'avion arrive à 4 h du matin. C'est _____.

POINTS DE GRAMMAIRE

Le verbe **finir** (2ème groupe)

finir

Singulier	Prononciation	Pluriel	Prononciation
je fi**nis**		nous fin**issons**	/isõ/
tu fi**nis**	/i/	vous fin**issez**	/ise/
il elle } fi**nit**		ils elles } fin**issent**	/is/

La forme négative est:

Je **ne** finis **pas,** tu **ne** finis **pas,** etc.

Pour la forme interrogative, placez le sujet après le verbe: **finis-tu? finit-il?** Mais pour la première personne utilisez **est-ce que:**

Est-ce que je finis?

Certains verbes en **–ir** du deuxième groupe correspondent à des verbes en *–ish* en anglais.

EXEMPLES: **finir**   *to finish*
           punir   *to punish*
           démolir   *to demolish*

Certains verbes en **–ir** indiquent un changement.

EXEMPLES: **grandir**   de l'adjectif   **grand**
           pâlir   **pâle**
           rougir   (*to blush*)   **rouge**

Remarquez aussi les verbes:

obéir   *to obey*
choisir   *to choose*
réfléchir *to reflect, to ponder*

Donnez la forme correcte du verbe.   *Exercice X*

1. Tu (finir)   5. Il (finir)   9. Les jardins (fleurir)
2. Vous (punir)   6. Nous (choisir)   10. Ils (démolir)
3. Vous (réfléchir)   7. Tu (obéir)   11. Je ne (grandir) pas
4. Les classes (finir) 8. Je (réfléchir)   12. Elle (pâlir)

Les adjectifs irréguliers

Les adjectifs **doux, gentil, frais, long, sec:**

SINGULIER		PLURIEL	
Féminin	*Masculin*	*Féminin*	*Masculin*
douce (*sweet, soft*)	doux	douces	doux
gentille (*nice, gentle*)	gentil	gentilles	gentils
fraîche	frais	fraîches	frais
longue	long	longues	longs
sèche (*dry*)	sec	sèches	secs

Accordez l'adjectif avec le nom.   *Exercice XI*

1. (doux) Jean-Pierre adore les jeunes filles _____ . Les garçons _____ sont rares mais appréciés.

2. (frais) Les fleurs du salon ne sont pas _____. J'aime le vin blanc _____.
3. (long) Les leçons sont _____. Le sermon du pasteur est _____ aussi.
4. (gentille) La petite amie de Jules est _____. Les étudiants du professeur de français sont _____.
5. (sec) J'aime le désert. J'aime le climat _____. Les chaussettes de l'archiduchesse sont _____!

Les adjectifs **beau, nouveau, vieux** ont deux masculins au singulier:

| | SINGULIER | | PLURIEL |
Féminin	*Masculin*	*Féminin*	*Masculin*
belle*	**beau** ou **bel**	belles	beaux
nouvelle*	**nouveau** ou **nouvel**	nouvelles	nouveaux
vieille*	**vieux** ou **vieil**	vieilles	vieux

*La prononciation de **bel, belle, belles; nouvel, nouvelle, nouvelles; vieil, vieille, vieilles** est identique.

Mardi-Gras à Nice.

EXEMPLE: un **beau** chapeau   un **nouveau** président   un **vieux** général

On emploie **beau, nouveau, vieux** devant un nom qui commence par une consonne.

EXEMPLE: un **bel** arbre   un **nouvel** emploi   un **vieil** ami

On emploie **bel, nouvel, vieil** devant un nom qui commence par une voyelle.

Mettez la forme correcte de l'adjectif: **beau, bel, belle; vieux, vieil, vieille; nouveau, nouvel, nouvelle.**   *Exercice XII*

1. (vieux) C'est un _____ avion. Vous aimez les _____ avions.
2. (beau) Voilà un _____ bébé. Ah! les _____ bébés.
3. (beau) C'est une _____ fille. Quel _____ enfant!
4. (nouveau) Le 1ᵉʳ janvier c'est le _____ an.
5. (nouveau) Elle a un _____ chapeau.
6. (vieux) Quel _____ idiot!
7. (vieux) Quelle _____ idiote!
8. (nouveau) Voilà une _____ actrice.
9. (beau) C'est un _____ dimanche. Ah! les _____ jours!
10. (vieux) Ces employés sont _____. Ces méthodes sont _____ aussi.

Voici d'autres adjectifs placés avant le nom. Ajoutez ces adjectifs à votre liste.

beau (belle)   gros (grosse)   nouveau (nouvelle)
dernier (dernière)   joli (jolie)   petit (petite)
gentil (gentille)   long (longue)   premier (première)
grand (grande)   mauvais (mauvaise)   vieux (vieille)
                                             bon (bonne)

Répétez avec l'adjectif avant le nom. Accordez l'adjectif.   *Exercice XIII*

1. (long) Une histoire.
2. (bon) Vous avez une idée.
3. (petit) Ils ont une maison à la campagne.
4. (mauvais) Quel temps!
5. (grand) C'est une cérémonie.
6. (gros) Tu préfères les bébés?
7. (nouveau) Nous avons un professeur.
8. (beau) Quelle auto!
9. (gentil) Les enfants ne parlent pas à table.
10. (premier) Les chapitres du livre sont faciles.
11. (dernier) C'est la phrase de l'exercice.

Mettez l'adjectif à sa place. Accordez l'adjectif.   *Exercice XIV*

1. (gris) Il y a des meubles au salon.
2. (vieux) Je préfère les arbres.
3. (froid) J'aime le café.

4. (beau) Vous aimez les garçons?
5. (nouveau*) Nous n'aimons pas les difficultés.
6. (neuf*) Ils ont une maison. *neuve*
7. (américain) L'histoire est passionnante.
8. (petit-rouge) Il a une auto.
9. (grand-noir) Dans la classe il y a deux tableaux.
10. (joli) Dans ma maison il y a une salle de bains.

LECTURES   1. Un jeune homme distrait

Georges a un rendez-vous avec Jacqueline, le vendredi douze mai, à cinq heures de l'après-midi, au jardin public, devant la statue de Vénus. C'est un endroit normal pour un rendez-vous. Georges est là à cinq heures moins le quart (il est en avance) avec des fleurs et un poème dans sa poche (c'est un jeune homme romantique, une espèce rare). Il n'est pas impatient, mais bientôt la pendule indique cinq heures dix. Jacqueline n'arrive pas. Georges est calme; il marche dans l'allée, il regarde les enfants, il passe et repasse devant la statue. Cinq heures vingt. Jacqueline exagère! Georges regarde ses fleurs: elles ne sont pas sensationnelles, maintenant. Jacqueline est en retard, évidemment. Georges est furieux. Et puis il réfléchit: Quel jour est-ce que nous sommes? Vendredi... mais... mais le rendez-vous est pour sept heures demain, pas aujourd'hui. Quel mois? Oui, le mois est correct aussi, mais... mais l'endroit du rendez-vous? Le jardin public, oui, mais devant ou derrière la statue de Vénus, de Vénus ou de Diane ou de... Quelle salade, quelle confusion! (C'est sans doute le premier rendez-vous de Georges avec une jeune fille.)

Georges est désespéré. Et ses fleurs, et son poème? Le poème est encore bon pour demain, ou un autre jour, c'est un poème sur la nature, la beauté, les jeunes filles, mais les fleurs?... Avec de l'eau peut-être. Mais Georges est obstiné. Il a son petit carnet dans sa poche avec des adresses et des numéros de téléphone. Il regarde, il cherche. «Voilà le numéro de Marguerite. Le poème est pour Jacqueline, mais si je change le nom, le résultat est le même.

Allons, demain est un autre jour. Demain, une décision est possible. Aujourd'hui, je téléphone... à Robert.»

Vocabulaire

allons   *here:* well
endroit, (*m.*)   place; **une place:** more often a square (*except in:* **chaque chose à sa place, la place de l'adjectif**)
évidemment /evidamã/   evidently

peut-être, sans doute   maybe
rendez-vous, (*m.*)   a date or an appointment
repasser   (**re** indique la répétition d'une action), **passer encore**

nouveau *new to someone*   **neuf** *brand new*

Bon anniversaire!

2. Fêtes françaises

Voici des dates et des fêtes importantes en France. L'année scolaire commence vers le 15 septembre; le mercredi est un jour de congé dans les écoles (pas à l'université). Au mois de novembre, il y a des vacances: le 1er novembre et le 2 novembre. Le 1er, c'est la Toussaint (*All Saints Day*) et le 2, le Jour des Morts: on va au cimetière et on porte des fleurs (des chrysanthèmes) sur les tombes des personnes aimées disparues. Le 11 novembre est aussi un jour de congé: on célèbre la fin de la première guerre mondiale et dans chaque petit village et dans chaque grande ville il y a un défilé (*parade*) d'anciens combattants.

Noël et le Nouvel An sont célébrés comme dans les autres pays chrétiens. En février, on fête Mardi Gras, surtout dans la ville de Nice où il y a un carnaval célèbre. En mars ou en avril, il y a Pâques (*Easter*) et les écoliers ont deux semaines de vacances. Le mois de mai a beaucoup de vacances: le 1er est la fête du Travail (les gens ne travaillent pas!); le 8 est l'armistice de 1945; le 2ème dimanche est la fête de Jeanne d'Arc et un jeudi de mai est l'Ascension. Souvent en mai (ou en juin) il y a le week-end de la Pente-Côte. Enfin le 14 juillet, c'est la fête Nationale (*Bastille Day*) et le 15 août, l'Assomption. En été les écoliers ne sont pas à l'école pendant 10 ou 11 semaines.

Mais chaque jour est une fête; c'est la fête d'un saint: Sainte Brigitte, Saint Jean, Sainte Anne, etc. Ce jour-là, vous apportez un petit bouquet à Brigitte, à Jean, à Anne, si votre ami a le nom du saint fêté.

Composition dirigée   Racontez vos activités de chaque jour, de chaque demaine: A quelle heure, quels jours est-ce que vous allez à l'université? Où est-ce que vous allez le lundi, le mardi, le week-end? Où est-ce que vous êtes à 8 h, à 9 h, à midi, à 6 h, à minuit?

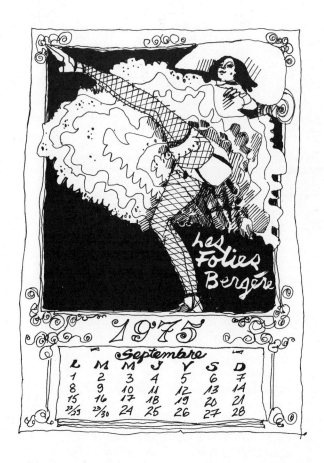

- ● PRÉSENTATION:　Le temps, les saisons

- ● PRONONCIATION:　les orthographes **oy** et **ay**
  la prononciation de la lettre **g**
  la lettre **m** non prononcée

- ● STRUCTURES:

  Constructions à retenir:　les prépositions **en** ou **au** + nom de saison
  les expressions **avoir froid, être froid, il fait froid**
  la cause: **pourquoi est-ce que...? parce que...**
  la préposition **sans** (without)

  Points de grammaire:　l'adjectif démonstratif
  l'article partitif
  choix de l'article
  la négation des articles
  le verbe **aller** pour le futur

- ● LECTURES:　1. «Refrains Enfantins» JACQUES PRÉVERT
  2. Les climats de la France

- ● PROVERBE: Après la pluie le beau temps

- ● EXPRESSION: Il fait un temps de chien

Automne

Francine Cockenpot
Paroles de J. Claude

Chapitre **6**

Col — chi — ques dans les　prés fleu — ris — sent,　fleu —

ris — sent, col — chi — ques dans　les　prés, c'est　la　fin de l'é —

té. La　feuil — le d'au — tom — ne em — por — tée par le　vent　en

ron — de mo — no — to — ne tombe　en tour — bil — lon — nant.

PRÉSENTATION   Le temps, les saisons

Nous sommes en octobre. Octobre, c'est en quelle saison? C'est en automne. Il y a quatre saisons dans l'année: l'automne, l'hiver, le printemps, l'été.

Quel temps fait-il? Je regarde dehors, je regarde le ciel, je regarde aussi le thermomètre et le baromètre.

Dehors, le ciel est bleu, il est clair, il est sans nuages: il fait beau. Le soleil brille: il fait chaud. Le baromètre indique «BEAU FIXE.»

Dehors le ciel est gris, il y a des nuages. Il fait du vent, il fait froid, il fait mauvais. Les nuages sont noirs: il pleut. Le baromètre descend et indique «TEM-PÊTE.»

Quel temps fait-il en automne? Il ne fait pas encore froid, il ne fait pas encore chaud: il fait frais. Quelquefois il pleut; souvent, il fait du vent. Les feuilles des arbres jaunissent et brunissent: elles tombent. C'est la saison de la rentrée.

En hiver, quel temps fait-il? Il pleut, il fait froid. On a froid. A la montagne, au Canada, dans l'Est du pays, il neige toujours. La terre blanchit. Les arbres n'ont pas de feuilles. Le paysage est triste et beau. C'est la saison des sports d'hiver, du feu dans la cheminée, des fêtes de Noël et du Nouvel An. Au printemps, il ne fait pas froid, il fait doux: les feuilles des arbres poussent, les jardins fleurissent. C'est la saison des promenades, du jardinage.

Et en été? Il fait chaud et beau; il ne fait pas de vent; le soleil brille. On va à la plage, à la piscine, on brunit au soleil. On a chaud. C'est la saison des vacances: on voyage, on va en camping.

Quelle saison préférez-vous? Moi, je préfère l'été. Pourquoi? Parce que je déteste le froid, je n'aime pas la pluie, je n'aime pas la neige. En hiver, il fait un temps de chien. Je ne déteste pas les sports d'hiver, mais j'adore le soleil et j'adore les vacances d'été.

Vocabulaire

automne, (*m.*) fall
avoir chaud to be hot, warm
beau fixe fair, clear
briller shine
brunir to turn brown
dehors outside
été, (*m.*) summer
feu, (*m.*) fire
feuille, (*f.*) leaf
froid (e) cold;
  froid, (*m.*) cold (*noun*)
hiver, (*m.*) winter
il fait beau the weather is nice
il fait du vent it is windy
il fait un sale temps,
  un temps de chien it's lousy weather
il neige it's snowing
il pleut it's raining
jaunir to turn yellow
jardinage, (*m.*) gardening

neige, (*f.*) snow
nuage, (*m.*) cloud
parce que because
pas encore not yet
paysage, (*m.*) landscape
plage, (*f.*) beach
pluie, (*f.*) rain
pourquoi why
pousser to grow
printemps, (*m.*) spring
quel temps fait-il?
  what is the weather like?
regarder to look at
rentrée, (*f.*) going back to school
sans without
souvent often
tempête, (*f.*) storm
tomber to fall
vacances, (*f. pl.*) vacation (toujours
  pluriel)

Les orthographes **oy** et **ay**

Un **y** est l'équivalent de deux **i.**

EXEMPLE: crayon = crai / ion

Coupez le mot en syllabes:

crayon:	crai / ion	/krɛ jõ/
voyage:	voi / iage	/vwa jaʒ/
employez:	emploi / iez	/ãplwa je/
payez:	pai / iez	/pe je/

Attention à la prononciation du mot **mayonnaise;** elle est spéciale: /majɔnɛz/.

La lettre **m** non prononcée

M n'est pas prononcé dans les mots **automne, damner, condamner.**

La prononciation de la lettre **g**

La lettre **g** devant **e, i** et **y** est prononcée /ʒ/ (comme *pleasure*).

> général   gymnastique
> gigi   Egypte

La lettre **g** devant **a, o** et **u** est prononcée /g/ (comme *garden*).

> garde   légume

Remarquez les deux prononciations de **g** dans **gorge.**

Pour le son /g/ devant **e** et **i** un **u** est nécessaire.

> guide   fatigue

Pour le son /ʒ/ devant **a, o, u** un **e** est nécessaire.

> Georges   geai (*blue jay*)   nuageux

Conséquence: Dans les verbes en **-ger (voyager, changer, manger, nager,** *to swim,* **plonger,** *to dive*) on a le son /ʒ/ à toutes les personnes.

> Je voya**g**e   Tu voya**g**es   Vous voya**g**ez   Il voya**g**e   Ils voya**g**ent
>
> Mais: Nous voya**geons**

Dans tous ces verbes, à la première personne du pluriel on a la terminaison **-geons** (avec **e** devant **o**).

Exercice I   Ecrivez et prononcez.

1. En automne, nous _____ (voyager).
2. Vous (changer) _____ de tabac?
3. Ils (manger) _____ trop: ils grossissent.
4. Nous (encourager) _____ les étudiants.
5. Nous (plonger) _____ dans la piscine, et nous (nager) _____.

STRUCTURES   CONSTRUCTIONS A RETENIR

Les prépositions **en** ou **au** + nom de saison

en octobre	Avec un nom de mois, la préposition est **en;** il n'y a pas d'article.
en automne	Avec les trois noms de saisons—**automne, hiver, été**—la préposition est **en;** il n'y a pas d'article.
au printemps	Avec le nom **printemps,** on utilise l'article contracté **au.**

le jour, le matin, le soir:

On utilise l'article **le** pour indiquer chaque jour, chaque soir, chaque matin, et **la** pour chaque nuit: **la nuit.** Attention: Il n'y a pas de préposition.

Mettez **en, au,** ou **le.**

1. Noël, c'est _____ décembre.
2. _____ automne, les classes commencent.
3. _____ hiver, les oiseaux ne chantent pas.
4. _____ printemps, les arbres ont des fleurs.
5. _____ week-end, nous allons à la plage.
6. _____ samedi, elle va au supermarché.
7. _____ été, les enfants sont à la mer.
8. _____ août, nous n'allons pas à l'université.
9. _____ matin, je vais à l'université à 8 heures.

Les expressions **avoir froid, être froid, il fait froid**

COMPAREZ: **Il fait chaud** (le temps). **J'ai chaud** (une personne). **Le café est chaud**
(une chose).

Le temps: Quel temps fait-il?
   Il fait beau, mauvais, chaud, ou froid.
   Le temps est beau, froid, chaud, etc.

Utilisez **fait-il** dans la question. Dans la réponse, on a le choix: **Il fait** (toujours **il**)
ou **Le temps est** avec le verbe **être.**

Une personne: **Elles ont froid.**   **Ils ont chaud.**

Employez le verbe **avoir** + l'adjectif au masculin singulier. La forme de l'adjectif
est invariable.

Une chose: **Le café est chaud.**   **La soupe est chaude.**

Employez le verbe **être** + l'adjectif. La construction est normale; accordez
l'adjectif.

Exercice II Mettez la forme correcte du verbe: **avoir, être,** ou **il fait.**

1. Dans un frigidaire, l'eau _____ froide.
2. Au Pôle Nord, il _____ froid.
3. Dans la neige, nous _____ froid.
4. Suzanne _____ chaud au soleil.
5. Il _____ chaud toute l'année au Sahara.
6. Le soleil _____ chaud.

La cause: **pourquoi est-ce que...? parce que...**

Pourquoi est-ce que vous êtes contente?
   Parce qu'il fait beau.
Pourquoi est-ce que vous avez froid?
   Parce qu'il pleut.

Remarquez l'élision de **que** devant une voyelle **(qu'il).**

Paris. Les Champs-Elysées.

Composez des phrases avec la question **pourquoi**, la réponse **parce que** et le   *Exercice III*
vocabulaire suivant:

1. avoir froid   il neige
2. transpirer   avoir chaud
3. voyager   être en vacances
4. habiter sous la tente   ne pas être riche
5. être rouge   rester longtemps au soleil

La préposition **sans** (*without*)

> Le ciel est **sans** nuages.   Le paysage est **sans** charme.

Avec la préposition **sans,** il n'y a pas d'article indéfini ou partitif (le ciel a des
nuages, le paysage a du charme).

> Il entre **sans** parler.

Avec la préposition **sans,** utilisez l'infinitif du verbe.

Ecrivez les phrases suivantes avec la préposition **sans:**   *Exercice IV*

1. Vous allez dehors avec un chapeau?
2. Avec de l'argent, il est content.
3. Les fleurs poussent avec de l'eau!
4. Nous n'allons pas au marché avec des paniers.
5. Ils voyagent, ils ne regardent pas le paysage.
6. Vous restez au soleil, vous ne transpirez pas?

POINTS DE GRAMMAIRE

L'adjectif démonstratif

> **ce** livre, **cette** table
> **cet** étudiant, **cette** étudiante
> **ces** étudiants, **ces** compositions

Avec l'adjectif démonstratif on montre une personne ou une chose.

> **ce** matin, **ce** soir, **cet** été

Avec l'adjectif démonstratif on indique un temps proche (*close*).

A. LES FORMES SIMPLES

Au masculin, on a deux formes:

> **ce** avec un nom qui commence par une consonne: **ce livre**
> **cet** avec un nom qui commence par une voyelle et on a une liaison: **cet‿arbre**

Au féminin, on a une forme unique, **cette:**   **cette dame.** On a un enchaînement
avec la voyelle initial du nom: **cetté‿opération.**

Au pluriel, on a une forme unique pour le masculin et le féminin: **ces.**

> **ces livres** (*masc.*)
> **ces dames** (*fém.*)

On a une liaison avec la voyelle initiale du nom.

> **ces‿arbres** (*masc.*)
> **ces‿opérations** (*fém.*)

Masculin **ce** + consonne **cet** + voyelle	*Féminin* **cette**	*Pluriel* **ces**

Exercice V Répétez avec la forme correcte de l'adjectif démonstratif.

1. le soleil
2. le gouvernement
3. la classe
4. les hommes
5. la prononciation
6. l'administration
7. les femmes
8. les étudiants
9. l'affaire
10. l'oiseau
11. le livre
12. la démocratie

B. LES FORMES LONGUES

	here	*there*
	ce livre-**ci**	**ce** livre-**là**
	ces arbres-**ci**	**ces** arbres-**là**

On distingue deux choses, séparées dans l'espace: l'une est **ici,** l'autre est **là.** On ajoute **-ci** ou **-là** après le nom.

Exercice VI Répétez avec **ce ...-ci** et **ce ...-là.**

la table	les vacances	le printemps	l'auto	les enfants
l'été	le tableau	la pendule	la fleur	

L'article partitif

> J'ai **une** auto, **un** appartement.
> Nous avons **des** enfants.
> Il aime **la** musique.
> **Le** français est **une** langue magnifique.
> **Les** oranges sont superbes.

En français, il y a presque toujours un article devant un nom commun.

Voici un nouvel article: l'article partitif.

> Il y a **du** feu dans la cheminée.
> Il y a **de la** bière dans le frigidaire.
> Il y a **de l'**eau dans la piscine.

> Le professeur a **de la** patience, **de l'**énergie.
> Les étudiants ont **du** travail.

Comparez avec:

> **Le** feu est agréable.
> **La** bière est fraîche.
> **L'**eau est bleue.

Les formes de l'article partitif:

> **du** feu: **du** + nom masculin qui commence par une consonne
> **de la** bière: **de la** + nom féminin qui commence par une consonne
> **de l'**eau: **de l'** + nom masculin ou féminin qui commence par une voyelle

L'article partitif indique une partie d'une chose, une quantité imprécise d'une chose.

Attention: En anglais, généralement il n'y a rien: *The students have work to do.* Une traduction possible est: *some* + un nom singulier.

(*a.*) Répétez le nom avec l'article partitif.   *Exercice VII*
(*b.*) Composez des phrases avec: **Il a** ou **Elle a** ou **Il y a** et le nom précédé de l'article partitif.

le courage	le thé	le talent	l'or
la patience	l'ambition	l'expérience	le réalisme
le progrès	la chance	la bière	l'autorité
la salade	l'importance	l'imagination	le champagne
le café			

Répétez avec l'article partitif.   *Exercice VIII*

1. Elle prépare _____ salade. 2. Il choisit _____ café. 3. Les astronautes trouvent _____ oxygène sur la Lune? 4. Vous avez _____ patience. 5. Il y a _____ eau dans la mer. 6. Tu choisis _____ chocolat? 7. Vous avez _____ énergie. 8. Le sculpteur a _____ imagination. 9. Le mineur trouve _____ or sous la terre. 10. Les étudiants ont _____ difficulté. 11. Elle a _____ argent à la banque. 12. Nous avons _____ courage. 13. Le philosophe a _____ intelligence. 14. L'éléphant a _____ mémoire. 15. Le dictateur a _____ autorité. 16. L'actrice a _____ talent. 17. Le président a _____ succès.

Choix de l'article

Le choix de l'article est un problème délicat et important. Quelquefois, les deux ou les trois articles différents sont possibles avec des significations différentes. Voici quelques mécanismes utiles:

> J'adore **le** pain, **la** musique, **les** oranges.
> Il déteste **l'**opéra.

1. Avec les verbes **aimer, adorer, détester,** et **préférer** on a généralement l'article défini.

> **Le** pain est délicieux.
> **La** musique classique est extraordinaire.

2. On commence une phrase avec un nom général d'espèce? On a l'article défini.

> **Il y a un** professeur dans la classe.
> **Il y a des** étudiants dans la classe.
> **Il y a de l'**argent dans la banque.

3. Avec **il y a** on a généralement l'article indéfini: **un, une, des**—ou l'article partitif: **du, de la, de l'.**

Exercice IX Mettez l'article correct; s'il y a un choix, expliquez le choix.

1. Je déteste _____ animaux. 2. Imaginez _____ situation spéciale. 3. Il compose _____ opéras. 4. Nous étudions _____ Leçon trois. 5. Elle cultive _____ jardin avec _____ fleurs. 6. Je préfère _____ café. 7. Ils adorent _____ bière. 8. Vous préparez _____ thèse? 9. Tu commences _____ Chapitre six. 10. _____ étudiants _____ classe sont intelligents. 11. Il y a _____ étudiants intelligents dans _____ classe. 12. Elle a _____ or à _____ banque. 13. Le professeur a _____ ténacité. 14. _____ français est _____ langue simple et logique. 15. Ils ont _____ enfants. 16. Nous avons _____ pommes. 17. L'acteur a _____ éducation. 18. L'artiste invente _____ théorie fantastique. 19. Le docteur examine _____ cas spécial. 20. Il y a _____ chocolat? 21. _____ thé et _____ café sont populaires. 22. Il y a _____ champagne dans _____ frigidaire (*m.*) de Claude? 23. _____ vin est excellent avec _____ bifteck. 24. Nous commençons _____ dîner. 25. _____ soupe est chaude. 26. Nous finissons _____ classe de français par _____ petite dictée.

La négation des articles

L'AFFIRMATION	LA NÉGATION
J'aime **l'**hiver, j'aime **la** neige, **les** sports.	Je n'aime pas **l'**hiver, je n'aime pas **la** neige, **les** sports.

La négation de **le, la, les** est **pas le, pas la, pas les.**

C'est un hiver terrible.	**Ce n'est pas un** hiver terrible.
C'est des nuages.	**Ce n'est pas des** nuages. (Voir Chapitre 2.)

La négation de **c'est un, c'est des** est **ce n'est pas un, ce n'est pas des.**

J'ai **un** ami.	Je n'ai pas **d'**ami.
Nous avons **des** enfants.	Nous n'avons pas **d'**enfants. (Voir Chapitre 3.)
Il fait **du** soleil.	Il ne fait pas **de** soleil.
Il y a **de la** bière.	Il n'y a pas **de** bière.
Tu as **de l'**ambition.	Tu n'as pas **d'**ambition.

La négation de **un, des, du, de la,** et **de l'** est **pas de.**

Affirmatif	Négatif	Affirmatif	Négatif
le	**pas le**	un	
la	**pas la**	une	
les	**pas les**	des	**pas de (d')**
c'est un	**ce n'est pas un**	du	
c'est des	**ce n'est pas des**	de la, de l'	

Mettez les phrases à la forme négative.   *Exercice X*

1. Vous avez des fleurs dans votre jardin.   2. Il y a des nuages dans le ciel.   3. Il fait du soleil.   4. C'est des vacances splendides.   5. Je mange des bonbons. 6. Nous aimons l'eau.   7. C'est un vent violent.   8. Tu as une petite amie? 9. Elle a de la famille.   10. Vous avez de l'argent à la banque.   11. Il y a de la bière au frigidaire.   12. J'aime le champagne.   13. Les jardins ont des fleurs cette année.   14. Elle déteste les fleurs artificielles.   15. Nous avons une fête ce mois-ci?   16. Les enfants préfèrent la fête de Noël.   17. Le professeur a de la patience.   18. Vous avez du feu?   19. Les jeunes respectent les vieux.   20. Ils ont du temps.

Le verbe **aller** pour le futur

EXEMPLE: Je **vais étudier** ma leçon.
              Nous **allons regarder** la télévision.
              Est-ce que vous **allez voyager** cet été?

Le verbe **aller** avec un infinitif indique une action future immédiate (en anglais *I am going to . . .*).

EXEMPLE: Tu **vas aller** au marché cet après-midi?

Il est possible d'avoir **aller** + **aller.**

Mettez les phrases suivantes au futur avec **aller.**   *Exercice XI*

1. Il retourne à l'université en septembre.
2. Vous voyagez cet été?
3. Elle reste au soleil. Elle brunit ou elle rougit?
4. Au printemps, les jardins fleurissent.
5. Dimanche, ils vont à la plage.
6. Cet hiver, il neige.
7. Tu as chaud à côté de la cheminée.
8. Ton café est froid.
9. Ils habitent à Paris.
10. Tu écoutes, oui ou non?

LECTURES   1. Poème   *REFRAINS ENFANTINS*

Des petites filles courent dans les couloirs du théâtre en chantant.

Ouh   ouh

ouh   ouh

C'est la chanson du loup garou

où   où

quand   quand

comment   comment

pourquoi   pourquoi

Ouh   ouh

ouh   ouh

C'est la chanson du loup garou

Il pleut   Il pleut

Il fait beau

Il fait du soleil

Il est tôt

Il se fait tard

Il

Il

Il

toujours Il

Toujours Il qui pleut et qui neige

Toujours Il qui fait du soleil

Toujours Il

Pourquoi pas Elle

Jamais Elle

Pourtant Elle aussi

souvent se fait belle!

JACQUES PRÉVERT,
Spectacle, p. 186

Vocabulaire

couloir, (*m.*) hallway
courent run
elle se fait makes herself
en chantant while singing
il se fait tard it is getting late
jamais never

loup garou big bad wolf
pourtant yet
tôt early
toujours always
souvent often

2. Les climats de la France

La France n'est pas un grand pays, et pourtant on trouve une variété de climats. Les régions près de la mer—la Normandie, la Bretagne—ont une température modérée, pas trop froide, pas trop chaude: il pleut souvent, mais le *Gulf Stream* réchauffe la mer et la côte. A Paris, les hivers sont brumeux, le printemps généralement humide et en été il y a de gros orages. Dans l'est et le centre, le climat est continental avec des hivers assez sévères, il neige; en été, il fait chaud.

En août, il fait beau à la plage.

Dans les Montagnes, les Alpes, les Pyrénées, le climat est montagnard. Il neige beaucoup et l'hiver est long, pour la grande joie des skieurs; on skie toute l'année au Mont Blanc. Les étés sont courts; il y a beaucoup d'orages. La région privilégiée de la France est la zone méditerranéenne. L'hiver, un vent froid souffle: le Mistral. Mais la Côte d'Azur est protégée; elle a du soleil toute l'année, des pluies rares, même en hiver. C'est la région où tous les Français rêvent d'habiter, et où on est sûr de trouver du soleil en vacances. Il n'y a pas, en France, d'ouragans et pas de tremblements de terre non plus.

Vocabulaire

brumeux foggy
brouillard, (*m.*), **brume**, (*f.*) fog

ouragan, (*m.*) hurricane
tremblement de terre earthquake

Composition dirigée

Quelle est votre saison favorite*?

   Ma saison favorite est _____. J'aime _____ et _____ mais je préfère le _____. Pourquoi est-ce que vous aimez cette saison? Quel temps fait-il (au) _____?

   J'aime cette saison parce qu'elle est _____. En (au) _____ il y a _____, il n'y a pas de _____, il fait _____, il ne fait pas _____.

   Où est-ce qu'on va en cette saison? _____ on va _____, on ne va pas _____. On mange _____, on prépare _____.

*favori, favorite, favoris, favorites

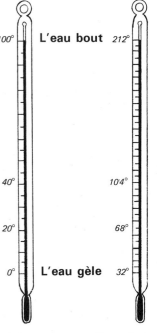

L'eau bout   100°   212°
40°   104°
20°   68°
L'eau gèle   0°   32°

Celsius   **Farenheit**

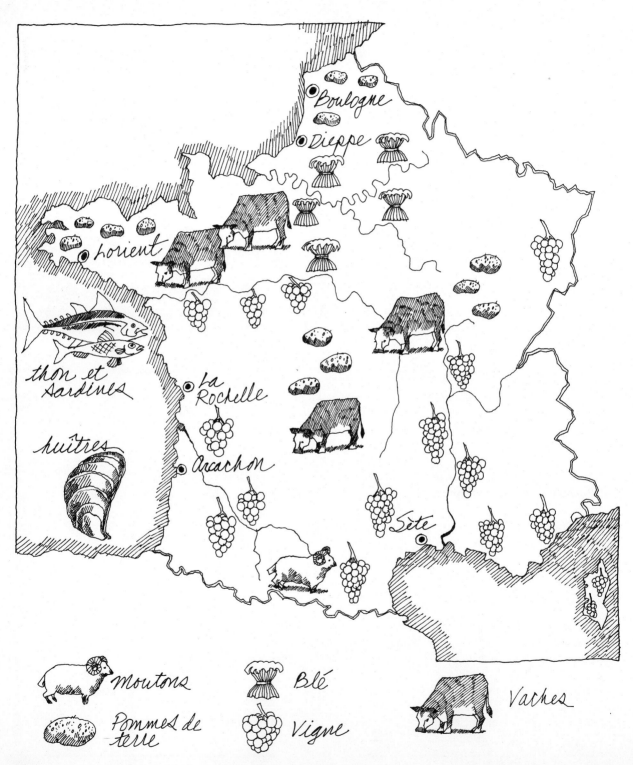

Boulogne

Dieppe

Lorient

thon et
sardines

huîtres

La
Rochelle

Arcachon

Sète

Moutons

Pommes de
terre

Blé

Vigne

Vaches

96

- **PRÉSENTATION:** Qu'est-ce que vous faites dans la vie?

- **PRONONCIATION:** **e** muet /ə/ ; les sons /e/ et /ɛ/ ; /ã/ et /õ/

- **STRUCTURES:**

  Constructions à retenir: la question **qu'est-ce que...?**
  l'adjectif **tout**
  les mots **an, année; jour, journée**
  les positions

  Points de grammaire: le verbe **faire**
  le pronom tonique: **moi, toi, lui, elle, nous, vous, eux, elles**
  la comparaison des adjectifs
  le pronom tonique dans une comparaison
  les nombres de 30 à l'infini

- **LECTURES:**
  1. Un jeune homme impatient
  2. Les activités en France suivant les régions
  3. «Familiale» JACQUES PREVERT

- **PROVERBE:** Une hirondelle ne fait pas le printemps

- **EXPRESSION:** Faut l'faire

Sur le pont d'Avignon

Chapitre 7

Sur le pont d'A – vi – gnon, l'on y dan—se, l'on y dan—se,

Sur le pont d'A – vi – gnon, l'on y dan—se, tout en rond. Les

beaux mes – sieurs font comm' ça, et puis en – cor comm' ça.

Sur le pont d'A–vi–gnon, l'on y dan – se, tout en rond.

PRÉSENTATION ## Qu'est-ce que vous faites dans la vie?

Moi? Je suis professeur. Et vous? vous êtes étudiants.
Et votre père, qu'est-ce qu'il fait?
Il est professeur? Il est pharmacien?
Et votre mère? Elle est docteur, ingénieur? Ou bien... elle ne travaille pas?
　Si, elle reste à la maison, elle fait la cuisine, le ménage.
Vous avez des frères, des sœurs? Qu'est-ce qu'ils font?

　　J'ai un frère qui fait des études de droit. Et puis, il va faire son service militaire. Il n'aime pas l'idée de faire la guerre, lui. Alors, il fait de la politique à l'université. Il dit toujours, «Faites l'amour, pas la guerre».

　　J'ai aussi une sœur. Elle, elle fait du théâtre et du cinéma. Regardez la chaîne 36 la semaine prochaine à 8 heures du soir; elle fait une petite apparition dans le programme: «Fais pas l'idiot». Elle va peut-être faire impression sur un gros producteur (elle espère).

Port de Toulon.

J'ai aussi un petit frère de 7 ans et une petite sœur de 5 ans. Eux, ils ne font rien, ils font du bruit, surtout.

Quelles sont vos activités de l'année? Que fait votre famille en hiver?

En hiver, nous allons faire du ski quelquefois. Généralement nous restons à la maison. S'il fait froid, nous faisons un bon feu dans la cheminée.

Et au printemps, qu'est-ce qu'on fait?

Au printemps, on fait des balades, on fait du jardinage. Le jardinage, c'est moins agréable que les balades.

Et en été?

En été, on fait des voyages, ou on fait du camping, parce que c'est plus économique.

Et en automne?

C'est la saison de la rentrée. On fait des préparatifs pour retourner à l'école. On refait du jardinage: on ramasse les feuilles mortes qui sont par terre.

Quelles sont vos activités de la journée?

Je suis debout à 7 heures. Je fais ma toilette. Je déjeune. Je vais à l'université. Toute la matinée je suis dans mes classes. L'après-midi je fais des expériences au laboratoire, ou des recherches à la bibliothèque. Je rentre à la maison. Je fais une petite sieste, et puis je fais mes devoirs. Le soir, si tout mon travail est fait, je passe la soirée devant la télé. Ce n'est pas une vie passionnante, mais c'est la vie d'un étudiant.

Vocabulaire

debout up
faire de la politique to dabble in politics
faire des études to go to college
faire des préparatifs to prepare
faire des recherches to do research
faire du bruit to make noise
faire du camping to go camping
faire du cinéma to be in the movies
faire du feu to build a fire
faire du jardinage to garden
faire du ski to ski
faire du théâtre to act
faire impression to make an impression
faire l'amour to make love
faire la cuisine to cook
faire la guerre to make war
faire la sieste to take a nap
faire le ménage to clean house
faire l'idiot to act silly
faire sa toilette to clean up
faire ses devoirs to do homework

faire son droit to study law; to go to law school
faire son service militaire to go to the army
faire un voyage to take a trip
faire une apparition to appear
faire une balade; faire une promenade to take a walk
faire une expérience to do experiments
il ne fait rien he does nothing (ne + verbe + rien: nothing)
journée, (*f.***)** day
matinée, (*f.***)** morning
par terre on the floor
passer la soirée to spend the evening
passionnant fascinating
ramasser to pick up
rentrer to come back home
soirée, (*f.***)** evening
surtout mostly
vie, (*f.***)** life

PRONONCIATION: **e muet** /ə/

Ce son est quelquefois épelé d'une manière bizarre: **on** dans mo**n**sieur, **ai** dans f**ai**sons et **ess** dans d**ess**ous et d**ess**us.

Répétez avec /ə/: dessous
dessus
dehors
dedans
debout

Contrastez les sons:

/e/	et	/ɛ/
fée		fait
dé		dais
mes		mai
les		laid
ré		raie
nez		nait

Contrastez les sons:

/ə/	/e/	/ɛ/
de	des	dais
me	mes	mais
le	les	laid
se	ses	sait
te	tes	tait

Contrastez les sons dans les mots du texte:

/e/	/ɛ/
j'ai	fait
activités	faites
l'année	êtes
cheminée	père
été	mère
rentrée	frère
journée	chaîne
matinée	guerre
université	terre
soirée	bibliothèque
la télé	sieste

Contrastez les sons:

/ã/	/õ/
banc	bon
dans	don
dent	dont
lent	long
franc	front
vent	vont
temps	ton

et dans les mots du texte:

généralement	font
étudiants	maison
printemps	apparition
expériences	impression
rentre	faisons
passionnante	saison

CONSTRUCTIONS A RETENIR **STRUCTURES**

La question **qu'est-ce que...?**

Qu'est-ce que vous faites?
Qu'est-ce que vous mangez?
Qu'est-ce que vous regardez?

> **qu'** (élidé) + **est-ce que*** + le sujet + le verbe

Faites une question avec chaque phrase.   *Exercice I*

EXEMPLE: Je mange du pain.
    Qu'est-ce que je mange?
    Qu'est-ce que tu manges?

1. J'aime cette musique.
2. Nous étudions le français.
3. Tu admires la peinture.

*Attention: Élidez **que** devant **il, elle, on, ils, elles: qu'il, qu'elle, qu'on,** etc.

4. Elle fait la cuisine.
5. Il regarde un programme à la télé.
6. Ils écoutent la radio.
7. Vous faites une balade.
8. On ramasse les feuilles.
9. Tu manges de la soupe.
10. Il fait ses exercices.

L'adjectif **tout**

Tout est un adjectif. Voici ses formes:

EXEMPLES: **tout** le monde
toute la classe
tous les étudiants
toutes les étudiantes

	Singulier	Pluriel
Masculin:	**tout**	**tous**
Féminin:	**toute**	**toutes**

Accordez **tout** avec le nom qui suit.

Exercice II   Répétez avec la forme correcte de l'adjectif **tout**.

le continent	la famille	les enfants	les filles
les exercices	les saisons	l'appartement	l'armée
les nations	l'université	les décisions	la science
l'histoire	l'or	la France	les États-Unis

Les mots **an, année; jour, journée**

Bonne **Année,** c'est le Nouvel **An**

On a deux mots pour traduire *year:* **une année, un an.** Employez **un an** avec les expressions **le Nouvel An, deux ans, trois ans, cinq ans, vingt ans,** etc. Employez **année** dans les expressions **Bonne Année, cette année, je passe une année for-midable** (*I spend*).

Je passe la **journée** au parc. Quelle bonne **journée!**
Le **jour** de mon anniversaire, je suis content.

On a deux mots pour traduire *day, morning* et *evening.* On utilise **la journée, la** matinée, et **la soirée** avec (*a.*) le verbe **passer** et (*b.*) un adjectif. On utilise **le jour, le matin**, et **le soir** pour indiquer la date précise (voir Chapitre 6).

REMARQUE: **ce matin** = *this morning;* **ce soir** = *this evening.*

COMPAREZ: toute l'année (*all year*)   tous les ans   (*every year*)
             toute la journée (*all day*)   tous les jours (*every day*)
             toute la matinée (*all morning*)   tous les matins (*every morning*)
             toute la soirée (*all evening long*)   tous les soirs (*every evening*)

Toute accompagne le nom féminin singulier en **-ée. Tous** accompagne les mots **ans, jours, matins**, et **soirs** au masculin pluriel.

REMARQUE: **le matin, le soir** = *in the morning, in the evening* or *every morning, every evening.*

Mettez le mot correct: **jour, journée, matin, matinée, soir, soirée, an, année.**   *Exercice III*

1. Qu'est-ce que vous faites le dimanche? Le dimanche, je reste toute _____ à la maison.   2. Quel _____ préférez-vous? Le dimanche.   3. _____ elle va à l'université à 9 heures.   4. Vous passez une _____ devant la télévision.
5. Qu'est-ce que tu fais de 7 h à midi? Je suis au labo de 7 h à midi. C'est une longue _____.   6. _____, il dîne à sept heures.   7. Le nouvel _____ est un lundi, cette _____ (*year*).   8. Bonne _____!   9. Je ne vais pas en France tous les _____ (*year*).   10. Je vais aller en France l'_____ prochaine.

Les positions

Il est debout.*

Elle est debout.*

Il est assis.

Elle est assise.

Il est couché.

Elle est couchée.

Il est par terre.

Elle est par terre.

*invariable

Il est assis entre Marie et Jacques.

Elle est assise entre la fenêtre et le tableau.

Il est sur la table.

Elle est dessous.

Il est dans la maison.
Il est dedans.

Exercice IV Indiquez la position ou la place des personnes.

POINTS DE GRAMMAIRE

Le verbe **faire**

faire

Singulier	*Pluriel*
je fais	nous faisons /ə/
tu fais /ε/	vous faites /εt/
il, elle fait	ils, elles font /õ/

Remarquez les quatre sons.

Le verbe **faire** est souvent utilisé dans des expressions idiomatiques:

il **fait** beau, froid, chaud

Pour le temps avec **il.**

faire la cuisine, la guerre
faire des études, du théâtre

Pour une activité avec un nom.

faire l'idiot, l'imbécile

Pour une attitude avec un adjectif et l'article défini.

Que **fait** votre père?

Pour la question sur la profession.

Mettez la forme correcte du verbe **faire.**   *Exercice V*

1. A la maison, ma mère _____ la cuisine. 2. Et vous, vous _____ les commissions? 3. Toi, tu _____ l'idiot. 4. Nous _____ des expériences. 5. Les hommes _____ la guerre. 6. Son frère _____ du théâtre. 7. En été, on _____ du camping. 8. En hiver, mes parents _____ du ski. 9. Cet hiver, je vais _____ un voyage en Europe. 10. En été, quand il _____ chaud, je _____ la sieste.

Le pronom tonique: **moi, toi, lui, elle, nous, vous, eux, elles**

EXEMPLES: Qu'est-ce que vous aimez? **Moi,** j'aime le vin.
　　　　　J'aime le vin, **moi.**
　　　　Toi, tu préfères le lait? Tu préfères le lait, **toi?**
　　　　Lui, il est Américain. Il est Américain, **lui?**
　　　　Elle, elle est Française.
　　　　Nous, nous sommes contents.
　　　　Vous, vous êtes tristes.
　　　　Jules et Jim? **Eux,** ils aiment la même femme.
　　　　Juliette et Justine? **Elles,** elles ne font pas la cuisine.

Utilisez ce pronom pour insister sur le sujet. Placez le pronom avant le sujet, ou à la fin de la phrase.

Exercice VI   Répétez les phrases avec le sujet renforcé, avant ou après.

1. Il n'aime pas le cigare.
2. Vous faites le ménage tous les jours.
3. Les végétariens? Ils ne mangent pas de viande.
4. Tu as trois autos.
5. Nous restons à la maison ce soir.
6. Je vais au cinéma.
7. Elle est impatiente.

La comparaison des adjectifs

plus ... que; moins ... que:

l'avion le train

L'avion est **plus** rapide **que** le train.

un appartement une maison

Un appartement est **moins** grand **qu'**une maison.

On place **plus ... que** et **moins ... que** autour de (*around*) l'adjectif. Accordez l'adjectif avec le premier nom. Attention à l'élision de **que** devant une voyelle.

Exercice VII   Faites des phrases de comparaison avec le vocabulaire suggéré.

EXEMPLE   un tigre   +   féroce   (un chat)
   Un tigre est plus féroce qu'un chat.

1. Gilberte   −   jolie   (Raymonde)
2. La Tour Eiffel   +   haute   (L'Arc de Triomphe)
3. Le camping   −   confortable   (un hôtel)
4. Le français   −   difficile   (le chinois)
5. Le professeur   +   vieux   (les étudiants)
6. Une Rolls   +   élégante   (une Renault)
7. Une bicyclette   +   pratique   (une auto)

aussi ... que:

Un train est **aussi** rapide **qu'**une auto.

On compare deux personnes ou deux choses égales avec l'expression **aussi ... que.**

Exercice VIII   Faites des phrases de comparaison avec **aussi ... que.**

1. La mer est agréable. La montagne aussi.
2. Robert est intelligent. François aussi.
3. Cet hôtel-ci est économique. Cet hôtel-là aussi.
4. Mon professeur d'histoire est difficile. Mon professeur de sciences aussi.

5. Le camembert est bon. Le roquefort aussi.
6. Les jeunes filles blondes sont jolies. Les brunes aussi.

Le pronom tonique dans une comparaison

> Il est **plus** grand **que moi.**
> Je suis **moins** intelligente **que lui.**

Utilisez le pronom tonique dans une comparaison. En anglais on a le pronom sujet: *than I, he, we*, etc.

Faites des phrases de comparaison avec **plus, aussi** ou **moins.**

Exercice IX

1. Les Mexicains sont gais.   (nous)
2. Je suis petite.   (tu)
3. Nous ne sommes pas intelligents.   (vous)
4. Vous avez un grand jardin.   (ils)
5. Elle est patiente.   (je)
6. Tu n'es pas grand.   (il)
7. Il est gentil.   (elle)

Les nombres de 30 à l'infini

30 trente	40 quarante	50 cinquante
31 trente et un	41 quarante et un	51 cinquante et un
32 trente-deux	42 quarante-deux	52 cinquante-deux
33 trente-trois	43 quarante-trois	53 cinquante-trois
34 trente-quatre	44 quarante-quatre	54 cinquante-quatre
35 trente-cinq	45 quarante-cinq	55 cinquante-cinq
36 trente-six	46 quarante-six	56 cinquante-six
37 trente-sept	47 quarante-sept	57 cinquante-sept
38 trente-huit	48 quarante-huit	58 cinquante-huit
39 trente-neuf	49 quarante-neuf	59 cinquante-neuf

60 soixante	70 soixante-dix	80 quatre-vingts*
61 soixante et un	71 soixante et onze	81 quatre-vingt-un**
62 soixante-deux	72 soixante-douze	82 quatre-vingt-deux
63 soixante-trois	73 soixante-treize	83 quatre-vingt-trois
64 soixante-quatre	74 soixante-quatorze	84 quatre-vingt-quatre
65 soixante-cinq	75 soixante-quinze	85 quatre-vingt-cinq
66 soixante-six	76 soixante-seize	86 quatre-vingt-six
67 soixante-sept	77 soixante-dix-sept	87 quatre-vingt-sept
68 soixante-huit	78 soixante-dix-huit	88 quatre-vingt-huit
69 soixante-neuf	79 soixante-dix-neuf	89 quatre-vingt-neuf

*Il y a **s** à **vingts.**   **Il n'y a pas **et.**

90 quatre-vingt-dix	99 quatre-vingt-dix-neuf
91 quatre-vingt-onze*	100 cent
92 quatre-vingt-douze	101 cent un, etc.
93 quatre-vingt-treize	200 deux cents
94 quatre-vingt-quatorze	1.000 mille**
95 quatre-vingt-quinze	2.000 deux mille
96 quatre-vingt-seize	1.000.000 un million
97 quatre-vingt-dix-sept	mille millions: un milliard
98 quatre-vingt-dix-huit	

REMARQUEZ: En anglais on a une virgule: 1,000   et un point: 1.50.
En français on a un point: 1.000   et une virgule: 1,50.

Exercice X Faites en français les opérations suivantes:

Combien font 48 + 25?
74 + 12?
66 + 87?
57 + 33?
91 + 8?

Pour les forts en maths!

1.686 − 925 =
50.392 − 743 =
8.579 + 11.020 =
74.581 + 6.976 =
12.345 + 54.310 =

Écrivez la date d'aujourd'hui (l'année aussi).

LECTURES   1. Un jeune homme impatient

Un jour, Jean-Paul est au restaurant universitaire, à l'heure du déjeuner, entre deux classes. Il est assis à une table, seul, avec un sandwich et un coca. Il est un peu triste. Tous ses copains sont occupés, en classe, au labo, à la bibliothèque. Et lui, il n'a pas de petite amie. Tout à coup, une jeune fille blonde, jolie, assise à une autre table, seule, attire son attention. Elle est vraiment plus élégante que toutes les autres jeunes filles. (Jean-Paul pense: Je vais parler à cette jeune fille charmante; voilà une petite amie possible). Il est debout et il parle à la jeune fille.

— Bonjour, Mademoiselle. Comment allez-vous? Je suis un ami de Jacques.
— Jacques? Quel Jacques?
— Mais Jacques Prévert. Vous n'êtes pas l'amie de Jacques Prévert? Tout le monde est l'ami de J. P. et lui, il est l'ami de tout le monde, l'ami des fleurs, des animaux, de l'amour. (Il pense: Bravo pour l'introduction!)
— Cette chaise est libre? Vous permettez?
Et voilà, il est assis à côté de la jeune fille.

*Il n'y a pas **et**.   **1.000 (**mille**) est invariable: 2.000 **deux mille**, 3.000 **trois mille**.

La jeune fille est choquée. (Elle pense: Je vais donner une leçon à ce jeune homme.) — Monsieur, je ne suis pas l'amie de Jacques Prévert, et je ne suis pas votre amie. Cette chaise est réservée pour....

— Oh pardon. Je vous fais mes excuses. Je m'appelle Jean-Paul et vous?

— Euh! Je m'appelle Thérèse... mais...

— Je suis étudiant. Je fais mon droit; et vous, qu'est-ce que vous faites?

— Moi, je fais de la psycho et si j'analyse votre personnalité, et votre attitude, et vos manières...

— Oh oui! Je vais être avocat et les avocats ont une réputation d'audace et de facilité de parole. Je suis moins timide qu'un jeune homme ordinaire.

— C'est évident.

— Je suis un garçon très actif; je fais du ski, de la moto et aussi du cheval et en été, je fais du ski nautique. J'aime les sports où on fait beaucoup d'exercice. Alors, qu'est-ce qu'on fait ce soir? Et demain, qu'est-ce que vous faites? On fait une balade en moto, ou on fait une escalade de rocher? et dimanche on va faire du surfing. La semaine prochaine...

— Écoutez, Jean-Paul, vous allez vraiment trop vite. Voilà dix minutes que vous êtes assis à côté de moi, et déjà vous faites des projets d'avenir. Pour faire connaissance, je demande une plus longue conversation.

— Oui, mais, voilà, j'ai une classe dans dix minutes et je ne vais pas passer toute la journée à vous faire la cour.

(Il exagère, pense Thérèse.) Elle regarde dans son petit carnet d'adresses et de rendez-vous. — Eh bien, nous sommes en novembre. J'ai une soirée libre le 23 mars. D'accord?

Vocabulaire

amour, (*m.*) love
attirer to attract
avocat, (*m.*) lawyer
escalade de rocher, (*f.*) rock climbing
faire connaissance to get acquainted
faire des excuses to apologize

faire des projets d'avenir to make plans for the future
faire du cheval to go horseback riding
faire du ski nautique to go waterskiing
faire la cour to woo, to court

2. Les activités en France suivant les régions

La variété du climat et de la géographie de la France a pour conséquence la variété des activités dans chaque région. Sur les côtes, au bord de la mer, on pêche: il y a la grande pêche (les bateaux vont jusqu'en Islande, à Terre Neuve) et la pêche côtière pour le thon, la sardine, le maquereau. Voici des ports de pêche importants: Boulogne, Dieppe, Lorient, La Rochelle.

Dans les plaines, on fait de l'agriculture et de l'élevage. On cultive les céréales, la pomme de terre, la betterave, les légumes, les fruits, et le raisin pour faire du vin. Le blé pousse dans la plaine au Nord et au Sud de Paris; la vigne, dans les régions où il y a du soleil, dans la vallée de la Loire, dans le Midi, autour de Bordeaux, dans la vallée du Rhône (le Bourgogne) et bien sûr en Champagne et en Alsace.

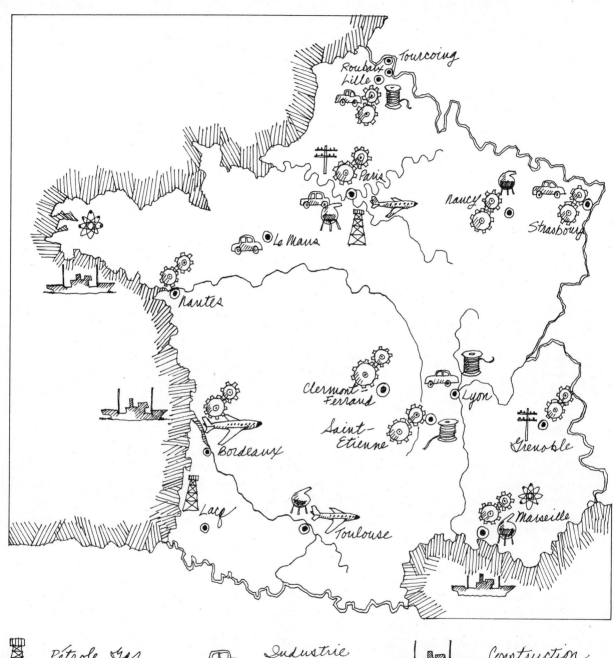

Pétrole, Gaz

Construction Mécanique

Industrie Textile

Industrie Automobile

Industrie aéronautique

Industrie Chimique

Construction Navale

Energie Nucléaire

Construction Electrique

L'industrie est importante et concentrée autour des grands centres miniers — le Nord (Lille) et l'Est (La Lorraine). On fait des autos dans la région parisienne (Citroën, Renault, Simca), et des tissus et des vêtements à Lyon et à Lille.

Dans les montagnes, la principale ressource est l'électricité (il y a des rivières et des barrages à Tignes, Serre-Ponçon). Et l'activité hôtelière est importante en hiver, parce que les sportifs font du ski: à Chamonix, à Courchevel, dans les Alpes, et à Super-Bagnères, dans les Pyrénées.

Vocabulaire

barrage, (*m.*) dam
betterave, (*f.*) beet
blé, (*m.*) wheat
élevage, (*m.*) cattle raising
maquereau, (*m.*) mackerel
pêcher to fish, to catch fish

plaine, (*f.*) lowland
pomme de terre, (*f.*) potato
port, (*m.*) harbor
raisin, (*m.*) grape
tissu, (*m.*) cloth
thon, (*m.*) tuna

3. Poème

FAMILIALE

La mère fait du tricot
Le fils fait la guerre
Elle trouve ça tout naturel la mère
Et le père qu'est-ce qu'il fait le père?
Il fait des affaires
Sa femme fait du tricot
Son fils la guerre
Lui des affaires
Il trouve ça tout naturel le père
Et le fils et le fils
Qu'est-ce qu'il trouve le fils?
Il ne trouve rien absolument rien le fils
Le fils sa mère fait du tricot son père des affaires lui la guerre
Quand il aura fini la guerre
Il fera des affaires avec son père
La guerre continue la mère continue elle tricote
Le père continue il fait des affaires
Le fils est tué il ne continue plus
Le père et la mère vont au cimetière
Ils trouvent ça tout naturel le père et la mère
La vie continue la vie avec le tricot la guerre les affaires
Les affaires la guerre le tricot la guerre
Les affaires les affaires les affaires
La vie avec le cimetière.

JACQUES PRÉVERT, *Paroles*

Vocabulaire

cimetière, (*m.*)   cemetery
elle trouve ça tout naturel   she thinks it is
very normal
faire des affaires   to be in business
faire du tricot   to knit

familiale, *short for* **vie familiale**   family life
il aura fini (*future past*)   when he is
finished
il est tué   he is killed
il fera   (*future of* **faire)**

Composition dirigée   Faites une liste de vos activités de chaque jour et de chaque saison. Qu'est-ce
que vous faites le matin, l'après-midi, le soir? En hiver, qu'est-ce que vous faites? et
au printemps, en été et en automne...?

J'aime la galette

J'ai — me   la   ga — let — te   Sa — vez   vous   com -ment?

Quand elle   est   bien   fait—e   A — vec   du   beurre de —dans   Tra-la—la —la

Tra—la—la—la —lai—re,   Tra—la—la —la,   Tra—la—la—la—la   Tra—la—la—la

Tra—la-la — la —lai — re,   Tra-la — la — la,   Tra-la-la — la — la.

Chapitre **8**

Un supermarché français.

PRÉSENTATION   Le supermarché

Le vendredi, mon frigidaire est vide. Ma famille a faim. Mes enfants ne sont pas contents: plus de lait, plus de pain, plus de chocolat, plus de fruits. Mon mari n'est pas content: plus de vin, plus de fromage, plus de bifteck. Le chat n'est pas content: plus de pâtée. Il faut faire des provisions. Le samedi, je vais au supermarché pour acheter toutes les choses qui sont nécessaires à l'alimentation de ma famille. C'est moi qui fais les provisions.

En France, généralement, on a un magasin spécial pour chaque sorte de produit. Un magasin spécial pour la viande: la boucherie, où le boucher vend du bœuf, du veau, du mouton; un magasin spécial pour le pain: la boulangerie (c'est le boulanger qui fait le pain); un magasin spécial pour le lait, le beurre: la crémerie, etc. Mais on a aussi des supermarchés, ou des libres-services, qui sont plus grands et plus modernes.

Aujourd'hui, je vais au supermarché; je fais une liste; j'attrape un caddie à l'entrée, et je marche dans les allées du magasin; je regarde, je choisis les produits qui sont sur les rayons: le rayon de l'épicerie (les choses sèches comme le riz, les pâtes, le sucre, le sel, le poivre). Puis, j'achète de la viande, du bifteck haché, du porc, un poulet bien tendre, des produits laitiers (du lait, des œufs, du fromage, de la margarine) et des fruits et des légumes frais (des pommes, des oranges, des bananes, des tomates mûres, des carottes, du céleri, des pommes de terre), ou des surgelés. Je passe aussi devant le rayon des produits d'entretien pour la maison (le

savon, les poudres, et les produits pour la toilette: le shampooing,* les kleenex).
Ah! Il ne faut pas oublier la pâtée pour le chat, dans des boîtes de conserve. C'est
lui qui n'est pas content quand le frigidaire est vide!

L'alimentation est chère. C'est souvent moins cher dans un grand supermarché.
C'est toujours plus cher dans des boutiques spécialisées. Ma liste varie avec les
saisons parce qu'il y a une saison pour les articles moins chers. Les légumes et les
fruits par exemple; les tomates, les pommes sont moins chères en automne, et les
oranges sont meilleures et bon marché en hiver. Les fruits exotiques sont toujours
très chers, et le bifteck est plus cher que le poulet. Quand on a une grande famille
et des enfants qui dévorent, il faut faire attention et faire son marché
économiquement.

Enfin, je passe à la caisse. Quelquefois il faut faire la queue, surtout le samedi.
C'est l'employé du supermarché, le caissier ou la caissière qui fait le compte et moi
je donne de l'argent ou un chèque, et il rend la monnaie. Je rentre à la maison.
Maintenant mon frigidaire est plein... pour quelques jours seulement et j'ai une
famille qui est enfin satisfaite.

Vocabulaire

alimentation, (*f.*)　food
argent, (*m.*)　money
attraper　to catch, grab
avoir faim　to be hungry
beurre, (*m.*)　butter
bifteck haché, (*m.*)　ground beef
bœuf, (*m.*)　beef
boîte de conserve, (*f.*)　can
boucher, (*m.*)　butcher
boucherie, (*f.*)　butcher shop
boulanger, (*m.*)　baker
boulangerie, (*f.*)　bakery
caddie, (*m.*)　cart
cher, chère　expensive
crémerie, (*f.*)　dairy store
crémier, (*m.*)　the shopkeeper of the
　dairy store
épicerie, (*f.*)　dry goods, also small gro-
　cery store
faire attention　to pay attention
faire la queue　to stand in line
il faut　it is necessary, one must; **il ne faut**
　pas　one must not
fromage, (*m.*)　cheese
lait, (*m.*)　milk
laitier　dairy (*adj.*)

légume, (*m.*)　vegetable
magasin (*m.*)　store
mouton, (*m.*)　lamb
ne ... plus de　no more, no longer
œuf, (*m.*)　egg; **un œuf**/œnœf/, **des œufs**
　/dezø/
pain, (*m.*)　bread
pâtée, (*f.*)　cat food
pâtes, (*f. pl.*)　noodles
poivre, (*m.*)　pepper
poulet, (*m.*)　chicken
produit, (*m.*)　product
produits d'entretien　maintenance prod-
　ucts, household cleaners, etc.
quelques　several
rayon, (*m.*)　aisle
riz, (*m.*)　rice
rendre la monnaie　to give back change
savon, (*m.*)　soap
surgelé, (*e*)　frozen
veau, (*m.*)　veal
vendre　to sell
viande, (*f.*)　meat
vide　empty; le contraire est **plein, pleine**
vin, (*m.*)　wine

*/ʃãpwɛ̃/

PRONONCIATION

Répétez les mots:

œuf	/œf/	œufs	/ø/
bœuf	/bœf/	bœufs	/bø/
heure	/œʀ/	eux	/ø/
cœur	/kœʀ/	queue	/kø/

Contrastez les sons:

/ɛ̃/	/ɑ̃/
vin	vend
vain	vent
saint	sang
sain	cent
sein	sans

Répétez les mots du texte:

faim	pain	magasin
plein	shampooing	entretien

Contrastez les sons:

/ɛ̃/	/ɛn/
pain	pleine
vilain	vilaine
américain	américaine
mexicain	mexicaine
canadien	canadienne

Contrastez les sons:

/ɛ̃/	/in/
magasin	magazine
divin	divine
cousin	cousine

e muet

Comparez les mots: madémoiselle   vendredi
                      bouchérie   surgelés

Dans les mots du premier groupe le **e** muet tombe. Dans les mots de deuxième groupe le **e** muet reste. La règle est la suivante: le **e** muet tombe si deux consonnes prononcées sont en contact:

madémoiselle	/dm/
bouchérie	/ʃr/

Le **e** muet reste si trois consonnes prononcées sont en contact:

vendredi /drd/
surgelés /rʒl/

Répétez les mots:

(pas d' **e** muet)	(avec **e** muet)
bouch̸erie	surgelés
boulang̸erie	entretien
crém̸erie	libres-services
sam̸edi	vendredi
cél̸eri	mercredi

Répétez les groupes:

plus d̸e pain	boîtes de conserve
plus d̸e lait	pommes de terre
pas d̸e chance	avec de l'argent
pas d̸e galette	avec de la chance
tout l̸e marché	pour le chat
tout l̸e pain	comme le riz
tout l̸e sucre	comme le sucre

e muet dans les verbes **acheter** (*to buy*), **lever** (*to raise*), **appeler** (*to call*) et **jeter** (*to throw*)

ach̸eter	nous ach̸etons	vous ach̸etez
lever*	nous l̸evons	vous l̸evez
app̸eler	nous app̸elons	vous app̸elez
jeter*	nous j̸etons	vous j̸etez

A l'infinitif, à la première et à la deuxième personnes du pluriel, le son final est /e/ ou /õ/. Dans la syllabe qui précède, le **e** est muet; il tombe généralement.

j'achète	tu achètes	il achète	ils achètent
je lève	tu lèves	il lève	elle lève

A ces personnes la finale est **e** muet, la syllabe qui précède a un accent grave parce que si on a le groupe **e** + *une consonne* + **e**, le premier **e** a un accent grave.

j'appelle	tu appelles	il appelle	ils appellent
je jette	tu jettes	il jette	ils jettent

A ces personnes, la finale est **e** muet, mais la consonne qui précède est double, alors un accent n'est pas nécessaire parce que si on a le groupe **e** + *deux consonnes* + **e**, le premier **e** n'a pas d'accent.

*Le **e** muet initial de groupe est prononcé: **lever**, **jeter**.

Exercice Donnez les formes des verbes.

1. Nous (levons) la main.
2. Elle (appeler) son chien.
3. Tu (jeter) un papier par terre.
4. Nous (appeler) le docteur au téléphone.
5. Vous (lever) la main.
6. Elle (acheter) des cigarettes.
7. Je (jeter) mon vieux livre.
8. Tu (lever) la tête?
9. Nous (jeter) nos boîtes de conserve vides.
10. Vous (acheter) du pain.

STRUCTURES CONSTRUCTIONS A RETENIR

L'expression **il faut, il ne faut pas**

En français, la construction qui correspond à l'anglais *I must go to the market, We must do this* or *that* est complexe et demande le subjonctif. On a la possibilité d'utiliser une construction simple pour traduire: *You must go to the market. You must not cry.*

Il faut aller au marché aujourd'hui. **Il ne faut pas** pleurer.

> **il faut** + *infinitif*   **il ne faut pas** + *infinitif*

Allons, Paul, **il faut apprendre** ces verbes.

Cette même construction exprime une nécessité personnelle: **Paul parle à Paul.**

En France, **il faut aller** au marché tous les jours.

Là, on parle en général (*one must*).

Exercice I Refaites ces phrases avec **il faut** ou avec **il ne faut pas.** Choisissez!

1. Achetez ces oranges!
2. Payez avec un chèque!
3. Ecoutez le professeur!
4. Faites votre ménage!
5. Je répète ma leçon vingt fois.
6. Je suis calme.
7. On choisit les fruits.
8. On fait la queue.
9. On va chez le boulanger.
10. Oubliez votre liste!
11. Ne pleurez pas!
12. N'allez pas dans les magasins le 24 décembre!

Les prépositions **chez, à**

EXEMPLE: **Chez** le boulanger   **A** la boulangerie.

On emploie la préposition **chez** devant le nom du marchand.
On emploie la préposition **à** devant le nom du magasin.

Vos oranges sont magnifiques!

Répétez avec **chez** ou **à**.   *Exercice II*

        (*le marchand*)   (*le magasin*)

Je vais _____ le boucher (la bouchère).   Je vais _____ la boucherie.
                le boulanger (la boulangère).   la boulangerie.
                le droguiste (la droguiste).   la droguerie.
                le crémier (la crémière).   la crémeire.
                l'épicier (l'épicière).   l'épicerie.

L'adjectif **cher**; l'expression **bon marché**

Une Rolls est **chère**.   Une bicyclette est **bon marché**.
Le filet mignon est **cher**.   Le bifteck haché est **bon marché**.
Les diamants sont **chers**.   Les perles en plastique sont **bon marché**.
Les perles noires sont **chères**.

Cher est un adjectif ordinaire. Il a des formes différentes au masculin et au féminin, au singulier et au pluriel:

    cher   **chère**   **chers**   **chères**

Bon marché est une expression invariable. Elle ne change pas. (*Cheaper =* **moins cher**; *more expensive =* **plus cher**)

Exercice III Répondez aux questions; faites des phrases: comparez les deux objets ou les deux situations.

1. Est-ce qu'une Cadillac est bon marché? Et une vieille Renault?
2. Est-ce qu'un voyage en Europe est bon marché? Et un pique-nique au parc?
3. Est-ce que le camping est bon marché? Et une nuit dans un hôtel de luxe?
4. Est-ce qu'un appartement est bon marché? Et une villa sur la Côte d'Azur?

POINTS DE GRAMMAIRE

Les verbes du 3ème groupe régulier: **vendre** (*to sell*)

L'infinitif est en **–dre**.

vendre

Singulier   *Pluriel*

Singulier		*Pluriel*	
je ven**ds**		nous ven**dons**	/vãdõ/
tu ven**ds**	/vã/	vous ven**dez**	/vãde/
il, elle ven**d**		ils, elles ven**dent**	/vãd/

Au singulier les terminaisons sont: **–ds, –ds, –d.** Le **d** n'est pas prononcé.
Au pluriel les terminaisons sont: **–dons, –dez, –dent.** Le **d** est prononcé.

Conjuguez sur ce modèle les verbes **entendre,** *to hear;* **descendre,** *to descend, to go down;* **perdre,** *to lose;* **rendre,** *to return;* **attendre,** *to wait for;* **répondre,** *to answer.*

Exercice IV Mettez la forme correcte du verbe.

1. Vous (entendre) _____ le téléphone? 2. Il (attendre) _____ sa petite amie. 3. Nous (descendre) _____ l'escalier. 4. (répondre) _____ à la question du professeur! (*impératif*) 5. Je (perdre) _____ mon temps. 6. (Attendre) _____! J'arrive. 7. Ils (entendre) _____ la neuvième symphonie à la radio. 8. Tu (rendre) _____ la monnaie au client. 9. Le boucher (vendre) _____ du bifteck. 10. Les enfants (répondre) _____ poliment.

Le comparatif de **bon: meilleur** (*better*)

EXEMPLE   Le bifteck haché est **moins bon que** le filet mignon.
                  Le poulet est **aussi bon que** le poisson.
                  Le pain français est **meilleur que** le pain Merveille.

L'adjectif **bon** a un mot spécial pour son comparatif.

La soupe est **meilleure.**
Les vins sont **meilleurs.**
Les tomates sont **meilleures.**

	Singulier	*Pluriel*
Masculin:	**meilleur**	**meilleurs**
Féminin:	**meilleure**	**meilleures**

Faites des phrases avec le comparatif de **bon.**   *Exercice V*

1. En été, les oranges sont (− bonnes) _____ abricots, mais le raisin est (+ bon) _____ les bananes.
2. Alain a des A, Richard a des B. Les notes d'Alain sont (+ bonnes) _____ les notes de Richard.
3. Mes professeurs de cette année sont (+ bon) _____ mes professeurs de l'année dernière.
4. Le vin de Californie est (− bon) _____ le vin de France.
5. Pour un chat, est-ce que le bifteck est (+ bon) _____ la boîte de conserve?
6. Souvent, les légumes surgelés sont (= bons) _____ les légumes frais.

Les adverbes en **–ment**

probablement *probably*
pratiquement *practically*

Il y a beaucoup d'adverbes en **–ment** en français, et souvent ils correspondent à des adverbes en *–ly* en anglais.

rapide	rapid**ement**
naïve (naïf *m.*)	naï**vement**
correcte (correct *m.*)	correct**ement**

On forme les adverbes en **–ment** de cette manière: on ajoute **–ment** à la forme du féminin de l'adjectif.

Attention: Les adjectifs qui ont une voyelle avant le **e** au féminin perdent ce **e.**

vraie: vrai**ment**   polie: poli**ment**

L'adverbe de **gentille** est **gentiment.**

Le **e** muet avant la syllabe **–ment** tombe quelquefois quand deux consonnes seulement sont prononcées ensemble.

EXAMPLE: **facil∕ement**

/lm/ est facile à prononcer; le son /ə/ tombe.

Mais si on a trois consonnes, alors le son /ə/ reste.

EXEMPLE   **simplement**

/plm/ est impossible à prononcer; le son /ə/ reste.

RÉPÉTEZ: /ə/ tombe   /ə/ reste

naturell*é*ment   horriblement
sèch*é*ment   calmement
général*é*ment   agréablement

Exercice VI   Faites des adverbes avec les adjectifs suivants; indiquez si **e** tombe ou reste.

sèche	nette	naturelle	exceptionnelle
complète	rare	difficile	nerveuse
première	générale	agréable	seule
économique	facile	horrible	familière
tranquille	timide	typique	simple
logique	négative	calme	formidable

Remarquez la forme et la prononciation de **forcément, précisément, énormément** (avec **é**).

évidemment (*adj.* évidente)
patiemment (*adj.* patiente)   Prononcez /amã/.
récemment (*adj.* récente)

La langue populaire et familière aime les adverbes nouveaux et colorés. Voilà deux adverbes modernes; ils signifient **très.**

drôlement: C'est drôlement joli.
vachement:*   C'est vachement difficile.

Il parle doucement. Elle est vraiment jolie.

On place l'adverbe **après** le verbe ou **devant** l'adjectif.

Exercice VII   Faites un adverbe avec l'adjectif entre parenthèses. Attention à la place de l'adverbe!

1. Il voyage. (rare) 2. Vous parlez. (facile) 3. Cette leçon est difficile. (horrible) 4. Ils étudient. (énorme) 5. Nous marchons dans le parc. (tranquille) 6. C'est une attitude française. (typique) 7. J'entre dans la maison. (timide) 8. Elle parle. (nerveuse) 9. La maison est décorée. (agréable) 10. Mes enfants sont calmes. (générale) 11. Vous êtes pâle. (drôle) 12. Ce film est intéressant. (vache)

Le pronom relatif **qui** (*who, which, that*)

Écoutez le professeur. Le professeur parle.
Écoutez le professeur **qui** parle.

*****une vache** = *a cow* (l'adverbe est familier)

Regardez le train. Le train passe.
Regardez le train **qui** passe.

Qui est le pronom sujet pour les personnes et pour les choses, au singulier et au pluriel. **Qui** n'est jamais élidé. Les mots **professeur, train** sont les antécédents.

Refaites les phrases avec le pronom relatif sujet **qui.**   *Exercice VIII*

1. Regardez la jolie jeune fille. Elle plonge dans la piscine.
2. Je n'aime pas les nouvelles. Elles sont dans le journal.
3. Ne punissez pas l'enfant. Il fait du bruit!
4. J'aime les chats. Ils restent à la maison.
5. Marc aime les jeunes filles. Elles font la cuisine.
6. Brigitte adore un jeune homme. Il skie comme Jean-Claude Killy.

Refaites ces phrases avec **qui.** Attention! Changez l'ordre des mots, parce que **qui**   *Exercice IX*
est inséparable de son antécédent.

EXAMPLE: Le journal a un article intéressant. Il est sur la table.
Le journal **qui est sur la table** a un article intéressant.

1. Les nouvelles sont déprimantes. Elles sont dans le journal.
2. Les étudiants ont des bonnes notes. Ils vont à la bibliothèque tous les jours.
3. Les gens ont de la chance. Ils habitent à la campagne.
4. Les jeunes filles sont élégantes. Elles achètent leurs robes chez Courrèges.
5. Les fleurs sont moins jolies. Elles poussent dans mon jardin.

C'est...qui

EXEMPLE: **C'est** le boulanger **qui** fait le pain.
C'est les chiens **qui** font du bruit.

On entoure un sujet important avec **c'est...qui.**

Répétez les phrases avec **c'est...qui.**   *Exercice X*

1. Paris est la plus belle ville du monde.
2. Le bœuf est la meilleure viande.
3. Claude parle au professeur.
4. Le chat mange mon bifteck.
5. A Noël, les enfants sont contents.

C'est le boulanger qui fait le pain.
C'est **lui** qui fait le pain.
C'est la boulangère qui vend le pain.
C'est **elle** qui vend le pain.
C'est **moi** qui explique. C'est **vous** qui comprenez.

Le groupe **c'est...qui** entoure le pronom tonique: **c'est moi qui; c'est lui qui.**

C'est **moi qui suis...**	C'est **nous qui sommes...**
C'est **toi qui es...**	C'est **vous qui êtes...**
C'est **lui qui est...**	C'est **eux qui sont...**
C'est **elle qui est...**	C'est **elles qui sont...***

Conjuguez le verbe avec le pronom sujet correspondant.

Exercice XI Répétez les phrases avec **c'est...qui** autour du pronom tonique.

1. Tu poses cette question.
2. Vous allez au marché.
3. Nous achetons leur auto.
4. Il a une bonne idée.
5. Ils prennent une bière.
6. Elle fait des provisions.
7. Je suis surprise.
8. Elles arrivent en retard.

LECTURES **1. Betty et Paulette**

Betty, une jeune femme américaine, et Paulette, une Française, vont faire des provisions au marché. Betty arrive d'Amérique. Elle n'a pas l'habitude des magasins français, elle, parce qu'en Amérique, elle fait ses provisions au supermarché. Mais Betty et Paulette habitent dans un petit village où il n'y a pas de supermarché, et il faut aller dans cinq magasins différents.

PAULETTE: Allons au marché ensemble, Betty, aujourd'hui.

BETTY: D'accord! Avec mon auto?

PAULETTE: Non, les rues sont pleines d'autos et de monde. Il n'y a pas de parking. Allons à pied.

BETTY: Bon. J'ai ma liste: des boîtes de conserve, des surgelés, du bifteck haché, des dîners-télé...

*Dans la langue plus élégante, on a: **ce sont les chiens..., ce sont eux qui...,** etc.

PAULETTE: Non, non, pas en France, ma chère. Ici, on ne mange pas tout ça; et puis, il faut aller dans des magasins différents pour chaque chose. Nous commençons par la boucherie. Aujourd'hui, je vais acheter du cheval.

BETTY: Ah oui! pour ton chien et ton chat.

PAULETTE: Pas du tout, du bifteck de cheval pour mes enfants. Ils adorent cela. C'est délicieux.

BETTY: !!!

PAULETTE: Ensuite, je passe à l'alimentation: des pommes de terre pour faire des frites avec le bifteck, des carottes pour la salade. Ensuite allons à la crémerie pour le fromage, indispensable...

BETTY: Mais, mais, tout cela pour midi?

PAULETTE: Eh oui! en France le déjeuner est très important, on mange beaucoup à midi. Le soir, le dîner est plus léger.

BETTY: Alors, pas de sandwiches?

PAULETTE: Rarement, en pique-nique peut-être, ou quand on voyage. Ah! Je vais aussi acheter des œufs pour une omelette, du beurre, et du lait.

BETTY: Ton panier est plein!

PAULETTE: Eh oui! C'est la même chose tous les jours. Maintenant je passe chez le poissonnier pour commander un poulet pour dimanche, et peut-être des huîtres.

BETTY: Mais le poulet n'est pas un poisson!

PAULETTE: C'est exact. Mais souvent en France le poissonnier vend des poissons, des huîtres et des poulets. Ah, bien. Allons à la droguerie!

BETTY: La droguerie!! Tu vas acheter de la drogue!! mais Paulette... mon amie, tu...

PAULETTE: Ah, ah, ah, comme c'est drôle. Le droguiste ne vend pas de drogue; il vend des produits d'entretien, du savon, des kleenex, etc.

BETTY: Ah! Quelle émotion!

PAULETTE: Enfin, la boulangerie, mon magasin préféré. Ah, le pain chaud, quelle odeur divine! Et les gâteaux, les éclairs, les babas au rhum... Adieu, mon régime!

BETTY: Oui, d'accord! C'est extraordinaire. Mais, Paulette, tu es pâle... ça ne va pas.

PAULETTE: Mes paniers sont pleins. Je suis fatiguée. Et puis, j'ai faim. Mon petit déjeuner est si petit.

BETTY: C'est vrai, en France, le petit déjeuner est très petit. Les Américains sont plus logiques, n'est-ce pas? des œufs, du bacon, des toasts, du café. En France on a un petit toast, un petit café au lait, c'est tout.

PAULETTE: Chaque pays a ses habitudes, et ses coutumes différentes...

BETTY: Oui, et toi, tu as faim à 10 heures du matin, et tu as «le coup de pompe» et tous les jours tu vas faire des courses dans dix magasins différents et il faut porter des paniers pleins. Quelle existence!

PAULETTE: Tu as raison. Vive le style de vie à l'américaine! Mais toi, tes paniers sont vides.

BETTY: Aujourd'hui, je vais aller à la charcuterie acheter un déjeuner tout préparé, ou bien, au restaurant.

Vocabulaire

alimentation, (*f.*) grocery store
aller à pied to walk
avoir l'habitude de to be used to
avoir raison to be right
charcuterie, (*f.*) store where pork meat and prepared dishes are sold, delicatessen
commander to order
coup de pompe, (*m.*) sudden feeling of tiredness

déjeuner, (*m.*) lunch
dîner, (*m.*) dinner
droguerie, (*f.*) variety store **(le, la droguiste)**
huître, (*f.*) oyster
panier, (*m.*) basket
petit déjeuner, (*m.*) breakfast
poisson, (*m.*) fish
poissonnier, (*m.*) fish seller
vive! long live!

2. Les repas en France

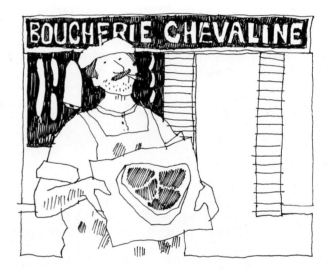

En France, il y a maintenant des supermarchés et des libres-services partout. Les Françaises font des provisions pour la semaine, si elles ont un grand frigidaire; mais souvent, il est trop petit, et puis, aller au marché tous les matins est une activité importante et nécessaire. Le pain frais est indispensable sur la table d'un Français pour le déjeuner. Les petits magasins sont encore nombreux dans les villages ou dans les vieux quartiers.

En France, la cuisine est un art, et un vrai repas est une cérémonie ordonnée comme une symphonie. Voilà sa composition:

les hors d'œuvre: de la charcuterie, une salade de tomates, du thon à l'huile, etc.
l'entrée: un poisson ou un soufflé
la viande garnie: un rôti et des légumes, du poulet et des frites
la salade: verte (uniquement à l'huile et au vinaigre)

les fromages: une ou deux des 350 variétés!
le dessert: un fruit ou une crème ou un yaourt

Voilà un repas à midi. Dans beaucoup de familles, où les membres travaillent, on ne mange pas d'entrée. Mais les autres plats sont traditionnels. Le soir, le dîner est plus léger:

un potage
une entrée: des œufs ou du jambon ou viande froide
un légume ou une salade
un fromage ou un dessert ou un fruit

Le petit déjeuner est toujours rapide: un café noir ou un café au lait avec des tartines beurrées. Le dimanche, des croissants. Les enfants, les paysans et les ouvriers ont aussi un casse-croûte à 9 h ou 10 h, et les enfants ont un goûter après l'école: du pain et du chocolat ou un pain au chocolat.

Manger est une des occupations favorites des Français. Souvent on ne mange pas, on bouffe. «Bouffer» est un verbe de la langue argotique, synonyme de manger vite, avec beaucoup de bruit et de satisfaction extérieure. Un cinéaste a fait un film: «La grande bouffe» qui décrit cet amour exagéré de la nourriture.

Bien sûr, beaucoup de Français ont des problèmes avec leur foie, leur tension ou leur cholestérol. Ils parlent de leur régime, ils mangent parfois des biscottes, des yaourts taille-fine, ou des fromages 1%. Mais souvent, c'est difficile de sacrifier les bons petits plats, le pain frais acheté chaque jour à la boulangerie, la charcuterie délicieuse. Un repas familial pour une célébration exceptionnelle—un mariage, un baptême—dure parfois quatre heures.

Vocabulaire

argotique, (from **argot**) slang
biscotte, (*f.*) zweiback
casse-croûte, (*m.*) snack
charcuterie prepared pork meats like:
   pâté, head cheese, salami, etc.
foie, (*m.*) liver

goûter, (*m.*) four o'clock snack
jambon, (*m.*) ham
quartier, (*m.*) section of town
taille fine, (*f.*) thin waist
tartine, (*f.*) slice of bread
viande froid, (*f.*) cold cut

Composition

Vous allez dans un supermarché américain avec une amie française qui n'a pas l'habitude des produits américains. Qu'est-ce que vous achetez? Comparez les produits.

Chevaliers de la table ronde

Chapitre 9

Che — va — liers de la ta — ble ron — de, goû — tons

voir si le vin est bon. Che — va — bon. Goû — tons

voir, oui, oui, oui, goû — tons voir, non, non, non, goû — tons

voir si le vin est bon, goû — tons bon.

PRÉSENTATION   Au restaurant

Aujourd'hui, c'est dimanche, le plus beau jour de la semaine. Je dis à mon mari: — Je n'ai pas envie de faire la cuisine. Allons au restaurant. — Où aller? Il y a «Chez Dupont» où tout est bon. — Non, il y a trop de monde. — Allons au «Restaurant du Marché»! — Non, il y a trop de bruit. — Bon, alors, au restaurant arabe de la rue du Désert. — Non! Je n'aime pas beaucoup la cuisine exotique. — Tu es vraiment difficile... Et le restaurant universitaire? C'est le moins cher de tous les restaurants. — Tu plaisantes! Il faut avoir vingt ans et une carte d'étudiant. — Bon, alors où? — Allons au «Restaurant des Amis»; on dit que la cuisine est excellente et qu'ils ont les prix les plus raisonnables de toute la ville. — Bon. Allons-y.

Nous entrons dans le restaurant. Nous choisissons une table dans un coin tranquille et nous prenons place. La nappe est propre. Devant nous, il y a le couvert: une assiette, un verre, une fourchette, un couteau, une cuillère et une serviette — miracle! — qui n'est pas en papier.

Voilà la conversation du restaurant.

LE MARI: Appelons le garçon. Garçon!

LE GARÇON: Oui, monsieur. Voilà. Bonjour, messieurs-dames!

LE MARI: La carte, s'il vous plaît! Nous allons commander.

LE GARÇON: Voilà, monsieur, vous avez le repas à la carte et le plat du jour. Qu'est-ce que vous allez prendre?

LE MARI: Le repas à la carte est plus cher que le plat du jour, probablement, n'est-ce pas?

LE GARÇON: Eh oui, monsieur.

LE MARI: Quel est le plat du jour?

LE GARÇON: Aujourd'hui, c'est le bœuf bourguignon.

LE MARI: Qu'est-ce que tu vas prendre, chérie?

LA FEMME: Oh! je n'ai pas envie de viande, aujourd'hui. Qu'est-ce que vous avez comme poisson?

LE GARÇON: La sole normande est extra, et la truite aux amandes est la plus délicieuse du monde.

LA FEMME: Je vais prendre la sole, alors; mais avant, donnez-moi un hors d'œuvre, un melon, et aussi un légume, des carottes Vichy. Pour le dessert, un yaourt.

LE MARI: Eh bien, moi, je vais prendre le pâté de foie, un steak frites, une salade verte; et après, apportez-moi le plateau de fromages.

LA FEMME: Chéri, du pâté, un steak. Tu manges trop de viande. Tu as tort, ce n'est pas bon pour toi.

LE MARI: Oh toi! avec ton régime!

LA FEMME: Mais chéri, j'ai peur pour ta santé.

LE GARÇON: Hum! Bien, et comme vin, qu'est-ce que vous préférez: un vin blanc pour la sole de madame et un rouge pour le steak de monsieur?

LA FEMME: Non! je ne bois pas de vin mais j'ai assez soif, alors donnez-moi de l'eau minérale: un quart Vichy, c'est vraiment la meilleure des eaux minérales.

LE MARI: Carottes Vichy, eau de Vichy — Vichy est à la mode, avec toi. Pour moi, oui, un bordeaux rouge pas trop sec.

LE GARÇON: Vous avez raison.

(Nous mangeons. Tout est délicieux.)

LE GARÇON: Tout va bien?

NOUS: C'est excellent.

LE GARÇON: Un petit dessert, monsieur?

LE MARI: Non, je n'ai plus faim. Donnez-moi un café et un pousse-café.

LA FEMME: Toute cette viande, tout ce vin, et encore un poussé-café. C'est du poison.

LE MARI: Allons, allons! Nous n'allons pas tous les jours au restaurant. Garçon, l'addition.

LE GARÇON: Voilà, monsieur.

Nous payons, nous laissons un pourboire généreux et nous rentrons à la maison.

Un choix difficile, au restaurant.

Vocabulaire

addition, (*f.*) bill
à la mode in the fashion
amande, (*f.*) almond
allons-y let's go there, let's go
apporter to bring
assiette, (*f.*) plate
avoir envie to feel like
avoir peur to be afraid
avoir soif to be thirsty
avoir tort to be wrong
avoir raison to be right
avoir vingt ans to be 20 years old
boire to drink
carte, (*f.*) menu
coin, (*m.*) corner
commander to order
couteau, (*m.*) knife
couvert, (*m.*) knives and forks
cuillère, (*f.*) spoon
difficile *here,* hard to please
dire to say
extra super
fourchette, (*f.*) fork
garçon, (*m.*) waiter (**la serveuse:** the waitress)

laisser to leave something
Messieurs — dames Ladies and gents (*familiar, unrefined way of speaking*)
nappe, (*f.*) tablecloth
n'est-ce pas isn't it?
plaisanter to kid
plat du jour the day's special
plateau, (*m.*) tray
propre clean
pourboire, (*m.*) tip
pousse-café, (*m.*) liqueur, brandy, or cognac that one drinks after the coffee
prendre place to take a seat
prix, (*m.*) price
quart a quarter of a liter
santé, (*f.*) health
serviette, (*f.*) napkin
tout everything
trop too much, too many
truite, (*f.*) trout
verre, (*m.*) glass
vraiment really

PRONONCIATION   Les sons /s/ et /z/

dessert   désert

Deux **s** sont toujours prononcés /s/. Un **s** entre deux voyelles est prononcé /z/. Répétez les mots suivants:

poisson   poison
coussin   cousin
cuisse   cuisine
assiette   raisonnable

choisissez
assaisonné
pas assez

Les lettres **i** ou **y** dans les verbes en **–ayer, –oyer, –uyer**

payer	nous payons	vous payez	(*to pay*)
employer	nous employons	vous employez	(*to use*)
s'ennuyer	nous nous ennuyons	vous vous ennuyez	(*to be bored*)

L'infinitif et les première et deuxième personnes du pluriel sont toujours épelés avec **–y.** Prononcez /ɛj/, /waj/, /ɥij/.

je paye *ou* je paie	j'emploie
tu payes *ou* tu paie	tu emploies
il paye *ou* il paie	il, elle emploie
elles payent *ou* elles paient	ils, elles emploient
PRONONCEZ /ɛj/ *ou* /ɛ/	/wa/

Aux autres personnes, lorsque le **–y** est en contact avec **e** muet de la terminaison, **y** se transforme en **–i.** Pour le verbe **payer** on a le choix entre les deux orthographes, **je paye** ou **je paie.** Pour les autres verbes on n'a pas le choix. Conjuguez de la même manière: **essayer** (*to try*); **envoyer** (*to send*).

Donnez la forme correcte des verbes. *Exercice*

1. (payer) Tu _____ la note.
2. (employer) _____ l'article partitif.
3. (envoyer) Ils _____ des fleurs à l'actrice célèbre.
4. (essayer) Nous _____ de prononcer, mais c'est difficile.
5. (payer) Vous _____ l'addition.

Mots difficiles

Articulez avec soin les mots suivants:

bœuf bourguignon /bœfbuʀgiɲõ/	à la mode /alamɔd/
hors-d'œuvre /ɔʀdœvʀ/	pourboire /puʀbwaʀ/
yaourt /jauʀt/	

VERBES IRRÉGULIERS STRUCTURES

prendre *to take, to have some kind of food*

je **prends** ⎫	nous **prenons** /pʀənõ/
tu **prends** ⎬ /pʀã/	vous **prenez** /pʀəne/
il, elle **prend** ⎭	ils, elles **prennent** /pʀɛn/

La conjugaison de ce verbe présente trois sons différents. Conjuguez de la même manière: **comprendre** (*to understand*); **apprendre** (*to learn*).

Exercice I Mettez la forme des verbes **prendre, comprendre, apprendre.**

1. Vous _____ une bière? 2. J'_____ le piano. 3. Georges est lent. Il _____ lentement. 4. Vous _____ la situation internationale? 5. Je ne _____ pas la leçon. 6. Elles _____ des vacances tous les ans. 7. Pierre _____ son dîner à cinq heures.

dire *to say*

je **dis**	} /di/	nous **disons** /dizõ/
tu **dis**		vous **dites** /dit/
il, elle **dit**		ils, elles **disent** /diz/

Conjuguez de la même manière **redire** (*to say again*).

Exercice II Mettez la forme correcte du verbe **dire** ou **redire.**

1. Le prêtre _____ la messe.
2. Nous _____ : «Garçon, une bière!»
3. Pardon, vous _____?
4. Je _____ et je _____, «Zut! (*shucks!*)» à mon frère.
5. Le professeur _____ la même chose dix fois.

boire *to drink*

je **bois**	} /bwa/	nous **buvons** /byvõ/
tu **bois**		vous **buvez**
il, elle **boit**		ils, elles **boivent** /bwav/

Remarquez les deux radicaux **boi** et **bu.**

Exercice III Mettez la forme correcte du verbe **boire.**

1. Nous _____ de la bière en été.
2. Il _____ beaucoup de whisky.
3. Mes enfants ne _____ pas de lait au dîner.
4. Vous _____ du vin de Californie, en France?

CONSTRUCTIONS A RETENIR

Expressions idiomatiques avec **avoir**

avoir faim	*to be hungry*	**avoir envie**	*to feel like doing something*
avoir soif	*to be thirsty*	**avoir raison**	*to be right*
avoir peur	*to be afraid*	**avoir tort**	*to be wrong*

EXEMPLES: J'ai faim.   Nous avons tort.
           Tu as soif.   Vous avez raison.
           Il a peur.   Ils ont envie de boire.

Tous ces fromages
délicieux. . .

Pour ces expressions idiomatiques, conjuguez le verbe **avoir** et ajoutez le nom **faim,
soif,** etc., sans article.

> **J'ai tort.**   Tu **as raison.**

Employez ces deux expressions pour des personnes uniquement. Pour une chose
on dit: **c'est vrai, c'est faux,** ou **c'est correct, c'est incorrect.**

> **J'ai envie de regarder** la télé.
> **J'ai envie d'**une bonne **bière.**

Employez **j'ai envie de** avec un infinitif ou avec un nom.

Mettez l'expression idiomatique avec **avoir.**   *Exercice IV*

1. J'_____, je vais manger un énorme bifteck.
2. Vous _____? Prenez une bière bien fraîche.
3. Je suis fatigué. Je n'_____ pas _____ étudier. J'_____ regarder la télé.
4. Il y a une tempête, du bruit, une tornade; Janine _____.
5. Mes amis fument trop de cigarettes. Ils _____, c'est mauvais pour la santé.
6. Vous aimez le pain français? Vous _____, c'est délicieux.

avoir...ans   *to be...years old:*

Employez le verbe **avoir** et le nom **ans** pour l'âge.

> Vous **avez** vingt **ans.** Quel **âge a** votre sœur?
> Elle **a** dix-neuf **ans.** Et votre professeur?
> Il **a** quatre-vingt-dix-neuf **ans.**
> Cette année il **va avoir** cent **ans.**

Exercice V   Répondez aux questions.

1. Quel âge avez-vous?   2. Quel âge a votre père; et votre mère?   3. Quel âge a votre petit(e) ami(e), ou votre mari ou votre femme?

Prendre ou avoir dans les questions

> **Qu'est-ce que vous prenez?** *What are you going to have?*
> **Qu'est-ce que vous avez comme poisson?** *What kind of fish do you have?*

Employez le verbe **prendre** pour traduire *to have food or drink, to eat or drink* et pour **prendre un taxi, le train.** Employez le verbe **avoir** pour une question sur le menu ou les produits du magasin.

Exercice VI   (*a.*) Faites des questions avec les deux expressions étudiées.

(*b.*) Répondez aux questions.

EXEMPLE: de la bière   **Vous prenez de la bière? Non, je prends de l'eau.**
   Qu'est-ce que vous avez comme bière? J'ai de la Schlitz et de la Michelob.

1. de l'eau minérale   2. des fruits   3. un dessert   4. un pousse-café

POINTS DE GRAMMAIRE

Le pronom tonique avec une préposition

> Devant **nous,** il y a le couvert.
> Georges est assis à côté de **moi.**
> Chez **eux,** il y a du bon vin.
> J'ai peur pour **toi.**

Employez le pronom tonique — **moi, toi, lui, elle, nous, vous, eux, elles** — avec une préposition: **chez, avec, sans, pour, à côté de, devant, derrière.**

Exercice VII   Remplacez le mot entre parenthèses par le pronom tonique correct.

EXEMPLE: Je suis devant (Paul).
   Je suis **devant lui.**

1. Christine fait une balade avec (Pierre).   2. André habite chez (ses parents).
3. Guy est à côté de (Marguerite).   4. Armand est entre (Janine et Simone).
5. Mon mari ne voyage pas sans (je).   6. Le professeur est devant (vous).   7. Il a
peur, je reste avec (il).   8. Chez (nous), il y a du bon vin.   9. Tes parents restent
chez (tu).   10. Il est triste sans (elle).

On étudie bien au café.

Le superlatif

EXEMPLES: **le plus beau** jour de la semaine
le restaurant **le moins cher**
les prix **les plus raisonnables**

Ce sont des superlatifs. On forme le superlatif de cette manière: Si l'adjectif est avant le nom, on a:

$$\text{l'article} + \frac{\textbf{plus}}{\textbf{moins}} + \text{l'adjectif} + \text{le nom}$$

le beau jour   **le plus beau jour**
le grand restaurant   **le moins grand restaurant**
la jolie fillette   **la plus jolie fillette**
                                 la moins jolie fillette

Si l'adjectif est après le nom, on a:

$$\text{l'article} + \text{le nom} + \text{l'article} + \frac{\textbf{plus}}{\textbf{moins}} + \text{l'adjectif}$$

le livre intéressant   **le livre le plus intéressant**
la viande chère   **la viande la moins chère**

On répète l'article après le nom, devant le superlatif.

Exercice VIII   Répétez au superlatif.

1. le vieux monument
2. le fromage délicieux
3. la grande pharmacie
4. les bananes mûres
5. les grosses oranges
6. les histoires extraordinaires
7. le garçon intelligent
8. les marchands aimables

EXEMPLE: le plus beau jour **de la semaine**

Le complément du superlatif commence par **de** (*in, of*):

Pierre est le garçon **le plus intelligent de** la classe.
C'est le restaurant **le moins cher de** la ville.

Attention à la contraction: Paris est la plus belle ville **du** (= de + le) **monde.**

Exercice IX   Complétez les phrases avec **de, de la, du, des.**

1. le vin le plus cher _____ magasin
2. le plus grand monument _____ New York
3. la viande la moins chère _____ supermarchés
4. le plus gros chat _____ ville

5. la partie la plus chaude _____ pays
6. les oranges les plus mûres _____ jardin
7. le film le plus fantastique _____ semaine
8. les produits les plus fins _____ épicerie

EXEMPLE: L'eau de Vichy, c'est **la meilleure** des eaux minérales.

L'adjectif **bon** a, comme superlatif, le même mot spécial que pour le comparatif, mais on ajoute l'article.

	Comparatif	*Superlatif*
Masc. Sing.	meilleur	le meilleur
Fém. Sing.	meilleure	la meilleure
Masc. Plur.	meilleurs	les meilleurs
Fém. Plur.	meilleures	les meilleures

Répétez au superlatif.

Exercice X

1. Un bon film; c'est _____ l'année.
2. Un bon fromage; c'est _____ France.
3. Les bons produits; ce sont _____ le supermarché.
4. Une bonne histoire; c'est _____ son répertoire.
5. Le bordeaux est un bon vin; c'est _____ ce restaurant.

Les expressions de quantité: **beaucoup, un peu, assez, trop, plus, moins**

Je mange. Je mange **beaucoup.**
J'aime le ski. J'aime **beaucoup** le ski.

Avec un verbe seul, avec un nom qui a l'article défini, **le, la, les,** on ajoute l'adverbe de quantité après le verbe.

Ils ont de l'argent. Ils **ont beaucoup d'**argent.
Nous avons des problèmes. Nous avons **moins de** problèmes que vous.

Avec un nom qui a l'article partitif, **du, de la, de l',** ou l'article indéfini **des,** l'adverbe de quantité est:

$$\left.\begin{array}{l} \text{beaucoup} \\ \text{un peu} \\ \text{assez} \\ \text{trop} \\ \text{plus} \\ \text{moins} \end{array}\right\} \textbf{de}$$

Comparez avec **pas de.**

Exercice XI Répétez les phrases suivantes avec les six expressions de quantité.

1. Il boit.
2. Elle aime les bébés.
3. Tu manges des bonbons.
4. Le professeur a de la patience.
5. Il y a du vent.

J'ai un peu soif, moins peur, trop envie.

Avec les expressions **avoir faim, soif, peur** et **envie** on garde **un peu, assez, trop, plus, moins** sans article et sans **de.**

J'ai très faim, très soif, très peur, très envie.

N'employez pas «beaucoup» avec ces expressions. Dites **très faim, très peur, très soif,** etc.

Exercice XII Répétez les expressions suivantes avec **un peu, assez, trop, moins, très.**

1. Il a faim.   2. Elle a soif.   3. Nous avons peur.   3. Ils ont envie.

LECTURES   ## 1. Gastronomie française

La vie moderne change les habitudes des Français. En général, les magasins et les bureaux ferment à midi et tout le monde rentre à la maison pour déjeuner. Dans certaines grandes villes, on commence à avoir la journée continue, à l'américaine, mais cette méthode n'est pas très populaire. Peu de Français aiment déjeuner d'un sandwich, sauf pour une occasion exceptionnelle, pique-nique, voyage, etc. Les écoliers, les employés qui habitent loin de leur travail, vont à la cantine ou au restaurant. Il y a des restaurants à tous les prix, à 10F ($2.00), à 12F, à 20F, à 25F, et les restaurants chic, avec des étoiles dans le Guide Michelin. Une, deux ou trois — c'est une distinction remarquable. A Paris, il y a un restaurant hors-classe (sans étoile) où la salade seule coûte 160F ($32.00): «Chez Denis». Un chef de restaurant s'est suicidé le jour où le Guide Michelin a mis deux étoiles devant son nom à la place de trois!

La gastronomie française est un voyage intéressant: dans chaque province il y a des spécialités. Vous trouvez 350 fromages différents: la Vache qui rit, le Bonbel, le Roquefort, le Camembert, le Port Salut sont les plus connus à l'étranger. Les vins varient de la même façon. Il faut essayer, un jour, le boudin du Dauphiné, les escargots de Bourgogne, la bouillabaisse de Marseille, et la tête de veau. Et que dire de la toupinade de béatilles, mot poétique inventé pour un plat... inventé par un grand cuisinier? Le «Cordon-bleu» est une décoration donnée aux meilleurs élèves d'une école spéciale. C'est aussi un compliment pour une cuisinière excellente.

Vocabulaire

a mis   *past of the verb* **mettre,** to put
boudin, (*m.*)   blood sausage
bouillabaisse, (*f.*)   fish soup
cuisinière, (*f.*)   cook

escargot, (*m.*)   snails
s'est suicidé   committed suicide
tête de veau, (*f.*)   calf head

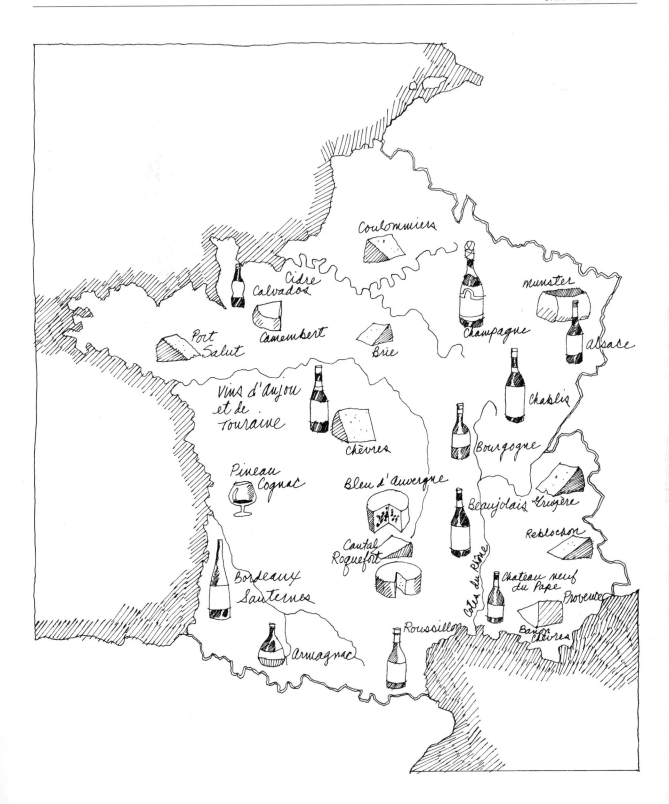

2. Poème

LA CHANSON DU CHAT

Chat, chat, chat,
Chat noir, chat blanc, chat gris,
Charmant chat couché,
Chat, chat, chat,
N'entends-pas les souris
Danser à trois des entrechats
Sur le plancher?
Le bourgeois ronfle dans son lit,
De son bonnet de coton coiffé,
Et la lune regarde à la vitre,
Dansez, souris, dansez, jolies,
· · · · · ·
Et tous les chats du vieux Paris
Dorment sur leur chaise,
Chats blancs, chats noirs ou chats gris.

TRISTAN KLINGSOR
Mercure de France

Vocabulaire

à trois   three by three
coiffé   his head covered
entrechat, (*m.*)   a step in ballet

plancher, (*m.*)   wooden floor
rongler   to snore
vitre, (*f.*)   window

3. Poème

IL EST TERRIBLE...

Il est terrible
le petit bruit de l'œuf dur
cassé sur un comptoir d'étain
il est terrible ce bruit
quand il remue dans la mémoire
de l'homme qui a faim...

JACQUES PRÉVERT

Vocabulaire

dur hard-boiled
étain, (*m.*) tin
remuer to stir

Il y a une fête spéciale chez vous: un anniversaire ou un mariage. Quel est le menu *Composition*
du repas? Ou bien vous invitez toute la famille au restaurant et vous composez un
menu fantastique.

Alouette

Chapitre **10**

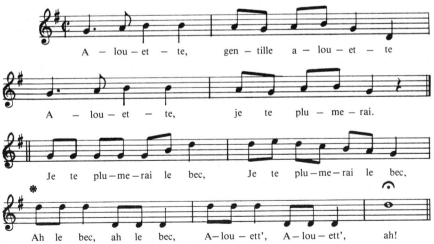

A — lou — et — te,   gen — tille   a — lou — et — te

A — lou — et — te,   je   te   plu — me — rai.

Je   te   plu — me — rai le   bec,   Je   te   plu — me — rai   le   bec,

Ah   le   bec,   ah   le   bec,   A — lou — ett',   A — lou — ett',   ah!

2. et les yeux . . .   3. et la tête . . .   4. et le cou . . .
5. et les ailes . . .   6. et le dos . . .   7. et les pattes . . .
8. et la queue

PRÉSENTATION   La description de la personne. Les parties du corps.

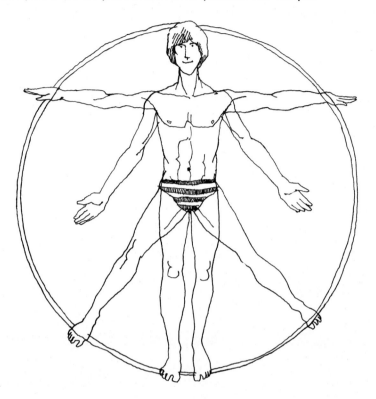

Regardez-moi: je vais décrire les parties de ma personne, de mon corps. Nous commençons par la tête. Voici les cheveux; ce nom est pluriel en français: un cheveu, c'est vraiment un cheveu, pas deux ou trois. Les yeux, deux yeux (un bon exercice de prononciation); au singulier, on dit: un œil. Voici le nez, la bouche avec les dents, au singulier: une dent (le dentiste les aime bien) et la langue, le cou, les oreilles (une oreille). Combien de dents est-ce que vous avez? Trente-deux généralement.

La poitrine, le dos, les épaules (une épaule), la taille, le derrière, les bras (un bras), les mains (une main) avec les doigts (un doigt), les jambes (une jambe), les pieds (un pied), et les doigts de pied. Combien de doigts et de doigts de pied? Vingt en tout.

Il y a beaucoup d'autres noms. Mais ce n'est pas une classe d'anatomie ici. Ce vocabulaire est suffisant, pour le moment.

Apprenons quelques expressions utiles pour décrire la personne: Combien est-ce que vous mesurez? En France, on compte en mètres et en centimètres. Je mesure un mètre cinquante six. Je suis petite mais vous êtes grand (on dit: une personne est grande, la Tour Eiffel est haute, une personne est petite, le mois de février est court). Quelle est votre taille (une autre signification du mot taille)? Combien est-ce que vous pesez? Je pèse environ 52 kilos. En France, on calcule le poids en kilos et en grammes. Un kilo fait environ *2.2 lbs*. Il y a 1.000 grammes dans un kilo. Une livre est un demi-kilo. Mon poids est moyen. Paul est fort. Jeanne est mince. Si on n'est pas très gentil, on dit «gros» à la place de «fort» et «maigre» à la place de «mince.»

Voilà. J'ai fini. Vous avez entendu ma description. Maintenant, à votre tour. Regardez-vous dans une glace. Qu'est-ce que vous voyez? Faites la description de votre personne et la description de votre voisin ou de votre voisine, et ajoutez des couleurs, des formes, des mesures. Quoi? Vous ne voyez pas bien? Prenez vos lunettes. Vous ne les avez pas? Vous les cherchez? Mais vous les avez sur votre nez!

Exemple: J'ai les cheveux gris. Mlle, vous avez les cheveux roux et longs. J'ai les yeux verts. M., vous avez les yeux bleus. J'ai un nez moyen. Elle a un petit nez. Cyrano de Bergerac a un grand nez.

Attention! Les humains ont des cheveux sur la tête, des poils (un poil) sur le corps. Les animaux n'ont pas de cheveux, ils ont des poils partout. Certains ont une fourrure. Les chats et les chiens n'ont pas de bras, pas de jambes: ils ont des pattes (une patte). Un oiseau, l'alouette par exemple, a des plumes (une plume), des ailes (une aile), une queue. Alouette! Je te plumerai.

Vocabulaire

aile, (*f.*) wing
à la place de instead
bouche, (*f.*) mouth
bras, (*m.*) arm
centimètre, (*m.*) centimeter
cheveux (*pluriel*) hair
cou, (*m.*) neck
corps, (*m.*) body
décrire to describe
demi-kilo, (*m.*) half a kilo, about a pound
dent, (*f.*) tooth
derrière, (*m.*) behind
doigt, (*m.*) finger; **doigt de pied,** (*m.*) toe
dos, (*m.*) back
épaule, (*f.*) shoulder
environ around, approximately
fort(e) strong (*or* fat)
fourrure, (*f.*) fur
glace, (*f.*) mirror (*also:* ice cream)
grand(e) tall (for people); large (for things)
gros(se) big, stout
haut(e) high, tall (for objects)
jambe, (*f.*) leg
langue, (*f.*) tongue (*or* language)
livre, (*f.*) pound
lunettes (*pluriel*) glasses
maigre skinny

main, (*f.*) hand
mesurer to measure
mètre, (*m.*) meter
mince thin
moyen average
nez, (*m.*) nose
oreille, (*f.*) ear
patte, (*f.*) animal leg
partout everywhere; le contraire est:
 nulle part nowhere
peser to weigh; *conjuguez comme* **lever:**
 je pèse, nous pesons
petit(e) small; short (for people)
pied, (*m.*) foot
plume, (*f.*) feather
poids, (*m.*) weight
poil, (*m.*) body hair, animal hair
poitrine (*f.*) chest
pour le moment for right now
queue /kø/, (*f.*) tail
roux(sse) red (for hair only)
taille, (*f.*) waist or size
tête, (*f.*) head
voisin, (*m.*) neighbor
voir to see
suffisant(e) sufficient
yeux (un œil) eyes

PRONONCIATION   Les sons /o/ et /ɔ/

Les lettres **o, au** représentent les deux sons /o/ fermé et /ɔ/ ouvert: **o, au, eau** sans consonne sont prononcés /o/; **o** avec **r, l, t, n** est prononcée /ɔ/.

	/o/	/ɔ/
RÉPÉTEZ:	stylo, moto, kilo	or, port
	cyrano	fort, corps, forme
	pot, dos	bol, sol, folle
	chaud, haut	note, botte, personne
	beau, château	

O, au avec **se** /z/ sont toujours /o/.

RÉPÉTEZ: rose, pose, chose, cause, pause

Beaucoup de mots en **-ome** sont prononcés /o/.

RÉPÉTEZ: atome, idiome, chrome, hippodrome, vélodrome, aérodrome.

Comparaison des sons /o/ et /ɔ/

/o/	/ɔ/
grosse	bosse (*bump*)
aube (*dawn*)	robe
Bône	bonne
paume (*palm*)	pomme
rauque (*hoarse*)	roc
Paule (une fille)	Paul (un garçon)

Mots particuliers avec /o/ et /ɔ/:

un os	/ɔs/	des os	/o/
alcool	/alkɔl/	les Vosges	/voʒ/
oignon	/ɔɲõ/	la Saône	/son/
automne	/otɔn/	Renault	/ʀəno/
rhum	/ʀɔm/	zoo	/zoo/

Contrastez les sons /o/, /ø/ dans les orthographes **o, au,** et **eu**

/o/	/ø/
dos	deux
pot	peux
vaut	veux
faut	feu
sot	ceux
mot	meut

Contrastez les sons /œ/, /ɔ/ dans les orthographes **eu, œu,** et **o**

/œ/	/ɔ/
leur	l'or
meurt	mort
sœur	sort
peur	pore
cœur	corps

Contrastez les sons /œ/ et /o/ dans les orthographes **eu** et **au**

/œ/	/o/
jeune	jaune
seul	saule
peur	Paule

Masques.

Mots difficiles

chevaux /ʃvo/, cheveux /ʃvø/
fourrure /fuʀyʀ/, rue /ʀy/, roux /ʀu/
poil, poids, poitrine, doigt, voisin /wa/
taille /aj/, oreille /ɛj/, derrière /jɛ/, œil /œj/, yeux /jø/
pied /je/, pays /ei/, ailes /ɛl/, ail (*garlic*) /aj/
Cyrano de Bergerac /siʀanodə bɛʀʒəʀak/

STRUCTURES   VERBES IRRÉGULIERS

	lire *to read*		**écrire** *to write*
je **lis**	nous **lisons**	j'**écris**	nous **écrivons**
tu **lis** /li/	vous **lisez** /liz/	tu **écris** /ekʀi/	vous **écrivez** /ekʀiv/
il, elle **lit**	ils, elles **lisent**	il, elle **écrit**	ils, elles **écrivent**

La conjugaison de ces deux verbes est parallèle. Seule la consonne du radical
change: **s,** nous lisons; **v,** nous écrivons. Conjuguez de la même façon: **relire** (*to
read over*), **décrire** (*to describe*).

Exercice I   Mettez la forme correcte des verbes **lire** ou **relire, écrire** ou **décrire.**

1. Nous _____ le journal.
2. _____ la lecture de la leçon quatre!
3. Je ne comprends pas cette lettre. _____ la lettre!
4. Ils _____ le même livre tous les mois!
5. _____ votre chambre!
6. J'_____ une lettre à mon petit ami.
7. Nous _____ le pays de nos vacances.
8. _____ un roman de six cents pages.
9. Ils _____ une composition.
10. Vous n'_____ pas à vos parents?

	voir *to see*		**croire** *to believe*	
	je **vois**		je **crois**	
	tu **vois**		tu **crois**	
	il, elle **voit**		il, elle **croit**	/wa/
	ils, elles **voient**		ils, elles **croient**	
	nous **voyons**		nous **croyons**	/wajõ/
	vous **voyez**		vous **croyez**	/waje/

La conjugaison de ces deux verbes est parallèle. Conjuguez de la même façon:
revoir (*to see again*).

Mettez la forme correcte du verbe indiqué.   *Exercice II*

(voir) 1. Je ne _____ pas sans mes lunettes.
            2. Vous _____ cette étoile dans le ciel?
            3. Les chats _____ la nuit.
            4. Nous _____ quelquefois des films intéressants à la télé.
(croire) 5. Tu _____ toutes ces histoires.
            6. Vous _____ que les hommes sont vraiment pacifistes?
            7. Je dis qu'il va faire froid demain. Il ne me _____ pas.

CONSTRUCTIONS A RETENIR

Expressions idiomatiques avec **avoir**

avoir les yeux bleus (*to have blue eyes*):

EXEMPLES: Elle **a les** yeux bleus.
            Il **a les** cheveux longs.

Employez le verbe **avoir** + une partie du corps avec l'article défini: **le, la, les.**
L'adjectif est après le nom, et accordé. La construction **Elle a des cheveux longs** est
possible mais moins idiomatique.
   Si l'adjectif précède le nom, l'article défini n'est pas possible. Il faut l'article
indéfini (**un** ou **des**): Elle a **un** petit nez.

Faites des phrases avec le vocabulaire suggéré.   *Exercice III*

1. Janine a   yeux   bruns
2. Vous   cheveux   roux?
3. Pierre (n'a pas) yeux   bleus
4. Il   yeux   verts
5. Les jeunes filles cheveux   longs
6. Céline   petite bouche   jolies dents

avoir l'air, avoir l'air de (*to look, to look like*):

EXEMPLE: Tu **as l'air triste.**   *You look sad.*
            Vous **avez l'air fatigué.**   *You look tired.*

Conjuguez **avoir.** Ajoutez le mot **l'air** (avec l'article). Ajoutez un adjectif au
masculin singulier.

Refaites les phrases avec l'expression **avoir l'air.**   *Exercice IV*

1. Jules est fort.
2. Cet exercice est facile.
3. Ces livres sont intéressants.
4. Tu es pâle, tu es malade?
5. Il a probablement un *A* à son examen, il est content.

EXAMPLE: Tu n'**as** pas **l'air de** travailler.   *You don't look like you are working* (*as if you were working*).

Conjuguez **avoir**, ajoutez **l'air de**; ajoutez l'infinitif.

Exercice V   Refaites les phrases avec **avoir l'air de** + infinitif.

1. Il dort.
2. Elle a des problèmes.
3. Vous comprenez.
4. Tu ne vois pas.

L'expression de quantité: **combien de, combien**

EXEMPLE: **Combien de dents** est-ce que vous avez?
Combien mesurez-vous?

Avec un nom employez **combien de** (comparez avec **beaucoup de**). Avec un verbe seul, sans objet, employez **combien.**

Exercice VI   Faites des questions avec les réponses suivantes.

1. J'ai quatre enfants.
2. Il a beaucoup d'argent.
3. Cette opération coûte cinq cent mille francs.
4. Il mesure un mètre quatre-vingt dix.
5. Elle pèse quatre-vingt-dix kilos.
6. Ils ont trois autos.

Le système métrique

EXEMPLES: Il mesure **1 m 80.**
Elle pèse **65 kilos.**
La Tour Eiffel mesure **300 mètres.**

1 centimètre = .3937 *inch*
1 mètre (100 centimètres) = 39.37 *inches* = 1 *yard* + 3.3 *inches*
1 kilomètre (1.000 mètres) = .6213 *miles*

1 gramme = .035 *ounces*
100 grammes = 3.52 *ounces*
500 grammes (une livre) = 17.6 *ounces* (*about* 1.1 *pounds*)
1.000 grammes (1 kilo) = 35.27 *ounces* (*about* 2.2 *pounds*)

1 litre = 1.05 *quarts*

Vive la simplicité du système métrique!

Exercice VII   Calculez votre poids et votre taille en français.

POINTS DE GRAMMAIRE

Le passé composé

EXEMPLES: Aujourd'hui je regarde la télévision.
Hier, j'**ai regardé** la télévision.
Aujourd'hui je mange du bifteck.
Hier **j'ai mangé** du bifteck.

C'est le temps d'une action accomplie, dans le passé.

Règle générale: On conjugue le verbe **avoir.*** On ajoute le participe passé: **regardé, fini, vendu.**

j'**ai** regardé	j'**ai** fini	j'**ai** vendu
tu **as** regardé	tu **as** fini	tu **as** vendu
il **a** regardé	il **a** fini	il **a** vendu
nous **avons** regardé	nous **avons** fini	nous **avons** vendu
vous **avez** regardé	vous **avez** fini	vous **avez** vendu
ils **ont** regardé	ils **ont** fini	ils **ont** vendu

Voici les formes des participes passés des verbes réguliers. Le participe passé des verbes en **-er** (1er groupe) est en **-é:**

Infinitif	*Part. Passé*	*Infinitif*	*Part. Passé*
parl**er**	parl**é**	aim**er**	aim**é**
étudi**er**	étudi**é**	mang**er**	mang**é**

Le participe passé des verbes en **-ir** (2ème groupe) est en **i:**

Infinitif	*Part. Passé*	*Infinitif*	*Part. Passé*
fin**ir**	fin**i**	chois**ir**	chois**i**
obé**ir**	obé**i**	pun**ir**	pun**i**

Le participe passé des verbes réguliers en **-dre** (3ème groupe) est en **u:**

Infinitif	*Part. Passé*	*Infinitif*	*Part. Passé*
ven**dre**	ven**du**	atten**dre**	atten**du**
enten**dre**	enten**du**	répon**dre**	répon**du**

Mettez les phrases suivantes au passé composé. Commencez la phrase par: **Hier...**   *Exercice VIII*
à la place de **Aujourd'hui.**

1. Aujourd'hui, je mange des pommes (**Hier,** _____). 2. Aujourd'hui, elle finit ses exercices avant le dîner. 3. Aujourd'hui, tu parles avec tes amis. 4. Aujourd'hui, il quitte la maison à 8 heures. 5. Aujourd'hui, ils choisissent un programme. 6. Aujourd'hui, nous dînons à 7 heures. 7. Aujourd'hui, vous écoutez la radio. 8. Aujourd'hui, tu réponds au téléphone. 9. Aujourd'hui, je rends mon livre à la bibliothèque. 10. Aujourd'hui, elles punissent leurs enfants. 11. Aujourd'hui, vous étudiez votre leçon.

*Voir Chapitre 12.

Le cheval aussi est fatigué.

A la forme négative, la négation entoure **avoir.**

EXEMPLES: Je **n'ai pas** mangé.   Nous **n'avons pas** aimé.
Tu **n'as pas** fini.   Vous **n'avez pas** choisi.
Il **n'a pas** vendu.   Ils **n'ont pas** entendu.
Elle **n'a pas** parlé.

Exercice IX   Mettez l'exercice VIII à la forme négative du passé composé.

Les fonctions des noms (objet)

Je fais **la cuisine.**
Tu téléphones **à Robert.**
Il habite **chez ses parents.**

Le nom **la cuisine** est objet direct (il est placé directement après le verbe). Le nom **Robert** est objet indirect (il y a la préposition **à** entre le verbe et le nom Robert). Le nom **ses parents** est objet de la préposition **chez** (c'est une autre préposition que **à**).

Le pronom objet direct

Je fais la cuisine.	Je **la** fais.
Tu vois le film.	Tu **le** vois.
Il punit les enfants.	Il **les** punit.

Le pronom objet direct est identique à l'article défini (masc. sing. **le**, fém sing. **la**, pluriel **les**). Il est placé avant le verbe.

J'entends **le** bus.	Je **l'entends.**
J'aime **la** musique.	Je **l'aime.**

Devant un verbe qui commence avec une voyelle, **le** et **la** sont élidés en **l'.**

La clé?	Je **la** cherche.
Les photos?	Je **les** regarde.
Le bus?	Je **l'attends.**
La musique?	Je **l'écoute.**

Attention aux verbes:

chercher	*to look for*	attendre	*to wait for*
regarder	*to look at*	écouter	*to listen to*

En anglais, ils ont une préposition; en français, ils ont un objet direct.

J'aime **mes enfants.**	Je **les** aime.
Il cherche **sa clé.**	Il **la** cherche.
Tu aimes **cette musique.**	Tu **l'aimes?**

Le nom objet direct est quelquefois défini par l'article ou par un autre mot: l'adjectif possessif ou l'adjectif démonstratif. Le pronom objet direct remplace le nom et ses adjectifs.

Mettez le pronom objet direct **le, la, l', les,** à la place du nom entre parenthèses.   *Exercice X*

1. Il trouve (ses chaussures).
2. Elle met (sa robe).
3. Nous faisons (notre toilette).
4. Vous prenez (l'autobus).
5. Je punis (mes enfants).
6. Vous aimez (les hippies).
7. Tu veux (le dernier gâteau)?
8. Ils aiment (le chocolat).
9. Elles ont (le temps).

Il **me** voit. Il **m'**attend.
Il **te** regarde. Il **t'**attend.
Il **vous** regarde. Il **vous** attend.
Il **nous** voit. Il **nous** attend.

Le pronom objet direct pour les autres personnes est: **me, m'; te, t'; nous; vous.**
Placez le pronom avant le verbe: **Il me regarde.**

Exercice XI Répétez les phrases avec les pronoms objets directs entre parenthèses.

1. Il comprend (me, te, nous, vous).
2. Elle aime (me, te, nous, vous).
3. Vous voyez (me, nous).
4. Ils croient (me, te, nous, vous).
5. Nous attendons (te, vous).

Utilisez le pronom direct avec **voici, voilà** pour traduire:

Here I am.   **Me voici.**
There they are.   **Les voilà,** etc.

Le pronom objet indirect

Elle **me** parle.
Il **te** téléphone.
Vous **nous** donnez votre adresse.
Elles **vous** écrivent.

Les verbes **parler, téléphoner, donner, écrire** prennent la préposition **à** devant le nom de personne. Ce nom est objet indirect. **Me, te (m', t'** devant une voyelle), **nous, vous** sont des pronoms objets indirects. Ils sont identiques aux formes du pronom objet direct. Comparez:

O.D.	O.I.
mon ami **me** comprend, il **m'**aime	il **me** parle et il **m'**écrit
ton ami **te** comprend, il **t'**aime	il **te** parle et il **t'**écrit
notre ami **nous** comprend, il **nous** aime	il **nous** parle et il **nous** écrit
votre ami **vous** comprend, il **vous** aime	il **vous** parle et il **vous** écrit

J'écris à Marie, je **lui** écris.
Il parle à son père, il **lui** parle.
Vous téléphonez à vos parents, vous **leur** téléphonez.

Lui, leur sont les pronoms objets indirects de la troisième personne, masculin et féminin. Ces formes sont différentes du pronom objet direct. Comparez:

O.D.	O.I.
son ami **le** comprend, il **l'**aime	il **lui** parle et il **lui** écrit
son ami **la** comprend, il **l'**aime	il **lui** parle et il **lui** écrit
leur ami **les** comprend, il **les** aime	il **leur** parle et il **leur** écrit

Répétez avec le pronom objet indirect qui correspond à la personne entre paren-   *Exercice XII*
thèses.

1. Votre enfant _____ parle en français? (vous)
2. Il _____ dit zut. (tu)
3. Elle _____ envoie des fleurs. (à sa mère)
4. Vous _____ écrivez. (à vos parents)
5. Ce chien _____ obéit. (à son maître)
6. L'étudiant _____ demande la permission de sortir. (je)
7. Vous _____ donnez votre composition. (au professeur)
8. Tu _____ lis une histoire. (à Suzanne et à Laurent)
9. Il _____ téléphone tous les jours. (à sa petite amie)
10. Elle _____ prête son auto. (à tous ses amis)

Le verbe pronominal

Je regarde mon image dans une glace.   Je **me** regarde.
Tu regardes ton image dans une glace.   Tu **te** regardes.
Il regarde son image dans une glace.   Il **se** regarde.
Elle regarde son image dans une glace.   Elle **se** regarde.
Nous regardons notre image dans une glace.   Nous **nous** regardons.
Vous regardez votre image dans une glace.   Vous **vous** regardez.
Ils regardent leur image dans une glace.   Ils **se** regardent.
Elles regardent leur image dans une glace.   Elles **se** regardent.

Je **me regarde** (infinitif: **se regarder**) est un verbe pronominal, un verbe toujours
conjugué avec un pronom. Les pronoms sont: **me, te, se, nous** et **vous.**

EXEMPLE: Je **m'**aime.   Nous **nous** aimons.
                 Tu **t'**aimes.   Vous **vous** aimez.
                 Il, elle **s'**aime.   Ils, elles **s'**aiment.

Si le verbe commence avec un voyelle, on a une élision de **me, te, se: m', t', s'.**
Remarquez:

1. Le deuxième pronom peut être objet direct ou objet indirect; ça dépend du
verbe. Comparez:

   il **me** regarde, je **me** regarde (O.D.)
   il **me** parle, je **me** parle (O.I.) **(parler à)**

2. Ce deuxième pronom est toujours **se** pour le 3ème personne (objet direct ou objet indirect). Comparez:

je l'aime   il **s'**aime   ⎫
je les aime   ils **s'**aiment   ⎬ O.D.
je lui parle   elle **se** parle   ⎫
je leur téléphone   ils **se** téléphonent ⎬ O.I.

je me regarde   *I look at myself*
tu te parles   *you talk to yourself*

Le verbe pronominal exprime quelquefois une action du sujet sur lui-même (*himself*). Il est réfléchi (*reflexive*).

nous nous aimons   *we love ourselves* (*each other*)
elles se téléphonent   *they phone* (*one another*)

S'il y a plusieurs (*several*) sujets le verbe pronominal est réciproque. Beaucoup de verbes pronominaux n'ont pas le sens réfléchi et n'ont pas le sens réciproque. Ils ont simplement la forme pronominale.

Conjuguez sur le même modèle: **se voir** (*to see oneself* or *each other*); **s'admirer** (*to admire oneself* or *each other*); **s'appeler** (*to be called*); **se raser** (*to shave* or *to be bored*); **se trouver** (*to be found* or *to be*).

Exercice XIII   Donnez les formes des verbes pronominaux.

1. Josette et Marguerite (se voir) tous les jours à l'école.
2. Nous (se téléphoner) après la classe.
3. Comment est-ce que vous (s'appeler)?
4. Elle (se regarder) dans la glace et elle (s'admirer).
5. Il (se raser) tous les matins.
6. Judith et David (s'aimer).
7. Tu (se trouver) beau?

LECTURES   1. Jolie Merveille et Julie Vilaine

«Je suis un être exceptionnel. Ma beauté est extraordinaire. Je regarde mon visage dans une glace, je me regarde, je vois une personne remarquable, et je m'admire. Regardez-moi, j'ai les cheveux longs, blonds et doux comme de la soie, des yeux bleus, immenses et rêveurs, des cils longs, longs (artificiels, bien sûr), une bouche délicate et rouge, des dents blanches et régulières, un cou élégant et des petites oreilles. Pour le corps, c'est encore plus merveilleux. Je suis admirablement proportionnée, avec une poitrine moyenne, des épaules et un dos bien droits. J'ai la taille fine, des mains adorables et des jambes de danseuse, des pieds ravissants, et des doigts de pied...

Bien sûr, je passe ma journée devant un miroir. Je suis si belle, je suis fascinée par ma personne et ma beauté. Un jour, c'est sûr, je vais faire du cinéma. Un producteur d'Hollywood va remarquer cette merveille 'moi,' et il va engager une nouvelle Greta Garbo. J'ai un nom, tout à fait ordinaire. Je le déteste: Je m'appelle Joséphine. Mais j'ai choisi mon nom d'actrice: c'est «Jolie Merveille.»

Dans une autre chambre, une autre jeune fille, la sœur de Jolie Merveille, regarde son visage dans la glace. Elle dit: «Comme je suis vilaine! Mes cheveux sont rares et maigres, mes dents ne sont pas droites. (Je les brosse, je vais chez le dentiste, mais le résultat est nul.) Je porte des lunettes épaisses. Mon nez est ridicule et j'ai les oreilles larges. Je suis trop petite et j'ai des complexes, alors j'ai faim et je mange des bonbons et des gâteaux toute la journée! Bien sûr, je suis grosse, mes pieds et mes mains sont énormes, et j'ai un gros derrière. Quelle horreur! Je suis une catastrophe de la nature. Ma sœur, elle, est bien plus belle que moi, elle a l'air d'une princesse: moi, je vais rester toute ma vie à la maison. Elle, elle va être une célébrité, un jour.» Pauvre «Julie Vilaine»!

Un paysan sympathique.

Le téléphone sonne: c'est un producteur de Hollywood qui appelle Mademoiselle Julie Vilaine. Jolie Merveille? Non, Julie Vilaine!! C'est une erreur? Mais non! Les jeunes filles comme Julie Merveille sont trop nombreuses, avec des cheveux trop blonds et des yeux bleus trop magnifiques. La Compagnie du Lion cherche une jeune fille pas belle du tout, avec des dents irrégulières et un caractère naturel, pour faire un film sur la «Fille de Frankenstein.»

C'est Vilaine qui a réussi. C'est une célébrité maintenant, et c'est Merveille qui reste à la maison, qui se regarde, s'admire, et se rase!

Vocabulaire

droit straight
engager to hire
épais(se) thick
être, (*m.*) being
fin thin (fine)

nombreux numerous
pas du tout not at all
ravissant ravishing, adorable
soie, (*m.*) silk
vilain(e) ugly

2. Le portrait du Français

L'histoire dit que la «race» française est un mélange aussi varié que la «race» américaine. Les invasions normandes du Nord, les Germains (les Francs) de l'Est, les Romains d'Italie et les Arabes et d'autres «Barbares» ont contribué à faire le «Français.» Alors le «Français moyen» n'est pas grand (mais le Général de Gaulle mesurait 1 m 90). Il est brun dans le Midi, mais blond avec les yeux bleus dans le Nord. Et les Français de la Martinique, de la Guadeloupe, de Tahiti et de Nouvelle Calédonie ont la peau brune, les yeux noirs.

Et le caractère? Le Français a une réputation: on dit qu'il est à la fois réaliste et idéaliste, généreux et avare, individualiste, sociable, gai, curieux, logique et fantaisiste, ingénieux. A l'étranger, on voit souvent le Français-type comme un homme charmant, charmeur, avec le visage d'Alain Delon ou de Jean-Paul Belmondo. Attention à son esprit! Il peut être très méchant, car il aime tout critiquer. Et la Française? Elle est grande et blonde comme Brigitte Bardot ou petite et brune. Elle est féministe et indépendante, comme Simone de Beauvoir, ou «popote,» bourgeoise, et souvent elle reste dans l'ombre de son mari.

3. La langue française dans le monde

On parle français dans certaines parties de la Suisse — à Genève, à Lausanne — et en Belgique, avec des expressions que les Français de France trouvent souvent «bizarres» ou amusantes. En Suisse, en Belgique on ne dit pas «soixante-dix, quatre vingt dix», on dit «septante, nonante,» comme dans le vieux français. Au Canada, à Québec, on parle aussi un français avec des expressions proches de la langue du XVIIe siècle, et avec beaucoup d'anglicismes, des expressions anglaises «traduites.» On «chèque» vos bagages et on mange des «chiens chauds.»

Une rue typique, au Maroc.

Mais regardez sur la carte du monde les pays où le français est la langue favorite des gens cultivés. Si la France n'a plus le rôle de «*leader*» qu'elle a gardé pendant des années, elle reste pourtant le symbole de la culture, de l'élégance, de l'esprit, d'un certain humour. L'animal emblème de la France est le coq. Cet oiseau fier, le roi de la basse-cour, se dresse sur ses pattes et chante «cocorico.» Il est un peu ridicule à côté de l'aigle américain, du lion britannique, et de l'ours russe. Mais son chant clair et joyeux a toujours réveillé les pays du monde

Vocabulaire

à l'étranger abroad
avare greedy, stingy
basse-cour, (*f.*) chicken yard
charmeur fascinating
coq, (*m.*) rooster
esprit, (*m.*) wit
Français moyen average Frenchman
fier proud
ingénieux skillful

méchant mean
mélange, (*m.*) mixture
ombre, (*f.*) shadow
ours, (*m.*) bear
peau, (*f.*) skin
«popote» she likes to stay at home and cook
réveiller to wake up

4. Poème

L'ESPÈCE HUMAINE

L'espèce humaine m'a donné
le droit d'être mortel
le devoir d'être civilisé
la conscience humaine
deux yeux qui d'ailleurs ne fonctionnent pas très bien
le nez au milieu du visage
deux pieds deux mains
le langage
l'espèce humaine m'a donné
mon père et ma mère
peut-être des frères on ne sait
des cousins à pelletées
et des arrière-grands-pères
l'espèce humaine m'a donné
ces trois facultés
le sentiment l'intelligence la volonté
chaque chose de façon modérée
trente-deux dents un cœur un foie
d'autres viscères et dix doigts
l'espèce humaine m'a donné
de quoi se dire satisfait.

RAYMOND QUENEAU
L'Instant Fatal, 1948.

Vocabulaire

à pelletées (**une pelle:** a shovel) full shovels of, in great quantity
arrière-grand-père (*m.*) great-grand father
cœur (*m.*) heart

d'ailleurs besides
espèce humaine (*f.*) human species
foie (*m.*) liver
fonctionner to work (*l'auteur porte des lunettes*)

Composition Décrivez votre personne. Décrivez votre petit ami (petite amie). Est-ce que vous vous admirez ou est-ce que vous vous détestez? Quels traits (*features*) aimez-vous particulièrement chez votre ami (amie)?

Le bon roi Dagobert

PRÉSENTATION   Les vêtements

Une étudiante parle:

Le matin je me réveille à 6 h 30. Je me lève; j'ai fait ma toilette le soir, alors je ne me lave pas le matin, juste le bout du nez; je m'habille: je mets mes sous-vêtements, puis, mes vêtements; généralement un pull et un pantalon: je préfère les jeans. Ce sont les vêtements de la mode actuelle, la mode unisexe. C'est tellement pratique. Je les achète dans des magasins pour filles ou garçons. Je mets des chaussettes et des souliers, et un manteau ou une veste, et s'il fait froid, je porte une écharpe, un bonnet et des gants. S'il pleut, je prends mon imper ou un parapluie. Mais un parapluie, ce n'est pas pratique à bicyclette. Un chapeau? pour se protéger du soleil. J'aime cette mode, les grosses ceintures, les gros bijoux, les colliers, les bagues, les bracelets.

Un étudiant parle:

Oui, moi aussi, je me lève à 6 h 30. Mais je travaille dans une banque, alors il faut «m'habiller»: pas de polo, pas de T-shirt, pas de jeans, pas de shorts, pas de tennis. Une chemise blanche et une cravate et un veston ou un costume, et des souliers. Quelle barbe! Ma petite amie travaille aussi, alors elle porte une jupe et une blouse, ou une robe et des bas de nylon. Surtout pas de mini, a dit le patron. Il les déteste, et les maxis aussi sont interdites; il dit que c'est la mode «hippie.» Ces gens sont conservateurs! Un jour, Suzie (mon amie s'appelle Suzie) a eu une idée bizarre: elle a mis un caftan pour aller travailler. Le patron lui a dit: «Pas de Carnaval à mon bureau.» Suzie n'a pas pu rester au bureau et on ne lui a pas compté cette journée dans son salaire! Maintenant, son caftan, elle ne le met pas pour aller au bureau.

Il faut aussi se raser, parce que la barbe donne un air suspect. Mon amie peut se maquiller, surtout les yeux, pour ça, le patron ne trouve pas que c'est exagéré. Moi, je crois que c'est terrible, cette autorité des patrons, des directeurs, sur la mode et les vêtements.

Bien sûr, on ne peut pas porter un maillot de bain ou un pyjama ou une robe de chambre au bureau, mais il faut être moins strict. Les patrons nous tyrannisent. Ils commencent à nous fatiguer.

Un jour, je veux être un patron libéral, avec des employés «hippies» et habillés comme ils veulent.

Vocabulaire

bague, (*f.*) ring
bas, (*m.*) stocking, hose
bijou, (*m.*) jewelry
bonnet, (*m.*) cap
bout, (*m.*) tip
ceinture, (*f.*) belt
bracelet, (*m.*) bracelet
chaussette, (*f.*) sock
chemise, (*f.*) shirt
collier, (*m.*) necklace
costume, (*m.*) suit

conservateur (-trice) conservative
cravate, (*f.*) tie
écharpe, (*f.*) scarf
faire sa toilette to wash oneself
gant, (*m.*) glove
gens, (*m. pl.*) people
imper(méable), (*m.*) raincoat
interdit; défendu forbidden
jupe, (*m.*) skirt
maillot de bain, (*m.*) swim suit
manteau (*m.*) coat

Une petite robe pratique
pour le bureau.

mettre to put on	**se lever** to get up
pantalon, (*m.s.*) pants	**se maquiller** to put make-up on
polo, (*m.*) T-shirt	**se réveiller** to awaken, to wake up
porter to wear	**soulier,** (*m.*) shoe
pull, (*m.*) sweater	**sous-vêtement,** (*m.*) underclothes
robe, (*f.*) dress	**suspect** suspicious
robe de chambre, (*f.*) robe	**tennis** (*pluriel*) tennis shoes
sac, (*m.*) purse	**veste,** (*m.*) girl's jacket, boy's sport jacket
s'habiller to get dressed	**veston,** (*m.*) jacket (top of suit)
se laver to wash, bathe	**vêtement,** (*m.*) clothes

PRONONCIATION L'enchaînement

> la mode̸ ‿actuelle
> il porte̸ ‿une cravate
> pas pratique̸ ‿à bicyclette

Dans un groupe, enchaînez la consonne avant le **e** muet final d'un mot et la voyelle qui commence le mot suivant.

Exercice I Entourez d'un cercle le groupe enchaîné.

EXEMPLE: mo (de̸ a) ctuelle

1. cette année
2. un bel été
3. quatre ans
4. un article indéfini
5. quelle heure
6. votre ami
7. la même idée
8. une table horrible
9. le peuple américain
10. notre époque

EXEMPLE: et̸ ‿un pull /e œ/
un manteau‿ou‿une /o u y/

En français, on enchaîne aussi les voyelles successives sans s'arrêter.

Exercice II Enchaînez les voyelles. Indiquez leurs symboles phonétiques.

1. Roger a un chien.
2. Elle va au marché.
3. Andrée a eu un bébé.
4. Il a eu une idée.
5. là-haut aussi
6. en haut et en bas
7. en mai et en juin
8. Il va à Arles.
9. Et où allez-vous?

La finale –er

Prononcez **–er** /ɛR/ dans les mots suivants; ce sont des exceptions à la règle de la page 11, Chapitre Préliminaire 2.

hiver   enfer   mer   fer   cher
cancer   imper   super   ver

Prononcez **–er** /e/ dans les mots suivants:

boucher   épicier   collier   soulier   papier
cahier   entier   léger   premier

Une succession de e muets

Étudiez les groupes suivants; un **e** muet tombe.

Je ne̸ /ʒən/   Je ne̸ sais pas.
Je ne̸ veux pas.
Je ne̸ crois pas.

Je mé /ʒəm/	Je mé lave.	Je mé rase.
	Je mé lève.	Je mé fâche.
Je lé /ʒəl/	Je lé veux.	
	Je lé crois.	
	Je lé peux.	
Jé m' /ʒma/	Jé m'habille.	Jé m'amuse.
	Jé m'assieds.	Jé m'approche.
Jé te /ʃtə/	Jé te vois.	Jé te dis.
	Jé te crois.	Jé te répète. (**t** change le /ʒ/ en /ʃ/)

Si on a une succession de **e** muets, on alterne: un **e** reste, un **e** tombe, un **e** reste, un **e** tombe, un **e** reste, etc.

EXEMPLES: Je né te rédemande pas. /ʒənətʀdəmãdpɑ/
Je né le répasse pas. /ʒənləʀpɑspɑ/
Je né me démande pas. /ʒənmədmãdpɑ/

VERBES IRRÉGULIERS STRUCTURES

mettre *to put*

je **mets**	nous **mettons**
tu **mets** /mɛ/	vous **mettez** /mɛt/
il, elle **met**	ils, elles **mettent**

Conjuguez de la même manière: **admettre** (*to admit*); **se mettre à** (*to begin*); **remettre** (*to put again, to postpone*).

Mettez la forme convenable du verbe **mettre, admettre, remettre.** *Exercice I*

1. _____ le livre sur la table. 2. Vous _____ l'usage de la drogue? 3. Il se _____ à pleurer. 4. Elles _____ des fleurs dans des vases. 5. Nous _____ nos papiers sur le bureau du professeur. 6. Je n'_____ pas le retard. 7. Tu _____ le même disque? 8. _____ ta robe bleue aujourd'hui!

vouloir *to want*	**pouvoir** *to be able to*
je **veux**	je **peux**
tu **veux**	tu **peux** /ø/
il, elle **veut**	il, elle **peut**
ils, elles **veulent**	ils, elles **peuvent** /œ/
nous **voulons**	nous **pouvons** /u/
vous **voulez**	vous **pouvez**

Remarquez les trois sons différents.

EXEMPLE: Tu **veux aller** au cinéma, ce soir?
Oui, si je **peux finir** mon travail avant.

Après ces deux verbes, mettez un infinitif direct (c'est-à-dire sans préposition).

Exercice II Répétez la phrase avec la forme correcte du verbe entre parenthèses.

(vouloir) 1. Tu vas à la plage dimanche?
2. Elle voit un bon programme à la télévision.
3. Nous passons une soirée tranquille à la maison.
4. Ils font un voyage en Grèce.

(pouvoir) 5. Tu regardes mon album de photos.
6. Je mange un autre gâteau?
7. Vous écrivez votre nom sur votre livre.
8. Elles disent non.

CONSTRUCTIONS A RETENIR

Les verbes **mettre** et **porter** (*to wear*)

Qu'est-ce que je vais **mettre** aujourd'hui?
Je vais **mettre** un pantalon, un pull et des sandales.
Qu'est-ce que vous **portez** aujourd'hui?
Je **porte** des blue jeans.

Employez **mettre** pour *to put on;* employez **porter** pour *to wear.*

Exercice III Répondez aux questions: Qu'est-ce que vous allez mettre pour...

1. aller à une soirée?   3. aller à la plage?
2. jouer au tennis?   4. la nuit?

Exercice IV Décrivez vos vêtements, les vêtements de votre voisin et de votre voisine avec le verbe **porter.**

Aujourd'hui je porte...
il porte...
elle porte...

L'expression **habillé de** (*dressed in*)

Comment est-ce qu'un boulanger **est habillé**?
Il **est habillé de** vêtements blancs.

Employez l'expression **habillé(e) de** pour *dressed in.*

Répondez aux questions. Choisissez l'expression appropriée dans la colonne de droite.   *Exercice V*

  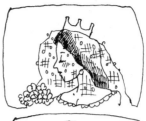 

Comment est-ce qu' 1. une Marocaine est habillée?
2. un prêtre
3. une mariée
4. un bonze bouddhiste
5. une dame riche
6. un étudiant pauvre
7. Mark Spitz aux Olympiques
8. Tarzan

un manteau de fourrure
une robe orange
un caftan
un T-shirt moche
un vêtement noir
un maillot de bain, 7
   médailles
une peau de panthère
une robe blanche

La question sur la matière: **en quoi est** (*what is... made of?*)

En quoi est votre robe? (le tissu: *material*)
Elle **est en** coton (le coton); elle **est en** soie (la soie: *silk*); elle **est en** tergal (le tergal); elle **est en** nylon (le nylon); elle **est en** laine (la laine: *wool*).

La construction est:

> le verbe **être** + en + un nom sans article

Voici les autres matériaux pour des articles divers:

l'or (*gold*), l'argent (*silver*), pour les bijoux; le bois (*wood*), le métal, le verre (*glass*), le cuir (*leather*), pour les ceintures, les souliers; le plastique, pour beaucoup de choses!

Répondez aux questions.   *Exercice VI*

1. En quoi est la maison?
2. En quoi est le livre?
3. En quoi sont vos bijoux?
4. En quoi sont vos souliers?
5. En quoi est la table?

POINTS DE GRAMMAIRE

Le passé composé

J'ai vu, j'ai pris, j'ai bu

Voici les participes passés et les passés composés des verbes irréguliers des leçons précédentes:

Infinitif	Part. Passé	Passé Composé
avoir	eu /y/	j'ai eu
être	été	j'ai été
faire	fait	j'ai fait
prendre	pris	j'ai pris
mettre	mis	j'ai mis
dire	dit	j'ai dit
écrire	écrit	j'ai écrit
lire	lu	j'ai lu
boire	bu	j'ai bu
voir	vu	j'ai vu
croire	cru	j'ai cru
pouvoir	pu	j'ai pu
vouloir	voulu	j'ai voulu

Exercice VII Mettez les phrases suivantes au passé composé. Commencez par «Hier,...» ou «L'autre jour...»

EXEMPLE: Aujourd'hui, tu fais tous tes exercices. **Hier** tu as fait tous tes exercices.

1. Nous écrivons une lettre.
2. Tu peux dormir toute la journée.
3. Il dit bonjour au professeur.
4. Je veux sortir.
5. Ils lisent un livre.
6. Nous voyons un film.
7. Vous entendez du bruit dans la rue.
8. Elle apprend sa leçon toute seule.
9. Elles ont un accident sur l'autoroute.
10. Pierre voit la comète.
11. Vous faites un bon voyage.
12. Tu prends l'avion?
13. Nous mettons une lettre à la poste.
14. Je finis un roman sensationnel.
15. Il boit du vin.

Répétez l'exercice VII à la forme négative du passé composé.   *Exercice VIII*

EXEMPLE: **Hier** tu n'as pas fait tous tes exercices.

La négation avec un pronom objet

Je **prends** mon imper.	Je **le** prends.	Je **ne le** prends **pas.**
Je **parle à** Paul.	Je **lui** parle.	Je **ne lui** parle **pas.**
	Je **me** lave.	Je **ne me** lave **pas.**

Remarquez l'ordre des mots si le verbe est à la forme négative:

$$\text{sujet} + \mathbf{ne} + \text{pronom} + \text{verbe} + \mathbf{pas}$$

Répétez à la forme négative.   *Exercice IX*

1. Elle les écoute. 2. Tu t'appelles Paul? 3. Ils se lavent le matin. 4. Nous leur téléphonons. 5. Vous vous réveillez à 5 heures. 6. Nous nous levons immédiatement. 7. Tu leur écris. 8. La Tour Eiffel se trouve à New York. 9. Vous la cherchez sur la carte. 10. Ils les achètent au marché.

L'impératif avec un pronom

Vous ne les regardez pas.	**Ne les** regardez pas!
Vous ne vous lavez pas.	**Ne vous** lavez pas!
Tu ne lui parles pas.	**Ne lui** parle pas!

Pour exprimer un ordre négatif, on supprime le sujet du verbe.

Répétez les phrases comme un ordre négatif (une défense).   *Exercice X*

1. Tu ne te lèves pas.   5. Nous ne leur parlons pas.
2. Nous ne nous habillons pas. 6. Vous ne vous levez pas.
3. Vous ne les écoutez pas.   7. Tu ne la mets pas.
4. Tu ne l'attends pas.   8. Vous ne lui écrivez pas.

Vous me regardez?	Regardez-**moi.**
Tu la regardes?	Regarde-**la.**
Nous les écoutons?	Ecoutons-**les.**
Vous vous regardez?	Regardez-**vous.**
Tu le mets?	Mets-**le.**
Vous lui parlez?	Parlez-**lui.**
Nous nous levons?	Levons-**nous.**
Tu te réveilles?	Réveille-**toi.**

Pour un ordre positif (*command*) le pronom est placé après l'impératif du verbe. Les pronoms sont: **moi, toi, nous, vous, le, la, les** (objets directs); **lui, leur** (objets indirects).

Exercice XI Répétez les phrases à l'impératif. Mettez un pronom à la place du nom.

1. Tu manges le bonbon.
2. Vous regardez ce programme.
3. Nous prenons les oranges.
4. Tu achètes ce gros bifteck.
5. Vous cherchez vos lunettes.
6. Nous apprenons la leçon 12.
7. Vous écrivez à vos parents.
8. Nous parlons à la vedette.

Exercice XII Répétez à la forme négative les phrases suivantes; exprimez une défense, ensuite un ordre positif.

EXEMPLE: Vous vous regardez.
       Vous ne vous regardez pas.
       Ne vous regardez pas!
       Regardez-vous!

1. Vous vous habillez.
2. Tu te maquilles.
3. Nous nous levons.

L'infinitif après un verbe: direct, avec **à**, avec **de**

Je **veux lire.** Je **peux lire.**
Je **commence** à lire.
J'**essaie de** lire.

Comme en anglais, un verbe comme **je veux, je commence, j'essaie** est suivi d'un infinitif. Mais en anglais, l'infinitif est *to read.* En français, c'est différent. Après le verbe **vouloir** l'infinitif est direct: **Je veux lire.** Après le verbe **commencer** il y a **à**: **Je commence à lire.** Après le verbe **essayer** il y a **de: J'essaie de lire.** Il n'y a pas de règle pour savoir si on n'a rien, ou **à**, ou **de.** Il faut apprendre la construction du verbe.

Voici une liste simple.

Verbes qui n'ont rien avant l'infinitif:

EXEMPLE: **J'aime lire.**

aimer	espérer (*to hope*)	il faut
préférer	vouloir	pouvoir

Verbes qui ont **à:**

EXEMPLE: **Je commence à écrire.**

commencer à
inviter (une personne) à
se mettre à (= commencer à)

avoir (une chose) à faire (*to have something to do*)
réussir à (*to succeed in*)

Verbes qui ont **de:**

EXEMPLE: . **J'ai envie de manger.**

avoir envie de   avoir peur de   décider de
défendre de (*forbid*)   essayer de   oublier de
refuser de

Répétez les phrases. Changez le verbe principal et la préposition.   *Exercice XIII*

1. J'aide Marie / à faire les exercices.
   Je commence / _____.
   J'oublie / _____.
   Pouvez-vous / _____ ?
2. J'aime / boire un verre de vin.
   J'invite Paul / _____.
   Ils décident / _____.
3. Nous espérons / aller mieux.
   Il commence / _____.

Essayez / _____ !
Nous nous mettons / _____.
Ils refusent / _____.

Le docteur me défend / _____.
Est-ce que vous voulez / _____ ?
J'ai envie / _____.
Vous refusez / _____.
Elle se met / _____.

Costumes régionaux en Bretagne.

L'infinitif avec un pronom

Le livre? Je **veux le** lire, je **commence à le** lire, j'**essaie de le** lire.

Si le verbe **(veux, commence, essaie)** est accompagné d'un infinitif, placez le pronom devant l'infinitif, après la préposition. Ne contractez pas **à + le**, **de + le** (ce **le** n'est pas un article, c'est un pronom).

Exercice XIV Répétez avec un pronom.

1. Nous pouvons comprendre la leçon.
2. J'ai peur de voir les films d'horreur.
3. Vous voulez regarder le match de football?
4. Elle se met à écouter la symphonie.
5. J'oublie d'apporter mon livre.
6. Ils réussissent à faire cet exercice.
7. Tu décides de manger le dernier gâteau.

LECTURES 1. Ken et Marcellin

Ken et Marcellin sont deux petits garçons qui habitent le même village. Ken est américain, Marcellin est français. Ils ont 12 ans, ils sont copains. Un dimanche matin, Marcellin arrive à la maison de Ken.

MARCELLIN: Salut, ça va?

KEN: Salut, ça va, et toi?

MARCELLIN: Moi, comme ci, comme ça.

KEN: Allez, on va s'amuser. On va jouer au foot?

MARCELLIN: Oui, je voudrais* bien, mais...

KEN: Mais quoi???

MARCELLIN: Regarde-moi, mes vêtements. C'est dimanche. Ma mère m'a dit qu'il faut «m'habiller». Alors je ne peux pas jouer! Je vais être tout sale si je joue au foot. Ma mère m'a dit: «Surtout, ne te salis pas».

KEN: Ah! Ah! S'habiller, bien sûr on «s'habille», on ne peut pas aller nu, c'est défendu.

MARCELLIN: Oui, mais «s'habiller» veut dire aussi mettre ses vêtements chic, ses vêtements du dimanche.

KEN: Ah! C'est pour ça que tu es si beau! Tu as mis un pantalon gris clair, une chemise blanche, une cravate, des souliers noirs, une veste, hou, là, là.

MARCELLIN: Ah! tu te moques de moi. C'est pas chic. Toi, tu as de la chance de pouvoir porter un blue jean et un polo et des vieilles tennis, le dimanche. C'est bien plus confortable. Moi, je ne peux pas le faire.

---

*La forme **voudrais** est un conditionnel plus fréquent que le présent: *I would like to; I wish I could.*

KEN: C'est vrai, en Amérique on s'habille plus simplement, on est plus pratique. Ma mère aussi porte des jeans et des pulls, mais, je trouve que ta mère est plus élégante, avec sa jupe et ses bas. Et puis, ma mère, elle a toujours des bigoudis sur la tête, même pour aller au marché. Les femmes, en Amérique, adorent les bigoudis...

MARCELLIN: Quelle barbe, alors! Je ne peux pas jouer au foot. Toute la famille va à l'église à 11 h.

KEN: Ah oui, c'est vrai, il y a l'église.

MARCELLIN: Tu ne vas pas à l'église, toi?

KEN: Non, ma famille est athée, mais mes cousins de Boston, ils vont à l'église le dimanche; alors, ils s'habillent: costumes, chapeaux et tout.

MARCELLIN: Un chapeau sur les bigoudis? Ah, Ah, Ah!

KEN: (*Vexé*) Ah. ça va. Regarde-toi, avec tes habits du dimanche.

MARCELLIN: Bon, alors, quand est-ce qu'on va pouvoir jouer?

KEN: Après la messe, dépêche-toi d'enlever tes vêtements chic, mets un short et un polo, et allons sur la place jouer au basket ou au foot.

MARCELLIN: Impossible. Après la messe, il y a le déjeuner qui dure 2 heures. Et les visites des cousins, des oncles, des tantes.

KEN: Flûte! A mercredi alors. Vive le mercredi! C'est le meilleur jour de la semaine!

Vocabulaire

athée atheist

basket, foot beaucoup de sports ont un nom anglais, mais les Français ne disent pas «*ball*» après, ou alors ils prononcent /bal/

bigoudi, (*m.*) curler

ça va; *ici*: **ça suffit** that's enough

c'est pour ça que that's why

c'est pas chic **ne** est absent dans la langue populaire

dépêche-toi (de **se dépêcher**) to hurry up

église, (*f.*) church

foot European football (soccer)

flûte shucks

habit, (*m.*) clothes

jouer à to play (a game)

nu naked

sale dirty

se moquer to mock, to make fun of

se salir (*2ème groupe*) to get dirty

2. La mode en France

Quand on voyage en France, quand on se promène dans les rues commerçantes d'une ville, on est frappé par l'élégance des magasins de vêtements et aussi par leur qualité et leur prix. Quelle tentation pour les gens qui aiment s'habiller! Et en France beaucoup de femmes — et d'hommes — sont très soucieux de leur toilette. Récemment encore les petits Français (et les grands) passaient leur dimanche habillés de leurs plus beaux vêtements et il fallait bien faire attention de ne pas se salir! Mais dans certaines familles, on est plus «relaxed,» on garde ses vieux vêtements pour le weekend, pour jardiner ou se reposer. Et les étudiants français copient les Américains, portent des jeans troués et passés et des T-shirts imprimés.

La mode de Paris.

Mais pour beaucoup de Français la mode est tyrannique. Et les journaux féminins sont très stricts sur ce qui «se fait», ce qui «date.» La Haute-Couture donne le ton, chaque saison, avec ses présentations de collection: les noms des couturiers «Yves Saint-Laurent, Pierre Cardin, Courrèges» sont connus dans le monde entier. Peu de femmes peuvent s'habiller chez eux: leurs prix sont exorbitants. Mais le «prêt-à-porter» est plus abordable, et il y a toujours une petite couturière de quartier qui peut copier un grand modèle (les Françaises font moins de couture que les Américaines). La «mode» du monde entier vient de Paris. Une année, c'est la mini-jupe, une autre la jupe qui touche par terre, le «new-look», et le pantalon; une Française se sent insultée et ridicule si elle n'est pas «à la mode.» Une mode qui ne change pas, c'est la mode régionale, les vieux costumes bretons, alsaciens, provençaux, avec leurs broderies délicates et leur charme provincial.

abordable raisonnable
ce qui date what is outdated
ce qui se fait what is being done
couturier, (*m.*) designer
couturière, (*f.*) seamstress
faire de la couture to sew
Haute-Couture, (*f.*) fashion
il fallait *imparfait de* **il faut**
on est frappé one is struck

passaient *imparfait* (voir Chapitre 14)
 used to spend
passés faded
prêt-à-porter, (*m.*) «ready-to-wear»
rue commerçante, (*f.*) une rue avec
 beaucoup de magasins
soucieux worried
troués with holes

Décrivez les vêtements que vous portez aujourd'hui. Quels vêtements portez-vous en hiver, en été, et pour les différentes activités de votre vie? Quels autres vêtements est-ce qu'il y a dans votre placard? Est-ce qu'il y a une mode, passée, ou future, qui a votre préférence?

Composition

● PRÉSENTATION: L'histoire d'une vie

● PRONONCIATION: la lettre **y**
                   h aspiré
                   le **e** muet
                   mots difficiles

● STRUCTURES:

Verbes irréguliers: **partir, sortir, dormir, venir**

Constructions à retenir: les verbes **visiter, aller voir** (*to visit*)
                               les verbes **sortir, partir, quitter, laisser** (*to leave*)
                               les expressions de temps: **l'année dernière, la semaine dernière, hier soir**

Points de grammaire: le passé composé avec **être**
                               le passé composé des verbes pronominaux
                               la forme négative de ces verbes
                               la place de l'adverbe
                               l'adverbe **y**
                               les prépositions **en, au, de** avec des noms de pays

● LECTURES: 1. «Pour toi mon amour» JACQUES PRÉVERT
                   2. Les études en France

● EXCLAMATION: Quelle vie de chien!
  EXPRESSION: Un rat de bibliothèque

A la claire fontaine

Chapitre 12

A la clai — re fon — tai — ne   m'en al — lant

pro — me — ner,   j'ai trou — vé   l'eau si bel — le

que je m'y suis bai — gnée.   Il y a long —

temps que je t'ai — me,   ja — mais je ne   t'ou — blie — rai.

PRÉSENTATION   L'histoire d'une vie

Sans paroles.

Je suis né à _____ dans l'état de _____ .

Mon amie Simone est née en France, dans un petit village.

J'ai habité dans cette ville pendant _____ ans, et puis nous ne sommes pas restés... Ma famille a déménagé et nous sommes allés en _____ dans la ville de _____ . Mon amie Simone est allée au Maroc, avec sa famille. Elle a passé son enfance dans ce pays magnifique.

Je suis allé à l'école élémentaire de _____ , puis à l'école secondaire. J'y ai étudié l'anglais, les maths, le latin, les sciences naturelles et l'histoire, et aussi le français. Mon amie Simone, vous l'avez deviné, est française; elle est allée à l'école élémentaire, puis au lycée: le lycée c'est l'école secondaire (*high school*) des Français. Elle y a étudié les langues classiques, le latin, le grec, le français, l'anglais, les maths (toujours les maths), l'histoire et le géographie, les sciences naturelles et aussi (quelle horreur!), la chimie et la physique. L'emploi du temps d'une lycéenne (ou d'un lycéen) est très lourd. On étudie ces matières pendant six ans, tous les ans. Il y a aussi la gymnastique, le dessin, le chant et la couture (pas pour les garçons, la couture; eux, ils étudient la mécanique ou l'électricité. Les écoles françaises sont sexistes!)

Bon. Nous avons beaucoup étudié, n'est-ce pas? Nous avons trop étudié et nous avons beaucoup oublié, aussi. Mais au moins, en Amérique, nous n'avons pas à passer un examen à la fin de nos études, comme le baccalauréat.

Pendant les années 1939–1945, il y a eu la guerre. Moi, je suis jeune; je ne suis pas allé à la guerre. Vous, vous êtes jeunes, vous êtes nés après la guerre, vous ne vous rappelez pas, peut-être. Mais mon amie, au Maroc, a vu l'arrivée des troupes américaines. La guerre au Maroc n'a pas été aussi terrible qu'en France. En France, il y a eu l'occupation, les restrictions. Beaucoup de gens ont été très malheureux et beaucoup sont morts.

Après l'école secondaire, j'ai déménagé et je suis allé au *college* à _____ dans l'état de _____. Mon amie Simone est revenue en France avec sa famille et elle est allée à l'université de Paris, à la Sorbonne, pour y faire des études supérieures.

Quand j'ai quitté ma famille pour la première fois, j'ai bien pleuré. J'ai laissé des objets familiers, mon chien, mes parents; mon amie a pleuré aussi parce qu'elle a perdu ses amis, et le soleil et les plages magnifiques du Maroc.

Mais au *college* je me suis bien amusé. Il y a eu des moments difficiles: les études, les examens; mais je me rappelle beaucoup de moments agréables: les bals d'étudiants, les matches de foot contre l'équipe de l'université voisine, et les visites à la grande ville proche où il y a des musées et des monuments intéressants. Et puis j'ai fait un voyage en Europe en 19—. J'ai visité tous les musées de Paris, enfin presque: j'ai visité le Louvre, le Jeu de Paume; je suis allé au théâtre, je me suis promené sur les grands boulevards, sur les Champs Élysées, aux Halles de Paris, je suis monté sur la Tour Eiffel et sur les tours de Notre-Dame, je suis descendu dans les Catacombes.

Et vous, pouvez-vous raconter l'histoire de votre vie? Où est-ce que vous êtes né? Ou est-ce que vous avez habité pendant votre enfance? Est-ce que vous avez déménagé? Est-ce que vous êtes resté dans la même ville? Est-ce que vous êtes allé à l'école élémentaire, à l'école secondaire? Est-ce que vous êtes allé à un *college,* ou à deux ou trois? Est-ce que vous êtes fiancé, marié? Si oui, quand est-ce que vous vous êtes fiancé, quand est-ce que vous vous êtes marié? Si non, quand est-ce que vous allez vous y mettre?

Vocabulaire

déménager to move (from a house)
deviner to guess
descendre to go down
enfance, (*f.*) childhood
lycée, (*m.*) (aussi **le musée**) high school (Ce sont des exceptions à la règle des mots en –ée.) On dit aussi **le collège** pour *high school*; un collège en France donne un enseignement technique, ou commercial, ou général (CEG). Le lycée prépare à l'université (*college*).
lourd heavy
malheureux (le contraire de **heureux**) unhappy
matière, (*f.*) *ici:* subject
monter to go up
mort dead

natale *ici:* où vous êtes né
né(e) born; **je suis né** I was born
oublier to forget
passer un examen to take an exam; to pass: **réussir (à)**
pendant for (avec passé composé, si l'action est finie)
proche voisin; qui est à côté
s'amuser to have fun
s'ennuyer to be or to get bored
se fiancer to become engaged
se marier to get married
se promener faire une promenade (conjuguez-le comme **lever: je me promène, nous nous promenons**)
se rappeler to remember

PRONONCIATION   La lettre **y**

Prononcez la lettre **y** /i/.

J'**y** suis allé.   Ils **y** vont.   lycée gymnastique

Prononcez **y** /ij/.

J'**y ai** étudié. /ijɛ/   il **y a** /ijɑ/
Il **y est** allé.   Ils **y ont** été.

H aspiré

Il y a des mots en français qui commencent par un **h** aspiré. Ce **h** n'est pas prononcé; mais on ne fait pas la liaison et on ne fait pas l'élision.

COMPAREZ: l'homme   **le/héros**
             les‿horreurs   **les/Halles**

Voici quelques mots courants:

une/**hache** (*hatchet*)   l'adjectif/**haut** (c'est/**h**aut)
une/**halte**   l'adverbe en/**haut**
le/**hareng** (*herring*)   les/**Hauts** de Seine
La/**Hollande**   les/**Hollandais**
le/**hasard**   le/**Havre**
la/**Hongrie**   les/**Hongrois**

COMPAREZ: les‿hommes   les/**Hongrois**
             les zéros   les/**héros**
             les‿auteurs   les/**hauteurs**
             en‿eau   en/**haut**

Le **e** muet

Dans les chansons et en poésie, il est nécessaire de prononcer certains **e** muets qui tombent dans la conversation.

EXEMPLE: A la claire fontaine
            J'ai trouvé l'eau si bell**e** qu**e** j**e** m'y suis baignée.

Dans le Sud de la France, on prononce aussi les **e** muets qui tombent dans le Nord.

EXEMPLE: Un**e** petit**e** fill**e** pass**e** sur la plac**e** publiqu**e**.

Comparez les prononciations:

dans le Midi	*à Paris*
plus de pommes de terre	plus de̸ pomme̸ṣ de terre̸
plus de petites tomates	plus de̸ petites tomate̸ṣ
pas de chance	pas de̸ chance̸
assez de remarques	assez de̸ remarque̸ṣ

Mots difficiles

lycéen /eɛ̃/, lycéenne /eɛn/; européen /eɛ̃/ européenne /eɛn/
baccalauréat /bakalorea/
Le Louvre /ləluvʀ/ (chuchotez **ʀ**!)
Le Jeu de Paume /ləʒø̸dpom/
Les Champs-Élysées /leʃãzelize/
Les Halles /leal/
La Tour Eiffel /laturefɛl/
Les Catacombes /lekatakõb/

STRUCTURES VERBES IRRÉGULIERS

partir *to leave*	**sortir** *to go out*	**dormir** *to sleep*
je pars̸	sors̸	dors̸
tu pars̸	sors̸	dors̸
il par̸t	sor̸t	dor̸t
nous partons	sortons	dormons
vous partez	sortez	dormez
ils partent	sortent	dorment

Ces trois verbes ont la même caractéristique: pour les personnes du singulier la consonne finale du radical (**t, m**) est absente.

Pour les personnes du pluriel (**nous, vous, ils-elles**), on entend la consonne du radical.

Conjuguez à la personne indiquée.   *Exercice I*

1. Ils (partir) _____ pour Paris? 2. Vous (sortir) _____ ce soir? 3. Il (dormir) _____ le dimanche matin? 4. Je (sortir) _____ avec ma sœur. 5. Nous (partir) _____ à midi. 6. Tu (dormir) _____ en classe? 7. Ils (sortir) _____ avec leurs amis. 8. Je (dormir) _____ toute la nuit?

Un verbe plus irrégulier que les autres:

venir *to come*

je **viens**	nous **venons**
tu **viens** /vjɛ̃/	vous **venez** /vn/
il, elle **vient**	ils, elles **viennent** /vjɛn/

Conjuguez sur ce modèle: **revenir** (*to come back*) et **devenir** (*to become*).

Exercice II   Mettez la forme correcte du verbe indiqué.

1. Il (revenir) _____ de France. 2. Nous (venir) _____ à l'école tous les jours.
3. Ils (venir) _____ à 8 heures. 4. Tu (venir) _____ au marché avec moi?
5. Vous (devenir) _____ très bons en français. 6. Je (revenir) _____ dans mon pays.

Note: Le passé composé de **dormir** est: **J'ai dormi.** Pour **partir, sortir, venir,** voir page 187.

CONSTRUCTIONS A RETENIR

Les verbes **visiter, aller voir** (*to visit*)

Je **visite** une ville, un musée, un pays.
Je **vais voir** des amis.

Employez **visiter** pour un endroit; **aller voir** pour une personne.

Exercice III   Mettez la forme correcte (au temps correct) du verbe **visiter** ou **aller voir.**

1. En 1973 nous sommes allés en Europe et nous _____ six pays.
2. Ils _____ l'Italie, la France, l'Espagne et l'Angleterre.
3. Si vous allez en France, _____ mes cousins à Paris.
4. Et aussi, il faut _____ la cathédrale de Chartres.
5. Est-ce que Brigitte _____ ses parents à la campagne?

Les verbes **sortir, partir, quitter, laisser** (*to leave*)

EXEMPLES: Je **sors.**
Ils **partent** lundi.
Je **quitte** la classe.
Je **laisse** mes livres ici.

Il y a beaucoup de verbes pour traduire *to leave.*

Sortir veut dire *to leave a room, to get out,* et aussi *to go out at night* ou *to date someone:*

Je **sors de la classe.** (Le contraire est: **j'entre dans** la classe)
Il **sort avec Marguerite.**

Partir veut dire *to leave, to depart, to take off.* Il n'y a pas d'objet direct avec **partir.**
On part pour un pays, pour une destination.

> Ils **partent** lundi **pour l'Espagne.** (Le contraire est: **ils arrivent**)

Quitter veut dire *to leave a place.* Il y a un objet direct obligatoire avec **quitter.**

> Je **quitte la France.**
> Je **quitte l'université.**

Attention! *I quit!* = **J'abandonne!**

Laisser veut dire *to leave behind* (*and to forget*). Il y a un objet direct obligatoire
avec **laisser.**

> **J'ai laissé mon livre** à la maison.

Mettez la forme correcte de *to leave.*   *Exercice IV*

1. Elle _____ ses affaires sur le divan du salon.
2. Est-ce que Josette _____ avec son petit ami, ce soir? (*to date*)
3. Mes parents _____ pour un voyage autour du monde.
4. Elle _____ de la classe et dit «ouf!»
5. Mon mari _____ son travail.

A l'intérieur du Louvre.

L'Arc de Triomphe du Carrousel.

Les expressions de temps: la dernière année, l'année dernière

L'adjectif **dernier** peut se placer après le nom. Il a un sens différent:

la dernière année veut dire *the last year* (*of his life, of your studies*)
l'année dernière veut dire *last year*
la dernière semaine veut dire *the last week* (*of a period*)
la semaine dernière veut dire *last week*

On dit: **lundi dernier, mardi dernier.**

Attention! *last night,* c'est **hier soir** (pour **la soirée**) ou **la nuit dernière** (pour **la nuit**).

Hier soir, j'ai regardé la télévision jusqu'à minuit.
La nuit dernière j'ai eu un rêve affreux.

Exercice V Mettez **dernier** dans ces phrases, à la place correcte.

1. (La semaine) de l'année est pleine d'activités pour les fêtes.
2. (Le mois) il a travaillé 140 heures.
3. (L'année) de sa vie, il a été très malade.
4. (La semaine) il a fait très beau.
5. (La nuit) il y a eu un orage terrible; je n'ai pas pu dormir.

POINTS DE GRAMMAIRE

Le passé composé avec **être**

Je **suis né.**   Je **suis allée.**   Nous **sommes arrivés.**
Il **est parti.**   Elle **est sortie.**

Certains verbes n'ont pas l'auxiliaire **avoir** au passé composé. Ils ont l'auxiliaire **être.** On conjugue le verbe **être,** on ajoute le participe passé:

Singulier	*Pluriel*
je **suis allé, allée**	nous **sommes allés, allées**
tu **es allé, allée**	vous **êtes allé, allée, allés, allées**
il **est allé**	ils **sont allés**
elle **est allée**	elles **sont allées**

Le participe avec **être** est comme un adjectif. Il s'accorde avec le sujet.

EXEMPLES: **Nous** sommes **pâles.**   **Elles** sont **grandes.**
            Nous sommes **allés.**   **Elles** sont **venues.**

Voici le participe passé des verbes qui se conjuguent avec **être:**

	Infinitif	*Part. Passé*	*Exemples*
en **é**	all**er**	all**é**	Je suis allé.
	arriv**er**	arriv**é**	Tu es arrivé.
	entr**er**	entr**é**	Il est entré.
	mont**er**	mont**é**	Nous sommes montés.
	rest**er**	rest**é**	Vous êtes restés.
	tomb**er**	tomb**é**	Ils sont tombés.
	rentr**er**	rentr**é**	Elles sont rentrées.
en **-i**	part**ir**	part**i**	Je suis parti.
	sort**ir**	sort**i**	Elle est sortie.
en **-u**	descend**re**	descend**u**	Elle est descendue.
	ven**ir**	ven**u**	Nous sommes venus.

Remarque: Cette liste est presque complète. Ce sont presque tous des verbes de mouvement — sauf **rester.** Il y a aussi les deux formes irrégulières:

Je **suis né (naître,** *to be born). I was born.*
Il **est mort (mourir,** *to die). He died.*

On peut résumer la liste de ces verbes par un dessin.

La Maison d'Être

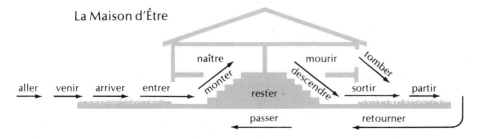

Exercice VI   Mettez les phrases suivantes au passé composé. Commencez la phrase par: **Hier,...**

1. Je vais au marché.
2. Il tombe dans l'escalier.
3. Elle arrive à midi.
4. Ils entrent à l'université.

5. Vous partez à 10 heures.
6. Elles sortent avec leurs amis.
7. Nous venons à l'école en taxi.
8. Je descends par l'ascenseur.

Le passé composé des verbes pronominaux

Je me lave.	Je me **suis lavé.**
Tu te réveilles.	Tu t'**es réveillé.**
Il se rase.	Il s'**est rasé.**
Elle se regarde.	Elle s'**est regardée.**
Nous nous coiffons.	Nous nous **sommes coiffés.**
Vous vous habillez.	Vous vous **êtes habillés.**
Elles se maquillent.	Elles se **sont maquillées.**
Ils se parfument.	Ils se **sont parfumés.**

Le verbe pronominal est conjugué avec **être.** Le participe passé est comme un adjectif, il est accordé avec le sujet: **Ils se sont aimés.** Il y a quelques exceptions. Rappelez-vous: **Ils se sont parlé; Elles se sont téléphoné.**

Exercice VII   Écrivez les phrases au passé composé.

1. Le matin il se réveille à 6 h. Hier,...
2. D'habitude je me lève à 7 h. Hier,...
3. Aujourd'hui nous nous couchons tôt. Hier,...
4. Tous les jours elle se maquille. Hier,...
5. Tu te rases? _____ ce matin.
6. Marie-Claude se parfume. _____ pour le bal.
7. Elles se coiffent élégamment. La semaine dernière...
8. Je m'amuse. Hier soir...
9. Il s'ennuie. A cette soirée...

Exercice VIII   Mettez les phrases suivantes au passé composé avec **être** ou **avoir.**

1. Elle lit un article intéressant.
2. Vous restez à la maison?
3. Je sors avec un ami.
4. Nous allons au match de foot.
5. Tu regardes la télévision.
6. Il voit un bon film.
7. Elle se lève.
8. Ils montent sur le Mont Blanc.
9. Vous comprenez la leçon?
10. Je pars à midi et j'arrive à deux heures.
11. Ils entrent dans un restaurant et ils commandent un repas.

12. Je m'habille.
13. Elle reste à la maison et dort toute la journée.
14. Ils payent à la caisse et la caissière rend la monnaie.
15. Elles font du ski et elles tombent souvent.
16. Nous nous réveillons.
17. Ils viennent en Europe et ils montent sur les montagnes.
18. Vous entrez à l'université et vous commencez vos études.
19. Vous vous baignez?
20. Tu te rases.

La forme négative de ces verbes

Nous avons vu.	**Nous n'**avons **pas** vu.
Je suis allé.	**Je ne** suis **pas** allé.
Il s'est baigné.	**Il ne** s'est **pas** baigné.

A la forme négative du passé composé, la négation est toujours à la même place:
ne immédiatement après le sujet; **pas** après l'auxiliaire.

Répétez les phrases suivantes à la forme négative.   *Exercice IX*

1. Tu as mangé.   6. Ils sont venus.
2. Ils sont partis.   7. Je me suis amusé.
3. Elle s'est parfumée.   8. Elles se sont promenées.
4. Nous avons voyagé.   9. Tu t'es rappelé.
5. Vous êtes descendus.   10. Il s'est moqué de son amie.

La place de l'adverbe

J'ai mangé.	J'ai mangé **simplement.**	J'ai **bien** mangé.
Tu es sorti.	**Hier** tu es sorti.	Tu es **beaucoup** sorti.

Les adverbes en **–ment** sont placés après le verbe; les adverbes de temps comme
hier, aujourd'hui sont placés au commencement de la phrase, ou à la fin.
   Certains adverbes sont placés entre l'auxiliaire et le participe passé du verbe.
Ces adverbes sont: **beaucoup, trop, assez, bien, mal, encore, déjà, toujours, souvent.**
A la forme négative, on a: **pas bien, pas mal, pas encore,** etc.

Répétez les phrases avec l'adverbe indiqué.   *Exercice X*

1. (beaucoup) Il a travaillé.
2. (trop) Tu as mangé.
3. (mal) Elle a compris.
4. (encore) Vous avez fait des fautes.
5. (déjà) J'ai entendu cette chanson.
6. (souvent) Ils n'ont pas voyagé.

7. (toujours) Elles ont été gentilles.
8. (bien) Tu as répondu.
9. (assez) J'ai aimé le film.
10. (mal) Elle est tombée.
11. (déjà) Elle s'est levée.
12. (encore) Est-ce qu'ils sont sortis?
13. (bien) Vous êtes arrivés.
14. (souvent) Elles sont venues.
15. (ne pas encore) Tu t'es promené dans la ville?
16. (toujours) Nous sommes restés amis.
17. (beaucoup) Ils sont tombés pendant leurs vacances de ski.
18. (trop) Tu es sortie avant ton examen.
19. (assez) Je ne me suis pas amusée.
20. (déjà) Est-ce qu'ils sont arrivés?

L'adverbe **y**

Vous allez en France.	Vous y allez.
Je vais à Paris.	J'y vais.
Nous sommes dans la classe.	Nous y sommes.
Le crayon n'est pas sur la table.	Il n'y est pas.

On emploie **y** à la place d'un nom objet des prépositions **en, à, sur** et **dans** qui indiquent la localisation.

Exercice XI   Refaites les phrases avec **y.**

1. Nous allons en France.
2. Vous restez à la maison, ce soir?
3. Elle parle des heures au téléphone.
4. Il n'a pas mis son argent à la banque.
5. Ils arrivent en retard au restaurant.
6. Elle envoie sa fille à l'université de Paris.
7. Nous sommes dans la classe.
8. Vous allez au cinéma ce soir?
9. Mes gants ne sont pas dans mon sac.
10. Ils ont fait un voyage merveilleux au Mexique.
11. Allez au marché sans moi.

Les prépositions **en** et **au** avec un nom de pays

Les noms de pays ont un genre: masculin ou féminin (**le Mexique, la France**). On emploie **en** devant les noms féminins et les noms masculins qui commencent par une voyelle. On emploie **au** devant les noms masculins qui commencent par une consonne.

en	Argentine	Bolivie	Colombie
	Egypte	Algérie	Tunisie
	Syrie	Grèce	Belgique
	Allemagne		

Ce sont des pays féminins.

en	Iran	Israël	Uruguay

Ce sont des pays masculins qui commencent par une voyelle.

au	Brésil	Chili	Luxembourg	**aux** Pays-Bas
	Danemark	Maroc	Portugal	
	Vénézuela	Pérou		

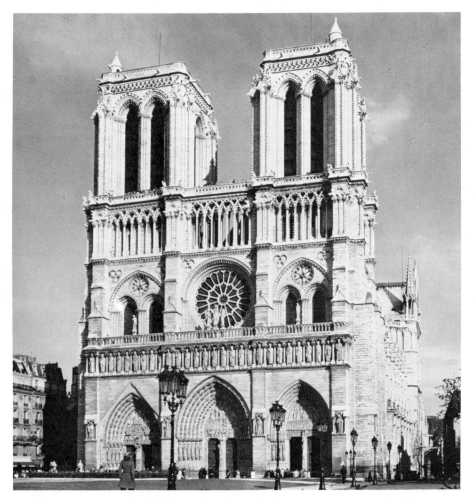

Notre-Dame de Paris.

Ce sont des noms de pays masculins avec une consonne initiale. La règle est la même pour les noms des provinces françaises.

la Bretagne	**en Bretagne**
la Normandie	**en Normandie**
la Province	**en Provence**

Ce sont des noms féminins.

l'Anjou	**en Anjou** (Anjou est masculin et commence par un voyelle.)
le Poitou	**au Poitou**
le Dauphiné	**au Dauphine**

Ce sont des noms masculins.

Les états américains sont francisés. Les noms d'états en **a** sont généralement en **e** en français, donc féminins:

la Californie	**en Californie**
la Louisiane	**en Louisiane**
la Floride	**en Floride**

L'Orégon est masculin mais commence par une voyelle: **en Orégon.** Les autres sont masculins:

le Wisconsin	**au** Wisconsin
le Connecticut	**au** Connecticut
le Montana	**au** Montana
le Névada	**au** Névada
le Texas	**au** Texas

Le Montana et **le Névada** sont des exceptions et ne sont pas francisés.

Pour les noms d'états qui sont des noms de ville on dit:

dans l'état de New York   **dans l'état de Washington**

Remarque: On peut toujours dire **dans l'état de** si on ne connaît pas le genre de l'état.

De + nom de pays

Après les verbes **arriver, venir, revenir** on emploie **de** sans article devant un nom féminin.

Il revient **de** France.   Il revient **d'**Italie.

Mais on emploie **du, des,** articles contractés, devant un nom masculin.

Elle revient **du** Japon   Elle revient **du** Mexique, **des** États-Unis.

Mettez la forme correcte: **en, au, dans l'état de.**   *Exercice XII*

1. Donald est né _____ Boston _____ Massachusetts.   2. Ses parents ont déménagé trois fois: ils sont allés _____ Floride, _____ Nouveau Mexique et _____ Louisiane.   3. Donald est allé à l'école primaire _____ Michigan, à l'école secondaire _____ New York et au *college* _____ Californie.   4. Il s'est marié _____ Orégon et maintenant il vit _____ Texas. Quelle vie!

Mettez la préposition correcte.   *Exercice XIII*

1. Il va passer ses vacances _____ Suède, _____ Pérou, _____ Chili, _____ Iran, _____ Grèce, _____ Pays-Bas, _____ Allemagne, _____ Danemark, ou _____ Maroc?
2. Je crois que je vais aller _____ Bretagne, _____ Auvergne, _____ Provence, _____ Corse, _____ Poitou.
3. Pendant leur voyage aux États-Unis, ils sont restés _____ Alabama, _____ Kentucky, _____ Michigan, _____ Vermont, _____ Virginie, et _____ New Jersey.
4. Ils reviennent _____ Egypte, _____ Indes, _____ Israël, _____ Pays-Bas, _____ Japon, _____ France, _____ Italie.

1. Poème   LECTURES

POUR TOI MON AMOUR

Je suis allé au marché aux oiseaux
Et j'ai acheté des oiseaux
Pour toi
mon amour
Je suis allé au marché aux fleurs
Et j'ai acheté des fleurs
Pour toi
mon amour
Je suis allé au marché à la ferraille*
Et j'ai acheté des chaînes
De lourdes chaînes
Pour toi
mon amour
Et puis je suis allé au marché aux esclaves
Et je t'ai cherchée**
Mais je ne t'ai pas trouvée**
mon amour

JACQUES PRÉVERT

*La ferraille = *junk;* ce mot vient de **fer** (*iron*).
**Voir p. 209

Les épreuves du baccalauréat
ont commencé.

2. Les études en France

Les petits Français commencent leurs études à l'âge de 3 à 5 ans (cela dépend des villes ou des villages). Certaines écoles maternelles acceptent les petits dès qu'ils sont «propres»; alors, comme les grands, ils vont à l'école tous les jours (sauf le mercredi et le dimanche) de 8 h 30 à 11 h 30 et de 1 h 30 à 4 h 30. Comme les «grands», ils rentrent à la maison pour déjeuner, ou ils vont à la cantine; mais seuls les petits font la sieste l'après-midi.

A l'école maternelle ils apprennent à lire et à écrire, à faire des petits objets en céramique, en papier, à faire du tissage, des bijoux de résine, etc. A l'école élémentaire, c'est plus sérieux, on y reste jusqu'à 10 ou 12 ans. Parfois l'école est mixte, parfois les garçons et les filles sont séparés.

Puis commence l'enseignement secondaire. Là, c'est plus compliqué, il y a plusieurs branches: le lycée, qui prépare au baccalauréat, un examen très difficile avec 40 pour-cent d'échecs (on le passe à 17 ou 18 ans); les collèges (CEG)* qui donnent un enseignement «court» ou un enseignement technique pour préparer les étudiants à entrer ensuite dans des écoles professionnelles (d'agriculture, de commerce, de comptabilité, etc.). A l'université on commence des études supé-rieures: on passe une licence, une maîtrise, une agrégation ou un doctorat. Ces examens sont souvent des thèses ou des concours. Chaque université a 3 ou 5 facultés: les sciences, les lettres et sciences humaines, le droit et les sciences économiques, la médecine et la pharmacie. Depuis Napoléon qui les a créées, il y a les «Grandes Écoles» où on prépare les ingénieurs, les hommes du gouverne-ment, l'élite de la nation: les plus célèbres sont l'École Normale Supérieure (pour les professeurs d'université), l'École Polytechnique (pour les grands ingénieurs, les généraux) et l'École Nationale d'Administration (d'où est sorti le président de la République).

L'enseignement français est laïque et gratuit, même l'université. Les droits d'inscriptions sont minimes ($36.00). Pourtant il y a peu d'étudiants en France qui viennent de milieux modestes (ouvriers, petits employés). C'est qu'il est plus difficile en France pour un jeune de travailler, et d'avoir assez d'argent pour vivre et faire des études. Et peu d'étudiants ont la possibilité de gagner leur vie en allant à l'université.

Depuis la révolution de mai 68, l'université française a subi beaucoup de changements et de réformes, dans le sens d'une participation des étudiants aux décisions. C'est la co-gestion. Il y a moins de cours ex-cathedra, plus de petites classes et de séminaires qu'autrefois.

La vie sur un *campus* américain est bien différente de la vie d'un étudiant français. Un étudiant français doit vivre en ville, payer un loyer pour une chambre et prendre ses repas dans un restaurant universitaire où la nourriture est bon marché (50¢) mais pas excellente. Les fraternités n'existent pas, et les universités sont plus politisées qu'en Amérique. Dans une grande ville, la vie d'un étudiant peut être très solitaire. Les classes sont données dans des amphithéâtres qui contiennent plus de 500 élèves, alors il est difficile de rencontrer des amis. Et les examens sont si difficiles, si sélectifs qu'on a peu le temps de se distraire: il y a des bals, des «chahuts» et les cafés. Mais les vrais étudiants sont à la bibliothèque occupés à étudier.

Vocabulaire

cantine, (*f.*)   cafeteria for elementary school
chahut, (*m.*)   rough housing
concours, (*m.*)   competitive exam
cours ex-cathedra, (*m.*)   lecture
dès que   as soon as
droits, (*m. pl.*)   tuition
échec, (*m.*)   failure

enseignement, (*m.*)   teaching
gratuit   free
laïque   non-religious
lycée, (*m.*)   high school
loyer, (*m.*)   rent
milieu, (*m.*)   family, social class
propre   *ici:* toilet trained
tissage, (*m.*)   weaving

*CEG = **Collège d'Enseignement Général**

Composition Racontez les événements de votre vie depuis (*since*) le jour où vous êtes né (née) jusqu'à aujourdhui. Où est-ce que vous êtes né (née)? Où est-ce que vous êtes allé (allée) à l'école maternelle, à l'école élémentaire, au lycée, à l'université? Est-ce que votre famille a déménagé une fois, deux fois, souvent? Dans quels états est-ce que vous avez habité? Où est-ce que vous avez voyagé, dans ce pays et dans d'autres pays?

- **PRÉSENTATION:** Une grippe
- **PRONONCIATION:** problèmes de consonnes
- **STRUCTURES:**

    Verbes irréguliers: ouvrir, couvrir, souffrir; savoir, connaître

    Constructions à retenir: les verbes **savoir** et **connaître** (*to know*)

        les expressions idiomatiques avec **avoir: avoir mal à, avoir besoin de, qu'est-ce que?**

        la traduction de *it, it is:* **ça, c'est, il est, elle est**

    Points de grammaire: l'imparfait

        les emplois de l'imparfait

        le pronom relatif: **que; c'est...que**

        l'accord du participe passé

- **LECTURES:**
  1. «Conversation» JEAN TARDIEU
  2. La médecine en France

- **EXPRESSIONS:** Il a une fièvre de cheval

        Je suis malade comme un chien

Bonjour belle Rosine

Chapitre **13**

Bon - jour bel - le Ro - si — ne, Com - ment vous por — tez — vous?

Vous me fai — tes la mi - ne, Di - tes — moi, qu'a — vez — vous?

C'est mon a — mi qu'est par - ti ce ma — tin, Ce qui me cau — se

Ce qui me cau — se, C'est mon a — mi qu'est par —

ti ce ma tin, Ce qui me cau — se bien du cha — grin.

Le professeur a l'air sévère.

PRÉSENTATION   Une grippe

La semaine dernière, quand je suis rentrée de l'université, je me suis sentie fatiguée; j'avais chaud, j'avais froid, j'avais des frissons, j'avais mal à la tête, j'avais mal aux jambes, mal au dos, mal à la gorge, mal au ventre, mal partout. J'avais envie de dormir. Je souffrais vraiment.

Je me suis couchée; j'ai pris ma température. Le thermomètre indiquait 39°5 (c'est un thermomètre français), j'avais de la fièvre! Ce n'était pas un petit rhume. C'était la grippe, évidemment. Quelle grippe? La grippe de 24 heures, ou la terrible grippe de Hong Kong, l'influenza de 1969 ou une grippe légère? J'ai pensé: «Quelle catastrophe! je vais être absente pendant 8 jours. Et mes classes et mes pauvres étudiants? Ils vont être tristes. Plus de cours, plus d'exercices.» Mon mari m'a dit: «Qu'est-ce que tu as? Il faut appeler le docteur.» Moi, je lui ai répondu (je pouvais encore parler): «Mais non, pas en Amérique. Ici on va chez le docteur. Il vient vous voir seulement à la dernière extrémité.» Mon mari a dit: «C'est vrai. Alors, allons à l'hôpital.» Moi, j'ai dit (ma voix était terrible): «Mais non, ce n'est pas sérieux. J'ai la grippe, tout simplement. J'ai besoin de repos, d'aspirine, de boissons chaudes, de vitamine C, c'est tout.»

Mon mari: «Alors, c'est toi le docteur, maintenant?» Moi (j'étais presque morte et j'avais envie de dormir): «Mais non, je ne suis docteur en rien du tout, et surtout pas en médecine. Mais j'ai déjà eu des grippes. Je connais les symptômes de la grippe; je sais que je ne suis pas sérieusement malade.» Mon mari a pris mon pouls: mais il n'y connaît rien, alors...

J'ai encore dit: «La dernière fois que j'ai eu la grippe, je suis allée chez le médecin; il m'a fait une piqûre, il m'a ordonné des tonnes de médicaments coûteux. Résultat: je suis restée au lit une semaine avec des douleurs terribles...» Mon mari a vu que je m'énervais, alors il s'est arrêté.

Je n'ai pas appelé le docteur, je ne suis pas allée à l'hôpital. Des médicaments? PFFT! J'ai pris de l'aspirine, j'ai bu de la citronnade chaude, j'ai pris des vitamines C, et surtout, avant de dormir, j'ai bu un grand grog! C'est le remède favori des Français (de l'eau bouillante, du sucre, du citron et du rhum! — les proportions dépendent de votre capacité de résister à l'alcool!).

J'ai beaucoup dormi. Après vingt-quatre heures — c'était la grippe de vingt-quatre heures — la fièvre est tombée, je n'avais plus de température. Je toussais un peu, j'étais encore très fatiguée, et faible, mais j'avais faim: c'était bon signe.

Je me suis encore reposée pendant une journée: c'était presque agréable; j'ai lu des magazines, je n'ai pas travaillé. Ma fille était l'infirmière. Mon mari et mes enfants ont fait la cuisine et le ménage. Tout n'était pas parfait, mais je leur ai fait beaucoup de compliments. Le troisième jour, le matin, je me sentais moins faible et le soir, j'étais complètement remise. J'étais guérie. Je suis revenue à mon travail, à mes chers étudiants qui étaient si tristes de mon absence. D'ailleurs on dit: «Le travail, c'est la santé.» Je suis en bonne santé.

Vocabulaire

avant de dormir before sleeping (il faut un infinitif en français)
avoir de la fièvre to have a fever
avoir envie de to feel like
avoir mal à la tête to have a headache; **à la gorge** a sore throat; **au cœur** nausea; **au ventre** a stomach ache
à votre santé Cheers!
boisson, (*f.*) drink
bouillant boiling
citronnade, (*f.*) lemonade; **citron** (*m.*) lemon
coûteux costly
docteur, (*m.*) doctor
douleur, (*f.*) pain, ache
faire des compliments to compliment
frisson, (*m.*) shiver
grippe, (*f.*) influenza, flu
grog, (*m.*) hot toddy
guéri to be cured
infirmière, (*f.*) nurse
maladie, (*f.*) sickness

médicament, (*m.*) medicine, remedy
médecin, (*m.*) doctor
médecine, (*f.*) medicine
n'y rien connaître to know nothing about it
piqûre, (*f.*) injection
pouls, (*m.*) pulse
prendre sa température to take one's temperature
remède, (*m.*) medicine, remedy
remis to be well again
repos, (*m.*) rest; **se reposer** to rest
santé, (*f.*) health
savoir; connaître to know (voir page 201)
s'arrêter to stop
s'énerver to become nervous, irritated
se sentir fatigué to feel tired; **déprimé** depressed; **fiévreux** feverish
tousser to cough (**la toux**)
triste sad
voix, (*f.*) voice

PRONONCIATION Problèmes de consonnes

Prononcez **t** final dans les mots suivants:

ouest   est   la ville de Brest
net (un poids net)   **brut** (un champagne brut)
intact (le trésor des pirates est intact)

Ne prononcez pas **t** dans

aspect   respect   Montréal   Montmartre

Prononcez **l** dans le mot

fil, fils (*thread, threads*)

Ne prononcez pas **l** final dans

gentil   fusil (*gun*)   **pouls** (*pulse*)
persil (*parsley*)   **sourcil** (*eyebrow*)   **fils** /fis/

Prononcez **ch** /ʃ/ dans

chat   chemin   bronchite   chèque   chemise, etc.

Prononcez **ch** /k/ dans

broncho-pneumonie   orchestre   chaos /kɑo/   **choeur   orchidée**

Prononcez généralement le **c** final:

sec   bac   sac

Où sont les malades?

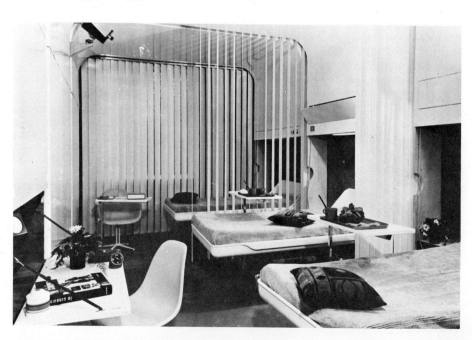

Ne prononcez pas le **c** final dans

blanc̸   **banc̸** (*bench*)   **franc̸**   **tabac̸**
estomac̸   **tronc̸** (*tree trunk*)   **porc̸**

Prononcez la **g** final de

grog   **gang**

Mais ne le prononcez pas dans

long̸   **sang̸**

Prononcez **rhum** /rɔm/ et **rhume** /rym/.

EXEMPLE: On prend du **rhum** quand on a un **rhume.**

VERBES IRRÉGULIERS   STRUCTURES

ouvrir *to open*	**couvrir** *to cover*	**souffrir** *to suffer*
j'ouvre*	je couvre	je souffre
tu ouvres*	tu couvres	tu souffres
il, elle ouvre*	il, elle couvre	il, elle souffre
ils, elles ouvrent*	ils, elles couvrent	ils, elles souffrent
nous ouvrons*	nous couvrons	nous souffrons
vous ouvrez*	vous couvrez	vous souffrez

Leur passé composé est: j'ai ouv**ert;** tu as couv**ert;** il a souff**ert,** etc.

Conjuguez sur ces modèles: **découvrir** (*to discover*), **offrir** (*to give a present, to offer*).

Mettez le verbe au présent.   *Exercice I*

1. Tu (ouvrir) la porte.
2. J'ai mal aux dents, je (souffrir).
3. Nous (ouvrir) le livre à la page 52.
4. La neige (couvrir) le sol.
5. Vous (ouvrir) l'enveloppe.
6. Elles (souffrir) du froid en hiver.
7. J' (offrir) des chocolats au professeur pour Noël.

Mettez les phrases de l'exercice 1 au passé composé.   *Exercice II*

savoir *to know*		**connaître** *to know*	
je **sais**	nous **savons**	je **connais**	nous **connaissons**
tu **sais** /sɛ/	vous **savez** /sav/	tu **connais** /ɛ/	vous **connaissez** /ɛs/
il **sait**	ils **savent**	il **connaît**	ils **connaissent**

Remarquez que le verbe **connaître** a l'accent circonflexe à la troisième personne du singulier seulement: il, elle **connaît.**

*Ces terminaisons sont identiques au présent d'un verbe du premier groupe (je parl**e**).

Exercice III   Donnez la forme du verbe au présent.

1. Vous (connaître) cette chanson?
2. Ils ne (connaître) pas la vie française.
3. Tu (connaître) Paris?
4. Je (savoir) ma leçon.
5. Elles ne (savoir) pas nager.
6. Nous (savoir) ce que nous faisons?

Le passé composé de **connaître** est: j'ai **connu,** tu as **connu,** etc. **Savoir** cst spécial au passé. Voir p. 207.

Exercice IV   Mettez le verbe au passé composé.

1. Le chien (reconnaître) Ulysse.
2. Hier, j'ai vu Paul et d'abord je (reconnaître négatif + le): il a une barbe!
3. Est-ce que vous (connaître) mon grand-père?
4. Non, mais je (bien connaître) votre grand-mère.

CONSTRUCTIONS A RETENIR

Les verbes **savoir** et **connaître** (*to know*)

EXEMPLES: Je **sais.** Je ne **sais** pas.
Je **sais** ma leçon. Il **sait** le latin.
Je **sais** que c'est difficile. Tu **sais** quand il arrive?
Je **sais** nager.

Employez **savoir** pour traduire *to know something for true, to know after learning, to know how to* avec l'infinitif du verbe; *to know that, if, when, what* (que, si, quand).

EXEMPLES: Je **connais** M. Dupont.
Il **connaît** bien la France.
Il la **connaît** très bien.

Employez **connaître** pour traduire *to know by acquaintance* (avec un nom ou un pronom objet direct).

Exercice V   Mettez la forme correcte du verbe **savoir** ou **connaître.**

1. Je _____ que le terre est ronde.
2. Nous _____ les coutumes des Français.
3. Elle ne _____ pas ses verbes irréguliers.
4. Est-ce que vous _____ si le courrier est arrivé?
5. Elles _____ la Provence.
6. Ils _____ ce qu'ils veulent.
7. Tu _____ Jean-Jacques?
8. Vous ne _____ pas la nouvelle boulangerie française?

Les expressions idiomatiques avec **avoir**

avoir mal à (*to hurt, to have a _____ ache*):

J'**ai mal à** la tête.
Il **a mal aux** oreilles.
Elle **a mal à** l'estomac.

On conjugue le verbe **avoir;** on ajoute **mal;** on complète la phrase avec la partie du corps précédée de **à.** (Attention à la contraction!)

Répétez avec **j'ai mal...**   *Exercice VI*

1. les dents 2. le ventre 3. le cœur 4. les yeux 5. le foie 6. la main 7. les pieds 8. la jambe droite

avoir besoin de (*to need*):

J'**ai besoin d'un** whisky.
Il **a besoin d'une** femme de ménage.
Nous **avons besoin du** livre de français.
Vous **avons besoin des** médicaments du docteur?

Tu **as besoin de** repos.
Elle **a besoin d'**argent.
Ils **ont besoin de** vacances.

Avec ce verbe, ajoutez l'article **un, une, le, l', la, les** à **de** et faites les contractions habituelles:

$$
\begin{array}{ll}
\text{de + un } = \textbf{d'un} & \text{de + le } = \textbf{\textit{du}} \\
\text{de + une} = \textbf{d'une} & \text{de + la } = \textbf{de la} \\
& \text{de + l' } = \textbf{de l'} \\
& \text{de + les} = \textbf{\textit{des}}
\end{array}
$$

Si **de** est en contact avec l'article **du, de la, des** on a seulement **de:**

$$
\begin{array}{ll}
\text{de + du } = \textbf{de} & \text{de + de l' } = \textbf{de} \\
\text{de + de la} = \textbf{de} & \text{de + des } = \textbf{des}
\end{array}
$$

Répétez les phrases avec **j'ai besoin de...** (Attention à la rencontre de **de** avec   *Exercice VII*
l'article):

1. J'ai des ami.   5. Elle a les notes des étudiants.
2. Tu as du temps.   6. Il a de l'énergie.
3. Ils ont la carte de France.   7. Nous avons un nouveau gouvernement.
4. Vous avez un stylo.   8. J'ai du travail.

qu'est-ce que...:

Qu'est-ce qu'il y a   *What is the matter?*
Qu'est-ce que tu as?   *What is the matter with you?*

On commence par **Qu'est-ce que...** et on conjugue le verbe **avoir** avec une personne différente.

Qu'est-ce qu'il a?

Exercice VIII   Répétez la question **Qu'est-ce que j'ai?** avec un sujet qui correspond à la réponse:

EXEMPLE: Qu'est-ce que j'ai?   Je me sens mal.

1. Elle est pâle. 2. Vous avez l'air fâché. 3. Nous sommes toujours fatigués.
4. Elles ne parlent pas. 5. Ils dorment en classe.

La traduction de *it, it is:* **ça, c'est, il est, elle est**

Ça va,   **Ça** arrive

Employez **ça** avec un verbe qui n'est pas **être**.

C'est la grippe.   **C'est** le président.
C'est un bon grog.   **C'est** ma sœur.

Employez **c'est** devant un nom pour identifier un objet, une personne (la question impliquée est **Qu'est-ce que c'est?** ou **Qui est-ce?**).

C'est beau, **cette** exposition.
C'est terrible, **ce** rhume!

Employez **c'est** avec un adjectif masculin (jamais féminin) si le véritable sujet est placé après. Souvent le véritable sujet est accompagné de l'adjectif démonstratif (**ce, cette**).

> Vous avez un chapeau? Oui, **il est** horrible.
> Où est ma composition? **Elle est** sur le bureau du professeur.

Employez **il est**, si le nom qui représente *it* est masculin et mentionné avant. Employez **elle est**, si le nom qui représente *it* est féminin et mentionné avant.

Mettez **ça** ou **c'est, il est** ou **elle est**.   *Exercice IX*

1. _____ extraordinaire, ce tableau de Picasso.
2. Tu as vu ce film? Oui, _____ idiot.
3. _____ un opéra de Mozart.
4. _____ me plaît.
5. Je ne trouve pas ma bague. _____ à votre doigt!
6. _____ veut dire. . .
7. _____ le père de Suzanne.
8. _____ compliqué, la grammaire française.
9. _____ devient difficile.
10. _____ le directeur de l'Institut.

POINTS DE GRAMMAIRE

L'imparfait

> Aujourd'hui, je suis fatigué. Hier, **j'étais** fatigué aussi.
> Hier, **j'avais** mal à la tête. Aujourd'hui, je vais très bien.

J'étais, j'avais sont des imparfaits. L'imparfait est un temps du passé qui décrit un état physique.

LA FORME

Pour former l'imparfait, on prend la forme **nous** du verbe au présent: **nous donnons, nous finissons, nous vendons;** on ôte la terminaisons –**ons** (donn–, finiss–, vend–); on ajoute les terminaisons suivantes: –**ais**, –**ais**, –**ait**, –**aient**; –**ions**, –**iez**. Voici l'imparfait des verbes des différents groupes:

1er groupe	*2ème groupe*	*3ème groupe*
je donn**ais**	je finiss**ais**	je vend**ais**
tu donn**ais**	tu finiss**ais**	tu vend**ais**
il donn**ait**	il finiss**ait**	il vend**ait**
ils donn**aient**	ils finiss**aient**	ils vend**aient**
nous donn**ions**	nous finiss**ions**	nous vend**ions**
vous donn**iez**	vous finiss**iez**	vous vend**iez**

A l'imparfait, on entend les sons /ɛ/, /jo/, /je/ à la terminaison pour tous les groupes et aussi pour les verbes irréguliers. Remarquez les orthographes spéciales:

1. les verbes en **–ger (manger, voyager)**

   je man**geais**   tu man**geais**   il man**geait**   ils man**geaient**

   Il y a un **e** après le **g** devant **–ais, –ait, –aient** pour garder le son /ʒ/ dans tout le verbe. Nous man**gions**, vous man**giez**: un **e** n'est pas nécessaire.

2. les verbes en **–cer (placer, commencer)**

   je pla**çais**, tu pla**çais**, il pla**çait**, ils pla**çaient**

   Il y a une cédille sous le **c** devant **–ais, –ait, –aient** pour garder le son /s/ dans tout le verbe. Nous pla**cions**, vous pla**ciez**: il n'y a pas de cédille.

3. le verbe **étudier** (et tous les verbes en **–ier** et **–yer**)

   nous étud**iions**   vous étud**iiez**   nous cro**yions**   vous vo**yiez**

   Il y a deux **i** ou **yi** à ces deux personnes.

4. le verbe **faire**

   je **fai**sais   nous **fai**sions

   Fai est prononcé /fə/ dans tout l'imparfait.

5. le verbe **être** est irrégulier. C'est la seule exception.

j'**étais**	nous **étions**
tu **étais**	vous **étiez**
il **était**	
ils **étaient**	

Exercice X   Donnez l'imparfait de:

1. je parle
2. tu rougis
3. elle entend
4. je brunis
5. tu regardes
6. elle va
7. nous allons
8. vous dormez
9. ils sont
10. vous montons
11. vous descendez
12. elles ont

Les emplois de l'imparfait

Hier soir, j'**étais** fatiguée, j'**avais** mal à la tête, j'**avais** mal à la gorge, je me **sentais** déprimée, mes jambes **étaient** douloureuses, je ne **pouvais** pas dormir,... c'**était** la grippe. Aujourd'hui, je reste au lit.

1. Employez l'imparfait pour indiquer un état physique ou mental qui dure, sans indication de limite de temps.

Hier, il ne **pleuvait** pas, le ciel **était** bleu, le soleil **brillait,** les oiseaux **chantaient** dans les arbres. Aujourd'hui, catastrophe, il pleut!

2. Employez l'imparfait pour faire la description du temps, du décor.

J'**étais** fatiguée; j'**avais** la fièvre, je **pensais** que je **pouvais** sortir.

3. Certains verbes sont employés plus souvent à l'imparfait qu'au passé composé. Ce sont **être:** j'étais, **avoir:** j'avais, **penser:** je pensais, **croire:** je croyais, **espérer:** j'espérais, **pouvoir:** je pouvais, **vouloir:** je voulais, **savoir:** je savais.

Répétez les phrases à l'imparfait.   *Exercice XI*

EXEMPLE: Aujourd'hui il fait froid. Hier il **faisait** froid.

1. Le ciel est gris. Hier...
2. Le vent souffle.
3. Il pleut.
4. Pierre est fatigué.
5. Est-ce que tu as de la fièvre?
6. Elle se sent déprimée.
7. Ses amis sont tristes.
8. Il ne peut pas travailler.
9. Je veux dormir.
10. Ça va très mal.
11. Il commence à m'énerver.
12. Vous étudiez.
13. Elle ne mange pas de viande.
14. Nous sommes à la cuisine.

Le pronom relatif **que; c'est...que**

Le livre est intéressant. Je lis le livre. Je le lis.
Le livre **que** je lis est intéressant.

Le professeur parle lentement. J'écoute le professeur.
Le professeur **que** j'écoute parle lentement.

Que est objet direct. Il représente une chose ou une personne. En anglais, il est possible d'oublier *that* ou *which,* mais en français, il faut toujours avoir **que.**

Que est placé aussitôt après l'antécédent: **le livre que...**

Que est élidé en **qu'** devant **il, elle, on, ils, elles: le livre qu'il lit.**

Récrivez les phrases avec le relatif **que.**   *Exercice XII*

EXEMPLE: Le film est stupide. Nous avons vu le film: **Le film que nous avons vu est stupide.**

1. La musique est divine. Nous entendons la musique.
2. Le tableau est de Cézanne. Tu regardes le tableau.
3. Le vin est de Bordeaux. Je préfère le vin.
4. La jeune fille s'appelle Suzanne. Il aime la jeune fille.
5. La lettre n'arrive pas. Vous attendez la lettre.
6. Les leçons sont difficiles. Le professeur explique les leçons.

Elle chante une chanson française.
C'est une chanson française **qu'**elle chante.

Il fait des recherches.

Elle achète des pommes.
C'est des pommes **qu'**elle achète.

Vous entourez l'objet direct important avec **c'est...que.*** Il faut toujours avoir **que.**
Cette construction est très idiomatique.

*Dans la langue élégante, on emploie **ce sont...que** devant un objet pluriel: **Ce sont des pommes
qu'elle achète.**

Répétez les phrases avec **c'est...que.**

1. Elle préfère le bourgogne.
2. Vous expliquez la leçon 5.
3. Nous achetons des oranges.
4. Ils veulent acheter une Cadillac.
5. Tu lis un livre stupide.
6. Je regarde ta photo dans l'album.
7. Les astronautes cherchent des nouvelles planètes.

L'accord du participe passé

Elle est charmante.	**Elle est allée.**
Ils sont riches.	**Ils sont venus.**

Accordez le participe passé d'un verbe conjugué avec **être** avec le sujet comme un adjectif.

J'ai mangé la salade.
La salade que j'ai mangée vient de mon jardin.
Quelle salade as-tu **mangée?**
La salade? Oui, je **l'ai mangée.**

Avec le verbe **avoir** le participe passé est invariable si l'objet direct est après le verbe. Si l'objet direct est avant le verbe, on accorde le participe passé avec cet objet direct qui précède. L'objet direct peut être: **que; quel** + un nom; un pronom O.D. Cet accord ne s'entend généralement pas. C'est une règle de la langue écrite.

Ma robe? eh oui, je **l'ai faite** moi-même.
Le professeur a expliqué **la leçon,** mais je ne **l'ai** pas **comprise.**

On entend l'accord avec des verbes comme **faire, prendre, mettre, comprendre, dire, interdire** (*forbid*), etc.

Accordez le participe passé avec l'objet direct qui est avant le verbe. Ne l'accordez pas avec l'objet direct qui est après.

1. Ils ont (acheter) une auto.
2. L'auto qu'ils ont (acheter) ne marche plus.
3. Elle a (entendre) les nouvelles à la radio.
4. Les nouvelles qu'elle a (entendre) sont mauvaises.
5. Vous avez (prendre) une fausse route.
6. Quelle route avez-vous (prendre)?
7. J'ai (mettre) les fleurs dans un vase.
8. Les fleurs que j'ai (mettre) dans un vase sentent bon.
9. Ce gouvernement a (interdire) la barbe et la mini-jupe.
10. Quelles autres choses est-ce qu'il a (interdire)?

LECTURES 1. Poème

CONVERSATION

(*Sur le pas de la porte, avec bonhomie*)

Comment ça va sur la terre?
— Ça va, ça va, ça va bien.

Les petits chiens sont-ils prospères?
— Mon Dieu oui merci bien.

Et les nuages?
— Ça flotte.

Et les volcans?
— Ça mijote.

Et les fleuves?
— Ça s'écoule.

Et le temps?
— Ça se déroule.

Et votre âme?
— Elle est malade.

Le printemps était trop vert
Elle a mangé trop de salade.

JEAN TARDIEU
Monsieur-Monsieur, 1957

Vocabulaire

âme, (*f.*) soul	**mijoter** to simmer	**s'écouler** to flow away
flotter to float	**pas de la porte,** (*m.*) doorstep	**se dérouler** to unroll

2. La médecine en France

En France, si on n'est pas très malade, si on souffre seulement d'un petit «bobo,» on ne va pas chez le docteur, on va d'abord chez le pharmacien qui vous donne des conseils, et qui vous vend, bien sûr, un médicament toujours très nouveau et coûteux. Si on peut encore marcher, on va à la consultation du médecin, ou du spécialiste, avec ou sans rendez-vous. Mais souvent, le docteur fait des visites à domicile. Il monte et descend les escaliers et couvre des kilomètres avec sa voiture. A la campagne surtout, cette vie est très dure: il se lève la nuit, et va par des routes mauvaises et noires voir un malade dans une ferme.

Il y a en France des équipes de médecins célèbres et excellents, mais il y a une crise dans le personnel hospitalier: les médecins ne sont pas assez nombreux (les études sont longues et coûteuses) et surtout les infirmiers et les infirmières manquent: ils sont surmenés et mal payés. Alors, il faut fermer les hôpitaux neufs qu'on a construits, parce qu'il n'y a pas assez d'infirmières pour soigner les

L'hôpital favori des vedettes.

malades! Certains hôpitaux existent depuis le Moyen-Age (ils ont été modernisés!): l'Hôtel-Dieu à Paris et les Hospices de Beaune. Mais à Paris, l'hôpital favori des gens riches, des vedettes de cinéma, est l'hôpital américain de Neuilly.

La Sécurité Sociale est l'équivalent de *Medicare* et rembourse tous les frais médicaux de 70 à 90%: visites médicales, opérations, séjours à l'hôpital, médicaments, et même dentistes, lunettes. On rembourse même les séjours dans une station thermale, à Vichy (pour le foie), à Royat (pour le cœur), très populaires en France. Mais la bureaucratie de la Sécurité Sociale est un cauchemar. Il faut remplir des papiers innombrables, faire la queue des heures devant des guichets où les employés harassés sont souvent hostiles. C'est l'univers de Kafka!

Vocabulaire

à domicile at home
à la campagne in the countryside
bobo, (*m.*) un mal pas très grave, mot d'enfant passé dans le vocabulaire adulte
cauchemar, (*m.*) nightmare
donner des conseils to give advice
dur hard, difficult

frais, (*m.*) expenses
guichet, (*m.*) booth, window
remplir to fill, fill out (forms), fill up (a glass)
soigner to take care of a sick person
surmené overworked

Composition Vous êtes malade. Vous avez de la température. Le docteur vient vous voir, ou vous allez à la visite. Racontez la scène.

Chapitre **14**

Bon voyage Monsieur Dumollet

Bon voy — a — ge Mon-sieur Du—mol — let, A Saint Ma—

lo dé—bar—quez sans nau — fra—ge; Bon voy — a—ge, Mon-sieur Du-mol-

let, Et re — ve — nez si le pa — ys vous plaît.

PRÉSENTATION   Les voyages, les vacances

Est-ce que vous aimez voyager? Est-ce que vous avez déjà voyagé? Oui, tout le monde aime voyager; tout le monde a voyagé. Les voyages sont faciles dans la vie moderne.

Moi, personnellement, j'ai beaucoup voyagé. Quand j'étais enfant, ma famille et moi nous faisions des voyages régulièrement: tous les étés nous allions à la ferme de ma grand-mère qui habitait à la campagne. Nous ne prenions pas le train, c'était trop cher; nous y allions en voiture: c'est mon père qui conduisait parce que ma mère n'aimait pas conduire.

Mon amie Simone, vous vous rappelez? Elle habitait au Maroc, et tous les ans, ses parents l'emmenaient en France pour voir ses grands-parents, ses oncles et ses tantes. (On aime beaucoup la famille en France!) Ils n'allaient pas en voiture, parce que l'Espagne — le pays qu'il fallait traverser — était en guerre. Ils prenaient le bateau. Mon amie n'aimait pas ces voyages parce qu'elle avait le mal de mer. Et puis, il y a eu la guerre, et ils ne sont plus allés en France pendant cinq ans.

Plus récemment, j'ai fait un voyage en Europe. Imaginez que vous avez fait un voyage. C'est-à-dire, imaginez que vous aviez assez d'argent pour en faire un. Où êtes-vous allé? Dans quel pays? En Europe? Par quel moyen? Par avion bien sûr. Vous avez pris l'avion — c'était un charter, c'est plus économique. Vous êtes allé à l'aéroport, vous avez enregistré vos bagages, vous êtes monté dans l'avion, vous vous êtes assis à votre place, vous avez souri à l'hôtesse qui vous disait d'attacher votre ceinture; vous avez vu du paysage? Non, on n'en voit pas beaucoup. L'avion vole trop haut. Le voyage a duré sept heures. Après votre arrivée, vous avez voyagé pendant quatre semaines à travers les pays, et puis vous êtes rentré.

Bon, je m'adresse à une autre personne: Mlle X. Je m'adresse à elle. Mlle, vous êtes allée au Canada en auto. Vous conduisiez? Votre chauffeur conduisait? Non, votre frère, votre petit ami? Vous avez emmené d'autres personnes? Votre vieille tante, vos trois chats, votre perruche? Non, vous n'en avez pas. Vous avez emporté beaucoup de bagages? Non, vous n'en avez pas emporté beaucoup. Est-ce que votre voiture était un break? Un break, c'est pratique pour emporter beaucoup de choses (on en met partout) ou pour rapporter des souvenirs. Vous n'en avez pas rapporté. Peut-être que vous aviez une caravane: une caravane, c'est une petite maison qu'on traîne derrière l'auto. C'est très confortable, quelquefois. On en voit souvent, l'été, sur les routes. Est-ce que vous avez eu une panne? Une panne, c'est quand l'auto ne marche plus. C'est désagréable, une panne. Non, vous n'en avez pas eu. Est-ce que vous avez rencontré des personnes bizarres sur le bord de la route, qui attendaient, le pouce en l'air. On les appelle les auto-stoppeurs: il font de l'auto-stop; ils voyagent très économiquement.

Moi, j'en ai rencontré des quantités; mais attention, ils ont une mauvaise réputation. Il y a eu des agressions par des auto-stoppeurs et maintenant les automobilistes en prennent rarement: ils n'ont plus confiance. Un jour j'ai vu des auto-stoppeurs qui tenaient une pancarte qui ne disait pas le nom de la destination mais qui disait: «Pas méchants».

Voilà un sujet de réflexion agréable, votre prochain voyage: vous allez en faire un bientôt, alors, pensez-y, songez-y, réfléchissez-y, mais n'y rêvez pas trop, n'oubliez pas vos études!

Vocabulaire

attacher to buckle, to tie, to fasten
automobiliste, (*m.*) driver
auto-stop, (*m.*) hitch-hiking
avoir confiance to have confidence
bagages, (*m. pl.*) luggage
break, (*m.*) station wagon
campagne, (*f.*) countryside
caravane, (*f.*) trailer
conduire to drive
disque, (*m.*) record
durer to last
emmener to take somebody somewhere
emporter to take things along
enregistrer to check
mal de mer, (*m.*) sea sickness
marcher to work, to run, to function properly

méchant mean
moyen, (*m.*) way, means
pancarte, (*f.*) sign, poster
panne, (*f.*) breakdown; **être en panne**
paysage, (*m.*) landscape
perruche, (*f.*) parakeet
pouce, (*m.*) thumb; **pouce en l'air** up
rencontrer to come across, to meet
route, (*f.*) road; **bord de la route,** (*m.*) roadside
s'adresser à to speak to
sourire to smile
tenir to hold; *conjuguez comme* **venir;** *mais passé composé:* **j'ai tenu.**
traîner to pull, to drag
traverser to cross; **à travers** across

Un aéroport moderne.

PRONONCIATION Les géminées

immense, **ill**ustre

Les deux **m**, les deux **l** se prononcent comme un seul. Mais dans la conversation, beaucoup de Français insistent sur les deux consonnes et prononcent /mm/, /ll/. C'est courant, surtout pour certains adjectifs. Répétez des deux façons: façon normale /m/, géminée /mm/.

immense	illogique
intelligent	imminent
illégal	illicite

Souvent la géminée est justifiée, et nécessaire quand un mot finit par une consonne et que le mot suivant commence par la même consonne.

RÉPÉTEZ:

ll	nn	rr	kk
il l'a dit	une nuit	pour refaire	avec qui
il l'a vu	une nouvelle	pour repasser	avec quoi
il l'a cru	une nécessité	pour redire	avec quel ami
il l'a fait	une nature	pour relire	avec courage
il l'a mis	une naissance	pour retrouver	avec quatre sous
il l'a acheté	une nation	pour revoir	avec confiance

A l'imparfait, en particulier, on a le son /jj/.

COMPAREZ:

/j/	/jj/
Présent: vous voyez	*Imparfait:* voyiez
nous croyons	croyions
vous envoyez	envoyiez
nous employons	employions
vous payez	payiez

Mots difficiles du texte

emmène /ɑ̃mɛn/	amène /amɛn/
en panne /ɑ̃pan/	Espagne /ɛspaɲ/
récemment /resɑmɑ̃/	un charter /ʃaʀtɛʀ/
en Europe /ɑ̃nøʀɔp/	un break /brɛk/

Pour les mots «franglais» en **-er**, on a deux prononciations:

un **starter**, un **charter** sont prononcés /ɛʀ/
un **leader**, un **speaker** sont prononcés /œʀ/

Pour aller en vacances, prenez le train.

VERBES IRRÉGULIERS **STRUCTURES**

conduire *to drive*

je **conduis**	nous **conduisons**
tu **conduis** /ɥi/	vous **conduisez** /ɥiz/
il, elle **conduit**	ils, elles **conduisent**

Imparfait: **je conduisais,** etc. (c'est la formation normale)
Passé composé: **j'ai conduit,** etc.

Conjuguez sur le même modèle **détruire** (*to destroy*) et **construire** (*to build*).

Mettez la forme correcte du verbe **conduire.** *Exercice I*

1. Il _____ vite.
2. Elle _____ une Rolls.
3. Nous _____ lentement.
4. Quand vous _____, vous buvez?

5. Vous avez eu un accident parce que vous _____ vite? (imparfait)

6. Toute la journée, ils _____ sous la pluie. (passé composé)

s'asseoir *to sit down*

je **m'assieds**	nous **nous asseyons**
tu **t'assieds** /sjɛ/	vous **vous asseyez** /sɛj/
il **s'assied**	ils **s'asseyent**

Imparfait: **je m'asseyais,** etc.
Passé composé: **je me suis assis,** etc.
Impératif: **assieds-toi, asseyez-vous, asseyons-nous**

Exercice II   Donnez la forme du verbe **s'asseoir.** Attention au temps!

1. Je m'assieds sur cette chaise. _____ (vous) sur le divan!

2. Il s'est assis par terre et elle _____ à côté de lui.

3. Les étudiants entrent dans la classe et ils _____ en silence.

4. Tous les jours nous entrions dans la classe et nous _____ en silence.

5. Vous _____ par terre parce qu'il n'y a plus de chaise libre.

CONSTRUCTIONS A RETENIR

Les verbes **conduire une auto, aller en voiture** (*to drive*)

Il **conduit** vite.
Nous **allons** à San Francisco **en voiture.**

Employez **conduire** pour *to drive* quand le verbe a un objet direct (une auto, un autobus) ou un adverbe (bien, vite, etc.). Employez **aller en voiture, en auto** quand *to drive* a un complément de destination (à Rome, à New York).

Je **marche** lentement.	Je **vais** à l'université **à pied.**
L'avion **vole** à 2.000 mètres.	Nous **allons** en Europe **par avion.**

Il y a une différence entre **marcher** (+ *adverbe*) et **aller à pied** (à un endroit). **Voler** (*to fly*) s'emploie si le sujet est l'avion ou l'oiseau, mais **Un passager va par avion.** En général, pour décrire la manière de voyager, on dit: **aller à bicyclette, à pied, en voiture, en bateau, par avion, par le train,** etc. ou **prendre l'avion, le bateau, le train.**

Exercice III   Mettez l'expression correcte.

1. (*to drive*) Nous _____ au Canada. C'est mon père qui _____.

2. (*to fly*) Moi, je préfère _____. C'est plus rapide. Les avions _____ si vite!

3. (*to go by boat*) Mes cousins _____ en Europe _____.

4. (*to walk*) Ils _____ au marché _____. Ils _____ tous les jours dans le parc.

5. (*ride a bike*) Moi, je _____ à l'université _____.

6. (*to go by train*). Pour aller de Paris à Marseille, nous _____ le train.

Les verbes **s'asseoir, être assis** (*to sit*)

Il est entré et il **s'est assis.**

S'asseoir décrit une action, un mouvement.

Il n'est pas debout, il n'est pas couché, **il est assis.**

Être assis décrit une position déjà prise.

 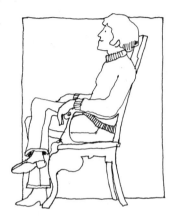

Mettez la forme correcte du verbe **s'asseoir** ou **être assis.**   *Exercice IV*

1. Le professeur est souvent debout et marche dans la classe. Mais aujourd'hui, il est fatigué, il _____.
2. Entrez dans le cabinet du docteur et _____.
3. Ma grand-mère est très vieille. Elle _____ toute la journée dans son fauteuil.
4. Les étudiants _____ sur leurs chaises pendant 50 minutes.
5. Bernard va au tableau, écrit l'exercice, revient à sa place et _____.
6. Au match de football, nous _____ sur des bancs bien inconfortables. Des gens apportent leur petit coussin (*pillow*).
7. Au cinéma, hier, Alice _____ derrière un hippie mal lavé. (imparfait)
8. Elle s'est levée, et elle _____ dix rangs (*rows*) derrière.

Les verbes **emporter, emmener; apporter, amener; rapporter, ramener**

Elle **emporte** une grosse valise de livres pour ses vacances.
Tu **apportes** du champagne pour mon anniversaire!
J'**emmène** mon petit frère au zoo.
Elle **amène** trois garçons à la soirée.

On **emporte, apporte** des objets inanimés (le verbe **porter** = *to carry*).
On **emmène, amène** des personnes (le verbe **mener** = *to lead*).
On **emporte** et on **emmène** (préfixe **em-**) quand on va quelque part (*one goes*

someplace). On **apporte** et on **amène** (préfixe **a-**) quand on vient quelque part (*one comes to a place*).

>Je reviens de Tahiti; je **rapporte** des photos.
>Il revient d'Europe; il **ramène** sa vieille mère.

On **rapporte** et on **ramène** quand on revient (*one returns*).

Exercice V Mettez le verbe qui convient: **emporter, emmener, apporter, amener, rapporter, ramener.**

1. Le samedi, il _____ sa petite amie au cinéma. 2. Le weekend, je vais à la campagne, j'_____ seulement quelques vêtements et des livres. 3. Si vous venez dîner chez moi, _____ une bouteille de vin et _____ des amis. 4. Elle _____ des fleurs d'Hawaii. 5. Ce jeune homme américain a fait son service militaire en Allemagne, il a rencontré une jeune fille et il l'a _____ aux U.S. pour l'épouser. 6. N'oubliez pas de _____ vos livres à la bibliothèque. 7. Le professeur dit: Si vous voulez _____ un invité en classe, il faut demander la permission.

POINTS DE GRAMMAIRE

Le passé composé seul dans une phrase

Employez le passé composé:

>Vous **avez fait** un voyage. Il **a pris** l'avion.

1. pour une action unique, terminée.

>Question: Qu'est-ce que **vous avez** fait?

>Vous **êtes allé** à l'aéroport, vous **avez pris** votre billet, vous **êtes monté** dans l'avion, vous **êtes parti...**

2. pour une succession d'actions rapides, comme dans un film.

>Vous **avez voyagé pendant six semaines.**
>Il **a dormi pendant dix minutes.**

3. pour une action qui a duré, qui est limitée dans le temps mais qui est terminée (*an action which lasted but is finished*).

>Je **suis allé** trois fois en Europe. **J'ai** souvent **visité** ce musée.

4. pour une action qui a été répétée mais qui est terminée (*a repeated but completed action*).

Exercice VI Mettez les phrases suivantes au passé composé. Indiquez si les actions des phrases sont: des actions uniques, des actions successives, une durée terminée, une répétition terminée.

1. Je sors à 7 heures.   2. Il quitte la maison, il attend une heure, il prend l'autobus. Il arrive en retard.   3. Le professeur répète deux fois le modèle de l'exercice.   4. Le directeur parle une heure.   5. Je visite le musée du Louvre. (dix fois)   6. Nous partons en avance.   7. Les étudiants entrent, vont à leur place, prennent leur livre, commencent à travailler.   8. Le film dure trois heures.   9. Le gangster entre dans la banque, attaque l'employé, prend l'argent et sort.   10. Je dors tout l'après-midi.

L'imparfait seul

Quand j'étais enfant, nous **voyagions** tous les étés, nous **allions** chez ma grand-mère; mon père **conduisait.** (En anglais: *we would travel, we used to travel; we used to go; my father would drive.*)

Employez l'imparfait pour des souvenirs d'enfance, des habitudes du passé.

(*a.*) Répétez les phrases suivantes à l'imparfait. Commencez le paragraphe par **Quand j'étais enfant....**   *Exercice VII*

1. A Noël, nous n'achetons pas d'arbre; nous allons en couper un dans la forêt.
2. Nous le décorons avec des objets que nous faisons nous-mêmes.
3. Ma mère fait des gâteaux et des bonbons spéciaux pour cette occasion.
4. Mes cousins de New York viennent nous voir et passent les fêtes avec nous.
5. Nous chantons des chants de Noël et nous allons à l'église à minuit.
6. Il y a un grand réveillon et nous mangeons une dinde magnifique et des huîtres. Nous buvons du vin chaud. C'est merveilleux.

(*b.*) Commencez le paragraphe par **Quand ma soeur était au Lycée...**

1. Elle rêve d'être une majorette.
2. Elle téléphone à ses amies pendant des heures.
3. Elle attend une lettre tous les jours.
4. Elle oublie de faire ses devoirs.
5. Elle écoute la radio d'un air absent.
6. Elle ne range pas sa chambre.

(*c.*) Une Française qui habite aux U.S.A. se rappelle sa vie en France. Commencez par **Quand j'habitais en France....**

1. Je vais faire mes provisions tous les jours.
2. J'achète du pain à la boulangerie.
3. Je porte des paniers lourds.
4. Je mange des choses différentes: des huîtres, des escargots.
5. Je n'ai pas de machine à laver.
6. Je suis une esclave ménagère.

Le passé composé et l'imparfait ensemble

TYPE 1:   Hier, j'**ai acheté** un journal français; et ensuite, je l'**ai lu**; après, je l'**ai prêté** à un copain.

Vous commencez un récit par une action unique et vous continuez par une suite d'actions.

> Hier, j'**ai acheté** un journal français; il **coûtait** $1.00.
> Je l'**ai lu**; il y **avait** trois articles sur les U.S.
> Je l'**ai prêté** à un copain; il **était** drôlement content.

Vous ajoutez un commentaire, une description d'un état après chaque action. L'action unique (terminée) est au passé composé. L'état, la description (qui dure) est à l'imparfait.

Exercice VIII   Sur le même modèle, écrivez les phrases au passé.

1. Vous allez à la plage.   Il fait beau mais il fait du vent.
   Hier _____   _____
2. Vous vous baignez?   Non, la mer est trop froide.
   Hier _____   _____
3. Je vois Bernard à la bibliothèque.   Qu'est-ce qu'il fait?
   Hier _____   Il lit? — Non.
                                                Il écrit? — Non.
                                                Il cherche un livre? — Non.
                                                Il est avec une jeune fille? — Oui.
                                                Il la regarde? — Oui.
                                                Il lui parle? Ils flirtent? — Oui.

TYPE 2:   **J'ai vu** un homme qui **conduisait** à 180 km à l'heure.

Dans une phrase de ce type, le 1er verbe qui exprime une action soudaine est au passé composé:

J'ai vu un homme...

Il y a un pronom relatif **qui** ou **que**:

qui

Le 2ème verbe est à l'imparfait (il indique un état, une description):

conduisait à 180 km à l'heure.

Exercice IX   Répétez les phrases avec un passé composé pour le premier verbe, un imparfait pour le deuxième verbe.

1. Pierre rencontre à la soirée une jeune fille qu'il ne connaît pas.
2. Nous mangeons des huîtres qui ne sont pas fraîches.
3. Ma mère achète des gants qui coûtent 100 F.
4. Je ne trouve pas les chaussures que je cherche.
5. Il voit un homme qui marche sur les mains.
6. Tu ne bois pas tout le vin qui reste.
7. Mon petit frère casse le vase que je préfère.
8. Le chat mange le bifteck que je vais faire cuire.

TYPE 3:   Je **suis sorti** de la pièce parce que j'**avais** mal à la tête.

Dans une phrase de ce type, il y a un premier verbe au passé composé:

Je suis sorti de la pièce

et:

parce que...

et un deuxième verbe à l'imparfait:

j'avais mal à la tête.

Mettez le 1ᵉʳ verbe au passé composé et le 2ème à l'imparfait.   *Exercice X*

  1. Il prend de l'aspirine parce qu'il a mal à la tête.
  2. Je prends ma température parce que j'ai de la fièvre.
  3. Vous vous couchez tôt parce que vous êtes fatigué.
  4. Elle appelle le docteur parce qu'elle a mal à un doigt de pied.
  5. Nous buvons un grog parce que nous avons la grippe.
  6. Son mari cède parce qu'elle s'énerve.
  7. Tu te lèves parce que tu vas mieux.
  8. Elles vont au travail parce qu'elles s'ennuient à la maison.
  9. Il est élu président parce qu'il est très populaire.
10. Les gens votent pour lui parce qu'il parle bien.
11. Il réussit parce qu'il a de la chance.
12. Le professeur se fâche parce que les étudiants n'écoutent pas.

TYPE 4:   Je vois que Georges comprend.
          J'ai vu que Georges **comprenait.**
          Il pense que nous sommes en vacances.
          Il **pensait** que nous **étions** en vacances.

Dans une construction avec la conjonction **que,** si on passe d'une situation au présent à une situation au passé le deuxième verbe, qui était au présent, est obligatoirement à l'imparfait. Le premier verbe est au passé composé ou à l'imparfait (cela dépend du contexte et de l'aspect du verbe: action soudaine? = passé composé; habitude, état mental indéfini? = imparfait).

Sur ce modèle, refaites les phrases suivantes au passé: *Exercice XI*

1. Je pense (*imp*) qu'ils partent ce soir.
2. Tu crois (*imp*) qu'il y a du vent.
3. Il voit (*p.c.*) que nous ne sommes pas fâchés.
4. Est-ce que les Américains trouvent (*p.c.*) que les Français mangent trop de pain?
5. Les Français pensent (*p.c.*) que les Américains boivent trop de whisky.
6. Il ne croit pas (*imp*) que je suis perdue.
7. Tu vois bien (*imp*) qu'il n'a pas peur.
8. Je pense (*imp*) qu'il me n'aime plus.

TYPE 5:   Quand **j'étais** enfant, **j'habitais** au Maroc.
Un jour la guerre **a commencé.**

Au milieu de vos souvenirs d'enfance (à l'imparfait) il y a un événement unique, une action spéciale (au passé composé).

Exercice XII   Sur le même modèle, écrivez des phrases avec (*a.*) l'imparfait de souvenir d'enfance, (*b.*) le passé composé d'action soudaine.

1. Jean-Jacques, quand il était jeune, (habiter) chez son oncle à la campagne. Un jour, toute la famille (faire) une excursion à la montagne.
2. Il (monter) à cheval tous les jours. Un jour il (tomber).
3. Mes deux cousins (travailler) à la ferme; ils (partir) pour l'armée.
4. Avant la guerre les provisions (être) abondantes; le gouvernement (faire) des restrictions.
5. Les prisonniers (souffrir) dans des camps; un jour les troupes alliées les (délivrer).

Choses et gens à St Trop'.

Le pronom **en**

Je mange la salade.	Je la mange.
Je mange **de la salade.**	J'**en** mange.
J'achète ce café.	Je l'achète.
Je veux **du café.**	J'**en** veux.
Elle aime les oranges.	Elle les aime.
Elle achète **des oranges.**	Elle **en** achète.

En est le pronom personnel qui remplace un nom précédé de **de** (sous la forme: **de la, de l', du** ou **des**).

$$\left.\begin{array}{l} \text{de} \\ \text{du} \\ \text{de la} \; + \; \text{nom} \\ \text{de l'} \\ \text{des} \end{array}\right\} \textbf{en}$$

Je **n'en** ai pas acheté. (avec élision de **ne** en **n'**)

Au passé composé, la négation entoure le groupe **en** + auxiliaire.

Les fleurs? Je **les** ai achet**ées.**
Des fleurs? J'**en** ai achet**é.**

Il n'y a pas d'accord du participe passé avec **en.**

Refaites les phrases avec **en** à la place du nom en italiques.   *Exercice XIII*

EXEMPLE: J'ai de l'argent.
             De l'*argent?* **J'en ai.**

1. Vous avez de la *fièvre?*   2. Le docteur prescrit des *médicaments.*   3. Le pharmacien n'a pas d'*aspirine.*   4. Son mari vend des *autos.*   5. Est-ce que l'étudiant envoie des *fleurs* au professeur?   6. L'enfant fait des *difficultés* pour manger sa soupe.   7. Il a du *courage.* Il n'a pas de *volonté.*   8. Tu as envie d'un *grog.*   9. Vous parlez de *politique.*   10. Je ne fais pas de *voyage.*   11. Vous mangez de la *salade.*

Vous mangez de la salade.	**N'en** mangez **pas.**
Vous **en** mangez.	**Mangez-en.**
Vous **n'en** mangez **pas.**	

A l'impératif négatif **en** reste devant le verbe. A l'impératif positif **en** est **placé** après le verbe.

(*a.*) Refaites les phrases suivantes avec **en.** (*b.*) Mettez-les à l'impératif négatif.   *Exercice XIV*

1. Achetez des pommes au marché.   4. Buvez du cognac.
2. Mangez de la soupe.   5. Envoyez des roses à votre petite amie.
3. Prenons de l'aspirine.   6. Dites des choses gentilles au malade.

J'ai **beaucoup de** travail.
J'en ai **beaucoup.**
Il veut **un verre de** bière?
Il **en** veut **un verre?**

De peut être une partie d'une expression de quantité:

beaucoup de	un verre de (*a glass*)
un peu de	une boîte de (*a box*)
trop de	une douzaine de
assez de	une bouteille de (*a bottle*)

On met **en** avant le verbe, on garde l'expression de quantité.

Exercice XV Répétez avec **en** et l'expression de quantité.

1. Nous avons trop d'exercices. 2. Elle a un peu de fièvre. 3. Ils n'ont pas assez d'argent. 4. Nous voulons plus de vacances. 5. Elle achète une douzaine d'œufs. 6. J'offre une boîte de chocolats aux enfants sages. 7. Il y a une bouteille de vin dans le bureau du professeur.

J'ai une auto.	**J'en** ai **une.**
Ils ont six enfants.	Ils **en** ont **six.**
Elle achète trois poulets.	Elle **en** achète **trois.**

On emploie **en** même quand **de** est absent, avec un nombre; on répète le nombre.

Exercice XVI Répétez avec **en** et le nombre.

1. Mon cousin a deux bicyclettes.
2. Ma sœur a quatre petits amis.
3. Son grand-père a mis dix mille francs à la banque.
4. Nous voulons six mois de vacances.
5. Est-ce que vous prenez un whisky avant le dîner?
6. Les étudiants écrivent dix exercices par jour.

Les pronoms **à vous, à lui, à elle** et **y** avec le verbe **penser**

Il pense **à moi, à toi, à vous, à elle, à lui, à nous, à eux, à elles.**

Si l'objet du verbe représente une personne, on garde la préposition **à** et on utilise le pronom tonique.

Il pense **à son futur, à ses vacances, à Paris.** Il **y** pense.

Si l'objet du verbe représente une chose, un endroit, on emploie **y.**

Pensez-y.

A l'impératif **y** suit le verbe.

Construisez de la même manière:

être à (*to belong to*): Ce livre **est à vous?** — Non, il **est à elle.**
s'habituer à (*to get used to*): Il s'habitue **à son travail;** il **s'y habitue.**
s'adresser à (*to address oneself to*): Je m'adresse **à vous,** mademoiselle.
songer à (*to think of*): Ne **songez** pas **à vos problèmes.** N'**y songez** pas trop.
faire attention à (*to pay attention to*): Elle ne **fait** pas **attention à moi.**
réfléchir à (*to reflect upon*): **Réfléchissez à** cette question. **Réfléchissez-y.**

Refaites les phrases avec la forme correcte: **à lui, à elle, à eux, à elles** ou **y.**   *Exercice XVII*

1. Il pense à sa petite amie.
2. Ce livre est au professeur.
3. Je m'adresse au bureau des renseignements.
4. Elle s'habitue à son mari.
5. Je ne pense pas à mes problèmes.
6. Est-ce que vous songez aux hommes de l'an 2000?
7. Elle s'est adressée à la secrétaire.
8. Ne pensez pas à l'avenir.
9. Faites attention à cette difficulté.
10. Est-ce que vous vous habituez à vos camarades de classe?

Mettez le pronom correct; objet indirect: **lui, leur;** à + pronom tonique: **à lui,**   *Exercice XVIII*
à elle, à eux, à elles; l'adverbe: **y.**

1. Il pose une question au professeur.
2. Nous allons au cinéma.
3. Vous pensez à vos parents.
4. Écrivent-ils à leurs petites amies?
5. Ce livre est à Marie.
6. Ma mère va au marché.
7. Les enfants obéissent à leurs parents.
8. Parlez à Marie.
9. Les jeunes ne pensent pas au futur.
10. Vous vous habituez à votre nouveau professeur?

Les Français en vacances   LECTURE

Les Français ont un véritable culte de l'automobile: ils adorent tout simplement
leur «voiture» (ils prononcent /watyʀ/), leur «bagnole.» L'humoriste Art Buchwald
a dit «si vous bousculez la femme d'un Français, il vous pardonne, si vous
égratignez sa voiture, il vous tuera.» C'est vrai. On voit couramment des Français
pris dans un embouteillage ou dans un petit accrochage descendre de voiture et se
battre à coups de poings et de mots: «Salaud, tordu, crétin, patate, conducteur du
dimanche». (Ils se donnent aussi d'autres noms moins corrects!)

Nice. La promenade des Anglais.

L'essence est horriblement chère en France: 2F le litre. Mais un Français fera de vrais sacrifices pour pouvoir rouler. Les Français conduisent très vite et c'est seulement récemment qu'on a institué une limite de vitesse sur les routes de France, mais elle est très impopulaire. Il y a peu d'autoroutes en France, comparativement avec l'Allemagne et l'Italie. Et les jolies petites routes bordées d'arbres sont meurtrières: il y a 13,000 tués par an sur les routes de France; chaque weekend apporte une hécatombe. Pourquoi? Il y a les ivrognes, et les fous du volant, les chauffards pour qui céder la priorité est comme une humiliation et qui ne pensent qu'à une chose: doubler tout le monde, battre un record. Le respect du code est une chose rare, la courtoisie aussi. Le résultat, c'est, chaque week-end, 200 ou 300 tués, des blessés graves, dans des accidents que causent l'absence de sobriété ou de discipline. Pourtant les gendarmes (les flics) sont là, à l'entrée des villages, avec leurs radars, leurs motards, l'alcotest, et leurs procès-verbaux.

Pour beaucoup de Français, un voyage et des vacances consistent à partir en famille dans une voiture, avec une caravane, pour camper dans un des villages de toile qui existent en France, en Italie et en Espagne. Les terrains sont généralement bien aménagés, avec douches, toilettes, magasins. Mais aussi ils sont bondés, en juillet et en août. Car les Français «n'étalent» pas leurs vacances. Il y a un véritable exode des villes vers les campagnes et surtout du Nord vers le Sud pendant ces deux mois, car tout le monde veut sa part de soleil, et du soleil, on est sûr d'en trouver sur la côte méditerranéenne. Alors, les trains (doublés ou triplés) sont réservés à l'avance, les routes deviennent encore plus encombrées et pleines d'accidents, et les petits villages calmes de Provence sont inondés de «vacanciers» qui font la fortune des commerçants: St. Tropez, Cannes, etc. On peut encore trouver des coins calmes à la montagne qui est moins populaire à cause du temps incertain, et sur certaines plages de Bretagne, où il pleut aussi. Et bien sûr, Paris au mois d'août est un désert où vous ne rencontrez que des étrangers, et où il faut faire des kilomètres pour trouver une blanchisserie, une boulangerie ouvertes. Mais les Français aiment aussi aller à l'étranger: il y a des clubs qui organisent des voyages forfaitaires dans des villages où tout est compris. Le plus célèbre est le Club Méditerranée avec ses villages au Maroc, en Sardaigne, à Tahiti.

Enfin, avec la dévaluation du dollar et la mode des charters, les jeunes Français commencent à arriver en Amérique: ils découvrent les joies du *Greyhound,* et mangent des hot dogs, des hamburgers. D'ailleurs, il y a maintenant un *Mac-Donald* à Paris, sur les Champs-Élysées, sans doute pour permettre aux Parisiens qui ont la nostalgie de l'Amérique de retrouver leurs plats favoris, et de déguster un *milk shake* après un bon *western* dans un cinéma.

Vocabulaire

accrochage, (*m.*) collision
aménagé set up
autoroute, (*f.*) freeway
blanchisserie, (*f.*) laundromat
blesser to wound
bondé jammed, filled up
bordé de lined with
bousculer to knock down
caravane, (*f.*) house trailer
chauffard, (*m.*) mauvais chauffeur
céder to yield
déguster to enjoy (food or drink)
doubler to pass, to overtake and pass a car
égratigner to scratch
embouteillage, (*m.*) bottleneck
essence, (*f.*) gasoline
étaler to spread
flic, (*m.*) cop
forfaitaire package deal
fou, (*m.*) madman

gendarme, (*m.*) highway patrol, policeman
grave serious
inondé(s) flooded
ivrogne, (*m.*) drunk
meurtrier murderous
motard, (*m.*) cop on a motorcycle
Moyen-Orient, (*m.*) Middle East
poing, (*m.*) fist
procès-verbal, (*m.*) ticket, citation
salaud filthy pig, bastard!
se battre to fight
terrain, (*m.*) ground
toile, (*f.*) canvas
tordu (twisted head) numbskull
tout est compris everything is included
tuera *future of the verb* «**tuer**» to kill
vacancier, (*m.*) vacationer
vitesse, (*f.*) speed
volant, (*m.*) steering wheel

Composition Vous venez de faire un voyage pendant vos vacances. Où êtes-vous allé? Quels endroits avez-vous visités? Qu'est-ce que vous avez emporté? Qu'est-ce que vous avez rapporté comme souvenir? Est-ce qu'il y a eu des incidents amusants dans votre voyage? Racontez-le, depuis les préparatifs jusqu'au retour. (Inventez, si c'est nécessaire.)

Meunier tu dors

Chapitre **15**

Une femme architecte.

PRÉSENTATION Les professions

Quel âge est-ce que vous avez? dix-huit ans, vingt ans? Dans deux ou trois ans,
vous finirez vos études à l'université, et vous recevrez votre diplôme final. Qu'est-ce
que vous ferez, ensuite? Dans quelle branche est-ce que vous vous dirigerez? Pour
beaucoup de jeunes gens, le choix d'une profession est un problème difficile, à
cause de l'embouteillage de certains domaines (l'enseignement par exemple), à
cause de la crise économique, et aussi parce que toute votre vie future dépend de
ce choix: si vous êtes mal orienté, vous ne serez pas heureux dans votre métier, et
vous ne serez pas une personne heureuse. Plus vous faites des études, plus vous
avez des chances de trouver une profession lucrative, mais ce n'est pas une règle
générale. Il est vrai qu'un diplôme ouvre des portes, mais aussi beaucoup de jeunes
gens qui ne font pas d'études supérieures se débrouillent très bien dans la vie.
Nous parlons des différentes professions. Je vous les décrirai.

Il y a des professions obscures, et modestes: employé de banque, vendeur
(vendeuse), représentant de commerce. Elles ne sont pas vraiment exaltantes, mais
elles sont nécessaires. D'un autre côté, il y a les professions de prestige: médecin,
architecte, avocat, directeur de compagnie. Il y a les occupations qui font rêver les
enfants: les garçons veulent être pilotes, capitaines de bateau, astronautes,

reporters; et les filles: hôtesses de l'air, actrices de cinéma, danseuses (étoiles, bien sûr).

Il y a aussi des occupations bien rebutantes: ouvrier à la chaîne, mineur (de fond), infirmier dans un asile d'aliénés ou dans un hôpital d'enfants arriérés, et d'autres où on peut se sentir libre: alpiniste, explorateur, gardien dans un parc national. Il y a un proverbe qui dit: «Il n'y a pas de sot métier»; et pourtant, parlons de différentes professions. D'abord la mienne: professeur. C'est aussi une profession de prestige, mais, croyez-moi, elle perd beaucoup de son intérêt: on est mal payé — dans certaines institutions; il y a les préparations, les corrections. Il y a des étudiants qui n'apprennent pas leurs leçons. Enfin chacun, une fois dans sa vie choisit une occupation; si on n'est pas content de la sienne, on peut toujours se recycler. Je dis «la mienne» quand je parle de ma profession, mais j'ai plusieurs métiers, alors je peux dire «les miens.» Je suis professeur, d'accord, mais aussi je suis femme de ménage, quand je rentre chez moi, le soir, parce qu'en Amérique on n'a pas de bonne. Je suis plombier quand je répare une conduite d'eau dans ma cuisine. Je suis mécanicien quand je regarde dans le moteur de ma voiture. Je suis jardinier quand je tonds ma pelouse et quand j'arrose mes fleurs et quand je les cueille. Je suis peintre en bâtiment quand je repeins ma cuisine et quand j'ai des loisirs, en vacances, je suis artiste-peintre. Je suis un peu écrivain, aussi, quand j'écris un roman, des poèmes. Je suis aussi un peu couturière quand je fais une robe, un pantalon (vous remarquez au passage qu'il n'y a pas de féminin pour beaucoup de ces noms de métiers; c'est qu'on ne concevait pas l'idée d'une femme mécanicien, plombier, etc.)

Je vous ai parlé de mes différentes occupations; parlez-moi des vôtres. Qu'est-ce que vous ferez, plus tard? Est-ce que vous serez flic, banquier, pompier, monsieur? pâtissière, speakerine à la télé, concierge, Mlle? J'ai fait mon choix; faites le vôtre. Décrivez les professions qui vous intéressent. Décrivez-les moi.

Vocabulaire

aliéné, fou crazy, mad

arroser to water

asile, (*m.*) asylum

bonne, (*f.*) maid

chacun each one, (*f.*) **chacune.** C'est un pronom; l'adjectif est **chaque** (*m. et f.*); il n'y a pas de pluriel.

chaîne, (*f.*) assembly line

concierge, (*f.*) house or apartment house manager

conduite d'eau, (*f.*) water pipe

cueillir to pick (flowers)

dépendre de to depend on

enfant arriéré, (*m.*) retarded child

enseignement, (*m.*) teaching profession

exaltant exciting, thrilling

femme de ménage, (*f.*) cleaning woman

gardien dans un parc, (*m.*) ranger

loisir, (*m.*) leisure

lucratif well-paying

moins...moins the less . . . the less

ouvrier, (*m.*) worker

peindre to paint (**je peins, nous peignons, ils peignent;** *passé composé:* **j'ai peint**)

plus...plus the more . . . the more

pompier, (*m.*) fireman

rebutant unattractive

recevoir un diplôme final to graduate

se débrouiller to manage, to muddle through

se diriger to direct oneself

sot stupide, (*f.*) **sotte**

tondre to mow (verbe régulier du 3ème groupe)

PRONONCIATION   Les sons *p* et *b*

Prononcez **p** initial dans

pneu   **p**saume   **p**sychiatre   **p**sychologie   **p**sychologue

Ne prononcez pas **p** intérieur dans

sculpter (sculpteur, sculpture)   baptiser (baptême)
compter (comptable, compte)   septième (sept)

Mais prononcez le **p** dans **septembre.**

P final n'est jamais prononcé dans

drap   trop   champ   temps   beaucoup

mais il est prononcé dans

cap   concept   stop

B final n'est pas prononcé dans **plomb, Colomb** mais il est prononcé dans **snob** et **club.** Le **b** du verbe **observer** est assourdi en **p** à cause du **s.** Prononcez /ɔpsɛRve/.

Les géminées (suite)

Deux consonnes identiques peuvent se rencontrer quand un **e** muet tombe.

	ss	**dd**
EXEMPLES:	et ce sac	pas de déjeuner
	et ce salon	pas de danger
	et ce supermarché	pas de douane
	et ce style	pas de douche
	et ce siècle	pas de défaut
	nn	**mm**
	je ne nage pas	je me mets
	je ne note pas	je me masse
	je ne nie pas	je me marie
	je ne nomme pas	je me moque
	je ne nettoie pas	je me mesure

Cette disparition du **e** est particulièrement importante au futur (voir p. 239).

Mots en /j/

cueillir /kœjiR/   bruyère (*heather*) /bRyjɛR/
Bayonne (*French town*) /bajɔn/   cobaye (*guinea pig*) /kɔbaj/
coyote /kɔjɔt/   Gruyère (*Swiss town, Swiss cheese*) /gRyjɛR/

VERBES IRRÉGULIERS **STRUCTURES**

recevoir *to receive*

Présent: je **reçois**   nous **recevons** /svõ/
tu **reçois** /swa/   vous **recevez** /sve/
il **reçoit**
ils **reçoivent**

Remarquez qu'il y a un **ç** devant le **o**; le **c** devant **e** est prononcé /s/.

L'imparfait: **je recevais, tu recevais,** etc.
Le passé composé: **j'ai reçu** (avec **ç** devant **u**)

Conjuguez sur le même modèle: **concevoir** (*to conceive*); **décevoir** (*to disappoint*); **apercevoir** (*to see in the distance*).

(*a.*) Conjuguez les verbes entre parenthèses au présent.   *Exercice I*

1. Il (recevoir) une lettre de sa petite amie.
2. J' (apercevoir) un bateau à l'horizon.
3. Nous (concevoir) une idée géniale.
4. Vous (recevoir) un mauvaise nouvelle.
5. Ils (apercevoir) l'autobus au coin de la rue.
6. L'architecte (concevoir) un projet pour un hôpital.

(*b.*) Mettez les verbes (1) à l'imparfait: **Tous les jours...** (2) au passé composé: **Un jour...**

cueillir *to pick* (*plants, flowers*)

je **cueille**   nous **cueillons**
tu **cueilles**   vous **cueillez** /kœj/
il, elle **cueille**   ils, elles **cueillent**

Au présent ce verbe a les terminaisons d'un verbe du 1ᵉʳ groupe.
Remarquez l'orthographe: **cue**ille (comme **que**).

L'imparfait est régulier:

je cueill**ais**   nous cueill**ions** /kœjjõ/*
tu cueill**ais** /kœjɛ/   vous cueill**iez** /kœjje/
il cueill**ait**
ils cueill**aient**

Le passé composé est:

j'ai cueilli   nous avons cueilli

Conjuguez sur le même modèle **recueillir** (*to collect* or *to give shelter to*); **accueillir** (*to welcome, to greet*).

---

*Remarquez les deux /jj/.

Exercice II Mettez la forme correcte du verbe **cueillir, recueillir, accueillir.**

1. Tous les jours elle va au jardin et elle _____ des fleurs fraîches.
2. Quand mes amis arrivent, tu les _____ avec un bouteille de champagne.
3. Quand j'étais enfant, je _____ tous les chats perdus du quartier.
4. Si vous _____ des plantes au bord de la route, le garde forestier va vous punir par une amende (*fine*).
5. J'ai _____ un chien abandonné.
6. Vous _____ toujours vos enfants avec un sourire?

CONSTRUCTIONS A RETENIR

La profession

A la question: **Qui êtes-vous?**
     On répond: Je suis **le** professeur.
                      Vous êtes **un** étudiant.
                      Nous sommes **des** étudiants.

A la question: **Qu'est-ce que vous faites?**
     On répond: Je **suis professeur.** (*sans article*)
                      Vous **êtes étudiant.**
                      Non, je **suis balayeur.**
                                  (*profession/état*)

A la 3ème personne, **il, elle, ils, elles,** on a aussi deux formules:

A la question: **Qui est-ce?**
     On répond: **C'est le** professeur.
                      C'est un professeur.
                      C'est un bon professeur.

On a **c'est** et un article ou un mot de qualification, souvent un adjectif. On identifie une personne ou on indique une qualification, une évaluation.

A la question: **Qu'est-ce qu'il (elle) fait?**
     On répond: Il **est professeur.**
                      Elle **est danseuse.**

On indique simplement la profession. Le verbe **être** est suivi du nom de profession, directement, sans article.

EXEMPLES: **C'est un** Allemand.   Il **est allemand.**
             C'est une Anglaise.   Elle **est anglaise.**
             C'est un protestant de Genève. Il **est protestant.**
             C'est une catholique fanatique. Elle **est catholique.**

Les constructions pour indiquer la nationalité ou la religion sont identiques.

Mettez **il est, elle est, ils sont, elles sont,** ou **c'est.**   *Exercice III*

1. _____ chanteuse.   _____ une chanteuse célèbre.
2. _____ journalistes.   _____ des journalistes connus.
3. _____ facteur.   _____ un facteur consciencieux.
4. _____ directeur.   _____ un directeur très autoritaire.
5. _____ vendeuse.   _____ une vendeuse honnête.
6. _____ architecte.   _____ un grand architecte.

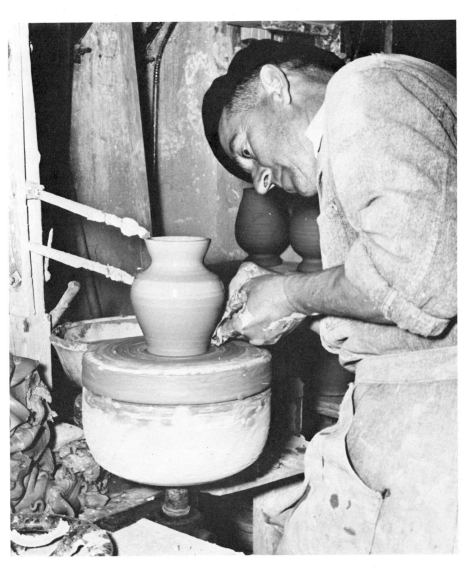

Un artisan potier

La proportion **plus...plus; moins...moins**

> **Plus** il travaille, **plus** il est fatigué.
> **Moins** elle mange, **moins** elle a faim.

Placez **plus** ou **moins** sans article au commencement de la phrase pour indiquer la progression proportionnelle.

Exercice IV   Faites des phrases avec le vocabulaire suivant et les deux expressions, sur ce modèle.

(*a.*) Avec **plus...plus**

1. le soleil brille   je suis heureuse
2. il fait froid   les marmottes dorment
3. il boit des grogs   il est malade

(*b.*) Avec **moins...moins**

4. vous travaillez   vous gagnez
5. il pleut   les fleurs poussent
6. elle étudie   elle a des bonnes notes

La préposition **à cause de**

> Pourquoi est-ce que tu es pâle?   Pourquoi est-ce que tu as peur?
> **Parce que** j'ai peur.   **A cause** de l'examen.

Employez **parce que** avec un verbe: **j'ai peur.** Employez **à cause de** avec un nom: ici **l'examen.** Attention à la contraction de **de** et l'article: **à cause du vent, à cause des nuages.**

Exercice V   Refaites les phrases avec **à cause de** à la place de **parce que;** faites les changements nécessaires.

EXEMPLE: Il a soif parce qu'il y avait du sel dans la soupe.
                Il a soif **à cause du** sel dans la soupe.

1. J'ai peur parce que tous les pays ont la bombe atomique.
2. Tu as sommeil parce que le soleil est chaud.
3. Elles sont contentes parce que c'est le printemps.
4. Nous sommes en retard parce qu'il y a une grosse circulation sur l'autoroute.
5. Jacqueline est nerveuse parce qu'elle a un rendez-vous chez le dentiste.

POINTS DE GRAMMAIRE
Le futur

Aujourd'hui vous ne pensez pas à votre futur, à votre avenir, mais bientôt vous y **penserez**: quelle profession est-ce que vous **choisirez?** Vous **serez** professeur ou balayeur? Vous **voyagerez** ou vous **resterez** dans votre ville? Vous vous **marierez**, vous **aurez** des enfants? etc.

Le futur avec **aller** est très pratique. Mais le temps futur est nécessaire pour faire des projets plus lointains, moins proches.

LA FORMATION DU FUTUR

On prend l'infinitif du verbe:

rester   **choisir**   **prendre**

On ajoute les terminaisons:

–ai		j'*ai*
–as		tu *as*
–a	Comparez avec le verbe	il *a*
–ons	**avoir:** C'est presque	nous av*ons*
–ez	identique.	vous av*ez*
–ont		ils *ont*

Le résultat est:

je rester**ai**	je choisir**ai**	je prend**rai**
tu rester**as**	tu choisir**as**	tu prend**ras**
il rester**a**	il choisir**a**	il prend**ra**
nous rester**ons**	nous choisir**ons**	nous prend**rons**
vous rester**ez**	vous choisir**ez**	vous prend**rez**
ils rester**ont**	ils choisir**ont**	ils prend**ront**

Remarquez la prononciation et l'orthographe des verbes au futur.

1. Il y a toujours les sons /ʀe/, /ʀa/, /ʀõ/.
2. **Prendre:** je pren**drai,** tu pren**dras;** le **e** final des verbes en **–dre** tombe.
3. **Finir:** je fin**irai,** tu fin**iras;** le **i** des verbes en **–ir** est toujours écrit et prononcé.
4. **Rester:** je rester**ai,** tu rester**as; donner:** je donn*e*rai, tu donn*e*ras. Dans les verbes du premier groupe (en **–er**) le **e** est écrit, mais souvent il tombe dans la prononciation. On entend /dɔnʀe/ je donn'rai; /dɔnʀa/ tu donn'ras. Si vous articulez avec soin, vous prononcez ce **e.** Si vous parlez vite, le **e** tombe.
5. Attention aux verbes en **–rer: montrer, rencontrer.**

   il mont**rera** /mõtʀəʀa/   vous rencont**rerez** /ʀãkõtʀəʀe/

   Ajoutez le son /ʀəʀa/, /ʀəʀe/, /ʀəʀõ/.

   il préfér*e*ra   espér*e*ra   explor*e*ra
   il admir*e*ra   prépar*e*ra

   Pour les verbes comme **préférer, espérer** le **e** muet tombe; on a une géminée /ʀʀ/.
6. Verbes en **–yer:** Le **y** se change en **i** dans le futur entier et le **e** est muet.

	Présent	*Futur*
	nous essayons	nous essai**erons** (j'essai**erai**)
	vous vous ennuyez	vous vous ennui**erez** (je m'ennui**erai**)

Envoyer est irrégulier: **j'enverrai.**

Exercice VI Répétez au futur.

1. Je prends un taxi.
2. Tu aimes ce livre.
3. Elle vend des bonbons.
4. Nous préférons le whisky.
5. Vous battez vos enfants.
6. Ils se téléphonent.
7. Je dis la vérité.
8. Tu rencontres Daniel.
9. Il ne rentre pas à la maison.
10. Est-ce qu'ils connaissent les réponses?
11. Je choisis un bonbon au chocolat.
12. Nous partons demain.
13. Ils ne changent pas de voiture.
14. Elle nous montre ses films de vacances.
15. Nous essayons de comprendre.
16. Vous payez la note?
17. Elles ne vendent pas leur maison.
18. Elle arrive à midi.
19. Est-ce que vous conduisez lentement?
20. Elle tombe dans la neige.

LES FUTURS IRRÉGULIERS

Pour certains verbes, on ne part pas de l'infinitif. On a un radical différent. Les terminaisons sont régulières.

Infinitif	*Futur*	*Infinitif*	*Futur*
aller	j'**irai**	avoir	j'**aurai**
savoir	je **saurai**	être	je **serai**
faire	je **ferai**	voir	je **verrai**
envoyer	j'**enverrai**	pouvoir	je **pourrai**
vouloir	je **voudrai**	venir	je **viendrai**
recevoir	je **recevrai**		(du présent: **je viens**)
falloir	il **faudra**	pleuvoir	il **pleuvra**

Exercice VII Répétez les phrases suivantes au futur: (*a.*) avec **aller,** (*b.*) au futur simple.

1. Je vais à l'université.
2. Tu parles au directeur.
3. Elle est charmante.
4. Nous n'avons pas de questions.
5. Il reste chez lui.
6. Vous faites du bon travail.
7. Je viens au restaurant en retard.
8. Tu sais toutes ces choses.
9. Est-ce qu'elle peut voyager seule?
10. Il faut être raisonnable.
11. Vous envoyez des fleurs à votre mère.
12. Il ne pleut pas au printemps.

EMPLOI DU FUTUR

Voici deux règles importantes pour le verbe subordonné, si le verbe principal est au futur.

1. Employez le futur après **quand,** si le verbe principal est au futur:

   Quand tu **seras** grand, qu'est-ce que tu feras?
   Quand je **serai** grand, je serai général.

2. Employez le présent avec **si,** si le verbe principal est au futur:

Si tu **es** général, qu'est-ce que tu feras?
Si je **suis** général, j'aurai un bel uniforme et je ferai la paix.

Si + **il** et **si** + **ils** deviennent **s'il** et **s'ils.** Il n'y a pas d'élision pour **si elle** et **si elles.**

Exercice VIII

Répétez les phrases au futur: (*a.*) avec **quand,** (*b.*) avec **si.**

1. Tu es sage, je t'achète une glace.
2. Il vient, je lui parle.
3. Elle téléphone, tu ne réponds pas.
4. Vous avez un enfant, vous voyez les problèmes.
5. Il reste chez lui, il fait la sieste.
6. Nous sommes en retard, nous avons des ennuis avec le directeur.
7. Ils ont une bicyclette, ils maigrissent.
8. Elles ont le temps, elles voient le film.

Le pronom possessif

votre profession et **la mienne**
mon travail et **le vôtre**

Le pronom possessif **le mien, la tienne, les nôtres** remplace un nom accompagné d'un adjectif possessif: **mon livre, ta femme, nos enfants,** etc. Pour les trois personnes du singulier (je, tu, il) la terminaison du pronom possessif est identique au nom de l'animal familier: **le chien** et sa femelle, **la chienne.** Comparez:

mon ch**ien**	le m**ien**	ma ch**ienne**	la m**ienne**
ton ch**ien**	le t**ien**	ta ch**ienne**	la t**ienne**
son ch**ien***	le s**ien***	sa ch**ienne***	la s**ienne***

Au pluriel, ajoutez un **s** et mettez l'article au pluriel:

les miens	**les miennes**
les tiens	**les tiennes**
les siens	**les siennes**

Pour les trois personnes du pluriel **vous, nous, eux,** et **elles** les formes sont:

notre chien	**le nôtre**	notre chienne	**la nôtre**
votre chien	**le vôtre**	votre chienne	**la vôtre**
leur chien	**le leur**	leur chienne	**la leur**

Au pluriel: **les nôtres** (*m.* et *f.*); **les vôtres; les leurs.**

Attention à la prononciation: Pour l'adjectif **notre, votre** on a un /ɔ/ ouvert. Pour le pronom **le nôtre, le vôtre** on a un /o/ fermé.

*(**à lui, à elle**) Remarquez qu'on accorde avec le nom (**chien**), pas avec le possesseur.

C'est un magicien.

Exercice IX Remplacez le groupe *adjectif possessif + nom* par le *pronom possessif*.

1. mon livre	7. nos occupations	13. vos amies
2. votre affaire	8. sa chambre	14. son travail
3. notre université	9. mes enfants	15. tes parents
4. ta raison	10. son adresse	16. votre pays
5. ma famille	11. leur patrie	17. leurs histoires
6. ton cœur	12. notre temps	

L'EMPLOI DU PRONOM POSSESSIF

Marie a son livre. Elle a **le sien.**
Pierre a sa moto. Il a **la sienne.**

On emploie **le mien, le tien, la nôtre, les vôtres,** etc. quand en anglais on a *mine, yours, ours,* etc. Attention cependant à l'accord avec le nom absent: **le livre = le sien; la moto = la sienne.** La personne (Marie) est la 3ème personne. C'est important, mais le genre de la personne est sans importance. Comme pour le possessif:

(Marie) ses parents: **parents** (*m. pl.*) = **les siens**
(Pierre) ses responsabilités: **responsabilités** (*f. pl.*) = **les siennes**

> Il parle **de** vos **parents?**   Non, il parle **des siens.**
> Tu penses **à** mes **problèmes?**   Non, je pense **aux miens.**

Attention à la rencontre possible de l'article **le mien, les siennes,** etc. avec les prépositions **à** ou **de.** Il y a une contraction:

à + le = **au**	**au mien**
à + les = **aux**	**aux tiens**
de + le = **du**	**du sien**
de + les = **des**	**des nôtres,** etc.

Au féminin singulier: **à la** sienne, **de la** nôtre, etc.
Remarque: *a friend of mine* = **un de mes amis.**

Remarquez la différence entre **à moi** et **le mien.** On dit **Ce livre est à moi,** si la question est **A qui est ce livre?** On dit **C'est le mien,** si la question est **C'est votre livre ou le sien?** (dans le deuxième cas, il y a deux ou plusieurs possesseurs, et il faut choisir).

Refaites les phrases avec un pronom possessif.   *Exercice X*

1. Il a pris ses valises et il a oublié mes valises.
2. Ton travail est plus intéressant que son travail.
3. J'écris à mes parents et à tes parents.
4. Pensez à votre avenir; ne pensez pas à notre avenir.
5. Ils ont parlé de votre profession et de leur profession.
6. Qu'est-ce que vous préférez? Mes tableaux ou ses tableaux?
7. Mes méthodes sont bien supérieures à leurs méthodes.
8. Ma mère et ta mère iront au marché ensemble.
9. Est-ce que ta profession est différente de ma profession?
10. Mon docteur et votre docteur sont excellents.

Les pronoms objets directs et objets indirects ensemble

> Je prête **mon livre à mon ami.**

En français, on a souvent la construction suivante:

prêter ⎫
donner ⎬ une chose (objet direct)   à   une personne (objet indirect)
envoyer ⎭

Si on veut remplacer les deux noms, le nom de chose et le nom de personne, par des pronoms, on a les phrases suivantes:

Je prête mon livre à mon ami.   Je **le lui** prête.
Il me donne le **livre**.   Il **me le** donne.
Elle envoie la **lettre** à **son père**.   Elle **la lui** envoie.

Voici l'ordre des pronoms.

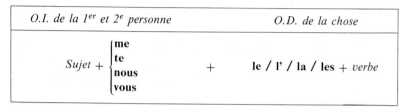

O.I. de la 1ᵉʳ et 2ᵉ personne		O.D. de la chose
Sujet + { me / te / nous / vous	+	**le / l' / la / les** + verbe

EXEMPLES: Le livre?   Il **me le** donne.
             La table?   Elle **te la** montre.
             Les crayons?   Je **vous les** prête.
             La lettre?   Tu **nous l'**envoies.

Exercice XI   Répétez avec les pronoms O.D. et O.I.

1. (L'heure?)   (moi   O.I.)   Il _____ demande.
2. (Les bonbons?)   (vous)   Je _____ donne.
3. (Son auto?)   (nous)   Il _____ prête.
4. (Ton adresse?)   (moi)   Tu _____ envoies.
5. (Le livre?)   (toi)   Nous _____ rendons.
6. (Notre argent?)   (nous)   On _____ vole.

EXEMPLES: Le livre?   Je **le lui** donne.   (à Jacques ou à Catherine)
             La leçon?   Tu **la lui** expliques.   (à Jacques ou à Catherine)
             Le livre?   Je **le leur** donne.   (aux étudiants)
             Les crayons?   Je **les lui** prêterai.   (à Jacques ou à Catherine)
                         Je **les leur** prêterai.   (aux étudiants)

Pour la troisième personne l'ordre des pronoms est différent.

O.D. de la chose		O.I. de la 3ᵉ personne
Sujet + **le / la / les**	+	**lui / leur** + verbe

Exercice XII   Remplacez les mots entre parenthèses par des pronoms.

1. (L'heure?)   (à Jacqueline)   Il _____ demande.
2. (Les bonbons?)   (aux enfants)   Je _____ donnerai.
3. (Ton adresse?)   (à Pierre)   Tu _____ envoies.
4. (Son auto?)   (à ses parents)   Il _____ prêtera.
5. (Leur argent?)   (les touristes = O.I.)   On _____ vole.
6. (Le livre?)   (à son propriétaire)   Nous _____ rendons.

Il **ne me le donne pas.**
Elle **ne le lui envoie pas.**

La négation entoure le groupe: *pronoms* O.D. + O.I. + *verbe simple.*

Répétez les exercices XI et XII à la forme négative.   *Exercice XIII*

Il **ne me l'a pas** donné.
Elle **ne le lui a pas** donné.

La négation entoure le groupe: *pronoms* O.D. + O.I. + *auxiliaire;* le participe passé
est placé après.

Répétez les exercices XI et XII au passé composé négatif.   *Exercice XIV*

Ne **me le** donne pas.
Ne **la lui** envoyez pas.

A l'impératif négatif, l'ordre des pronoms est identique à l'ordre du présent
négatif. Il n'y a pas de sujet.

Répétez la phrase (*a.*) à la forme négative, et (*b.*) à l'impératif négatif.   *Exercice XV*

1. L'adresse?   Tu la lui donnes.
2. Vos livres?   Vous les leur montrez.
3. Son stylo?   Nous le lui rendons.
4. Ton auto?   Tu me la prêtes.
5. Les journaux?   Vous les lui envoyez.
6. La question?   Tu nous la poses.

Le livre?   **Donne-le-moi.**
La lettre?   **Envoyez-la-leur.**

A l'impératif positif les pronoms sont après le verbe. Certaines formes sont
différentes (**moi** et **toi** pour **me** et **te**). L'ordre est le suivant:

O.D. *de la chose*		O.I. *de la personne*
Verbe + **le / la / les**	+	**moi, toi** **nous vous** **lui leur**

Placez des traits d'union (*hyphens*) entre le verbe et les pronoms.

Répétez à l'impératif positif.   *Exercice XVI*

1. Le cahier?   Tu me le donnes.
2. Le numéro de téléphone?   Vous nous le demandez.
3. Ton auto?   Tu nous la prêtes.
4. Cette question?   Vous vous la répétez.
5. Les journaux?   Tu me les envoies.
6. Les raisons?   Tu te les expliques.

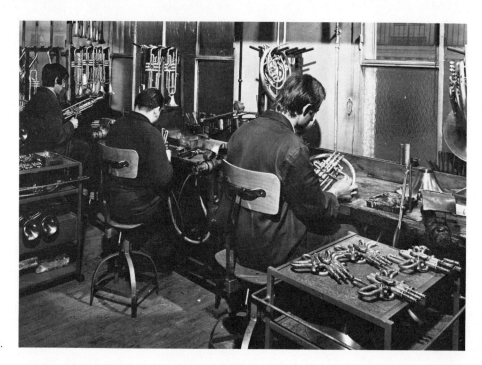

Ils font de la musique.

LECTURES   1. Les travailleurs en France

Sur 50 millions d'habitants la France compte environ 21 millions «d'actifs,» c'est-à-dire de gens qui travaillent. 35 pour cent des travailleurs actifs sont des femmes (une femme sur deux travaille). La population active compte aussi 1,6 million d'étrangers = 8 pour cent des actifs. 16 millions de Français sont salariés (ils reçoivent un salaire mensuel): 2 millions sept cent mille travaillent pour l'État; 1M. pour des entreprises nationales; le reste est dans des industries du secteur privé. Il y a beaucoup d'agriculteurs en France: 14 pour cent de la population active. Ils forment le secteur primaire. Le secteur secondaire, ce sont les industries (38 pour cent). Le secteur tertiaire représente les gens qui travaillent pour les transports, le commerce, les administrations, les banques.

Une enquête récente du journal *le Nouvel Observateur* (16 sept, 1974) montre qu'on peut diviser la France en 5 grandes familles de travailleurs: il faut, pour chaque famille, considérer les diplômes, l'héritage, les qualités personnelles du travailleur et bien sûr, comme résultat, le revenu (combien d'argent on gagne). Le niveau le plus bas, ce sont les exploités: les femmes de ménage, les domestiques, les manœuvres, les ouvriers, les employés dans les services médicaux ou sociaux. Les employés de commerce représentent 50 pour cent de la population active: ils n'ont pas de diplômes, pas de spécialité; leurs revenus sont faibles (les femmes surtout).

La deuxième catégorie, ce sont les «petits capitalistes»: ils représentent 18 pour cent des travailleurs. Ce sont les petits commerçants, les artisans, les agriculteurs. Ils sont leurs propres patrons et ils sont plus indépendants. Il y a en France environ un établissement de commerce pour 65 habitants; les petites boutiques sont encore nombreuses mais les gros supermarchés, les coopératives et les grands magasins les font disparaître.

Les artisans existent depuis le Moyen-Age: ils sont environ 5 M. Ils représentent une sorte de caractéristique de la mentalité française: individualisme, liberté dans le travail, souci de la qualité. Il y a les potiers, les travailleurs du cuir, du bois, des meubles, les cordonniers, les mécaniciens (autos, motos, bicyclettes), etc.

La troisième famille, ce sont les classes moyennes: les professeurs, les instituteurs, les techniciens, et les «cadres» moyens (c'est-à-dire les gens qui sont «entre» l'ouvrier et le patron, et qui ont une certaine responsabilité. Ce sont les «cols blancs»: 26 pour cent.

La quatrième catégorie, 2 pour cent seulement, c'est le capitalisme traditionnel: les industriels, les gros commerçants, les gros agriculteurs, et les professions libérales (avocat, dentiste, docteur, etc.). Pour ces gens, à part les professions libérales, les diplômes ne sont pas très importants, mais l'héritage compte, et surtout les qualités personnelles.

Enfin la cinquième classe, 4 pour cent des travailleurs, c'est la technocratie: les cadres supérieurs, les ingénieurs, les hauts fonctionnaires. Ils forment la classe dirigeante; beaucoup viennent des grandes écoles (Polytechnique, ENA, voir Chapitre 12). Il n'y a pratiquement pas de femmes dans ce groupe.

La durée du travail est officiellement de 40 heures par semaine. En fait, elle est en moyenne de 46 h. et beaucoup de travailleurs font des heures supplémentaires pour augmenter leur salaire (jusqu'à 57 h.) La loi a institué un jour de repos obligatoire par semaine, le dimanche, le lundi pour beaucoup de commerces (ne vous étonnez pas si vous trouvez des magasins fermés le lundi en France). La

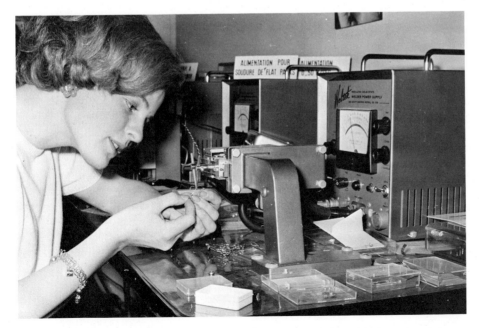

Elle a les doigts agiles.

semaine «anglaise» (repos le samedi et le dimanche) s'est répandue en France, mais dans les administrations on ne commence le week-end que le samedi à midi. Les congés payés annuels sont de quatre semaines depuis 1969.

La hiérarchie sociale existe plus en France qu'en Amérique. Il y a au moins 12 groupes ou milieux distincts dans l'échelle sociale: chacun a son mode de vie, ses habitudes, sa culture et même son langage. L'un se sent facilement supérieur à l'autre: un «cadre moyen» se sent supérieur à un ouvrier; un directeur de compagnie, c'est «mieux» qu'un employé de bureau, et un professeur est «plus» qu'un instituteur. Ces milieux ne communiquent pas entre eux et un fils d'ouvrier a une chance sur dix de faire des études et de devenir «cadre supérieur.»

Vocabulaire

bois, (*m.*) wood
boutique, (*f.*) small shop
commerçant, (*m.*) shop owner
cordonnier, (*m.*) cobbler, shoe repairman
en moyenne on the average
établissement de commerce, (*m.*) shop
fonctionnaire, (*m.*) civil servant
loi, (*f.*) law

instituteur, (*m.*) elementary school teacher
manoeuvre, (*m.*) unskilled laborer
niveau, (*m.*) level
potier, (*m.*) potter
revenu, (*m.*) income
secteur privé, (*m.*) private enterprise
se répandre to spread

2. Poème

L'ADIEU

J'ai cueilli ce brin de bruyère
L'automne est morte, souviens-t'en
Nous ne nous verrons plus sur terre
Odeur du temps, brin de bruyère
Et souviens-toi que je t'attends

GUILLAUME APOLLINAIRE

Vocabulaire

brin, (*m.*) a twig
bruyère, (*f.*) heather
se souvenir (de) = **se rappeler** to remember

Composition Décrivez les professions qui vous attirent; quelle profession allez-vous choisir et pourquoi?

La boulangère a des écus

Chapitre **16**

La bou – lan – gèr' a des é – cus qui ne lui

coû – tent guè – è – re La bou – lan – gèr a des é – cus qui ne lui

coû – tent guè – è – re Elle en a je les ai vus j'ai vu la

bou – lan – gèr' aux é – cus. j'ai vu la bou – lan – gè – è – re J'ai vu la

bou – lan – gèr' aux é – cus j'ai vu la bou – lan – gè – è – re.

PRÉSENTATION   L'argent

L'argent est un problème pour la majorité des gens. Les sous — les sous — on a
des problèmes si on en a, si on est riche. La richesse peut être un inconvénient. On
a des problèmes si on n'en a pas, si on est pauvre. La pauvreté est toujours un
inconvénient. Comment est-ce qu'on peut être riche? Si vous avez des parents
riches, ou une vieille tante sans enfants, il est probable que vous hériterez un jour
leur fortune. C'est commode, un héritage, c'est facile. On attend, c'est tout!

Si vous n'avez pas d'héritage, vous pouvez devenir riche si vous travaillez, si
vous gagnez de l'argent dans votre profession. Nous l'avons vu dans le chapitre
précédent, le choix d'une profession est important. Mais il y a les gens qui sont
exploités, il y a ceux qui travaillent mais qui n'arrivent pas au minimum vital, et
les pauvres, les économiquement faibles, et puis, il y a ceux qui ne travaillent pas,
les paresseux ou les chômeurs. Le chômage est un problème grave dans certains
pays.

Alors, vous êtes étudiant; vous avez une bourse peut-être. Non? vous vivez avec
vos parents et ils payent vos études et vous donnent de l'argent de poche. Ou bien
vous vivez seul et vous avez votre budget. Est-ce que vous êtes économe ou
dépensier? Est-ce que vous faites attention à vos dépenses, ou est-ce que vous jetez
l'argent par les fenêtres?

Quand vous aurez fini vos études, vous aurez un job, et vous serez économiquement indépendant, alors, il faudra faire attention. Qu'est-ce que vous ferez de
votre argent chaque mois quand vous aurez reçu votre chèque? Vous pouvez en
mettre une partie de côté, à la banque, qui vous donnera un intérêt. Vous pourrez
le placer, l'investir dans une affaire, acheter des actions à la Bourse (Mais attention, c'est dangereux! Il y a les hausses et les baisses.). Est-ce que vous ferez des
économies? Oui, it faut faire des économies; être économe, c'est utile, mais il ne

faut pas devenir avare; l'avarice, ça c'est laid. Connaissez-vous des avares célèbres dans la littérature?

Attention, si vous avez trop d'économies, vos amis voudront vous emprunter de l'argent. Est-ce que vous leur en prêterez? Vous êtes généreux, mais il ne faut pas être stupide ou alors ils ne vous rembourseront pas ce que vous leur aurez prêté. Dans ce pays, on achète beaucoup à crédit: une auto, un nouveau frigidaire, une télé. Allez, on achète, on paie plus tard. Mais chaque mois, il y a des traites à payer, et souvent, c'est la catastrophe. Ah! les cartes de crédit, quelle invention diabolique!

Attention, sur votre salaire il faudra payer des impôts, et le percepteur est là pour percevoir (= recevoir) des impôts sur vos gains, si ceux-ci sont trop importants.

Et puis, il y a les joueurs, ceux qui ont la passion du jeu: les courses, les cartes, la roulette — et qui perdent leur argent sur les champs de course, dans les casinos, dans les machines à sous, ou les maisons de jeux.

Enfin, que dire des voleurs, des escrocs? Des «hold-ups», il y en a tous les jours, on le lit dans les journaux.

Alors, qu'est-ce que vous serez plus tard? Un jeune retraité, un millionnaire avec des économies dans une banque suisse, un Américain avec des cartes de crédit, un hippie «fauché,» joyeusement inconscient de ses problèmes d'argent et de ceux du reste du monde?

Vocabulaire

action, (*f.*) stock
affaire, (*f.*) business, *also* bargain
avare greedy
avarice, (*f.*) greed
baisse, (*f.*) fall
bourse, (*f.*) scholarship; **La Bourse,** (*f.*) stock market
chômage, (*m.*) unemployment
chômeur, (*m.*) one who is unemployed
courses, (*f. pl.*) races — mostly horse races
dépenser to spend
économe ≠ **dépensier** thrifty ≠ extravagant
économiquement faible underprivileged
emprunter to borrow (de l'argent à une personne)
escroc, (*m.*) crook
fauché (*fam.*) broke
gain, (*m.*) earnings
gagner to earn
hausse, (*f.*) rise
hériter to inherit

impôt, (*m.*) tax
jeter l'argent par les fenêtres dépenser tout son argent
joueur, (*m.*) gambler; **jouer** to gamble
laid ≠ **beau**
machine à sous, (*f.*) slot machine
mettre de côté; faire des économies to save
minimum vital, (*m.*) subsistence wage
paresseux lazy
pauvre poor
pauvreté, (*f.*) poverty
percepteur, (*m.*) tax collector
prêter to lend (de l'argent à une personne)
rembourser to reimburse
retraite, (*f.*) retirement; **prendre sa retraite** to retire
retraité, (*m.*) retired person
richesse, (*f.*) wealth
sous, (*m. pl.*) popular word for money
traite, (*f.*) bill
vivre to live
voleur, (*m.*) thief

PRONONCIATION Les sons des groupes **gue, gui, gua; qui, qua; gn, ing**

1. Les groupes **gue, gui** sont prononcés /g/, /gi/ dans les mots **fatigue, guitare.**
   Le groupe **gui** est prononcé /gyi/ dans **linguistique.**
   Le groupe **gua** est prononcé /gwɑ/ dans **Guadeloupe, jaguar.**

2. Les groupes **qui, qua** sont prononcés /ki/, /ka/ dans **quitter, quatre.** Mais ils
   sont prononcés /kyi/ dans **équidistant;** /kwa/ dans **équateur, quatuor, square.**

3. Le groupe **gn** est prononcé /ɲ/ (*canyon*) dans:

   magnifique   ignorer   ignorant   peignons   Espagne

   Mais il est prononcé /gn/ dans:

   diagnostic   agnostique

   Remarquez le mot **oignon** /ɔɲõ/.

4. Le groupe **ing** est prononcé /ŋ/ dans des mots franglais:

   camping   parking   smoking (*tuxedo*)   **footing** (*jogging*)

Les sons /u/, /i/, /y/

Contrastez les sons:

/u/	/i/	/y/
doux	dit	du
sous	si	su
loue	lit	lu
fou	fit	fut
joue	j'y	jus
nous	ni	nu
vous	vit	vu

STRUCTURES VERBES IRRÉGULIERS

devoir *to owe*

Présent: je **dois**   nous **devons** /dvõ/
tu **dois** /dwa/   vous **devez** /dve/
il, elle **doit**
ils, elles **doivent**

Futur, irrégulier: je **devrai,** tu **devras,** etc.
Imparfait, régulier: je **devais,** tu **devais,** etc.
Passé Composé: j'**ai dû,** etc.

vivre   *to live*

Présent:	je **vis**	nous **vivons**
	tu **vis**	vous **vivez**
	il **vit**	ils **vivent**

Futur, régulier: je **vivrai,** tu **vivras,** nous **vivrons,** etc.
Imparfait, régulier: je **vivais,** nous **vivions,** etc.
Passé composé: j'**ai vécu,** etc. (sans cédille, le son est /ky/)

Mettez le verbe au temps indiqué.   *Exercice I*

(devoir)

1. Si tu m'empruntes de l'argent, tu me le _____ (*futur*). Et vous aussi, mes
   enfants, vous me le _____ .
   Ils _____ (*présent*) dix mille dollars à la banque.
   Elle _____ (*imparfait*) beaucoup à ses parents. Nous _____ (*imparfait*)
   beaucoup à nos parents.

(vivre)

2. Quand j'étais en France, je _____ (*imparfait*) à la campagne. Et vous, où est-ce
   que vous _____ (*imparfait*)?
   Quand je serai vieille, je ne _____ (*futur*) pas seule.
   Il _____ (*passé composé*) toute sa vie en Afrique.
   Ils sont morts à 99 ans: ils _____ (*passé composé*) assez longtemps.

CONSTRUCTIONS A RETENIR

Le verbe **devoir** avec un infinitif

1. Il **doit faire** beau à Tahiti.
   Elle a **dû oublier** notre rendez-vous.
   Tu n'as pas mangé pendant 2 jours? Tu **devais avoir** faim.

Le verbe **devoir** avec un infinitif donne un sens de probabilité au verbe (en
anglais — *it must be nice, she must have forgotten, you were probably feeling
hungry*). **Devoir** peut être conjugué au présent, au passé composé, ou à l'imparfait.

2. Mes parents **doivent faire** un voyage en Europe.
   Nous **devions sortir** ce soir, mais je suis fatigué.

Ici le verbe **devoir** au présent donne un sens de futur, d'action projetée. Il est
l'équivalent de **aller** + *infinitif:* **Mes parents vont faire un voyage.**

   A l'imparfait, le projet est manqué (*it failed*): Nous **devions sortir** mais je suis
fatigué. (*We were going to go out, but I am tired.*) Il y a souvent **mais** après le projet
manqué.

3. Les adjectifs **doivent s'accorder** avec le nom.
   En France les jeunes gens **doivent faire** leur service militaire a vingt ans.
   On **doit respecter** ses parents.

Le sens d'obligation, de nécessité existe aussi pour un sujet impersonnel, une idée, une abstraction. Pour les personnes, il est plus rare, sauf si les personnes sont un groupe (les jeunes gens, les professeurs) ou «**on.**»

Pour un individu, on préfère la construction avec **il faut** + *infinitif* et **il faut que** + *subjonctif* (Chapitre 20).

Exercice II   Répétez avec **devoir** au temps qui convient.

EXEMPLE: Ils viendront ce soir: Ils doivent venir ce soir.

1. Elles iront au Mexique pour Noël.
2. Gérard n'est pas à notre rendez-vous. Il a oublié probablement.
3. On recommence ce chapitre cinq fois. C'est nécessaire.
4. Les verbes pronominaux se conjuguent avec «être» au passé composé.
5. Ils allaient se marier en décembre, mais elle a changé d'avis.
6. Nous reverrons les Smith la semaine prochaine.
7. Une jeune fille, autrefois, baissait toujours les yeux (c'était une obligation).
8. Vous êtes fatigué (probablement).
9. Il faisait froid à la montagne.
10. Tu allais écrire à tes grands-parents, et tu ne l'as pas fait.

Les expressions de temps: **il y a** (*ago*), **il y a...que**

Il y a un an, ils ont adopté une petite fille.

La formule est:

> **il y a** + la durée,
> l'expression de temps + le verbe au passé composé ou à l'imparfait

Il y a peut aussi être placé à la fin de la phrase:

Ils l'ont adoptée **il y a un an.**

Exercice III   Complétez les phrases avec **Il y a.**

1. (10 minutes) Il est sorti.
2. (une heure) Elle a téléphoné.
3. (6 mois) Ils ont acheté une maison.
4. (une semaine) Ma cousine a eu deux bébés.
5. (3 ans) Nous avons fait un voyage en Europe.
6. (2 semaines) Le pauvre, il vivait encore.

Il y a...que:

Il y a une heure que j'étudie ce chapitre.
I have been studying this chapter for an hour.

En anglais on a le *present perfect progressive form.* Cela veut dire: «J'ai commencé à étudier il y a une heure, et je travaille encore maintenant.»

La formule est:

> **il y a** + la durée + **que** + le verbe au présent seulement

Refaites les phrases avec **Il y a...que.**   *Exercice IV*

1. (10 minutes) elle téléphone
2. (3 heures) il parle
3. (longtemps) je t'aime
4. (dix ans) ils habitent dans la même maison
5. (deux mois) vous avez un rhume

Il y a deux ans que je ne l'ai pas vu.
I have not seen him for two years.

En anglais on a le *present perfect,* mais pas la forme progressive. En français on a:

> **il y a** + la durée + **que** + le passé composé

Répétez avec **Il y a...que.**   *Exercice V*

EXEMPLE: Elle est partie il y a dix minutes.
            Il y a dix minutes qu'elle est partie.

1. J'ai fait mon dernier voyage en Europe il y a trois ans.
2. Elle a téléphoné il y a une heure.
3. Ils sont partis il y a huit jours.
4. Mes parents sont morts il y a dix ans.
5. Vous avez perdu votre chien il y a deux semaines?

Le passé récent: **venir de**

Paul **vient de** sortir.
Il est sorti il y a une seconde. (*He just left.*)
Je **viens de** dîner (= j'ai fini de dîner il y a une minute.)
Ils **viennent de** rentrer.

C'est un passé récent, une façon commode de dire *He just went out, I just ate dinner,* etc.

La formule est:

| le verbe **venir** au présent + **de** + l'infinitif d'un autre verbe |

Exercice VI Refaites les phrases avec le verbe **venir de.**

1. Ils ont acheté une ferme.
2. Les Indépendants ont gagné aux élections.
3. Les astronautes ont atterri sur la lune!
4. L'année scolaire est finie. (Vive les vacances!)
5. Je suis rentré d'une croisière à Tahiti.
6. Elle a eu un bébé.

Le chien est bien élevé.

POINTS DE GRAMMAIRE

Le futur antérieur

Je finis mon travail à 6 h 30, je dîne à 7 h.
Je dîne quand j'ai fini mon travail.
Je finirai mon travail à 6 h 30, je dînerai à 7 h.
Je dînerai quand j'**aurai fini** mon travail.

J'aurai fini est un futur antérieur. C'est le passé composé du futur. Il exprime une action future qui a lieu avant une autre action future.

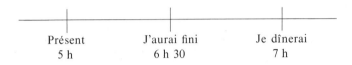

Présent	J'aurai fini	Je dînerai
5 h	6 h 30	7 h

FORMES

On prend le passé composé:

        j'**ai** fini   je **suis** arrivé   je me **suis** reposé

On conjugue l'auxiliaire au futur:

j'**aurai fini**	je **serai arrivé(e)**	je **me serai reposé(e)**
tu **auras fini**	tu **seras arrivé(e)**	tu **te seras reposé(e)**
il **aura fini**	il **sera arrivé**	il **se sera reposé**
nous **aurons fini**	nous **serons arrivés (ées)**	nous **nous serons reposés (ées)**
vous **aurez fini**	vous **serez arrivés (ées)**	vous **vous serez reposés (ées)**
ils **auront fini**	ils **seront arrivés**	ils **se seront reposés**

EMPLOI

Mettez le futur antérieur après **quand** même si en anglais il n'y a pas de *future past*. Le français est plus strict que l'anglais pour cette concordance de temps.

Répétez avec le *futur* et le *futur antérieur* à la place du présent et du passé composé.

Exercice VII

1. Je me lève quand mon réveil a sonné. 2. Je réponds quand on m'a posé une question. 3. Il est fâché quand il a manqué son train. 4. Elle est contente quand elle a économisé 1.000 dollars. 5. Nous allons en France quand nous avons terminé nos études. 6. Vous vous reposez quand vous avez fait tous vos exercices. 7. Ils pleurent quand ils ont perdu à la Bourse. 8. Elles achètent des robes quand elles ont gagné quatre sous. 9. Tu fais un emprunt à la banque quand tu as depensé tes économies.

Le pronom démonstratif

Ce livre-ci est intéressant, ce livre-là est idiot.
Celui-ci est intéressant, **celui-là** est idiot.

Cette jeune fille-ci est simple, cette jeune fille-là est compliquée.
Celle-ci est simple, **celle-là** est compliquée.

Ces garçons-ci sont sympas. Ces garçons-là sont snobs.
Ceux-ci sont sympas, **ceux-là** sont snobs.

Ces lettres-ci sont longues. Ces lettres-là sont courtes.
Celles-ci sont longues, **celles-là** sont courtes.

Celui-ci, celui-là, celle-ci, etc. sont des pronoms démonstratifs. Vous montrez des personnes ou des objets. Voici les formes du pronom démonstratif:

	Singulier		*Pluriel*	
Masculin:	celui-ci	celui-là	ceux-ci	ceux-là
Féminin:	celle-ci	celle-là	celles-ci	celles-là

On les appelle les formes longues.

Exercice VIII Répétez le pronom démonstratif à la place du nom.

EXEMPLE: cet homme-ci: **celui-ci**

1. ces oiseaux-là
2. cette maison-ci
3. cet appartement-là
4. ces châteaux-là
5. ces oranges-là
6. cet enfant-ci
7. cette dame-là
8. ces questions-ci
9. ce monsieur-là
10. ces livres-là

Exercice IX Remplacez l'expression en italiques par le pronom démonstratif.

1. Est-ce que vous allez à cette banque-ci ou à *cette banque-là?*
2. J'aime mieux ce casino-ci que *ce casino-là.*
3. Nous achetons à ce magasin-ci plutôt qu'à *ce magasin-là.*
4. Ces articles-là sont plus chers que *ces articles-ci.*
5. Ces pommes-ci et *ces pommes-là* sont bon marché.
6. Combien coûte cette auto-ci? Et *cette auto-là?*

Prenez **ceci** et laissez **cela.**
C'est **ça.**

C'est la forme neutre du pronom démonstratif: **ceci** et **cela** (*this* and *that*). On montre un objet indéfini. **Ça** est la contraction de **cela.**

Le professeur de Pierre est intéressant.
Celui de Bernard est plus amusant.

La montre de Marie marche bien.
Celle de Catherine ne marche pas.

Les parents de Bob sont américains.
Ceux de Jean-Claude sont français.

Les notes de Maurice sont acceptables.
Celles de Richard sont terribles.

Les formes courtes du pronom démonstratif			
mas. sing.	**celui**		
fém. sing.	**celle**	**de**	nom de
mas. pl.	**ceux**		personne
fém. pl.	**celles**		

Dans les exemples ci-dessus, on n'a pas **-ci** ou **-là** après le pronom mais on a **de** et un nom de personne. C'est la traduction de la forme possessive anglaise: *Pierre's, Paul's, Marie's,* etc. Remarquez qu'il n'y a pas de pronom neutre.

Le train qui part à 5 h est un rapide.
Celui qui part à 6 h est un omnibus.

La leçon que j'explique est facile.
Celle que j'expliquerai demain est difficile.

Les étudiants qui comprennent sont contents.
Ceux qui ne comprennent pas sont mécontents.

Les réponses que vous donnez aujourd'hui sont incorrectes.
Celles que vous avez données hier étaient correctes.

Les mêmes formes courtes sont suivies de **qui** ou **que,** pronoms relatifs.

celui
celle | **qui**
ceux | **que**
celles

C'est la traduction en français de *the one who, that; the ones who, that.*

Remplacez les groupes en italiques par un pronom démonstratif, forme courte: *Exercice X*
celui de ou **celui qui,** etc.

1. Mon argent est à la banque. Où est *l'argent* que je vous ai prêté?
2. Marie a fait un voyage avec ses économies. *Les économies* que Pierre a faites, il les a mangées!
3. Les impôts qu'on paie aux U.S.A. sont plus élevés que *les impôts* qu'on paie en France.
4. Les ouvriers des U.S.A. sont mieux payés que *les ouvriers* de France.
5. Je ne crois pas cette histoire. Quelle histoire? *L'histoire* que vous me racontez.
6. Le prix du beurre est plus haut que *le prix* de la margarine.
7. Le salaire d'un plombier est plus intéressant que *le salaire* d'un professeur!
8. Cette auto-ci est plus rapide que *l'auto* que je viens d'acheter.

Les pronoms personnels ensemble

> Elle me donne du travail, elle **m'en** donne.
> Vous lui envoyez des fleurs, vous **lui en** envoyez.

Voici l'ordre des pronoms avec l'objet indirect de la personne et l'objet partitif **en**: **m'en, t'en, nous en, vous en, lui en, leur en.**

> Il **ne m'en donne pas.**
> Vous **ne leur en prêtez pas.**

Comme pour les autres pronoms, la négation entoure le groupe *pronoms + verbe simple*.

> Il **ne m'en a pas** donné.
> Vous **ne leur en avez pas** prêté.

La négation entoure le groupe *pronoms + auxiliaire*. Le participe passé est placé après **pas**.

> **Ne m'en donne pas.**
> **Ne leur en prêtez pas.**

A l'impératif négatif, on supprime le sujet.

> **Donne-m'en!**
> **Prête lui-en!**
> **Demande leur-en!**

A l'impératif positif, l'ordre est le même et les pronoms sont après le verbe.

Exercice XI   Refaites les phrases avec les pronoms corrects pour les mots entre parenthèses.

1. (du courage)   (vous = o.i.) Il _____ montre.
2. (des nouvelles)   (me = o.i.) Vous _____ envoyez.
3. (du vin)   (aux amis) Nous _____ servons.
4. (de la patience)   (nous = o.i.) Il _____ faut.
5. (de l'argent)   (à ta cousine) Tu _____ prêtes.
6. (des histoires)   (à son ami) Elle _____ raconte.
7. (du travail)   (me = o.i.) Vous _____ donnez.

Exercice XII   Répétez les phrases que vous aurez obtenues:

(*a.*) à la forme négative du présent,   (*c.*) au passé composé, négatif.
(*b.*) au passé composé, affirmatif,

Exercice XIII   Répétez à l'impératif négatif, puis à l'impératif positif.

Des photos?

1. Tu m'en envoies.   4. Tu lui en donnes.
2. Vous leur en montres.   5. Vous nous en montrez.
3. Nous lui en envoyons.

> Vos parents vous envoient à l'université. Ils **vous y** envoient.
> Ses amis la retrouvent à la cafétéria. Ils **l'y** retrouvent.

La sieste du clochard.

Voici l'ordre des pronoms avec l'objet direct de la personne et l'adverbe **y: m'y, t'y, l'y, nous y, vous y, les y.** Cette combinaison est possible après un verbe comme:

envoyer	une personne	à un endroit
expédier	une personne	à un endroit
adresser	une personne	à un endroit
emmener	une personne	à un endroit
rencontrer	une personne	à un endroit
(*to meet by accident*)		
retrouver	une personne	à un endroit
(*to meet with a date*)		

Mettez le pronom O.D. de la personne et **y.**   *Exercice XIV*

1. (au cinéma) (toi = O.D.)   Tes amis _____ emmènent.
2.   (moi = O.D.)   Moi, il ne _____ emmène pas.
3. (dans le bureau du directeur) (les élèves qui font du bruit)   Le professeur _____ envoie.
4. (au diable) (cette femme impossible)   Il _____ expédiera.
5. (au café de la Paix) (nous = O.D.)   Les Giscard _____ ont rencontrés.
6. (à ce bureau) (vous = O.D.)   Vous _____ adresserez de ma part.
7. (à la cafétéria) (te = O.D.)   Je _____ retrouve à midi?

A l'impératif négatif, on dit:

Ne les y envoyez **pas.**

Exercice XV   Répétez à l'impératif négatif.

1. Tu les y emmènes.   3. Vous nous y rencontrez.
2. Nous l'y expédions.   4. Vous les y envoyez.

A l'impératif positif, ces formes sont rares, parce qu'on ne termine pas, en français, une phrase par **m'y, t'y, l'y** pour des raisons d'euphonie et de confusion. On dit simplement:

Emmenez-moi.   **Retrouvez-nous là-bas.**

Le groupe **y en** est souvent appelé *donkey's rule.* On le trouve surtout dans l'expression **il y en a, il n'y en a pas** (*there are some, there are none*).

Il y a du pain. Il **y en** a.
Il **n'y en** a **pas.**

Exercice XVI   Répétez les questions avec **il y en a** ou **il n'y en a pas** et répondez aux questions.

EXEMPLE: Des étudiants intelligents dans la classe? **Il y en a?**
Oui, **il y en a.**

1. Du lait dans votre café?   4. Du sucre dans la soupe?
2. Des Français sur la lune?   5. Des moustiques au Wisconsin?
3. De la neige au Sahara?   6. Des skunks en France?

RÉVISION: Tableau des pronoms

Sujet renforcé	*Sujet*	*Objet direct*	*Objet indirect*	*Objet de préps*
moi	je	me, m'	me, m'	(avec) moi
toi	tu	te, t'	te, t'	(avec) toi
lui	il	le, l'	lui	(avec) lui
elle	elle	la, l'	lui	(avec) elle
nous	nous	nous	nous	(avec) nous
vous	vous	vous	vous	(avec) vous
eux	ils	les	leur	(avec) eux
elles	elles	les	leur	(avec) elles
y		**en**		

Combinaisons possibles:

O.I.	O.D.	O.D.	O.I.
me			
te	le	le	lui
nous	la	la	
vous	les	les	leur
se			

avec **en**	avec **y**
m'en	m'y
t'en	t'y
nous en	nous y
vous en	vous y
s'en	s'y
lui en	l'y
leur en	les y

y en

Le passé composé et l'imparfait ensemble

Dans une composition, dans un récit, dans une lettre employez le passé composé pour les actions qui ont lieu une fois et qui répondent à la question: **Qu'est-ce qu'il (ou elle) a fait? Qu'est-ce qui est arrivé?** (*What did he do, what happened?*); employez l'imparfait pour les états, les descriptions (*what was going on, what was it like,* etc.)

Dans ce récit, mettez le temps correct, *imparfait* ou *passé composé*.   *Exercice XVII*

Quand j' (être) étudiante à Paris, je n' (avoir) pas beaucoup d'argent. J' (avoir) une bourse, mais ce n' (être) pas suffisant. Alors je (travailler) avec une agence qui (organiser) des visites des différents quartiers de Paris. Un jour, l'agence m' (charger) d'emmener un groupe dans un quartier de Paris: le Marais. Ce groupe (se composer) de deux professeurs américains. Le Marais, c'est un vieux quartier qui se trouve rive droite, au centre de la ville. Mais je ne (aller) jamais là-bas parce que j' (habiter) au Quartier Latin. Je ne (connaître) pas du tout ce quartier. Mais j' (être) consciencieuse, alors je (prendre) le guide Michelin et je (lire) attentivement tout le chapitre sur ce quartier: il (contenir) plusieurs églises, des musées et des vieux hôtels, et une communauté juive y (vivre).

Nous (partir), mes deux «clients» et moi. Nous (voir) l'église St Gervais, la place des Vosges, les Archives, et les petits magasins «yiddish.» Mais dans ce dédale de petites rues, nous (se perdre). C'est-à-dire que tout à coup je (se dire): «Où est-ce que nous sommes?» La rue (être) calme. Nous (se trouver) devant un «hôtel,» sûrement très ancien; une jolie grille (laisser) voir un jardinet charmant, avec des statues. Un des Américains me (demander): «Comment s'appelle ce bâtiment?» Je (dire): «Euh! euh!» Je (regarder) dans mon guide. Où (être) ce musée? J' (être) bien perdue. Les deux professeurs (regarder) dans le guide avec moi, mais nous (ne pas réussir) à trouver le renseignement. Enfin! L'un d'eux (arrêter) un homme qui (passer) et lui (demander) «Comment s'appelle cette maison?» « — C'est le musée Carnavalet, monsieur, (répondre) le passant. A Paris, tout le monde le connaît, c' (être) la demeure de Mme de Sévigné, qui (être) un écrivain célèbre au XVIe siècle.» J' (expliquer) à mes deux compagnons que je n' (être) pas une vraie

Parisienne. Ils (sourire). Dans le fond, ils (être) très fiers d'avoir trouvé le renseignement seuls.

Puis nous (continuer) notre promenade. Nous (arriver) dans une petite rue obscure, la rue Quincampoix. Mon guide (dire) que c' (être) une rue célèbre à cause d'une panique financière et de la banque qui s'y (trouver) autrefois. Mes deux Américains et moi (entrer) dans la rue, mais tout à coup nous (apercevoir) des femmes, très maquillées, très vulgaires, qui (se tenir) debout, devant leurs maisons. Mon guide ne (dire) pas que cette rue (être) maintenant célèbre pour ses prostituées. J' (être) terriblement embarrassée. Mes deux compagnons m' (attraper) chacun par un bras et nous (courir) à l'autre bout de la rue, suivis par les remarques violentes de ces dames.

J' (avoir) très peur. Sans doute ils (aller) faire des réclamations à l'agence car ce n' (être) pas le vrai Paris qu'ils (vouloir) voir. Et moi, j' (aller) perdre mon job. Mais non, ils (rire) et (trouver) l'aventure amusante. Nous (revenir) dans un quartier plus familier, le Quartier Latin, et nous (boire) à la santé de Mme de Sévigné et des dames de la Rue Quincampoix.

Vocabulaire

attraper   to seize, to catch
autrefois   in the old times
bâtiment, (*m.*)   building
dédale, (*m.*)   maze
demeure, (*f.*)   maison
faire des réclamations   to complain

grille, (*f.*)   gate
hôtel, (*m.*)   *here,* a big mansion
juive, juif   jewish
laisser   to let
passant, (*m.*)   passer-by
suivi par   followed by

LECTURE   Les salaires en France

Les salaires en France correspondent évidemment à la profession qu'on exerce; et la façon de dépenser aussi. Il y a encore de grands écarts entre le salaire d'un «cadre supérieur» par exemple, et celui d'un ouvrier; il y a aussi des inégalités entre le salaire d'un homme et celui d'une femme, pour un travail identique. Le salaire d'un cadre supérieur masculin est en moyenne de 8.200 F par mois.* L'ouvrière, elle, reçoit 1.354 F.** Les statistiques montrent qu'il y a 50% de la population active qui est dans la section des «exploités», c'est-à-dire ceux qui ont tout juste de quoi vivre. Pourtant le SMIG (salaire minimum interprofessionnel garanti) fixe un salaire minimum pour les travailleurs, mais le coût de la vie augmente plus vite.

Il y a des travaux que les Français ne veulent plus faire, car ils les trouvent trop durs ou dégradants; ces travaux sont alors confiés à des «travailleurs immigrés» (ils sont environ 1 M ½), des Algériens, des Marocains, des Portugais, des Italiens. Ils

---

*about $1,600   **about $260.00

sont balayeurs, éboueurs, et le salaire qu'ils reçoivent est quand même supérieur à celui qu'ils reçoivent chez eux. Et une femme de ménage ne gagne que 8 F de l'heure ($1.50).

Les professions où on gagne bien sa vie sont celles de docteur, de dentiste, d'avocat, de cadre supérieur et de haut fonctionnaire. Certains hauts fonctionnaires vivent presque gratuitement, car beaucoup de leurs dépenses sont remboursées par le gouvernement. C'est une profession très recherchée.

Comment est-ce que les Français dépensent leur argent? Les étrangers qui visitent la France, avec leurs poches pleines de «chèques de voyage» sont unanimes: comment font les Français pour vivre dans un pays où il y a tant de bonnes choses à acheter et où tout est si cher? Bien sûr, on ne voit pas, quand on est touriste, les clochards des quartiers pauvres, les taudis et les bidon-villes, ni les «économiquement faibles,» les petits vieux et les petites vieilles qui font les poubelles tôt le matin, avant le passage des éboueurs.

Pourtant, certains Français vivent bien. La nourriture est importante, et une bonne table est un signe de confort: mais la viande est chère (40 F le kilo de

Dans un restaurant chic.

bifteck = \$8.00!). Les vêtements aussi sont chers, mais élégants, et les Français (et surtout les Françaises) aiment suivre la mode.

Pendant longtemps les Français ont négligé leur logement et dépensé peu d'argent pour leur maison. Aussi on trouve des maisons en France qui n'ont pas de salle de bains! Mais la construction se développe, dans toutes les directions, dans des styles plus ou moins harmonieux: les «grands ensembles,» les HLM (habitations à loyer modéré) sont horribles, mais certaines maisonnettes charmantes. Les Français achètent même un appartment, plutôt qu'ils ne louent. Et les gens riches ont une résidence secondaire, une fermette à la campagne, ou un châlet à la montagne.

Acheter à crédit est une coutume récente. Autrefois, on achetait seulement si on avait assez d'argent pour payer comptant. Mais le crédit, le «tempérament», pousse à la dépense. Alors les Français achètent: des frigos, des autos, des télés, des mixeurs, etc.

Achetez maintenant, payez plus tard! Mais attention, il faut songer aux impôts. Le percepteur est un personnage puissant et redouté. Chaque Français adulte et qui travaille doit faire sa déclaration d'impôts, puis il doit payer en trois fois, s'il veut; pas de déduction automatique sur votre salaire, alors, il faut être prévoyant. Bien sûr, «tricher» est toujours possible, et même un Premier Ministre s'est fait prendre. Des impôts indirects, la T.V.A., «taxe à la valeur ajoutée», est la plus impopulaire; elle peut augmenter votre achat de 15 à 20%. Les Français aiment jouer aussi, aux courses de chevaux surtout. Il y a le «tiercé» tous les dimanches; et la Loterie Nationale est une institution du gouvernement.

Alors, remplissez vos poches de chèques de voyage et allez voir comme ils fondent au soleil de France!

Vocabulaire

achat, (*m.*) purchase
balayeur, (*m.*) street sweeper
bidonville, (*m.*) shantytown
châlet, (*m.*) une petite maison à la montagne
clochard, (*m.*) tramp (especially in Paris)
de quoi vivre enough to live
éboueur, (*m.*) garbage collector
écart, (*m.*) une différence
faire la poubelle to collect things in garbage cans
fermette, (*f.*) une petite ferme

fondre to melt
grand ensemble, (*m.*) large housing development
louer to rent
payer comptant to pay cash
plutôt que rather than
prévoyant prudent
redouté feared
taudis, (*m.*) slum house
tiercé, (*m.*) one bets on three horses in a certain order at the races
tricher to cheat

Composition Comment organisez-vous votre budget? Combien dépensez-vous d'argent pour votre loyer, votre nourriture, vos vêtements, vos distractions? Aimez-vous l'argent, le jeu, les cartes de crédit? Économisez-vous ou êtes vous dépensier?

Chapitre **17**

J'ai descendu dans mon jardin

J'ai de — scen — du dans mon jar — din, j'ai de — scen—

du dans mon jar — din pour y cueil — lir du ro — ma — rin.

Gen-til coq'-li — cot, mes-da-mes, gen — til coq'-li — cot nou-veau.

PRÉSENTATION   Les femmes

Ce chapitre est sur les femmes, mais les hommes ne sont pas exclus de la classe! Ils sont invités à écouter, à prendre des notes, à donner leur opinion. En écoutant, ils seront peut-être indignés et certaines vérités les rendront furieux... mais c'est un sujet qui doit être traité, car la libération des femmes est un problème très important dans notre société moderne.

Bien sûr, en lisant des livres d'histoire, on rencontre des femmes «libérées» avant l'heure: Jeanne d'Arc, Calamité Jane; mais elles sont rares. Il faut dire que les femmes n'ont pas toujours eu une vie facile. Nos grands-mères, comment étaient-elles traitées? Elles étaient considérées comme des êtres inférieurs. Elles n'étaient bonnes qu'à fabriquer des enfants, à les faire manger, à les élever... Elles étaient exclues des conversations, des occupations, des activités des hommes. Elles se sont battues pour obtenir le droit de voter, la permission d'aller à l'université. On ne leur permettait pas d'y aller. Savez-vous que le droit de vote n'a été accordé aux Françaises qu'en 1945, par le Général de Gaulle? Voyons, mesdemoiselles, comment avez-vous été élevées?

Mlle: est-ce qu'on vous a dit, quand vous étiez une petite fille: «Il ne faut pas jouer avec un revolver, porter un chapeau de cow-boy, des bottes... ce n'est pas féminin?» Est-ce qu'on a dit à votre frère: «Ne joue pas avec la poupée de ta sœur... ce n'est pas masculin. Tu veux tricoter, mais c'est ridicule pour un garçon.»

Oui? alors vous voyez, vous avez été conditionnée par les jeux autorisés par vos parents; il y avait, il y a encore, des jeux pour les garçons et des jeux pour les filles. Pour les filles: les poupées, les chiffons, le service à thé. Pour les garçons: les fusils, les épées, les soldats de plomb, le train électrique.

Mlle: est-ce qu'on vous a dit encore: «Ce sport (le football, la boxe, par exemple) est trop violent pour une fille; la bicyclette, oui, ça va, mais le foot, la boxe, ce ne sont pas des sports féminins! Ils rendent les femmes masculines et ce n'est pas joli?»

Sports féminins ou sports masculins? Autrefois, il y avait un choix. Depuis quelques années tout a changé, et on a vu aux Olympiques des femmes soviétiques, américaines ou françaises, par exemple, qui étaient des athlètes supérieures à beaucoup d'hommes, et qui étaient couvertes de médailles.

Quels sont généralement les travaux réservés aux femmes, dans une maison? Laver la vaisselle, faire le ménage, faire la cuisine, faire la lessive. Bien sûr, si on est riche, on peut faire faire tous ces travaux par une bonne; si on n'a pas de bonne, on peut les faire exécuter par les merveilleuses machines américaines. Et quels sont les travaux qui sont faits par les hommes dans une maison? Couper du bois, faire du feu, bricoler au garage, jardiner, arranger la voiture. Mais je connais beaucoup de femmes qui sont obligées de faire même cela. Une femme qui élève des enfants en travaillant au dehors, qui s'occupe de la maison en ayant un job, c'est une chose très courante. Et dans les professions, est-ce que le même salaire est accordé aux femmes et aux hommes pour un travail identique? Pas toujours.

Enfin, il y a des lois qui sont votées pour supprimer les injustices, pour rendre les femmes plus heureuses, mais il en reste beaucoup à voter pour arriver à l'égalité complète. Et puis il y a encore des quantités de femmes qui ne veulent pas être libérées. C'est plus facile d'être commandée, d'être dépendante que d'être un individu autonome et indépendant.

Peut-être que dans un avenir proche, les tâches seront équilibrées, les salaires seront ajustés, et les femmes seront enfin traitées comme des êtres humains «à part entière.»

Vocabulaire

à part entière full-fledged
arranger to fix
avant l'heure before their time
bonne, (*f.*) maid
bricoler to putter
chiffon, (*m.*) rag (*here*, cloth and patterns)
choix, (*m.*) choice
couper du bois to cut wood
droit, (*m.*) right
épée, (*f.*) sword

équilibrer to balance
faire la lessive to do the laundry
fusil, (*m.*) shot gun
indigné indignant
laver la vaisselle to wash the dishes
poupée, (*f.*) doll
rendre + *adj.* to make + adj. (voir p. 281)
se battre to fight
tâche, (*f.*) chore

PRONONCIATION   Les sons /a/ et /ɑ/

Il y a deux sons *a* en français. Le plus courant est /a/:

madame   partage   village

L'autre est rare. Il est postérieur: /ɑ/, prononcé dans la partie postérieure de la bouche. On le trouve dans certains mots écrits avec **â**. Il est surtout entendu dans des mots presque semblables, pour les distinguer.

COMPAREZ: Anne   âne
               patte   pâte
               bac   Pâques
               tache   tâche
               halle   hâle
               balle   Bâle
               malle   mâle
               lame   l'âme

Une femme libérée, en 1432: Jeanne d'Arc.

Contrastez /ə/, /a/, /e/:

il **le** dit	il **l'a** dit	il **les** dit
il **le** fait	il **l'a** fait	il **les** fait
il **le** voit	il **la** voit	il **les** voit
il **le** prend	il **la** prend	il **les** prend
il **le** croit	il **la** croit	il **les** croit

Prononcez **femme** /fam/.
Prononcez les adverbes en **–emment** /amã/. Ces adverbes viennent d'adjectifs en **-ant, -ent**. Répétez:

méch**ant**	méch**amment**
pati**ent**	pati**emment**
réc**ent**	réc**emment**
évid**ent**	évid**emment**

Les mots en **–en**

La majorité des mots en **–en** sont prononcés /ã/:

enfant   d**en**t   cli**en**t   pati**en**t

Certains sont prononcés /ɛ̃/ (généralement des mots avec **i** ou **y** devant **en**):

ch**ien**   m**ien**   b**ien**   mo**yen**   cito**yen**   exam**en**

D'autres sont prononcés /ɛn/ (ces mots ne sont pas nombreux):

abdom**en**   cyclam**en**   hym**en**

Et bien sûr, **–ent** n'est pas prononcé dans les verbes.

COMPAREZ: ri(ent)   riant   rien
             /ʀi/   /ʀjã/   /ʀjɛ̃/

VERBES IRRÉGULIERS   STRUCTURES

battre *to beat*

Présent:

je **bats**	nous **battons**
tu **bats** /ba/	vous **battez** /bat/
il **bat**	ils **battent**

Futur: je **battrai**

Imparfait: je **battais**

Passé Composé: j'**ai battu**

Conjuguez **se battre** (*to fight*) comme **battre**.

Exercice I   Mettez le verbe au temps indiqué.

battre

1. (*p.c.*) L'équipe de foot de Toulouse _____ celle de Bordeaux. (*futur*) Si Cendrillon rentre après minuit, sa belle-mère la _____ . (*présent*) Ma cousine me _____ toujours aux cartes. (*p.c. nég.*) Le Général Grant _____ le Général Lee.

se battre

2. (*présent*) Gilles et sa femme _____ une fois par semaine. Hier ils _____ encore une fois. (*futur*) Les hommes _____ toujours pour la liberté.

suivre   *to follow, to take* (*a class*)

Présent:	je **suis** (Attention!)	nous **suivons**
	tu **suis** /sɥi/	vous **suivez** /sɥiv/
	il, elle **suit**	ils, elles **suivent**

Futur:	je **suivrai**
Imparfait:	je **suivais**
Passé Composé:	j'**ai suivi**

Conjuguez **se suivre** (*to follow each other*) comme **suivre.**

Exercice II   Mettez les verbes **suivre** et **se suivre** au temps logique.

1. Nous _____ un cours de français.
2. Et vous, quel cours est-ce que vous _____?
3. L'année dernière elle _____ un cours de danse classique.
4. Les jours _____ et ne se ressemblent pas.
5. Hier le petit chien _____ sa maîtresse au marché.
6. Je ne _____ pas la mode; et toi, tu la _____?

rire   *to laugh*

Présent:	je **ris**	nous **rions** /ʀjõ/	
	tu **ris**	vous **riez** /ʀje/	
	il **rit**	ils **rient** /ʀi/	

Futur:	je **rirai**		
Imparfait:	je **riais**	nous **riions***	vous **riiez***
Passé Composé:	j'**ai ri,** etc.		

Conjuguez sur ce modèle **sourire** (*to smile*).

Exercice III   Mettez la forme correcte du verbe.

1. Les parents sont sévères, mais ces enfants (rire/*présent*) _____ tout le temps.
2. Elle était triste, mais j'ai fait une plaisanterie et finalement elle (sourire/*passé composé*) _____ .

*Remarquez les deux **i**; dans la prononciation, on entend deux **j**: /ʀijjõ/.

3. Quand tu entendras cette blague, tu (rire/*futur*) _____ .
4. Le bébé (rire/*imparfait*) _____ dans les bras de sa mère.
5. Chez le photographe, (sourire/*impératif*) _____ !

CONSTRUCTIONS A RETENIR

L'article à valeur possessive: **se laver les dents**

Je **me** lave **les** dents.   **Mes** dents sont blanches.
I brush my teeth.   *My teeth are white.*

J'ai **les** dents blanches.
My teeth are white.

Employez un article défini à la place du possessif en anglais devant une partie du corps, si le verbe est pronominal, ou si c'est le verbe **avoir.** Employez le possessif si le verbe n'est pas pronominal.

EXCEPTIONS: Levez **la** main.   *Raise your hand.*
Ouvrez **la** bouche.   *Open your mouth.*
Fermez **les** yeux.   *Close your eyes.*

Le verbe n'est pas pronominal, mais il n'y a pas de doute sur le possesseur.

Complétez avec l'article ou le possessif.   *Exercice IV*

1. Elle se brosse _____ cheveux. _____ cheveux sont magnifiques.
2. Il s'est cassé _____ jambe. _____ jambe droite est plus courte que _____ jambe gauche.
3. Elle se lave _____ mains. _____ mains sont fines et longues.
4. Lucille se teint _____ cheveux. _____ cheveux ont une couleur orange.
5. Est-ce que vous vous maquillez _____ yeux? _____ yeux sont jolis sans bleu ou vert.
6. Je lave _____ chaussettes. Je me lave _____ pieds.

L'expression de restriction: **ne... que**

Laurent est végétarien.
Il mange **seulement** des légumes.
Il **ne** mange **que** des légumes.
Toute sa vie il **n'a** mangé **que** des légumes.

Ne... que est l'équivalent de **seulement.** C'est une restriction. Placez **ne** devant le verbe; placez **que** devant le mot ou le groupe qui est affecté par la restriction.

Elle **ne se promène** dans le parc avec ses enfants **que le dimanche.**

Ce groupe peut être loin du verbe.

> Il **ne mange pas de** légumes.
> Il **ne mange que des** légumes.

Ne... que n'est pas une négation, alors l'article **du, de la, des** ne change pas.

Exercice V (*a.*) Répétez avec **seulement**. (*b.*) Répétez avec **ne... que**.
Mettez **que** devant le groupe en italiques.

1. Elle boit *de l'eau*. 2. Je dors *le dimanche matin*. 3. Ils sortent *le samedi*. 4. Il pleut *en été*. 5. Le président a voyagé *huit jours*. 6. Les Françaises ont obtenu le droit de vote *en 1945*. 7. Elle sont bonnes *à élever des bébés*. 8. Pendant son voyage, elle a trouvé des souvenirs intéressants *en Grèce*. 9. Vous avez emporté des cadeaux *pour les enfants*.

L'expression idiomatique: **il reste** (*there is left*)

> Il **reste** du gâteau. *There is some cake left.*
> Il **reste** des pommes. *There are some apples left.*

Il est impersonnel, le verbe est toujours singulier.

> Il **me** reste trois dollars. *I have 3 dollars left.*
> Il **lui** reste cent dollars. *He* (or *she*) *has a hundred dollars left.*

Me, lui sont des pronoms objets indirects.

> Il reste un gâteau? Il **en** reste **un.**
> Il ne reste que deux pommes. Il ne **m'en reste** que cinq.

Employez les pronoms **en, m'en,** et combinez l'expression de restriction avec ces pronoms comme avec un autre verbe.

Exercice VI Refaites les phrases suivantes avec **il reste, il me reste, il en reste,** etc. Conjuguez le verbe **rester** au temps nécessaire.

EXEMPLE: Tu auras encore du travail après ceci?
          Il **te restera** encore du travail après ceci?

1. Il y a trois bonbons dans la boîte.
2. Nous avons encore trente assiettes à laver.
3. Il y a beaucoup de lois à voter pour l'égalité des femmes.
4. J'avais quatre dollars pour finir le mois.
5. Trois de leurs enfants sont mariés. Ils ont deux filles à la maison.
6. Vous avez du temps pour lire à la fin de la journée?
7. Tu n'auras pas d'énergie après dix heures de travail.

POINTS DE GRAMMAIRE

Le gérondif

LA FORME

Les petites filles courent **en chantant.**

En chantant est un gérondif. On prend **nous chantons;** on enlève la terminaison **-ons;** on ajoute **-ant** à la forme **chant- = chantant.** Il y a toujours la préposition **en** pour former le gérondif (en anglais, la préposition peut changer: *in singing, while* *singing, by singing*). La forme **en chantent** est invariable; elle ne s'accorde pas avec le sujet.

> Elle a dit oui en roug**issant.**

Remarquez la forme du gérondif pour les verbes du 2ème groupe: **nous rougissons: en rougissant.** Elle est régulière, mais il ne faut pas oublier –**iss.**

Exercice VII   Donnez les gérondifs des verbes indiqués.

1. nous allons	4. nous gardons	7. nous tombons
2. nous rions	5. nous sortons	8. nous faisons
3. nous parlons	6. nous étudions	9. nous finissons

> Ne parlez pas en mang**eant.**
> En commen**çant** à 4 h, vous finirez à 6.

Remarquez l'orthographe des verbes en –**ger** et des verbes en –**cer: nous mangeons, en mangeant** avec **ge** devant **ant** pour garder le son /ʒ/; **nous commençons, en commençant** avec **ç** devant **ant** pour garder le son /s/.

> **En étant** à l'heure, vous faites plaisir à votre professeur.
> **En ayant** l'air de comprendre...
> **En sachant** votre leçon...

Remarquez les trois gérondifs irréguliers pour les verbes **avoir, être,** et **savoir:**

avoir:	le présent est **nous avons,** le gérondif est	**en ayant**
être:	**nous sommes**	**en étant**
savoir:	**nous savons**	**en sachant**

L'EMPLOI

1. Les petites filles courent en chantant.
2. Il est tombé en courant.
3. En étant à l'heure, vous faites plaisir à votre professeur.

Le gérondif exprime toujours une action du sujet principal.

1. Le sujet fait des actions en même temps: **les petites filles courent et elles chantent.**
2. Le sujet fait une action dans certaines circonstances: **il est tombé comment? dans quelles circonstances?**
3. Le gérondif exprime une condition: **si vous êtes à l'heure, vous faites plaisir à votre professeur.**

Exercice VIII   Refaites les phrases en mettant le verbe en italiques au gérondif.

1. Tu parles et tu *manges.*
2. Vous buvez et vous *conduisez?*
3. Ils se promènent et ils *se tiennent* par la main.
4. Les soldats marchent et *chantent.*
5. Elle *faisait* du ski, elle s'est cassé la jambe.

6. Nous *cherchions* un appartement, nous avons trouvé cette petite maison adorable.

7. Ils *passaient* devant une bijouterie, ils ont vu dans la vitrine un diamant vraiment bon marché.

8. Si vous *marchez* plus vite, vous arriverez peut-être à l'heure à votre cours.

Le passif

La classe **est finie**, je **suis fatigué**.

Le verbe **être** avec un participe passé indique un état, un résultat; en réalité, c'est la forme passive du verbe **finir** ou du verbe **fatiguer**. La classe est finie parce que le professeur et les élèves ont fini (passé composé de **finir**). Je suis fatigué parce qu'une chose m'a fatigué (passé composé de **fatiguer**). **La classe, je** ne font pas l'action. Le passif signifie que le sujet du verbe ne fait pas l'action, il la subit.

LES FORMES

Les cannibales mangent l'explorateur.

L'explorateur **est mangé** par les cannibales.

Le verbe passif a toujours l'auxiliaire **être**. Vous conjuguez le verbe **être** au temps nécessaire. Vous ajoutez le participe passé du verbe, accordé comme un adjectif.

Le présent passif du verbe **aimer**

je **suis aimé (aimée)**	nous **sommes aimés (aimées)**
tu **es aimé (aimée)**	vous **êtes aimés (aimées)**
il **est aimé**	ils **sont aimés**
elle **est aimée**	elles **sont aimées**

Donnez la forme passive des verbes suivants.   *Exercice IX*

1. Je bats.	6. Vous battez.	11. Il conjugue.
2. Tu acceptes.	7. Ils font.	12. Elle ferme.
3. Il choisit.	8. Elles apprécient.	13. Nous punissons.
4. Elle regarde.	9. J'écoute.	14. Vous conduisez.
5. Nous voyons.	10. Tu entends.	15. Ils finissent.

Voici les autres temps de la forme passive:

Futur:	je **serai obligé**
Imparfait:	tu **étais accepté**
Passé Composé:	elle **a été aimée***

Donnez la forme passive, au temps indiqué, du verbe entre parenthèses.   *Exercice X*

1. (*futur:* obliger)   Vous _____ de travailler.
2. (*présent:* accompagner)   Tu _____?

*Attention, il y a trois mots: deux pour le passé composé de l'auxiliaire, un pour le participe passé.

3. (*imparfait:* fermer)   La porte _____?
4. (*passé composé:* donner)   La bénédiction _____.
5. (*futur:* battre)   Les soldats _____.
6. (*présent:* casser)   Mon vase préféré _____.
7. (*imparfait:* punir)   Les petites filles insolentes _____.
8. (*passé composé:* interroger) Les prisonniers _____.

LE COMPLÉMENT D'AGENT

1. Les travaux ménagers fatiguent les pauvres femmes.
2. Les pauvres femmes sont fatiguées **par les travaux ménagers.**

Le groupe **par les travaux ménagers** s'appelle l'*agent.* On a la préposition **par** devant le véritable agent de l'action.

Dans la construction 1. on a: *sujet + verbe +* O.D.
Dans la construction 2. on a: *sujet* (ancien O.D.) *+ verbe + agent* (avec **par =** ancien sujet)

Exercice XI   Sur ce modèle, répétez les phrases en formant une construction passive (attention au temps du verbe).

1. Les bombardements ont détruit la ville de Rouen.
   La ville de Rouen....
2. Un journal littéraire critique le jeune écrivain.
3. Les nouvelles lois libéreront les femmes.
4. Ce projet m'enthousiasme. Je...
5. Le bruit de la circulation l'énervait. Il (ou elle)...
6. Les bombes au napalm ont tué la population.

Une question **a été posée** à l'étudiant.
On a posé une question à l'étudiant.

Si on a une phrase comme celle-ci, à l'actif: **Le professeur a posé une question à l'étudiant,** on peut dire au passif: **Une question a été posée à l'étudiant par le professeur.** Mais «l'étudiant» ne peut pas devenir le sujet d'un verbe passif comme en anglais *The student was asked a question,* parce qu'il y a **à.** Il faut employer une construction avec **on: On a posé une question à l'étudiant.**

Pour la même raison, *I am asked, I am forbidden, I am permitted* ne peuvent pas être traduits par un passif en français. On dit: **On m'a demandé, on m'a défendu, on m'a permis.**

Le MLF est composé de femmes courageuses.

Certains verbes ont la préposition **de** à la place de **par.** L'article est absent après **de.** Voici des verbes qui ont cette construction:

être rempli de   **être composé de**
être couvert de   **être formé de**
être entouré de   **être décoré de**
être orné de

Mettez dans ces phrases un des verbes de la liste ci-dessus.　　　　*Exercice XII*

EXEMPLE: A midi, la cafétéria _____ étudiants: A midi, la cafétéria est remplie d'étudiants.

1. La bouteille _____ vin.
2. Notre maison _____ arbres magnifiques.
3. L'arbre de Noël est _____ boules de couleurs.
4. Sa robe de mariée sera _____ rubans roses.
5. En hiver, le sol _____ neige.
6. Le gouvernement _____ ministres et de députés.
7. Le théâtre _____ spectateurs.

Ces femmes protestent.

Le verbe pronominal à sens passif

Un verbe **se conjugue** (est conjugué).
Un adjectif **s'accorde** (est accordé).

Se conjuguer, s'accorder, se trouver (pour **être**), etc. sont des verbes pronominaux à sens passif. Ils sont très idiomatiques. Employez-les quand c'est possible.

Exercice XIII Répétez les phrases avec le verbe pronominal suggéré, au temps correct.

EXEMPLE: **se vendre** Les journaux sont vendus dans la rue. Les journaux se vendent...

1. s'accorder L'adjectif est accordé avec le nom.
2. s'appeler Cet animal préhistorique est appelé dinosaure.
3. se trouver La cathédrale de Notre Dame est à Paris.
4. se conjuguer Ces verbes sont conjugués au passif!
5. se former Le défilé sera formé devant le monument aux morts.
6. se composer La classe était composée d'étudiants de tous les âges.
7. se chanter Cette chanson a été chantée pendant longtemps.

Ça se fait, ça se dit, ça se voit, ça se comprend, ça se mange sont traduits par *that is done, that can be said, it is easily seen, it is understandable, it is edible.*

Exercice XIV Mettez une de ces expressions dans les phrases suivantes.

1. Tu as les yeux rouges — J'ai pleuré. _____ !
2. Son mari la bat; elle va divorcer. _____ !
3. Enlever ses souliers dans la classe! _____ (forme négative)
4. «Tchao» à la place de «Au revoir»? _____ en France.
5. Manger avec les doigts, à un pique-nique, _____ .
6. Vous aimez les escargots? _____ .

Le verbe **faire** causatif

Le bébé ne peut pas manger seul.
La maman **fait manger** le bébé.

La construction **faire** + *infinitif* est l'expression en français de *to have someone do something.* L'ordre des mots est:

> *le sujet* + *le verbe* **faire** + *l'infinitif du verbe* + *le sujet de l'infinitif*

L'infinitif est placé immédiatement après **faire,** ne les séparez pas.

Exercice XV Avec le vocabulaire suggéré, faites des phrases sur le modèle: **La maman fait manger le bébé.**

1. (Le professeur) Les étudiants lisent.
2. (Ces comédiens) Les spectateurs rient.
3. (Un compliment) La jeune fille timide rougit.

4. (La peur)   Le chien court.

5. (Mes problèmes)   Ma mère pleure.

> Elle **le fait** manger.
> Vous **me faites** rire.

Le pronom qui représente le sujet de l'infinitif est placé devant le verbe **faire;** sa forme est le pronom objet direct.

Exercice XVI

(*a.*) Répétez les phrases de l'exercice XV avec un pronom (**les étudiants = les: Le professeur les fait lire.**)

(*b.*) Répétez les phrases suivantes en mettant à sa place le pronom entre parenthèses.

1. Il fait pleurer (vous).   3. La pluie fait changer d'avis (me).

2. Vous faites rire (nous).   4. Cet accident n'a pas fait réfléchir (te).

> **Fais**-le manger. **Ne les fais pas** manger.

A l'impératif positif, le pronom est placé entre **faire** et *l'infinitif.* A l'impératif négatif, l'ordre des mots est régulier.

Exercice XVII

Répétez à l'impératif positif puis à l'impératif négatif.

1. Tu le fais courir.   4. Vous la faites réfléchir.

2. Vous nous faites rire.   5. Nous les faisons travailler.

3. Tu la fais pleurer.

> Je **fais écrire** ma **lettre par** la **secrétaire.**
> (*I have the secretary write my letter.*)

La formule est:

> le verbe **faire** + *infinitif* + *l'objet de l'infinitif* + **par** + *le véritable agent de l'action*

Exercice XVIII

Sur ce modèle, faites des phrases avec **Je fais..., Il fait..., Nous faisons,** etc.

EXEMPLE: Un chauffeur conduit votre auto!
             Vous **faites conduire** votre auto **par** un chauffeur!

1. Le mécanicien répare son auto.

2. La bonne prépare notre dîner.

3. Vos enfants font votre ménage.

4. Les étudiants corrigent la dictée.

5. Un assistant explique la leçon.

Le verbe **rendre** + adjectif

> Cette histoire **me rend** malade.
> Jules ne **rend** pas **sa femme** heureuse.

Le verbe **rendre** + O.D. + *adjectif* est la traduction de l'expression *to make someone sick, happy, sad,* etc.

Exercice XIX Faites des phrases avec l'expression **rendre** et un adjectif avec le vocabulaire suggéré.

EXEMPLE: Cette histoire.   Je suis malade.
Cette histoire **me rend** malade.

1. Les événements politiques.   Elle est furieuse.
2. Le printemps.   Nous sommes amoureux.
3. Cette mauvaise nouvelle.   Jacques est triste. (passé composé)
4. Robert.   Ses enfants ne sont pas malheureux.
5. Votre travail.   Je suis mécontent. (imparfait)

Remarque: Certains verbes ont le sens de *to make* + *adjectif*. Le verbe seul est suffisant.

EXEMPLE: Ça me fatigue. *It makes me tired.*
Ça te déprime. *It makes you depressed.*
Ça vous dégoûte. *It makes you disgusted, it disgusts you.*

LECTURES   1. Les femmes en France

La tradition représente la Française comme une épouse docile («La femme doit suivre son mari»), une bonne cuisinière plus soucieuse de mijoter des petits plats que de commenter les dernières élections. Alors que les Américaines sont soulagées de bien des tâches ménagères par leurs machines: machines à laver la vaisselle, à laver le linge, séchoir, etc. — la Française est encore souvent esclave des travaux ménagers parce que les machines sont coûteuses et pas encore aussi répandues qu'aux U.S. Une Française sur deux travaille. Si elle ne travaille pas, elle passe ses matinées à faire son marché et à préparer un grand repas pour midi; elle doit conduire ses gosses à l'école le matin, aller les chercher à 11 h 30, les reconduire à 1 h 30 et les récupérer à 4 h 30, puis il y a le repas du soir. Si elle travaille, sa vie est une course perpétuelle contre la montre, car elle a les mêmes occupations ménagères, et sa journée ne se termine qu'à 9 ou 10 h du soir. Le MLF (Mouvement de Libération des Femmes) n'a été créé que récemment. Comme aux U.S. le *Women's Lib,* on reproche à ses membres d'être des femmes trop agressives, trop masculines ou «bas-bleus». Pourtant, certaines femmes qui l'animent sont admirables, comme Gisèle Halimi, une avocate, et Simone de Beauvoir, écrivain célèbre qui s'acharne depuis des années à faire sortir les femmes de leur condition minoritaire (il faut lire «*Le Deuxième Sexe*»).

En ce qui concerne la contraception, ce sujet brûlant, il y avait un grand problème en France: la grande quantité d'avortements clandestins (3000.000 par an) causés par une loi ancienne, rigide et conservatrice sur la contraception. Jusqu'au 28 novembre 1974, l'avortement était illégal et puni par la loi; mais des milliers de femmes mouraient chaque année dans des conditions affreuses. Grâce à Madame S. Veil, ministre de la Santé, la loi vient d'être changée et les Françaises ont maintenant, comme les Anglaises et les Américaines, le droit de décider si elles veulent être mères ou non.

Mme Françoise Giroud.

Il y a peu de femmes au gouvernement français, mais petit à petit, elles y viennent. L'une d'elles est une journaliste connue, Françoise Giroud: elle est Secrétaire à la Condition Féminine. C'est une femme généreuse et intelligente et on peut espérer qu'elle fera faire des progrès à la libération des Françaises.

Il y a encore des quantités de magazines féminins: «Elle,» «Marie-Claire» qui expliquent aux femmes comment se maquiller, être jolies, être des objets sexuels pour attirer un homme dans leurs filets. La «chasse à l'homme» est encore l'activité principale de beaucoup de jeunes filles. Et d'autres magazines masculins décrivent les femmes comme des objets sexuels, uniquement. Bien sûr, c'est important pour une femme de rester jeune, élégante, mais ce n'est pas tout: être féministe en restant féminine, c'est peut-être la formule parfaite pour la femme moderne.

Vocabulaire

avortement, (*m.*) abortion
bas-bleu, (*m.*) blue stocking
chasse, (*f.*) hunt
filet, (*m.*) net
gosse, (*m.* ou *f.*) kid
mijoter, cuire doucement *here,* to cook carefully and lovingly

répandu commonly used
s'acharner to work hard on something
séchoir, (*m.*) dryer
soucieux worried
soulagé unburdened, relieved
tâche ménagère, (*f.*) household chore

2. Poème

SI TU T'IMAGINES

Si tu t'imagines
si tu t'imagines
fillette fillette
si tu t'imagines
xa va xa va xa
va durer toujours
la saison des za
la saison des za
saison des amours
ce que tu te goures
fillette fillette
ce que tu te goures

Si tu crois petite
si tu crois ah ah
que ton teint de rose
ta taille de guêpe
tes mignons biceps
tes ongles d'émail
ta cuisse de nymphe
et ton pied léger
si tu crois petite
xa va xa va xa
va durer toujours
ce que tu te goures
fillette fillette
ce que tu te goures

les beaux jours s'en vont
les beaux jours de fête
soleils et planètes
tournent tous en rond
mais toi ma petite
tu marches tout droit
vers sque tu vois pas
très sournois s'approchent
la ride véloce
la pesante graisse
le menton triplé
le muscle avachi
allons cueille cueille
les roses les roses
roses de la vie
et que leurs pétales
soient la mer étale
de tous les bonheurs
allons cueille cueille
si tu le fais pas
ce que tu te goures
fillette fillette
ce que tu te goures

R. QUENEAU

Vocabulaire

xa va orthographe phonétique pour **que ca va**

des za **des** amours — orthographe phonétique de la liaison

ce que tu te goures argot (*slang*) pour comme tu te trompes

teint, (*m.*) complexion

guêpe, (*f.*) wasp

mignon cute

ongle, (*m.*) nail

email, (*m.*) enamel

cuisse, (*f.*) thigh

sque ce que

sournois sly

ride, (*f.*) wrinkle

véloce quick coming

graisse, (*f.*) fat

menton, (*m.*) chin

avachi flabby

que... soient may they be (*subjunctive of wish*)

mer étale, (*f.*) slack water = *ici,* the perfection

Vous êtes une jeune fille ou une jeune femme: est-ce que vous estimez que vous êtes libérée ou préférez-vous l'esclavage, la dépendance?

Vous êtes un garçon: quelles sont vos opinions sur la libération des femmes, sur la «femme au foyer» et sur la femme qui travaille? Comment voyez-vous votre future épouse?

Brave marin revient de guerre

Bra — ve ma — rin re –vient de guer — re,— tout doux! —

— Bra — ve ma — rin re –vient de guer — re,— tout doux! —

— Tout mal chaus — sé, tout mal vê — tu —

pau — vre ma — rin, d'où re — viens tu— tout doux!

PRÉSENTATION   L'amour; l'amour familial

De quoi allons-nous parler aujourd'hui? Quel est le thème de cette leçon? Nous avons touché à beaucoup de sujets importants, mais il en reste un qui intéresse les jeunes gens: lequel? Ah! je vais vous faire deviner; je vais vous poser des questions. Qu'est-ce qui vous permet d'exister? Qu'est-ce qui intéresse le monde entier, sans exception? Qu'est-ce que chacun espère rencontrer au moins une fois dans sa vie? A quoi est-ce que vous pensez, quand vous ne l'avez pas? Qu'attendent tous les jeunes gens, les jeunes filles, les jeunes hommes? De quoi rêvons-nous, avant de l'avoir? Que regrettons-nous, après l'avoir perdu? Qu'est-ce qui cause les plus grandes joies et les plus grandes peines? Qu'est-ce qu'on lit dans les journaux? De quoi parle-t-on dans les livres? Qu'est-ce qui peut causer des catastrophes ou des miracles?

Mais oui, bien sûr, c'est l'amour, toujours l'amour. Qu'est-ce que j'entends? Que dites-vous? Il paraît que je suis un professeur romantique, vieux jeu; il paraît que c'est «dépassé»? Mais de tous les films qui sont sortis ces derniers temps, lequel a eu le plus de succès, a fait le plus d'argent? «*Une histoire d'amour.*» Ah! vous voyez? Je ne mentais pas.

On naît, on vit, on grandit, on devient un adulte, une grande personne, on vieillit, on meurt, mais tout ce temps-là, la grande affaire de la vie, c'est l'amour. Vous êtes né — il n'y a pas très longtemps —, vous vivez, vous êtes dans la force de l'âge, vous vivrez et vous vieillirez et vous mourrez, comme tout le monde. Mais la chose la plus importante, c'est que vous aimerez.

Une soirée devant la télé.

Bien entendu, il y a plus d'une sorte d'amour: l'amour entre un homme et une femme, l'amour des enfants pour les parents et des parents pour leurs enfants, l'amour quand on est jeune, l'amour quand on est vieux, l'amour de l'humanité.... Je m'arrête: vous ne paraissez plus intéressés. Pourtant, savez-vous que les mariages d'amour sont une institution récente? Autrefois, en France en tout cas, une jeune fille épousait le jeune homme que ses parents avaient choisi pour elle: quand on avait comparé sa fortune et celle du jeune homme, le mariage était une affaire financière que les parents avaient étudiée, décidée. L'amour venait ensuite, quelquefois.

Maintenant, c'est le contraire; on se marie un peu trop vite — en deux minutes, c'est fait. On se rencontre, on se voit deux ou trois fois, et voilà, pas le temps de se connaître, on se marie. Les jeunes gens qui vivent ensemble avant de se marier ont un autre point de vue: après avoir vécu ensemble quelque temps, ils se connaissent mieux, alors le mariage devient un engagement plus solide. Mais que deviennent la morale, les traditions? Qu'est-ce qui compte le plus? La qualité de l'amour ou la respectabilité et l'opinion publique?

L'amour familial: certains parents disent qu'ils aiment leurs enfants, pensent qu'ils aiment leurs enfants, ils paraissent affectueux, mais ils sont ou trop autoritaires ou trop «coulants»: ils donnent à leurs enfants les choses matérielles nécessaires, mais ils ne leur donnent pas un véritable intérêt, un véritable amour. Et après, ils sont très étonnés quand les enfants font tout le contraire des choses qu'ils avaient apprises.

Écoutez un père de famille: «Regardez mon fils: je lui avais fait faire de bonnes études, et il ne veut plus travailler; il a décidé de vivre dans une communauté. Et ma fille, qui avait étudié le piano, la danse classique, l'opéra, est devenue une chanteuse pop, et elle joue de la guitare électrique. Ma femme est un modèle d'élégance, elle s'habille chez Courrèges et notre fille a donné aux pauvres tous les vêtements qu'on lui avait achetés: maintenant elle ne porte plus que des blue jeans et des vieux pulls.»

Cette révolte peut aller plus loin et être plus dangereuse, si les enfants se trouvent exposés à la drogue et aux «paradis artificiels.» Et c'est le gouffre entre les générations, l'absence de communication et d'amour qui conduit les jeunes gens à faire des bêtises... Et enfin les vieux, qui s'intéresse à eux? Quelle est leur place dans la famille? Souvent, ils sont «de trop», inutiles. Ils sont condamnés à attendre la mort, si on ne les aime pas. Est-ce que vous pensez à votre vieillesse quelquefois?

Vocabulaire

communauté, (*f.*) commune
coulant permissive
croulant falling apart
danse classique, (*f.*) ballet
épouser se marier avec
être de trop to be in the way (unwanted)

faire des bêtises to do silly things, wrong things
gouffre, (*m.*) gap
mentir to lie (*comme* **sentir**)
peine, (*f.*) sorrow, trouble, grief
vieux jeu old fashioned

PRONONCIATION   Le tréma (¨)

On le trouve sur un **i**, un **u**, ou un **e**. Il indique que la voyelle est articulée séparément.

ï dans **haïr** /aiʀ/ (*to hate*):

> nous haïssons   vous haïssez   ils haïssent

Mais on dit: je **hais** /ɛ/, tu **hais**, il **hait**.

ü dans **Saül** /sayl/.   Mais: **saule** /sol/.

ë dans **Noël, Joël** /ɔɛ/.   Mais: **œil** /œj/, **œuf** /œf/.

RÉPÉTEZ: hais   haïr   mais   maïs
            nais   naïf   oui   ouïe

Ecoliers parisiens.

L'accent circonflexe

fen**ê**tre   s**û**re   p**â**le   h**ô**pital

L'accent circonflexe apparaît sur les voyelles **e, u, a, o.** Généralement il n'affecte pas le son.

h**ô**pital   *hospital*

Il est quelquefois le signe d'un **s** qui a disparu.

nous conna**i**ssons   il conna**î**t

Dans les verbes en **–aître (paraître, naître)** l'accent circonflexe est sur le **i** qui précède un **t.**

l'**ê**tre   lettre
m**aî**tre   mettre
b**ê**le   belle

Dans quelques mots, il y a un contraste de sons entre le **ê** et le **e** sans accent. La syllabe qui contient l'accent circonflexe est longue /ɛ:/; celle qui n'a pas d'accent circonflexe est normale /ɛ/.

l'**â**ge, village   **â**ne, Anne

Le **â** est /ɑ/ postérieur. Le **a** est /a/. (Voir Chapitre 17.)

VERBES IRRÉGULIERS STRUCTURES

	naître *to be born*		**paraître** *to appear*	
Présent:	je **nais**	nous **naissons**	je **parais**	nous **paraissons**
	tu **nais**	vous **naissez**	tu **parais**	vous **paraissez**
	il **naît***	ils **naissent**	il **paraît***	ils **paraissent**

Futur: je **naîtrai**, je **paraîtrai**, etc.
Imparfait: je **naissais**, je **paraissais**, etc.

Passé composé: Le passé composé est différent.

je **suis né(e)**	j'**ai paru**	j'**ai apparu, disparu**
tu **es né(e)**	tu **as paru**	
il **est né**	il **a paru**	
elle **est née**	elle **a paru**	
nous **sommes nés(ées)**	nous **avons paru**	
vous **êtes né(és, ée, ées)**	vous **avez paru**	
ils **sont nés**	ils **ont paru**	
elles **sont nées**	elles **ont paru**	

*Il y a un circonflexe sur le **î** devant le **t**, uniquement.

Apparaître (*to appear*) et disparaître (*to disappear*) sont conjugués sur le modèle de paraître.

Exercice I Mettez la forme correcte du verbe entre parenthèses.

1. (naître *futur*) Ma sœur attend un bébé: Il _____ au mois d'août.

2. (paraître *imparfait*) Vous _____ fatigué hier soir.
3. (disparaître *passé composé*) Tiens, le soleil _____.
4. (apparaître) Ces acteurs _____ dans des films stupides.
5. (naître) Mes grand-parents _____ en Suisse. Moi, je _____ aux U.S.A.

6. (paraître) Il _____ qu'ils arrivent demain.
7. (disparaître) Je ne veux plus vous voir: _____!

mourir *to die*

Présent:	je **meurs** /mœʀ/	nous **mourons** /muʀɔ̃/
	tu **meurs**	vous **mourez** /muʀe/
	il **meurt**	
	ils **meurent**	

Futur: je **mourrai**, nous **mourrons** (les deux **r** sont prononcés)
Imparfait: je **mourais**, vous **mouriez**
Passé Composé: je **suis mort**, elle **est morte**, nous **sommes morts**, elles **sont mortes**

Remarque: On a rarement l'occasion de conjuguer le verbe **mourir** à la première personne, excepté au sens figuré:

Je **meurs de faim!** (J'ai très très faim.)
Je **mourais de froid!** (J'avais grand froid.)

Exercice II Mettez la forme correcte du verbe **mourir.**

1. Il fait moins vingt (degrés). On _____ de froid dans ce pays.
2. Napoléon _____ à St. Hélène.
3. Quand elles voient une souris, elles _____ de peur.
4. Tu auras une petite opération, tu n'en _____ pas!
5. Cette mère possessive _____ d'anxiété chaque fois que son fils quittait la maison.
6. Ils ont reçu les possessions de leur fils qui _____ au Vietnam.

CONSTRUCTIONS A RETENIR

Les expressions **il paraît que** (*it seems*); **il paraît triste** (*he looks sad*)

Il **paraît que** je suis un professeur vieux-jeu.

Il paraît que (toujours au présent) signifie: **voilà la nouvelle, la rumeur,** ou **on m'a dit...** (*it seems*); il est impersonnel.

Il paraît triste.

Paraître + *adjectif* conjugué avec un sujet personnel (**je, tu, il,** etc.) signifie **avoir l'air.**

Répétez la première phrase avec **il paraît que;** la deuxième avec la forme correcte du verbe **paraître** (accordez l'adjectif). *Exercice III*

1. Elle a eu la grippe. Elle a l'air fatigué.
2. Ils ont acheté une nouvelle maison. Ils ont l'air contents.
3. Votre fils a eu une opération. Il n'avait pas l'air malade.
4. Vous avez envoyé des fleurs au professeur. Elle a eu l'air flatté.
5. Tu as eu un A à ton examen. Tu es satisfait.

Les prépositions de temps: **dans, en**

Il est maintenant 2 h.
Pierre finira son examen à 4 h.
Il finira son examen **dans deux heures** (*2 hours from now*).

Il a commencé à écrire sa composition à 2 h.
Il l'a finie à 4 h.
Il a écrit sa composition **en deux heures** (2 heures est le temps nécessaire pour écrire la composition).

Mettez **dans** ou **en.** *Exercice IV*

1. Nous sommes mardi. Les vacances commencent samedi. Les vacances commencent _____ 3 jours.
2. Ils ont commencé leur voyage en Europe le 1ᵉʳ juin. Ils ont terminé leur voyage le 15 juin. Ils ont visité l'Europe _____ 15 jours.
3. Nous sommes le 15 mai. Nos amis d'Oregon arrivent le 25 mai. Ils arrivent _____ 10 jours.
4. La princesse s'est piquée au doigt. Elle s'endort. La méchante fée lui dit: «Tu te réveilleras _____ cent ans.»
5. Jacques est superintelligent. Ses deux années de français, il les a faites _____ une seule année.

Les prépositions **après** et **avant**

après la fin de la classe   **avant** la fin de la classe

Avec un nom, la construction de **après** et de **avant** est identique.

après avoir fini   avant **de finir**

Avec un verbe, la construction est différente. **Après** est suivi de l'infinitif passé.

L'infinitif passé est le passé composé de l'infinitif. On prend l'auxiliaire à l'infinitif; on ajoute le participe passé:

avoir parlé	**être allé**
avoir vu	**être venu**
avoir compris	**être sorti**

Après être **restée** debout, **elle** est fatiguée.

Le participe passé avec **être** s'accorde avec le sujet.

Avant de voir   avant de finir

Avant est suivi de l'infinitif présent avec **de**.

Exercice V   Mettez la forme correcte de l'infinitif avec **avant** et **après**.

1. (apprendre)   Avant _____ ses verbes irréguliers, il fait la sieste.
   Après _____
2. (voir)   Avant _____ le film «Papillon» elle a lu le livre.
   Après _____
3. (sortir)   Avant _____, ils remarquent qu'il pleut.
   Après _____
4. (faire)   Avant _____ mes provisions pour la semaine, je compte mon
   agent.
   Après _____
5. (devenir)   Avant _____ vieux, il faut profiter de la vie.
   Après _____

Les mots **temps, heure, fois** et **moment**

Le temps:	Quel **temps** fait-il? (*weather*)
	Il passe son temps à la plage.
	Le temps passe.
	Il est arrivé **juste à temps.**
	Dans **les temps anciens:** autrefois...
L'heure:	**Quelle heure est-il? Il est** quatre heures.
	C'est l'heure de dormir.
La fois:	**Une fois, deux fois, trois fois....**
	C'est la première et la dernière **fois** que je lis.
	Il était une fois... (*once upon a time...*)
Le moment:	**Les bons moments** (*the good times*)
	Les mauvais moments (*the bad times*)
	En ce moment (*at this time*)
REMARQUEZ:	**S'amuser** = to have a good time

Mettez le mot qui correspond à «*time*»: **temps, heure, fois, moment.**   *Exercice VI*

1. Je n'ai pas le _____ de lire des romans policiers.
2. Il était tellement intéressé par sa lecture qu'il a oublié _____.
3. C'est la troisième _____ qu'elle se marie.
4. Ma montre est arrêtée. Je ne sais pas quelle _____ il est.
5. Il pleut encore; quel mauvais _____! (*weather*)
6. Un conte de fées commence toujours par ces mots: _____.
7. Dans son enfance, il y a eu la dépression: c'étaient des mauvais _____.
8. Dans les _____ anciens, on ne se mariait pas par amour.
9. Nous avons rencontré nos vieux amis et nous avons parlé des bons _____ que nous avons eus au *college*.
10. Il passe son _____ à rêver aux femmes.

Ont-ils l'air heureux?

POINTS DE GRAMMAIRE

Le plus-que-parfait

LA FORME

La jeune fille épousait le jeune homme que ses parents **avaient choisi.**
Ma fille a donné aux pauvres les vêtements qu'on lui **avait achetés.**

Avaient choisi, avait achetés sont des plus-que-parfaits. Ce temps correspond à l'anglais *pluperfect,* ou *past perfect.*

On prend le passé composé. On conjugue l'auxiliaire à l'imparfait.

PLUS-QUE-PARFAIT

		Singulier	*Pluriel*
Passé Comp.	j'**ai** mangé	j'**avais mangé**	nous **avions mangé**
		tu **avais mangé**	vous **aviez mangé**
		il **avait mangé**	ils **avaient mangé**
	je **suis** parti	j'**étais parti(e)**	nous **étions partis(es)**
		tu **étais parti(e)**	vous **étiez parti(e,s,es)**
		il **était parti**	ils **étaient partis**
		elle **était partie**	elles **étaient parties**
	je **me suis** lavé	je m'**étais lavé(e)**	nous **nous étions lavés(ées)**
		tu t'**étais lavé(e)**	vous **vous étiez lavés(ées)**
		il s'**était lavé**	ils s'**étaient lavés**
		elle s'**était lavée**	elles s'**étaient lavées**

Exercice VII   Donnez la forme du plus-que-parfait des verbes suivants.

1. J'ai fini.
2. Tu as vu.
3. Il est sorti.
4. Elles se sont vues.*
5. Je tombe.
6. Vous faites.
7. Elle se dépêche.
8. Nous avons voulu.
9. Vous êtes allés.*
10. Ils sont venus.
11. Nous allons.
12. Il parle.
13. Elles arrivent.
14. J'ai eu peur.
15. Il a été malade.
16. Elle a dormi.
17. Tu vois.
18. Ils se rencontrent.

L'EMPLOI

Je me suis habillée; **j'avais fait** ma toilette avant.

Employez le plus-que-parfait pour une action qui a lieu avant une action passée.

Exercice VIII   Refaites les phrases, en mettant le verbe entre parenthèses au plus-que-parfait.

1. Elle est partie en voyage: elle (faire) des préparatifs pendant un mois. 2. Ils ont eu un bébé, c'est enfin un garçon; avant, ils (avoir) cinq filles. 3. Jean-Claude a eu un A en français; c'est la première fois; avant, le professeur ne lui (donner) que des C. 4. J'ai emmené des touristes dans le quartier du Marais: avant, je (lire) tous les détails dans le guide Michelin. 5. Mes cousins ont acheté des meubles neufs. Avant, ils (repeindre) tout leur appartement.

*Les règles d'accord du participe passé sont identiques pour le passé composé et le plus-que-parfait.

Elle m'a rendu le livre **que je lui avais prêté.**

Ils ont reçu une lettre **qui était restée** huit jours à la poste.

Employez le plus-que-parfait après le relatif **qui** ou **que** si l'action qui suit le relatif a eu lieu avant.

Remplacez l'infinitif entre parenthèses par le temps correct.   *Exercice IX*

1. J'ai vu un accident qui _____ (avoir lieu) cinq minutes avant.
2. Tu n'as pas aimé le film que je te (recommander)?
3. Elle n'a pas encore reçu la carte postale que je lui (envoyer) d'Espagne.
4. Ils ont adopté la petite fille qui leur (sourire) pendant leur visite à l'orphelinat.
5. Mes voisins ont hérité la fortune de leur grand-père qui (être) chercheur d'or en Amérique.
6. Vous avez oublié les résolutions que vous (prendre).
7. Elle a lu tous les livres que le professeur (mettre) au programme.

Je pense qu'il **a bu.** ou:	**J'ai pensé** qu'il **avait bu.**
	Je **pensais** qu'il **avait bu.**

Employez le plus-que-parfait à la place d'un passé composé après la conjonction **que**, si le premier verbe est au passé (au passé composé ou l'imparfait).

Refaites les phrases suivantes mais employez la forme du verbe suggéré en faisant   *Exercice X*
les changements nécessaires.

1. Je crois que vous avez eu des difficultés. Je croyais...
2. Tu trouves que nous avons beaucoup changé? Tu as trouvé...
3. Le docteur lui dit qu'elle a trop mangé. Le docteur lui a dit...
4. La maman croit que les enfants se sont endormis. La maman croyait...
5. Mais elle voit qu'ils se sont amusés toute la nuit. Mais elle a vu...
6. Ils comprennent qu'ils ont eu tort. Ils ont compris...

Un paragraphe de Raymond Devos:

> Je suis sévère, mais je suis juste... je suis juste. Hier, je rentre chez moi... Qu'est-ce que j'apprends? — Que le chat avait mangé la pâtée du chien! Dehors, le chat! — Là-dessus, qu'est-ce que j'apprends? — Que le chien avait mangé la côtelette de ma femme! — Dehors, le chien! Là-dessus, qu'est-ce que j'apprends? — Que ma femme avait mangé mon bifteck! Dehors, la femme! Et là-dessus, qu'est-ce que je découvre? — Que le lait que j'avais bu le matin était celui du chat! Alors, j'ai fait rentrer tout le monde et je suis sorti.

Les adverbes et adjectifs interrogatifs

Où habitez-vous?	**Quand** partez-vous?
Comment allez-vous?	**Pourquoi** dites-vous cela?

Où, quand, comment, pourquoi sont des adverbes.

Quel âge avez-vous?   **Quelle** heure est-il?

Quel (quelle, quels, quelles) est un adjectif. Il est accompagné d'un nom. «**Quelle est** la différence...» Le verbe **être** est entre **quelle** et le nom.

Les pronoms interrogatifs

Qu'est-ce que
Qui est-ce que

> **Qu'est-ce que** vous dites?   **Qu'est-ce que** vous faites?
> **Qui est-ce que** tu regardes?   Je regarde Catherine.

On dit une chose. On fait une chose. **Qu'est-ce que** est le pronom interrogatif objet direct pour une chose.

On regarde une personne. **Qui est-ce que** est le pronom interrogatif objet direct pour une personne.

Exercice XI   Complétez les questions avec **qui est-ce que** pour une personne et **qu'est-ce que** pour une chose.

1. _____ vous écoutez?   J'écoute le président qui parle à la radio.
2. _____ elle écoute?   Elle écoute de la musique pop, c'est plus drôle.
3. _____ nous admirons?   Nous admirons Marlon Brando.
4. _____ vous admirez?   Vous admirez une statue de Rodin.
5. _____ je préfère?   Je préfère Jean-Paul Belmondo.
6. _____ je préfère?   Je préfère les éclairs au chocolat.
7. _____ elle comprend?   Elle comprend ses enfants.
8. _____ elle comprend?   Elle comprend les problèmes de la jeunesse.

Avec qui est-ce que
Avec quoi est-ce que

> **Avec qui est-ce qu'**il sort? Il sort avec Justine.
> **Avec quoi est-ce qu'**il sort? Il sort avec son parapluie.

Qui est-ce que est le pronom interrogatif, objet d'une préposition, pour une personne. La phrase commence par la préposition.

Quoi est-ce que est le pronom interrogatif, objet d'une préposition, pour une chose. La phrase commence par la préposition.

Exercice XII   Complétez les questions avec une *préposition* + **qui est-ce que** pour une personne et une *préposition* + **quoi est-ce que** pour une chose.

1. De _____ ils parlent?   Ils parlent de la situation internationale.
2. De _____ ils parlent?   Ils parlent de l'actrice qui a eu l'Oscar.
3. Avec _____ vous dormez?   Je dors avec un tas de pilules.
4. Avec _____ vous dormez?   Je dors avec mon mari, bien sûr!

Une concierge.

5. Pour _____ elle s'est jetée dans le lac en plein hiver? Pour l'homme qu'elle aimait.
6. Pour _____ elle s'est jetée dans le lac? Pour une histoire d'amour.
7. A _____ tu penses? A Elizabeth et Richard.
8. A _____ tu penses? A la vieillesse.

Qui
Qui est-ce qui
Qu'est-ce qui

> **Qui** parle?
> **Qui est-ce qui** parle? C'est le professeur.
> **Qu'est-ce qui** intéresse le monde entier? C'est l'amour.

Quand le sujet de l'action est une personne, le pronom est **Qui** ou **Qui est-ce qui** par redondance. Quand le sujet est une chose, le pronom est **Qu'est-ce qui.**

Exercice XIII   Mettez la forme correcte du pronom interrogatif: **Qui?** ou **Qui est-ce qui?** ou **Qu'est-ce qui?**

1. _____ éclaire le monde? C'est le soleil.
2. _____ éclaire vos esprits obscurs? C'est le professeur.
3. _____ pollue la mer? C'est les produits chimiques.
4. _____ énerve une mère? Les enfants insupportables et bruyants.
5. _____ empoisonne l'atmosphère? L'oxyde de carbone.
6. _____ a empoisonné la victime? L'héritier qui voulait son argent.

Tableau récapitulatif:

	PERSONNE	CHOSE
Sujet:	**Qui?**	**Qu'est-ce qui?**
	(Qui est-ce qui)	
Objet direct:	**Qui est-ce que?**	**Qu'est-ce que?**
Objet de préposition:	**Avec** / **De** } **qui est-ce que?**	**Avec** / **De** } **quoi est-ce que?**

Remarque: Pour une personne le pronom est toujours **qui.**

Exercice XIV   Mettez le pronom qui convient.

1. Chez _____ ils habitent? Chez leurs cousins.
2. Avec _____ vous faites la cuisine? Avec du beurre.
3. _____ vous a dit cela? Mon coiffeur.
4. _____ fait pousser les plantes? Le soleil.
5. _____ les vieux regrettent? Le temps de leur jeunesse.
6. _____ tu as vu à la bibliothèque? J'ai vu Joël.

Formes longues, formes courtes:

> Qui est-ce que tu regardes? **Qui** regardes-tu?
> Qu'est-ce que nous faisons? **Que** faisons-nous?
> Avec qui est-ce qu'il sort? **Avec qui** sort-il?
> Avec quoi est-ce que vous écrivez? **Avec quoi** écrivez-vous?

Qui est-ce que est une forme longue. **Qui** est une forme courte. La formule pour une forme longue:

---

pronom interrogatif avec **est-ce que** + verbe à la forme énonciative est l'équivalent de la formule suivante pour une forme courte:

> pronom interrogatif + verbe à la forme interrogative

Tableau des formes courtes:

		PERSONNE	CHOSE
Sujet:		**Qui?**	
		Qui est-ce qui*?	**Qu'est-ce qui*?**
O.D.		**Qui?**	**Que?**
Objet de prép.		**Avec** } **qui?** **De**	**Avec** } **quoi?** **De**

Mettez le pronom qui convient, forme courte ou forme longue.

Exercice XV

1. _____ cherchez-vous? Je cherche mes clés.
2. _____ il attend? Il attend le train.
3. _____ vous prenez? Je prends un café.
4. _____ nous aimons? Nous aimons notre président.
5. _____ ils parlent? Ils parlent de leurs enfants.
6. _____ sors-tu? Je sors avec Jacqueline.
7. _____ en a assez? Les vieux en ont assez!
8. _____ protestent-ils? Ils protestent contre l'injustice.
9. _____ vous intéresse? Cet orateur m'intéresse.
10. _____ nous a rendus malades? Des huîtres pas fraîches.

Lequel, laquelle, le pronom de choix:

> **Lequel** de vos professeurs préférez-vous?
> De tous les films récents, **lequel** a eu le plus de succès?
> De toutes les jeunes filles de la classe, **laquelle** est la plus intelligente?
> J'ai trois jolies maisons: **laquelle** préférez-vous?

Lequel (*masc.*); **laquelle** (*fém.*); **lesquels** (*masc. pl.*); **lesquelles** (*fém. pl.*) sont des pronoms de choix: vous choisissez entre deux ou plusieurs personnes ou objets; vous accordez **lequel (laquelle)** avec le nom absent.

Mettez le pronom de choix.

Exercice XVI

1. Tous les étudiants n'ont pas compris: _____ n'ont pas compris?
2. Regardez les jeunes filles: _____ est la plus charmante?
3. De tous ces livres, _____ sont à vous?
4. Je donne mes petits chats à celui qui les veut: _____ voulez-vous?
5. Admirez les fleurs de mon jardin? _____ préférez-vous?

Duquel, auquel; desquels, auxquels, le pronom de choix contracté:

> Je parle **de** cet étudiant: **duquel** parlez-vous?
> Je parle **à** mes étudiants: **auxquels** parlez-vous?

*Ces formes ne changent pas.

Le, les dans **lequel, lesquels** sont des articles. S'ils sont en contact avec la préposition **de** ou **à,** il y a une contraction. Les formes contractées sont:

de + lequel = **duquel**	à + lequel = **auquel**
de + lesquels = **desquels**	à + lesquels = **auxquels**
de + lesquelles = **desquelles**	à + lesquelles = **auxquelles**
de laquelle et **à laquelle** ne sont pas contractés.	

Exercice XVII   Mettez la forme contractée de **lequel, laquelle,** etc.

1. Je pense à mes problèmes. _____ en particulier pensez-vous?
2. J'ai besoin de ce livre. Précisez: _____ avez-vous besoin?
3. Vous parlez de la forme des pronoms. _____ parlez-vous, de la courte ou de la longue?
4. Vous avez peur des événements. _____ surtout avez-vous peur?
5. Elle s'adresse aux jeunes filles de l'université. _____ est-ce qu'elle s'adresse?

LECTURE   **L'amour, les relations familiales en France. Les jeunes et les vieux.**

Les Français ont une curieuse réputation, quand on parle d'amour: ils sont, paraît-il, les plus grands amoureux de la terre; les petites femmes de Paris sont célèbres; Brigitte Bardot est un symbole; Alain Delon est le type du séducteur; les ménages à trois sont fameux, les rendez-vous clandestins aussi. La littérature, le théâtre, les chansons ont beaucoup contribué à faire cette réputation. Pour certains touristes, c'est une attraction, et on va en France, à Paris surtout, avec une curiosité impatiente; on est sûr qu'on va avoir des aventures extraordinaires. Pour d'autres, c'est une mauvaise réputation et on critique très fort ces vilains Français, qui sont le peuple le plus coquin de la terre. Eh bien, la réalité est tout autre. Il y a en France, comme partout ailleurs, des gens qui s'aiment, des mariages d'amour, mais aussi des divorces, des ruptures, des familles «bourgeoises» et très traditionalistes, et des couples «illégaux.» On parle beaucoup d'amour, c'est vrai, et une certaine presse, «la presse du cœur», entretient chez les jeunes filles pas très cultivées des rêves de princes charmants, de millionnaires, de romanesque. On est aussi très libre et il n'est pas rare de voir des amoureux s'embrasser dans la rue.

Dans les familles, c'est aussi comme dans le reste du monde. Les rapports familiaux ont beaucoup changé. Autrefois les parents étaient très stricts et très autoritaires. Les enfants devaient obéir, respecter. On ne s'occupait pas trop de leurs idées, de leurs désirs. Ils étaient, c'est tout. Par exemple, les enfants ne devaient pas parler à table, quand les «grandes personnes» avaient une conversation. Mais la psychologie moderne a fait évoluer les rapports parents-enfants. Et aussi la révolution de mai 68 a jeté les jeunes dans la rue. Les jeunes sont beaucoup plus conscients des problèmes sociaux, et ils revendiquent des libertés qu'on avait refusées à leurs parents. Ainsi, même les jeunes des lycées font des grèves, et en ont «ras le bol.» C'est une expression qui traduit l'insatisfaction des jeunes et un sentiment d'insécurité devant une société qui ne leur garantit pas l'avenir — car il y a de moins en moins de débouchés pour ceux qui font des études. Autrement, les jeunes Français ressemblent beaucoup aux jeunes Américains: comme distractions ils aiment les «surboums,» la musique «yéyé,» ils ont leurs idoles: Johnny Halliday ou Sheila. Ils mettent des posters sur les murs de leurs chambres: champions de motocyclette ou chanteurs à la mode. Ils chantent des «tubes,» ils ont les cheveux longs. Ils aiment les jeans avec des badges et les T shirts imprimés. Ceux qui ont trop de conflits avec leurs parents, ou certains qui habitent dans des «grands ensembles,» ont des problèmes; ils deviennent des voyous, des délinquants. D'autres se tournent vers la drogue, l'herbe d'abord, la marie-jeanne ou le haschich, puis la «neige» (la cocaïne). Malheureusement Marseille est un des grands centres de trafic de drogue, protégé par des puissances politiques! Il y a aussi les pacifistes, les non-violents qui prêchent le retour à la nature: ils vont en Inde, ou ils forment des communautés, loin des villes et de la civilisation.

Les vieux, eux, ne sont pas toujours bien traités. Souvent, leur pension est ridiculement basse, et ils arrivent difficilement à vivre, avec l'augmentation du coût de la vie. Beaucoup sont abandonnés à eux-mêmes, ils vivent dans un état proche de la misère, ou bien dans une maison de retraite, où ils sont entre eux, mais n'ont qu'à attendre la mort.

On semble s'intéresser un peu à leur sort, mais dans certains milieux seulement — ceux qui ont de l'argent. Il y a des groupes et des clubs pour organiser des voyages, des activités, des distractions et des sports. Les personnes âgées peuvent retourner à l'université, faire du ski de fond, apprendre à danser. On ne dit plus «les croûlants» comme les jeunes gens les avaient baptisés, on parle «du 3ème âge.» Mais il y a encore trop de vieux que ces efforts de recyclage ne touchent pas et qui végètent sans espoir — surtout les vieux ouvriers et les vieux à la campagne. On n'a pas encore trouvé de solution à ce problème: vieillir.

Vocabulaire

amoureux, (*m.*) lover
croulant, (*m.*); **crouler** to fall apart (for a building or an old ruin)
débouché, (*m.*) opportunity
en avoir ras le bol to have it up to here, to be fed up with the whole thing
entretenir to keep up
ménage à trois, (*m.*) le mari, la femme et un autre homme sont très amis

embrasser to kiss
ski de fond, (*m.*) cross-country skiing
surboum, (*f.*) dance, party
tube, (*m.*) famous song, hit
vilain; coquin naughty
voyou, (*m.*) hoodlum
yéyé comes from Beatle-type music (*I love you, heh, heh*)

Composition Choisissez:

1. Avez-vous vécu une grande histoire d'amour? Racontez-la. Si non, inventez-la.
2. Quels rapports avez-vous avec vos parents? Y-a-t-il des vieux dans votre famille? Comment voyez-vous votre âge mûr? votre vieillesse? votre retraite?
3. Aimez-vous votre jeunesse?

Chapitre

Le roi a fait battre tambour

Le roi a fait bat—tre tam — bour, Le roi a

fait bat—tre tam—bour, pour voir tou—tes ses da — mes et la pre—

miè—re qu'il a vue lui a ra—vi son â — me.

PRÉSENTATION Rien ne va

Hier il pleuvait, je me sentais terriblement déprimé. J'étais tellement maussade et triste que j'avais envie de pleurer et même envie de me tuer. Ça arrive à tout le monde, ces humeurs dépressives. J'étais vraiment de mauvaise humeur. Je pensais: rien ne va bien, personne ne m'aime, je n'ai plus d'énergie, je n'ai jamais eu de chance dans ma vie. J'ai cherché quelque chose d'intéressant à faire, mais je n'ai rien trouvé. Tout était négatif. Je voyais la vie en noir. J'avais le cafard. J'ai essayé d'écouter un disque, de boire un petit verre de vin. Rien à faire. Ni la musique, ni le vin n'ont pu changer mon état d'esprit. Vraiment, j'étais dans un état terrible. J'ai téléphoné à un de mes amis qui est psychiatre pour lui demander conseil. Voici notre conversation.

MOI: Allô! C'est toi, Charles? Est-ce que tu as une minute? (Tout le monde sait que les psychiatres n'ont pas une minute, mais si on pose la question de cette manière, ils n'ont pas le temps de réfléchir et de dire non.)

CHARLES: Euh!

MOI: Ici, Thomas. Voilà, j'ai besoin d'un conseil: je me sens affreusement déprimé: tout va mal, rien ne me plaît, personne ne fait attention à moi, personne ne m'écrit et puis, quand j'écoute les nouvelles c'est encore pire. On ne parle que de la pollution, de la surpopulation, de la famine, de la crise économique, de la course aux armements, de la guerre, du racisme, du chômage, des révoltes dans les prisons, de l'augmentation des crimes. Vraiment ce n'est plus drôle de vivre. J'ai la tentation de me tuer.

CHARLES: Voyons, tais-toi, mon vieux. Ne parle pas comme cela. Tu es fatigué. Tu travailles trop sans doute. Tu devrais te reposer. C'est le repos qui te manque.

MOI: Ah, tu me fais rire; se reposer quand on est professeur. Il est préférable de se taire.

CHARLES: Voyons, tu t'es couché tard hier soir? Tu as lu jusqu'à minuit, tu as corrigé des copies d'élèves?

MOI: Cette question! mais je ne fais rien d'autre de mes soirées, et même je manque tous les bons programmes à la télé à cause de ces copies.

CHARLES: Voilà, c'est ça. Tu aurais dû te coucher plus tôt. Tu devrais te coucher plus tôt ce soir.

MOI: Non, non, je crois que ce n'est pas la raison. C'est quelque chose de plus profond.

CHARLES: Ah... bon! Examinons tes raisons de découragement. (Là, il faut dire que Charles est un type formidable. Il prend des notes, toujours, même au téléphone. Moi, je ne sais jamais ce que les gens viennent de dire, lui, il est toujours organisé.) N° 1: la pollution. Il faut admettre que le gouvernement a essayé de la stopper: les usines contrôlent les déchets; le lac Érié est de nouveau plein de poissons.

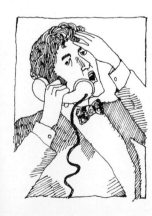

MOI: Plein! Tu exagères; ni le lac Érié, ni un autre des grands lacs ne sont pleins de poissons.

CHARLES: Nº 2: la population est limitée par la pilule, le contrôle des naissances.

MOI: Oui, mais pas encore dans les pays sous-développés, et le monde va exploser...

CHARLES: Nº 3: la famine. Une juste distribution de la nourriture du monde entier pourrait la supprimer.

MOI: «Pourrait,» c'est le mot, «si» le monde était mieux organisé, pour le moment ce n'est pas une réalité.

CHARLES: Nº 4: la crise économique. Si nous avions été plus prévoyants nous aurions pu l'éviter.

MOI: Ah! tu vois, tu parles au conditionnel passé, tu commences à constater que rien ne va.

CHARLES: Quant aux numéros 5, 6, 7, 8, 9, 10 — la course aux armements, la guerre, le racisme, le chômage, les révoltes dans les prisons, l'augmentation des crimes, je dois avouer que tu as raison: personne ne paraît s'intéresser à ces problèmes et rien n'est fait pour les considérer sérieusement. Ah! si j'étais quelqu'un au gouvernement, je changerais tout cela.

MOI: Tu ne changerais rien du tout, tu n'aurais pas assez d'autorité, et d'ailleurs tu es un optimiste.

CHARLES: Tu n'aurais pas dû me téléphoner, toutes ces pensées me dépriment horriblement.

MOI: En bien, moi je me sens beaucoup mieux. Je suis ravi de ne pas avoir hésité à te téléphoner. Merci mille fois.

CHARLES: Mais, et moi? Qui va me guérir de mon cafard?

MOI: Si j'étais toi, je téléphonerais à Eric. C'est un jeune psychologue qui monte; il pourrait peut-être t'aider. Au revoir, mon vieux!

Vocabulaire

avoir le cafard to have the blues
cafard, (*m.*) cockroach
copie d'élève, (*f.*) student paper
déchets, (*m. pl.*) wastes
de cette manière in this way
demander conseil à quelqu'un to ask someone for advice
de nouveau again
état d'esprit, (*m.*) state of mind (mood)
éviter to avoid
famine, (*f.*) hunger

humeur, (*f.*) mood, **être de mauvaise humeur** to be in a bad mood ≠ **être de bonne humeur**
maussade cranky, glum
monter to be on his way up
nourriture, (*f.*) food
mon vieux old chap
profond deep
quant à as for
type, (*m.*) guy
usine, (*f.*) factory
voir la vie en noir ≠ **voir la vie en rose**

PRONONCIATION   L'intonation d'une phrase négative

Nous avons vu l'intonation d'une phrase énonciative simple (p. 27) et l'intonation d'une phrase interrogative (p. 28). Voici quelques principes pour l'intonation d'une phrase négative.

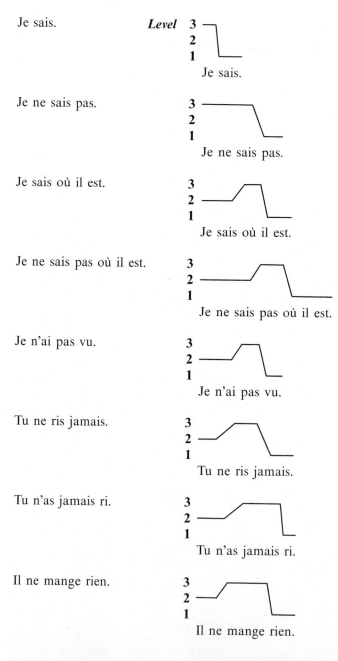

Je sais.

Je ne sais pas.

Je sais où il est.

Je ne sais pas où il est.

Je n'ai pas vu.

Tu ne ris jamais.

Tu n'as jamais ri.

Il ne mange rien.

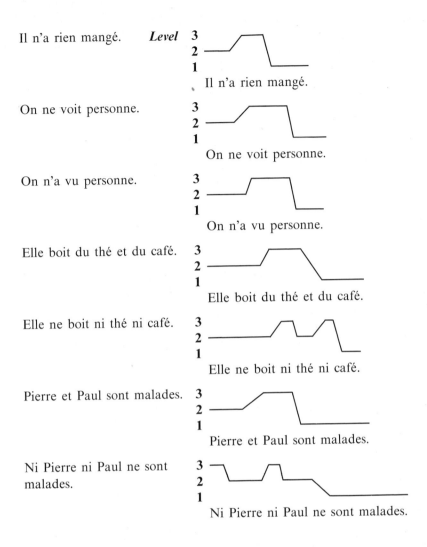

Il n'a rien mangé.   *Level* **3**

Il n'a rien mangé.

On ne voit personne.

On ne voit personne.

On n'a vu personne.

On n'a vu personne.

Elle boit du thé et du café.

Elle boit du thé et du café.

Elle ne boit ni thé ni café.

Elle ne boit ni thé ni café.

Pierre et Paul sont malades.

Pierre et Paul sont malades.

Ni Pierre ni Paul ne sont malades.

Ni Pierre ni Paul ne sont malades.

VERBES IRRÉGULIERS **STRUCTURES**

se taire *to be quiet, to stop talking*

Présent:	je **me tais**	nous **nous taisons**
	tu **te tais** /tɛ/	vous **vous taisez** /tɛz/
	il **se tait**	ils **se taisent**

Futur:	je **me tairai**
Imparfait:	je **me taisais**
Passé Composé:	je **me suis tu**
Impératif:	**Tais-toi!** **Taisez-vous!** **Taisons-nous!**

se tuer   *to kill oneself*

Présent:	je **me tue**, nous **nous tuons**
Futur:	je **me tuerai**
Imparfait:	je **me tuais**
Passé Composé:	je **me suis tué**

Se tuer est un verbe régulier du premier groupe.

Ne confondez pas au passé composé: il **s'est tu** /ty/ (de **se taire**)

il **s'est tué** /tɥe/ (de **se tuer**)

Exercice I   Mettez la forme correcte des verbes **se taire** ou **se tuer**.

1. Quand le professeur parle, les étudiants _____ .
2. Je dis aux enfants: _____ .
3. Elle _____ dans un accident d'auto. (*passé composé*)
4. Je n'entends plus le bébé pleurer. Il _____ . (*passé composé*)
5. S'ils ne s'attachent pas avec une corde (*rope*) pour l'ascension de cette montagne, ils _____ . (*futur*)
6. Quand vous serez fatigué de parler, vous _____ .

plaire   *to please*

Présent:	je **plais**, il **plaît**, nous **plaisons**, etc.
Futur:	je **plairai**, etc.
Imparfait:	je **plaisais**, etc.
Passé Composé:	j'**ai plu**, il **a plu**, etc.

Conjuguez ce verbe sur le même modèle que **se taire**, mais avec un accent circonflexe sur le **i** devant **t**.

On rencontre souvent ce verbe sous cette forme:

Ça me plaît.   **Ça lui a plu.**   **S'il vous plaît.**

Le verbe **se plaire** (*to please one another, to like each other*) a la forme suivante au passé composé pluriel: **ils se sont plu,** sans accord du participe passé.

Pleurer et **pleuvoir** sont deux verbes souvent confondus.

pleurer   *to cry, to weep*

Présent:	je **pleure**, il **pleure**, nous **pleurons**
Futur:	je **pleurerai**, tu **pleureras** (on entend deux /ʀ/)
Imparfait:	je **pleurais**, tu **pleurais**, etc.
Passé Composé:	j'**ai pleuré**, tu **as pleuré**, etc.

C'est un verbe régulier du 1er groupe.

pleuvoir   *to rain*

Présent:	il **pleut**
Futur:	il **pleuvra**
Imparfait:	il **pleuvait**
Passé Composé:	il **a plu**

C'est un verbe irrégulier et impersonnel. Il n'existe que sous la forme **il...**

EXEMPLE: Michel **a plu** aux parents de sa petite amie.
Hier il y a eu une tempête, et il **a plu** toute la journée.

Le verbe **plaire** et le verbe **pleuvoir** ont la même forme au *passé composé*.

Mettez les verbes **pleurer, pleuvoir** ou **plaire** au temps qui convient.   *Exercice II*

1. Vous avez vu cette pièce de théâtre. Elle vous _____?
2. Pendant mes vacances en Orégon, il _____ tous les jours. (*passé composé*)
3. Pourquoi n'as-tu pas acheté ce chapeau? — Il ne me _____ pas. (*imparfait*)
4. Quand je suis triste, je ne _____ pas.
5. Est-ce que vous prenez votre imper quand il _____?
6. Nous _____ quand vous partirez.
7. Demain il fera beau, il ne _____ pas.
8. L'été dernier, j'étais en Bretagne: il _____ constamment. (*imparfait*)
9. Ça ne me _____ pas; alors, je _____ .

CONSTRUCTIONS A RETENIR

Le verbe **manquer** (*to miss, to lack*)

Ce verbe a plusieurs constructions et des significations différentes:

1. **Je manque mon autobus (l'avion, le train, la classe).** *I miss my bus* (*the plane, the train, the class*).

    La construction est:

    > sujet + **manquer** + objet direct du nom de chose

2. **Je manque de courage.** *I lack courage.*

    La construction est:

    > sujet + **manquer de** + nom

3. **Vous me manquez.** *I miss you.*

    En français l'ordre est inverse. **Me** est objet indirect. On manque **à** une personne, on **lui** manque. La signification est: **Je regrette votre absence.** La construction est:

    > sujet + pronom O.I. de la personne + **manquer**

Exercice III   Complétez avec le verbe **manquer** et sa construction correcte.

1. Quand Janine sera au *college*, elle _____ ses parents.
2. Jean-Pierre? Il _____ toujours _____ argent à la fin du mois.
3. Hier soir vous _____ (*p.c.*) une partie sensationnelle.
4. Les étudiants sont toujours absents. Ils _____ régularité dans leurs études.
5. Vous partez en voyage? Nous vous regretterons. Vous _____.
6. Tu n'as pas regardé la télé hier soir? Tu _____ un bon programme.
7. (*Did you miss me?*)
8. (*Will she miss you?*)

Les mots indéfinis: **quelqu'un, quelque chose**

Il y a sûrement **quelqu'un** qui vous aime.
Parmi les jeunes filles de la classe, est-ce qu'il y a **quelqu'un** qui veut parler du M.L.F.?

Quelqu'un = une personne indéfinie = *someone*. **Quelqu'un** n'a pas de féminin. Employez **quelqu'un** même dans un groupe composé de femmes.

Quelqu'un d'important.
Une **personne** importante.

Le mot **personne** est un nom féminin, l'adjectif est féminin. Si **quelqu'un** est modifié par un adjectif, il faut la préposition **de.** L'adjectif est au masculin.

Exercice IV   Sur le modèle **quelqu'un d'important** ou **une personne importante,** répétez avec les adjectifs suivants:

1. intéressant   2. fascinant   3. charmant   4. sportif   5. ennuyeux

Tous mes étudiants ne sont pas stupides: **quelques-uns** comprennent.
Parmi les jeunes filles, **quelques-unes** comprennent.

Quelqu'un a deux formes au pluriel: un masculin, **quelques-uns,** et un féminin, **quelques-unes.** Le sens est *un petit nombre*.

C'est une **bonne chose.** C'est **quelque chose de bon.**

Le nom **chose** est féminin, l'adjectif s'accorde. L'expression **quelque chose** (*something*) est suivie de la préposition **de** et de l'adjectif au masculin.

Exercice V   Sur le modèle, refaites les phrases en changeant l'adjectif. Attention à la place de l'adjectif.

EXEMPLE: **grand:** C'est **une grande chose.**
                      C'est **quelque chose de grand.**

1. beau   2. mauvais   3. important   4. exceptionnel   5. normal
6. positif   7. gentil   8. remarquable 9. passionnant

Un petit embouteillage.

POINTS DE GRAMMAIRE

Le conditionnel présent

LA FORME

> Qu'est-ce que je **pourrais** bien faire pour vous?

Pourrais est un conditionnel présent. Le conditionnel présent, c'est le futur avec les terminaisons de l'imparfait:

je parler**ais***   nous parler**ions** /ʀjõ/

tu parler**ais** /ʀɛ/   vous parler**iez** /ʀje/

il parler**ait**

ils parler**aient**

---

* La différence de prononciation entre le futur **parlerai** et le conditionnel **parlerais** n'est pas très grande. Le futur est un /e/ fermé, le conditionnel est /ɛ/ ouvert. Quand on parle vite, on ne fait pas la différence.

Voici d'autres formes:

finir:	je **finirais**	avoir:	j'**aurais**
prendre:	tu **prendrais**	faire:	je **ferais**
dormir:	il **dormirait**	pouvoir:	je **pourrais**
être:	je **serais**		

Les futurs irréguliers donnent des conditionnels présents irréguliers.

Exercice VI (*a.*) Donnez le conditionnel correspondant à ces futurs:

1. nous choisirons
2. il fera
3. je verrai
4. vous aurez
5. elle ira
6. ils finiront
7. il pleura
8. je pourrai

(*b.*) Donnez le conditionnel correspondant à ces présents. Trouvez d'abord le futur:

1. je reste
2. nous sommes
3. vous finissez
4. ils peuvent
5. vous venez
6. je suis
7. tu as
8. il faut
9. nous allons
10. tu cours
11. je vois
12. elle envoie
13. vous vendez
14. ils prennent

L'EMPLOI

Si j'en **avais** la possibilité, je **changerais** tout cela.

Le conditionnel présent s'emploie comme la forme verbale anglaise *I would change... You would take...* etc. dans un système avec **si** = *if.* Attention: le verbe avec **si** est à l'imparfait, c'est le verbe principal qui est au conditionnel présent. Dans ce cas, ne mettez jamais un conditionnel après **si.** L'ordre des deux groupes peut varier:

si + imparfait	conditionnel présent
conditionnel présent	**si** + imparfait

Exercice VII Répétez, en mettant les verbes aux temps corrects:

(*a.*) conditionnel présent, (*b.*) **si** + imparfait, ou
(*a.*) **si** + imparfait, (*b.*) conditionnel présent

1. Si tu _____ (aller) à Paris, tu _____ (voir) toutes les boîtes de nuit.
2. Nous _____ (manger) du riz tous les jours, si nous _____ (habiter) en Chine.
3. Si elles _____ (vivre) en France, elles _____ (boire) du vin à tous les repas.
4. Il ne _____ (avoir) pas de difficulté, s'il _____ (apprendre) mieux ses verbes.
5. Si vous _____ (mettre) un tigre dans votre moteur, votre auto _____ (marcher) mieux.
6. Si je ne _____ (trouver) pas des phrases si amusantes, mes étudiants _____ (dire): Quelle barbe, la grammaire!
7. Si vos enfants ne vous _____ (entendre) pas, ils ne _____ (répéter) pas ces gros mots (*bad words, swear words*).

Remarquez le sens spécial de **si nous allions au cinéma?** (*How about going to the movies?*) **Si** + imparfait en question = *How about...?*

Le conditionnel passé

LA FORME

> **Si j'avais su,** je **serais venu.**

Je serais venu est un conditionnel passé. Voici les formes de ce temps:

Verbes avec auxiliaire **avoir**	*Verbes avec auxiliaire* **être**	
j'**aurais aimé**	je **serais allé**	je **me serais lavé**
tu **aurais fini**	tu **serais venu**	tu **te serais regardé**
il **aurait vu**	il **serait sorti**	il **se serait coiffé**
nous **aurions regardé**	nous **serions partis**	nous **nous serions compris**
vous **auriez compris**	vous **seriez morts**	vous **vous seriez téléphoné**
ils **auraient couru**	ils **seraient rentrés**	ils **se seraient aimés**

Pour le conditionnel passé, on prend le futur antérieur, mais on conjugue l'auxiliaire au conditionnel présent: **aurais** ou **serais.**

(*a.*) Donnez les formes du conditionnel passé correspondant à ces futurs antérieurs.   *Exercice VIII*

1. vous aurez fait
2. il sera arrivé
3. je me serai amusé
4. tu auras appris
5. elle sera partie
6. j'aurai conduit
7. nous serons restés
8. elles se seront écrit

(*b.*) Donnez les conditionnels passés des verbes suivants. Trouvez d'abord le futur antérieur.

1. elle dit
2. je dors
3. tu envoies
4. il se lève
5. ils vivent
6. nous allons
7. tu parles
8. tu sors
9. ils comprennent
10. elles savent
11. vous faites
12. j'entends
13. elle revient

L'EMPLOI

> L'été dernier, **si j'avais eu** de l'argent, **j'aurais fait** un voyage à Tahiti.

Le conditionnel passé correspond à la forme verbale anglaise *I would have* (*done, gone, been, written,* etc.) dans un système avec **si** = *if.* Le verbe après **si** est au plus-que-parfait, le verbe principal est au conditionnel passé. Dans ce système, ne mettez jamais le conditionnel passé après **si.**

si + plus-que-parfait	conditionnel passé
conditionnel passé	**si** + plus-que-parfait

Exercice IX Répétez les phrases suivantes sur le modèle: **S'il avait eu... il aurait fait**

1. S'ils (savoir) ils ne (se marier) pas si jeunes.
2. Je (prendre ma retraite) à 30 ans, si je (pouvoir).
3. Si la guerre ne pas (avoir) lieu, il n'y (avoir pas) des millions de morts.
4. Si Roméo et Juliette (ne pas se tuer) est-ce qu'ils (pouvoir) être heureux?
5. Si le nez de Cléopâtre (être) plus court, la face du monde (être) changée.
6. Si le *streaker* ne (avoir) pas si froid, il (continuer) sa course plus longtemps.
7. Vous (manger) des rutabagas, si vous (vivre) en France pendant la guerre.

Le conditionnel de **devoir**

Vous êtes malade? Vous **devriez** rester chez vous. (*You should*)
Vous avez sommeil? Vous **auriez dû** vous coucher plus tôt. (*You should have*)

Voici les formes du conditionnel de **devoir:**

Présent: je **devrais,** tu **devrais,** nous **devrions,** etc.
Passé: j'**aurais dû,** tu **aurais dû,** nous **aurions dû,** etc.

Le verbe **devoir** a un sens spécial au conditionnel présent et au conditionnel passé.

je devrais: *I should*
j'aurais dû: *I should have*

Exercice X Répétez les phrases suivantes avec (*a.*) **tu devrais, elle devrait,** (*b.*) **tu aurais dû, vous auriez dû,** etc.

EXEMPLE: Elle lit ce livre: Elle **devrait** lire ce livre.
            Elle **aurait dû** lire ce livre.

1. Tu te reposes. 2. Elle fait la gymnastique. 3. Il ne boit pas en conduisant.
4. Vous payez vos dettes avant de partir en voyage. 5. Ils adoptent un enfant.
6. Nous célébrons votre succès.

La négation

Je **ne** parle **pas** italien.
Il **ne** fume **plus.**
Elle **ne** boit **jamais** de vin.

FORMES

La négation est toujours en deux mots; les deux mots entourent le verbe: **ne... pas, ne... plus, ne... jamais.**

---

ne + verbe + un autre mot (**pas, plus, jamais,** etc.)

L'EMPLOI

Je parle italien. Je **ne** parle **pas** italien.

La négation simple est **ne... pas.**

J'ai **encore** du travail. Je **n'ai plus** de travail.

La négation de **encore** est **ne... plus.**

Tu dors **déjà?** Tu **ne** dors **pas encore.**

La négation de **déjà** est **ne... pas encore** (*not yet*).

Il est **toujours** fatigué. Il **n'est jamais** fatigué.

La négation de **toujours** est **ne... jamais.**

Tu aimes **quelqu'un.** Tu **n'aimes personne.**

La négation de **quelqu'un** est **ne... personne.** Remarquez que **personne** ici est neutre, pas féminin. Il y a toujours **ne** devant le verbe. **Personne ne regarde ce programme. Personne** peut être sujet.

Vous comprenez **quelque chose?** Vous **ne** comprenez **rien.**

Le négation de **quelque chose** est **ne... rien.**

Rien ne va.

Rien peut être sujet.

Qui a téléphoné? — **Personne.**
Qu'est-ce que tu as? — **Rien.**
Vous fumez? — **Jamais.**

Il faut toujours avoir **ne,** excepté dans une réponse avec un seul mot.

Mettez les phrases suivantes à la forme négative.   *Exercice XI*

1. Elle parle toujours de son argent.
2. Vous dormez encore?
3. Nous écoutons quelqu'un.
4. J'achète quelque chose.
5. Ils travaillent.
6. Elles sont déjà debout.
7. Quelqu'un vous parle.
8. Quelque chose te plaît?

Je **n'ai pas** vu ce film.
Il **n'a jamais** voyagé.
Tu **n'as rien** compris.
Ils **ne sont pas** encore arrivés.
Elle **n'est plus** allée à l'université.

Au passé composé, les négations entourent l'auxiliaire. Le participe passé est placé après.

Je **n'ai rencontré personne.**

Ne... personne est une exception; **personne** est placé après le participe passé.

Exercice XII   Mettez les phrases suivantes à la forme négative.

1. Nous avons encore parlé de son succès.   2. Tu as déjà pris ton petit déjeuner?
3. J'ai vu quelqu'un.   4. Quelque chose est arrivé.   5. Elles ont gagné à la
Loterie.   6. Quelqu'un a téléphoné.   7. J'ai acheté quelque chose.   8. Tu as
toujours eu peur des chiens.

Tu as **un** ami.	Tu **n'**as **pas d'**ami.
Je bois **du** café.	Je **ne** bois **pas de** café.
Il fume toujours **des** cigares.	Il **ne** fume **jamais de** cigares.
Elle a encore **du** travail.	Elle **n'a plus de** travail.

Rappelez-vous! Avec la négation (**ne... pas, ne... jamais, ne... plus**) l'article indéfini
un, une, des et l'article partitif **du, de la, de l'** sont réduits à **de** (**pas de, jamais de,
plus de**).

«Bidonville» près de Paris.

J'aime l'opéra. Je n'aime **pas** l'opéra.

Il fait toujours la vaisselle. Il ne fait **jamais** la vaisselle.

Elle se coupe encore les cheveux. Elle ne se coupe **plus** les cheveux.

L'article défini — **le, la, les** — ne change pas avec la négation (voir Chapitre 6).

pas le	**pas la**	**pas les**
jamais le	**jamais la**	**jamais les**
plus le	**plus la**	**plus les**

Il **n'a pas un** ami. (*not a single friend*)

Attention au sens spécial de **pas un** = **pas un seul.**

Répétez à la forme négative.   *Exercice XIII*

1. Elle a toujours eu de la chance. 2. Vous mangez encore des bonbons? 3. Tu entends du bruit. 4. J'ai aimé la 8ème symphonie. 5. Ils ont un sou. 6. Elles regardent encore les actualités. 7. Vous lisez le journal. 8. Nous avons toujours visité les U.S.A.

Il aime Catherine **et** Elizabeth.

Il **n'**aime **ni** Catherine **ni** Elizabeth.

Il épouse Georgette **ou** Célestine, je ne sais plus.

Il n'épouse **ni** Georgette **ni** Célestine.

Jules **et** Jim sont Anglais?

Ni Jules **ni** Jim **ne** sont Anglais.

Robert **ou** Bernard téléphoneront.

Ni Robert **ni** Bernard **ne** téléphoneront.

La négation de **et** et de **ou** est: **ne... ni... ni**

ou: **ni... ni... ne.**

Il aime le thé **et** le café.

Il **n'**aime **ni** le thé **ni** le café.

Il boit du thé **et** du café.

Il **ne** boit **ni** thé **ni** café.

Avec **ni... ni** on garde l'article **le, la, les.** L'article **de la, du, des** disparaît.

Refaites les phrases à la forme négative avec **ne... ni... ni** ou **ni... ni... ne.**   *Exercice XIV*

1. Les maths et les sciences l'intéressent.
2. Elle achète des pommes et des oranges.
3. Nous avons des chiens et des chats.
4. Nous lisons le journal du matin et le journal du soir.
5. Ils veulent des garçons ou des filles.
6. Tu bois de la bière ou du vin?
7. Roger et Odette sont malades.

Elle **ne sort pas.**

Je lui dis **de ne pas sortir.**

Il ne **fume plus.**

Il promet **de ne plus fumer.**

Elle **ne ment jamais.**

Elle jure **de ne jamais mentir.**

Devant l'infinitif, les deux mots de la négation **ne pas, ne plus, ne jamais, ne rien** ne sont pas séparés.

Exercice XV Répétez avec l'infinitif et la négation pas séparée.

EXEMPLE: Ne pleurez pas. Je vous dis **de ne pas pleurer.**

1. Il ne comprend pas. Il a peur de _____ .
2. Elle ne fait rien. Elle aime _____ .
3. Je n'écris plus à Rachel. Je préfère _____ .
4. Nous n'allons pas voir ce film. On nous a dit de _____ .
5. Vous n'êtes jamais en retard. Je vous prie de _____ .
6. Ils ne disent rien. Je leur demande de _____ .

Ces ouvriers protestent.

Ce qui ne va pas en France

Nous avons déjà parlé de certains problèmes qui existent en France, et de choses qui ne vont pas: les salaires et les retraites qui ne suivent pas le coût de la vie, le chômage, l'insuffisance du personnel hospitalier, la misère des vieux.

La France n'est plus en guerre, mais les deux guerres «coloniales» qu'elle a soutenues, la guerre d'Indochine et la guerre d'Algérie, ont fait beaucoup de mal à son économie, à son prestige, et à la force morale du pays. Beaucoup de jeunes hommes sont morts dans les rizières d'Indochine, dans les djebels d'Algérie, pour rien, puisque la France a finalement perdu ces deux provinces. Les conséquences de ces guerres sont encore ressenties, parce qu'une grande quantité d'Algériens, français et musulmans, se sont réfugiés en France. Les Européens qu'on appelle les «Pieds-Noirs» se sont plus ou moins adaptés, mais les Arabes ont du mal à s'intégrer. Groupés en villages créés pour eux (les villages harkis) ou installés dans des petites villes du Sud de la France, ils présentent un curieux contraste de coutumes héritées de leur vie africaine — leurs femmes sortent peu, portent le costume de leur pays; ils respectent le jeûne de leur religion — et de modernisme: les jeunes gens qui sont allés dans les écoles françaises veulent plus de libertés, les jeunes filles veulent aller danser au bal du dimanche. Il faudra sans doute plusieurs générations pour qu'ils s'intègrent complètement.

Le problème du racisme aussi est important. En plus des musulmans qui sont maintenant considérés comme Français, il y a 1.600.000 travailleurs étrangers: des Portugais, des Espagnols, des Italiens, et des Africains d'Afrique noire. Ils font les travaux que les Français ne veulent pas faire: balayeurs, ramasseurs d'ordures, ouvriers à la chaîne. Ils vivent à 10 ou 12 hommes dans de misérables chambres d'hôtel, ou dans des «bidonvilles» dans la banlieue des grandes villes. Ils parlent mal le français et ne s'intègrent pas à la vie française. Ils souffrent de toutes les difficultés créées par la paperasserie, la bureaucratie, et surtout des ratonnades! Y-a-t-il un vol dans le quartier? Les Français — qui ont eu pendant longtemps la réputation d'être le peuple le plus accueillant de la terre, pour les étrangers, mais qui, hélas, sont devenus xénophobes — soupçonnent «les gens à la peau brune et aux cheveux frisés» et on accuse ou on punit arbitrairement un Arabe ou un Noir.

Un autre problème que le gouvernement a à résoudre, c'est celui du «régionalisme.» Certaines provinces ont été maintenues dans l'ombre dans un désir d'unification du pays: la Bretagne, l'Alsace, la Corse. Mais ces régions ont une personnalité très vivante. Le breton, l'alsacien, l'occitan, le provençal ne sont pas de simples patois, ce sont des langues qui ont une littérature, qui transmettent une culture originale. Ces provinces ont enfin obtenu qu'on enseigne leur langue dans leurs universités. Elles demandent aussi qu'on se penche sur leurs problèmes économiques: la Bretagne, très agricole, se sent défavorisée par les lois qui viennent de Paris. Les Alsaciens se tournent ver l'Allemagne où l'industrie leur offre de bons jobs. Les protestations sont parfois violentes, pour attirer l'attention de «Paris.» Les Bretons à la veille des élections présidentielles de 1974 ont détruit à la bombe un relai de télévision; en été, ils ont jeté une récolte d'artichauts sur les routes de vacances! Et en Corse il y a eu des morts et des blessés dans une véritable révolution d'autonomistes.

La France a sa place dans la course aux armements et si certains Français sont fiers de leurs sous-marins atomiques aux noms sonores: «Le Foudroyant, le Redoutable, le Terrible, l'Indomptable, et le Tonnant,» d'autres sont moins contents de savoir que leur pays est un des premiers marchands d'armes de guerre d'Europe. Les tanks français et les Mystères se vendent bien au Moyen-Orient, et la «bombinette» qui a explosé à Muruora il y a quelques années a beaucoup fait parler d'elle.

Il y aurait encore beaucoup à dire sur l'alcoolisme chez les adultes et les enfants; les révoltes dans les prisons qui ont amené des changements timides dans leur administration et les conditions de vie des prisonniers; la destruction de l'environnement par les promoteurs du bâtiment (la Côte d'Azur en particulier est défigurée par la construction désordonnée des HLM et de «Marina» prétentieuses) et la pollution des côtes par les marées noires (des bateaux — pas tous français — vident leur huile au large), des rivières par les déchets des usines et les ordures ménagères (on y voit flotter des poissons morts et des bouteilles en plastique), et des endroits de pique-nique par des campeurs inconscients qui abandonnent papiers gras, boîtes de yaourts, bouteilles vides...

Assez! Assez!

Vocabulaire

à la veille de on the eve of
banlieue, (*f.*) suburb
bombinette, (*f.*) petite bombe
coutume, (*f.*) custom
djebel, (*m.*) montagne (en Algérie)
faire du mal to hurt
Foudroyant, (*m.*) Lightning
Indomptable Untamable
jeûne, (*m.*) fast
marée, (*f.*) tide

ombre, (*f.*) shade
patois, (*m.*) local language
raton North African in slang
ratonnade, (*f.*) beating up of North Africans
résoudre to solve
ressentir to feel
rizière, (*f.*) rice paddy
Tonnant Thunderbolt
urne, (*f.*) ballot box

Composition Quels sont, à votre avis, les problèmes les plus sérieux dans la société ou nous vivons? La pollution, la surpopulation, la famine, le chômage, la guerre? Choisissez-en trois ou quatre, décrivez-les et donnez votre opinion, et des solutions, si vous en avez.

Passant par Paris

Chapitre **20**

Pas — sant par Pa — ris, vi — dant la bou — teil — le, pas — sant par Pa — ris, vi — dant la bou — teil — le, un de mes a — mis me dit à l'o — reil — le, bon, bon, bon, _____ le bon vin m'en — dort, l'a — mour me ré — veil — le. Le bon vin m'en — dort, l'a — mour me ré — veille en — cor.

L'ESCARGOT

Est-ce que le temps est beau?
　　　Se demandait l'escargot
Car, pour moi, s'il faisait beau
C'est qu'il ferait vilain temps.
　　　J'aime qu'il tombe de l'eau,
　　　Voilà mon tempérament

Combien de gens, et sans coquille,
N'aiment pas que le soleil brille.
　　　Il est caché? Il reviendra!
　　　L'escargot? On le mangera.

ROBERT DESNOS
Chante fables et Chante fleurs,
© *1944 Gallimard*

PRÉSENTATION   Tout va bien

Vous non plus vous n'aimez pas qu'il pleuve, vous aussi vous aimez qu'il fasse beau. Vous détestez qu'il fasse froid et mauvais. Mais c'est la vie! Il est ridicule de se rendre triste, malade ou de s'indigner pour des choses dont on ne peut pas changer le cours: le temps, la suite des saisons.

C'est vrai qu'il y a des choses inacceptables dans le monde et il faut que nous fassions tout notre possible pour qu'elles cessent. C'est triste que les hommes se fassent la guerre, se battent et s'entretuent, c'est insupportable que des enfants meurent de faim et que des adultes soient si bien nourris qu'ils soient obligés de suivre un régime. C'est tragique que l'humanité soit sur le point d'épuiser les ressources naturelles de la terre. C'est absurde que les hommes aient amassé assez de bombes et d'armement pour faire sauter 20 fois toute la planète.

Toutes ces injustices, dont nous sommes responsables plus ou moins, il est bon qu'on en parle, pour les dénoncer, et pour qu'un jour elles soient supprimées. Mais les choses naturelles, auxquelles on ne peut rien changer, il est ridicule de les regretter. Il faut que chacun, pour être heureux, soit un peu philosophe, un peu fataliste. Tenez, comme les escargots pour qui la pluie c'est le beau temps, malgré les catastrophes et le mauvais fonctionnement de la planète, nous allons nous enfuir dans des projets d'avenir.

J'ai entendu dire que toutes les compagnies aériennes viennent de décider que les professeurs de français et tous leurs étudiants ont droit à un voyage gratuit aller et retour en France. Vous doutez que ce soit vrai? Vous n'avez pas entendu parler de cette décision? Vous avez peur que ce soit une blague? Bon, mais nous souhaitons que cela arrive, n'est-ce pas? Alors faisons comme si...

Je voudrais que nous parlions de tous les préparatifs dont il faut s'occuper avant un départ en voyage. Pardon, monsieur? Qu'est-ce que vous dites? Je n'entends pas bien ce que vous dites. Quoi? Vous dites que, avant que nous puissions prendre l'avion, il faut que nous sachions avec quoi nous allons vivre, quand nous serons en France? Mais, j'ai oublié de vous donner tous les détails sur les conditions dans lesquelles ce voyage aurait lieu. Le professeur et ses élèves seraient complètement pris en charge par le gouvernement français: hôtels, restaurants, pourboires, visites de musées, théâtres, déplacements en trains ou en autobus; tout... sauf le vin. C'est dommage que le vin ne soit pas inclus, mais, soyons philosophes, on ne peut pas tout avoir. Le gouvernement français a beau être généreux, il faut qu'il récupère un petit bénéfice sur notre visite.

Pardon, mademoiselle, qu'est-ce que vous dites? Décidément, je n'entends pas bien aujourd'hui. Je deviens sourde. Ce que vous dites n'est pas clair. Répétez. Ah, vous dites qu'après avoir lu la lecture de la leçon 19, vous avez peur que tout aille mal en France et que votre voyage soit une catastrophe. Eh bien, rassurez-vous. Il faut admettre que malgré les imperfections dont nous avons parlé, il y a des choses

qui vont bien en France. Et surtout il y a Paris, la Ville-Lumière, la merveille des merveilles. Mais jusqu'à ce que nous y allions, vous avez la permission de douter de tout, et même de ce projet.

Vocabulaire

aller et retour, (*m.*)   round trip
amasser   to heap up, to stockpile
avoir droit   to be entitled
avoir lieu   to take place
blague, (*f.*)   joke
déplacement, (*m.*)   trip
épuiser   to wear off, to exhaust (*here,* the supplies)
faire sauter   to explode
gratuit   free

non plus   neither (*négation de* **aussi**)
projets d'avenir, (*m.*)   plans for the future
sauf   excepté
s'occuper de   to take care of
sourde   deaf (*m.,* sourd)
sur le point   on the verge of
tempérament, (*m.*)   constitution (or disposition)
vilain temps   mauvais temps

PRONONCIATION   L'intonation de la phrase implicative

Une phrase implicative peut avoir une forme énonciative (*statement*), ou une forme impérative, ou une forme interrogative, ou une forme exclamative, mais son intonation ne suit pas la forme traditionnelle, parce qu'elle exprime une idée différente de ce qu'elle dit en réalité; il y a dans les mots une implication que le vocabulaire seul n'exprime pas. C'est le ton de la voix qui exprime le véritable sens de la phrase. Il faut suivre les modèles, car c'est un vrai travail d'acteur. Répétez les phrases suivantes avec les intonations suggérées (ou en écoutant la bande magnétique au laboratoire).

Tu sors, par ce temps.

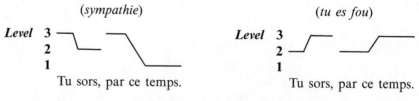

(sympathie)

Tu sors, par ce temps.

(tu es fou)

Tu sors, par ce temps.

Elle est arrivée ce matin.

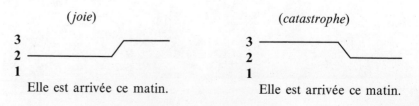

(joie)

Elle est arrivée ce matin.

(catastrophe)

Elle est arrivée ce matin.

Tu as encore oublié.

(*lassitude*) (*colère*)

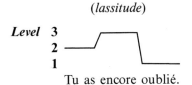 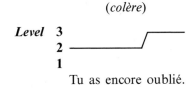

Elle a trente ans.

(*simple énonciation*) (*elle en a au moins 60*)

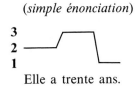 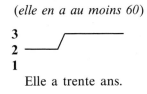

Avec qui sort-elle?

(*je ne le sais pas*) (*je le sais*)

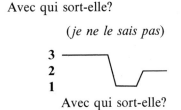 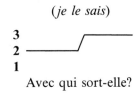

Qu'est-ce que vous dites?

(*Je n'entends pas.*) (*Je ne vous crois pas.*)

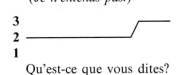 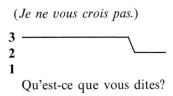

Regardez dans le dictionnaire.

(*Je ne suis pas sûre du sens moi-même.*) (*Vous ne me croyez pas.*)

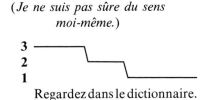 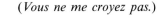

Appelez la police.

(*Vous êtes calme.*) (*Panique!*)

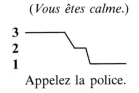 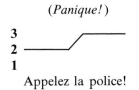

Vous avez vu son chapeau?

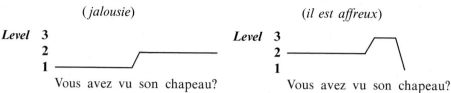

(jalousie)

Vous avez vu son chapeau?

(il est affreux)

Vous avez vu son chapeau?

C'est formidable.

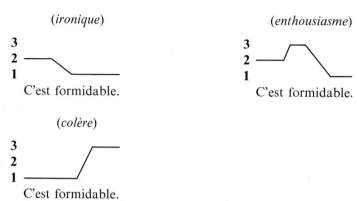

(ironique)

C'est formidable.

(enthousiasme)

C'est formidable.

(colère)

C'est formidable.

STRUCTURES   VERBES IRRÉGULIERS

fuir   *to flee*

Présent:	je **fuis**	nous **fuyons** /fɥijõ/
	tu **fuis** /fɥi/	vous **fuyez** /fɥije/
	il **fuit**	
	ils **fuient**	
Futur:	je **fuirai**	
	tu **fuiras**	
Imparfait:	je **fuyais**	nous **fuyions** /jj/
	tu **fuyais**	
Passé Composé:	j'ai **fui**	
	tu as **fui**	

Le verbe **s'enfuir** (*to run away*) se conjugue comme **fuire**. Le verbe **se sauver** a la même signification que **s'enfuir**.

Exercice I   Mettez la forme correcte du verbe **fuir, s'enfuir** ou **se sauver**.

1. Elle aime la solitude et elle _____ les réunions mondaines.
2. Le concert était tellement terrible que je me _____ (*p.c.*).

3. Quand le volcan fera éruption, les gens du village se _____.
4. Dans cette ville du Sud, les gens étaient racistes, nous les _____.
5. Vous _____ quand vous l'entendrez chanter!

CONSTRUCTIONS A RETENIR

Les verbes **entendre dire** et **entendre parler** (*to hear*)

> J'ai **entendu dire qu'**on a trouvé des êtres vivants sur Mars.
> Vous avez **entendu parler de** la communication des consciences?

Employez **entendre dire que** devant un groupe avec un verbe.
Employez **entendre parler de** devant un nom.

Refaites les phrases avec la formule correcte pour *to hear*. *Exercice II*

1. Tu dis que Claude et Bernadette vont divorcer?
2. Nous parlons de l'homme de Cros-Magnon.
3. Elle dit qu'il n'y a pas d'examen final dans cette classe.
4. Ils ne parlent pas de la nouvelle centrale nucléaire.

L'expression **il s'agit de...**
(*it is about, it is a question of, it concerns*)

> Dans ce livre **il s'agit de** sorcellerie. (*This book is about sorcery.*)

Cette expression est impersonnelle, elle commence par **il**. Le futur est: **il s'agira de**.... L'imparfait est: il **s'agissait de**....

Refaites les phrases avec **il s'agit de** au temps correct. *Exercice III*

1. (Ce livre parle) d'amour. Dans ce livre...
2. (Il faut) savoir ce que vous voulez.
3. (Elle ne pouvait pas) décider quelle robe elle allait mettre.
4. (Ce film parlera) d'un homme et d'une femme qui s'aiment. Dans ce film...

La contradiction: **quand même, malgré, avoir beau**

Ces trois expressions expriment la même idée, l'idée d'une contradiction.

> Jacqueline est pauvre; elle est toujours gaie.
> Jacqueline est pauvre, elle est **quand même** toujours gaie.

Ajoutez **quand même** après le verbe.

L'Opéra à Paris.

Malgré sa pauvreté, Jacqueline est toujours gaie.

La préposition **malgré** est employée avec un nom. Il faut faire un nom avec l'adjectif: **pauvre = pauvreté.** Ajoutez un possessif: **sa, leur, votre,** etc. si c'est nécessaire.

Jacqueline **a beau être pauvre,** elle est toujours gaie.

Voici la construction de cette expression idiomatique:

> sujet + **avoir** (conjugué) + **beau** (invariable) + l'infinitif du verbe + l'adjectif ou l'objet du verbe + une virgule + la deuxième partie de la phrase

Exercice IV   Faites des phrases en employant (*a.*) **quand même,** (*b.*) **malgré,** (*c.*) **avoir beau.**

EXEMPLES: Christiane a du succès, elle est maussade.
Christiane a du succès, elle est **quand même** maussade.
Malgré son succès, Christiane est maussade.
Christiane **a beau avoir du succès,** elle est maussade.

1. J'ai faim, je refuse de manger (pour maigrir).
2. Les Français ont des accidents de voiture, ils conduisent vite.
3. Le président est critiqué, il continue à gouverner de la même manière.
4. Les étudiants font tous les exercices, ils font des fautes.

POINTS DE GRAMMAIRE

Le subjonctif

GÉNÉRALITÉS

Tout va bien?	Je suis content que tout **aille** bien.
Nous arrivons en retard.	J'ai peur que nous **arrivions** en retard.
Elle fait la cuisine.	Il faut qu'elle **fasse** la cuisine.
Vous pouvez venir.	Je voudrais que vous **puissiez** venir.
Son père est mort.	Je suis navré que son père **soit** mort.

Dans la deuxième colonne, le verbe est au subjonctif parce qu'il suit une expression comme:

Je suis content (un sentiment)   **Il faut**   (une nécessité)
J'ai peur (un sentiment)   **Je voudrais** (un désir)
Je suis navré (un sentiment)

Le subjonctif est un mode (*a mood*). Il a deux temps courants:

Présent: aille, arrivions, fasse, puissiez
Passé: soit mort, ait fait

Le subjonctif présent

On part de la troisième personne du pluriel:

ils arrivent: **que j'arrive**
      que tu arrives
      qu'il arrive
      qu'ils arrivent

La terminaison de ces personnes est toujours: **–e, –es, –e, –ent.**

Pour les personnes **nous** et **vous,** on prend l'imparfait, on ajoute **que.**

nous arrivions: **que nous arrivions**   vous arriviez: **que vous arriviez**

Verbes du 1er groupe: **arriver**

COMPAREZ:	*Indicatif Présent*	*Subjonctif Présent*
	j'arriv**e**	que j'arriv**e**
	tu arriv**es**	que tu arriv**es**
	il arriv**e**	qu'il arriv**e**
	ils arriv**ent**	qu'ils arriv**ent**

Ces formes sont identiques. Mais:

nous arriv**ons**	que nous arriv**ions**
vous arriv**ez**	que vous arriv**iez**

Verbes du 2ème groupe: **finir** — il finissent

Subjonctif Présent

que je finiss**e**   que nous fin**issions** /issjõ/
que tu finiss**es** /is/   que vous fin**issiez** /issje/
qu'il finiss**e**
qu'ils finiss**ent**

Verbes du 3ème groupe: **vendre** — ils vendent

Subjonctif Présent

que je ven**de**   que nous ven**dions** /vãdjõ/
que tu ven**des** /vãd/   que vous ven**diez** /vãdje/
qu'il ven**de**
qu'ils ven**dent**

Verbes irréguliers:

courir: ils cour**ent**   que je cour**e**
voir: ils voi**ent**   que je voie

Exercice V   Répétez les verbes suivants au subjonctif avec **il faut que...**

1. Tu manges davantage. 2. Elle parle toujours de ses enfants. 3. Nous achetons une nouvelle voiture. 4. Je choisis un plus gros diamant. 5. Vous sortez moins souvent. 6. Ils dorment pendant la journée. 7. Elles prennent l'avion pour Tahiti. 8. Il vient nous voir. 9. Je traduis cette blague en anglais. 10. Tu lis un bon roman. 11. Elle apprend ses verbes. 12. Nous nous lavons tous les jours. 13. Vous arrêtez de fumer.

Certains verbes ont un subjonctif irrégulier. Voici les plus courants:

aller

que j'aille   que nous **all**ions
que tu ailles   que vous **all**iez
qu'il aille
qu'ils aillent

faire

que je fasse   que nous fassions
que tu fasses   que vous fassiez
qu'il fasse
qu'ils fassent

pouvoir

que je puisse   que nous puissions
que tu puisses   que vous puissiez
qu'il puisse
qu'ils puissent

vouloir

que je veuille   que nous **vou**lions
que tu veuilles   que vous **vou**liez
qu'il veuille
qu'ils veuillent

savoir

que je sache   que nous sachions
que tu saches   que vous sachiez
qu'il sache
qu'ils sachent

être

que je sois   que nous **soy**ons
que tu sois   que vous **soy**ez
qu'il soit
qu'ils soient

	avoir	pleuvoir
que j'aie	que nous **ayons**	
que tu aies	que vous **ayez**	
qu'il ait		qu'il pleuve
qu'ils aient		

Remarquez: **qu'il soit** et **qu'il ait** sont les seules formes de subjonctif qui ont un **t**.

Refaites les phrases suivantes avec **J'ai peur que...** *Exercice VI*

1. Il est malade.
2. Elle a trop de problèmes.
3. Ils vont seuls à San Francisco.
4. Vous faites des fautes.
5. Nous ne pouvons pas prendre de vacances.
6. Elles veulent acheter toutes les robes du magasin.
7. Tu ne sais pas ta leçon.

> **Soyons** raisonnables.
> **Ayez** du courage.
> N'**aie** pas peur.

Sois, soyons, soyez; aie, ayons, ayez sont les formes de l'impératif de **être** et **avoir**.

Le subjonctif passé

> Je suis désolé que son père **ait eu** un accident.
> Je suis désolé que son père **soit entré** dans un mur.

Ait eu, soit entré, c'est le passé composé du subjonctif. Conjuguez l'auxiliaire au subjonctif: il **a** eu — qu'il **ait** eu; il **est** entré — qu'il **soit** entré.

Répétez les verbes suivants au passé du subjonctif avec **il est possible que...** *Exercice VII*

EXEMPLE: Il a téléphoné. Il est possible qu'il **ait téléphoné.**

1. Elles ont oublié.
2. Tu n'as pas bien dormi.
3. Je me suis perdu.
4. Nous avons mal voté.
5. Vous êtes allé au marché trop tard.
6. Ils se sont vus.
7. J'ai mangé une mauvaise huître.

L'emploi du subjonctif

> **Il faut** que la guerre **finisse.**
> **Nous souhaitons** que la guerre **finisse.**

Employez le subjonctif après **Il faut que...** et après un verbe de volonté: **je veux que, je voudrais que*, je préfère que, je souhaite que** (*I wish*), **j'aime mieux que** (*I'd rather, I prefer*).

---

*Remarquez la construction différente de l'anglais *I want you to, I would like you to.*

Je suis heureux que les pays civilisés **aient limité** leur armement.

Employez-le après un verbe de sentiment: **je suis heureux** que, **je suis content** que, **je suis triste** que, **je suis fâché** que, **j'ai peur** que.

Je doute que les hommes **fassent** la promesse de ne plus se battre.

Employez-le après le verbe **douter** (*to doubt*).

J'attendrai que vous me téléphoniez.

Employez-le après le verbe **attendre** (*to wait until*).

C'est dommage qu'il soit sourd!

Employez-le après l'expression **c'est dommage** (*too bad!*).

Tu viendras? Je veux que tu **viennes.**

Il n'y a pas de futur au subjonctif. C'est le présent du subjonctif qui donne l'idée du futur.

Exercice VIII Combinez les phrases suivantes.

EXEMPLE: Nous sommes contents. La guerre est finie.
Nous sommes contents que la guerre **soit finie.**

1. (je préfère) Elle ne met pas son chapeau à fleurs.
2. (je suis fâché) Elles sont parties sans dire au revoir.
3. (sa mère a peur) Il aura trop chaud avec son pull.
4. (elle voudrait) Nous lui faisons des compliments.
5. (il doute) Tu prendras une décision rapide.
6. (attendez) La joie revient.

Subjonctif présent ou subjonctif passé?

Vous comprenez?
Vous comprendrez? Je doute que vous **compreniez.**

Vous comprenez?
Vous comprendrez? Je doutais que vous **compreniez.**

On emploie le subjonctif présent si l'action est présente ou future (par rapport à l'action principale).

Vous avez compris? Je doute que vous **ayez compris.**
Vous avez compris? Je doutais que vous **ayez compris.**

On emploie le subjonctif passé si l'action est passée (par rapport à l'action principale).

Le Louvre.

Faites des phrases avec le vocabulaire suggéré.   *Exercice IX*

1. Il est venu?   Je suis content...
                    J'étais content...
2. Elle reviendra?   Nous souhaitons...
                    Nous souhaitions...
3. Vous êtes parti.   Elle est triste...
                    Elle était triste...
4. Nous n'avons pas compris.   Le professeur a peur...
                                 Le professeur avait peur...
5. Il pleuvra.   Je doute...
               Je doutais...
6. Il fait beau.   Nous attendons...
                 Nous attendions...

Subjonctif ou infinitif?

1) **Je** suis heureux. **Je comprends. Je suis heureux de comprendre.**
2) **Je** suis heureux. **Vous** comprenez. **Je suis heureux que vous compreniez.**

Dans la phrase 1) les sujets des deux verbes représentent la même personne, on a un infinitif. Dans la phrase 2) les sujets des verbes représentent deux personnes différentes. Si on combine les deux phrases, on a un subjonctif.

Elle est heureuse de venir.   Elle a peur de dormir seule.
Je voudrais dormir.

Après **il faut,** un verbe de volonté, **préférer, aimer mieux,** l'infinitif est direct (sans préposition). Avec une expression verbale de sentiment, le verbe **douter,** le verbe **attendre,** on emploie **de** devant l'infinitif.

Exercice X   Combinez les phrases. Utilisez un subjonctif si les sujets sont différents ou un infinitif si on a le même sujet.

1. (Je doute)   Il peut partir à l'heure.
                       Je peux partir à l'heure.
2. (Evelyne attend)   La cabine téléphonique est libre.
                       Evelyne est libre pour se remarier.
3. (Tu voudrais)   Ta femme fait tout le travail.
                       Tu fais tout le travail, toi?
4. (Bruno a peur)   Son jeune frère part à la guerre.
                       Bruno part à la guerre.
5. (Nous aimons mieux) Vous savez la nouvelle tout de suite.
                       Nous savons la nouvelle tout de suite.

Je répéterai mes explications **jusqu'à ce que** vous compreniez.
Il a repeint sa voiture **pour que** personne ne sache qu'il avait eu un accident.
Elle s'est coiffée **avant que** vous arriviez.
Il est sorti **sans que** je l'entende.

Employez le subjonctif après certaines conjonctions composées avec **que:**

jusqu'à ce que...	(*until*)	**avant que**	(*before*)
pour que	(*in order to...*)	**sans que**	(*without*)

Exercice XI   Combinez les phrases suivantes avec la conjonction indiquée.

EXAMPLE: **(sans que)** Elle entre. Tu la vois. Elle entre **sans que** tu la **voies.**

1. (jusqu'à ce que) J'écris mon roman. Ma main me fait mal.
2. (pour que)   Elle enferme son chien la nuit. Il ne va pas dans la rue.
3. (avant que)   Elle avait fini ses bagages 5 minutes. Le taxi vient la chercher.
4. (jusqu'à ce que) Nous avons fait le ménage. La maison est impeccable.
5. (pour que)   Tu prendras un bon grog. Ton rhume disparaîtra.
6. (avant que)   Il vous a donné un coup de poing. Vous avez eu le temps de réagir.

Les pronoms relatifs: **dont, lequel, auquel, duquel**

La pièce **dont** elle parle ne se joue plus.
Le livre **dont** j'ai besoin n'est plus à la bibliothèque.

Dont est le pronom relatif qui remplace **de** + un nom. (Elle parle **de la pièce**.)
Placez **dont** immédiatement après l'antécédent, puis les autres mots dans l'ordre
normal:

> **dont** + sujet + verbe

Voici des verbes et des groupes qui sont construits avec **de** et avec **dont**: **j'ai besoin,
je parle, j'ai peur, j'ai envie, je me sers** (*I use*), **je suis fatigué, je suis content, je
m'occupe, je suis fier** (*I am proud*).

Sur l'île Saint-Louis.

Exercice XII   Répétez les phrases avec **dont**.

1. Les vêtements / j'ai envie de ces vêtements / coûtent trop cher.
2. Le beurre / elle s'est servie de ce beurre pour faire son gâteau / était rance!
3. Le job / il m'avait parlé de ce job / est déjà pris.
4. Ma visite au directeur / j'avais peur de cette visite / s'est bien passée.
5. Elle m'a donné une robe toute neuve / elle était fatiguée de cette robe.
6. L'écrivain a écrit un chapitre /il est très content de ce chapitre.
7. Les vieilles personnes / vous vous occupez de ces personnes / vous adorent.

L'auto dans **laquelle** il a eu son accident est irréparable.
Les cousins chez **lesquels** il habite se disputent tout le temps.

Lequel (féminin: **laquelle;** masculin pluriel: **lesquels;** féminin pluriel: **lesquelles**) est le pronom relatif qu'on emploie après une préposition.

Les cousins chez **qui il** habite se disputent tout le temps.

Pour les personnes et pour les personnes seulement, on peut avoir **qui** à la place de **lequel, laquelle, lesquels, lesquelles.**

Remarquez: **Qui il; qui** n'est jamais élidé.

Exercice XIII   Refaites les phrases avec la forme correcte de **lequel, laquelle, lesquels, lesquelles** ou **qui,** si l'antécédent est une personne.

1. La banque / il travaille pour cette banque / a été cambriolée.
2. Le chèque / je comptais sur ce chèque / n'est pas arrivé; catastrophe!
3. La firme / nous sommes associés avec cette firme / est très connue.
4. Pierre a perdu la valise / il avait mis tous ses vêtements dans cette valise.
5. Il a un oncle / il passe tous ses étés chez cet oncle.
6. Voilà la table / j'avais mis mes cigarettes sur cette table/ elles n'y sont plus.

Le motel / **auquel** j'ai écrit / était complet.
Le sénateur / **à qui** j'ai écrit / ne m'a pas répondu.

Attention à la préposition **à.** Il y a des contractions avec **lequel:**

à + lequel = **auquel**
à + lesquels = **auxquels**
à + lesquelles = **auxquelles**
à + **laquelle** reste à **laquelle**

Pour les personnes, **à qui** remplace toutes les formes avec **lequel.**

Exercice XIV   Répétez (*a.*) avec **auquel, à laquelle, auxquels, auxquelles;** (*b.*) avec **à qui** (si l'antécédent est une personne).

1. Le tableau / je pense à ce tableau / est exposé au Louvre.
2. La jeune fille / il a envoyé des fleurs à cette jeune fille / ne lui téléphone pas.
3. Le vieux bonhomme / tu parles à ce bonhomme / est complètement sourd.
4. Je n'ai pas eu de réponse de l'amie / j'avais écrit une longue lettre à cette amie.
5. L'étudiant / j'ai donné un F à cet étudiant / était furieux.

Le jeune homme à propos **duquel (de qui)** elles se battent toujours...
Les fenêtres à côté **desquelles** vous êtes assis...
Les jardins autour **desquels** il y a une palissade...
La jeune fille près **de laquelle (de qui)** je suis placée...

Si la préposition est **de** seul, on emploie **dont**, mais si la préposition est longue et terminée par **de**, par exemple: **à côté de, près de, autour de, à propos de, à l'intérieur de, à l'extérieur de, au-dessus de, au-dessous de**, on emploie **lequel**, avec les contractions suivants:

de + lequel = **duquel**   de + lesquelles = **desquelles**
de + lesquels = **desquels**   **de + laquelle** reste **de laquelle**

Remarque: On emploie **de qui** si l'antécédent est une personne.

Répétez avec **duquel, desquels,** etc. ou **qui**.   *Exercice XV*

1. Le jeune homme / je suis assise à côté de ce jeune homme / dort en classe.
2. Le parc / nous habitons près du parc / est plein de hippies.
3. Il a acheté une belle maison / autour de cette maison / il a construit un grand mur.
4. C'est une histoire sans importance / ils se sont disputés à propos de cette histoire.
5. Je ne veux pas dormir dans le lit / il y a un miroir au-dessus de ce lit.

Le discours indirect

Je dis: «Il fait beau aujourd'hui.»

C'est le discours direct. La phrase est entre guillemets /gijmɛ/.

Je dis qu'il fait beau aujourd'hui.

C'est le discours indirect. Il n'y a pas de guillemets. On commence la phrase avec **je dis que, je sais que, je ne sais pas,** etc.

Qu'est-ce qui se passe?
Je me demande **ce qui** se passe.
Qu'est-ce que vous regardez?
Il ne sait pas **ce que** vous regardez.

Dans le discours indirect gardez les deux derniers mots des pronoms interrogatifs **qu'est-ce qui** et **qu'est-ce que: ce qui** et **ce que**.

Qui vous a écrit? Je vous demande **qui** vous a écrit.
Avec qui irons-nous au cinéma? Je ne sais pas **avec qui** nous irons au cinéma.
De quoi s'agit-il? Elle cherche **de quoi** il s'agit.

Les autres pronoms sont ceux de la forme courte — **qui, avec qui, de quoi** — mais l'ordre des mots n'est pas interrogatif.

Exercice XVI   Répétez au discours indirect.

1. Qui a téléphoné? Je vous demande...
2. Qu'est-ce qu'il a dit? Je ne sais pas...
3. De quoi parlez-vous? Dites-nous...
4. Qu'est-ce qui se passe? Je sais bien...
5. Avec qui sort-elle? Vous ne voulez pas me dire...
6. Qu'est-ce que nous faisons ce soir? Nous devions décider...

LECTURE   Un voyage à Paris

Eh bien, voilà, vous y êtes! Vous êtes à Paris. Votre vœu le plus cher s'est réalisé. Vous voilà dans la Ville-Lumière. Vous êtes arrivé hier soir à l'aéroport Charles de Gaulle, tout nouveau et moderne, à Roissy-en-France. Vous avez trouvé un petit hôtel pas cher, du côté de la Gare de Lyon, et vous vous préparez, le guide Michelin en poche, à visiter Paris. Mais Paris c'est un monde, c'est immense. Par où commencer? Suivez-moi! Je vais vous conduire à travers le Paris que je connais et que j'aime.

A mon avis, il faut commencer par le cœur de Paris; et le cœur de Paris, le berceau de la ville, c'est l'île de la Cité, c'est Notre-Dame. Prenez le métro, si pratique et si rapide. Vous sortez du métro près de la Préfecture de Police et vous longez le Marché aux fleurs (qui devient le dimanche le Marché aux oiseaux). Une pensée amicale à Jacques Prévert et vous arrivez sur le parvis de Notre-Dame. Une première visite à Notre-Dame est toujours un choc: la majesté de ce bâtiment, la multitude des sculptures, la beauté des vitraux ne laissent personne indifférent. Vous pouvez passer des heures à regarder, à écouter, à admirer. Ne manquez pas, surtout, de monter sur les tours; on y a une vue incomparable de Paris. Vous vous orientez; en regardant vers l'ouest, vous voyez la Tour Eiffel, l'Arc de Triomphe et le cours de la Seine. Vers le Nord vous voyez la colline de Montmartre, vers l'est le cours de la Seine, encore, et partout des dômes, des tours, et des... gratte-ciel qui commencent à envahir le vieux Paris. La cité est comme un bateau, dont Notre-Dame serait la partie la plus haute, et qui descend le long de la Seine. La pointe du Vert-galant en est la proue, et ce jardinet et les rives du fleuve, ici, sont le dernier refuge des amoureux et des promeneurs — on ne peut plus comme autrefois, traverser Paris en suivant les quais: ceux-ci ont été transformés en «voies rapides,» sortes d'autoroutes au cœur de la ville. Quelle horreur! Le Vert-Galant, c'est Henri IV, dont la statue équestre garde le Pont-Neuf, «son» pont, et l'entrée de la Place Dauphine.

Du haut de votre observatoire, vous verrez aussi, à vos pieds, dans l'île, le Palais de Justice, et la flèche élégante de la Sainte Chapelle, construite sous Saint-Louis et qu'il faut aussi visiter à cause de ses superbes vitraux. La Conciergerie, qui était le premier palais des rois de France, est devenue une prison pour femmes, et c'est là que Marie-Antoinette passa les dernières heures de sa vie. Si vous regardez maintenant vers l'est, vous voyez que le bateau de la Cité a une remorque, un autre bateau plus petit, qu'il traîne derrière lui: c'est l'île St. Louis; cette île est pleine de

Prenons le métro.

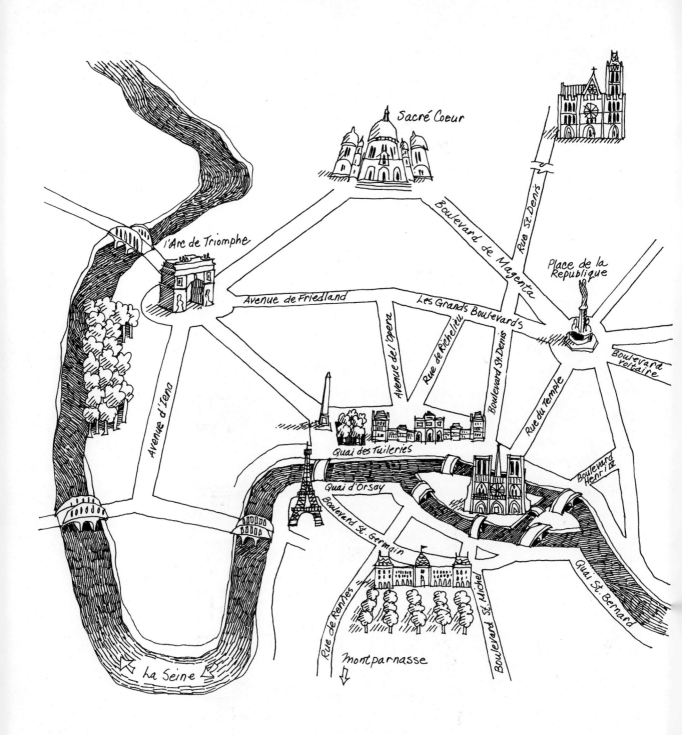

Sacré Coeur

l'Arc de Triomphe

Boulevard de Magenta

Rue St. Denis

Place de la Republique

Avenue de Friedland

Les Grands Boulevards

Boulevard Voltaire

Avenue de l'Opera

Rue de Richelieu

Boulevard St. Denis

Rue du Temple

Avenue d'Iena

Quai des Tuileries

Boulevard Henri IV

Quai d'Orsay

Boulevard St. Germain

Rue de Rennes

Boulevard St. Michel

Quai St. Bernard

La Seine

Montparnasse

vieux hôtels du XVIIᵉ et du XVIIIᵉ, restaurés et habités — certains — par de riches propriétaires et des artistes qui apprécient le calme villageois de ce coin. Ne quittez pas les tours de Notre-Dame sans saluer les gargouilles et sans évoquer devant la grosse cloche — le bourdon — la mémoire de Quasimodo et de Victor Hugo.

En route, pour la suite. Quoi? Vous êtes déjà fatigué? Alors, reposez-vous dans le jardin de l'Archevêché, ou dans le square qui forme la poupe du bateau. Vous pourrez même y déguster le lunch que vous aurez acheté auparavant dans un Prisunic: du jambon blanc, du fromage, avec une baguette achetée à la boulangerie, une bouteille de vin ou d'eau minérale, et des fruits que vendent les marchands des quatre-saisons. Les pigeons et les moineaux vous aideront à finir les miettes!

Traversez le pont au sud de Notre-Dame. Par un dédale de vieilles rues charmantes, ou en suivant le quai et en flânant devant les étalages des bouquinistes, vous arrivez place St. Michel et vous remontez le Boul Mich. C'est le Quartier Latin, le quartier des étudiants. Ce boulevard, toujours animé, vous conduit jusqu'au Luxembourg, qui est en quelque sorte le «campus» de cette partie de l'université de Paris. Faites un détour pour visiter le Musée de Cluny et bien sûr, la vénérable Sorbonne. Quoi, vous êtes encore fatigué? Alors, arrêtez-vous dans un des nombreux cafés, ou asseyez-vous près de la fontaine Médicis, à l'ombre des platanes; c'est là que les étudiants viennent étudier, quand il fait beau et quand les bibliothèques sont trop pleines. Allez, en route! Vous laissez derrière vous le Panthéon, la Montagne Ste Geneviève, le Jardin des Plantes, et vous vous dirigez vers St. Germain des Prés. A l'ombre de la tour romane de la plus vieille église de Paris, les cafés des Deux-Magots et de Flore étaient, juste après la guerre, le rendez-vous des existentialistes, et dans les «caves» on écoutait du jazz *New Orleans* et on dansait le *be-bop.* La petite place Furstenberg mérite le détour; ses quatre arbres et son réverbère en font un des coins les plus harmonieux et les plus poétiques de Paris. Par des petites rues calmes où vous trouverez des antiquaires et des libraires, vous rejoignez la Seine.

Là, deuxième choc: vous arrivez au Louvre dont les façades nettoyées se colorent de rose ou de jaune pâle aux différentes heures de la journée. Il faudrait des mois pour tout voir dans le Louvre, et je ne doute pas que vous y passerez plusieurs heures. La Joconde, la Victoire de Samothrace, les antiquités égyptiennes vous occuperont un moment. De l'Arc de Triomphe du Carrousel vous pouvez voir la magnifique perspective du Jardin des Tuileries, de la Place de la Concorde (ancienne place de Grève, où la guillotine fonctionna activement), des Champs-Elysées et de l'Arc de Triomphe de l'Étoile, une ligne droite de cinq kilomètres. Vous laissez sur votre droite le Palais Royal dont les bâtiments du XVIIIᵉ encadrent des jardins charmants recherchés par les amateurs de calme (Colette y a habité) et sur votre gauche le Palais Bourbon où siège l'Assemblée Nationale. On ne vous laissera pas entrer au Palais de l'Élysée, où réside de Président de la République, mais sur les Champs-Élysées vous trouverez une foule cosmopolite attirée par les beaux magasins, les cafés et les cinémas.

Vous pouvez monter sur l'Arc de Triomphe, et admirer Paris dans une autre perspective. La Tour Eiffel n'est pas loin, et vous voudrez aussi y grimper; c'est presque une obligation pour un touriste. Vous verrez la colline de Chaillot, et les «beaux quartiers» qui se sont développés dans cette partie de la ville. Dans l'alignement de l'Arc de Triomphe, l'avenue de la Grande Armée conduit au quartier d'affaires, tout neuf, de la Défense.

Les rues en branches d'étoile, qui partent de l'Arc, ont donné son nom à cette place, mais elle s'appelle maintenant place du Général de Gaulle. Au loin vous apercevrez la verdure du Bois de Boulogne, ce grand parc si populaire le dimanche; ses lacs, ses hippodromes, ses clubs sportifs, ses restaurants de luxe, son Jardin d'Acclimatation (sorte de zoo) en font le rendez-vous des gens chic qui habitent à proximité dans des immeubles dits de «grand standing.» De la Tour Eiffel vous aurez une autre vue de Paris et à vos pieds, le Champs de Mars et le Palais du Trocadéro achèvent un ensemble harmonieux unique au monde.

Par le Faubourg St. Honoré, le domaine des grands couturiers, des parfumeurs, de luxe, vous arrivez à la Madeleine et en suivant les Grands Boulevards vous longez le pied de la Butte Montmartre. L'Opéra mérite un arrêt, mais vous ne pourrez y entrer que le soir, si vous avez pris un billet pour un spectacle.

Le long des Grands Boulevards, la foule est populaire, les magasins nombreux, et c'est aussi là qu'on trouve le plus grand nombre de théâtres. Je sais; Montmartre vous attire. Il faut y aller, de jour et de nuit: de jour pour grimper les escaliers de ses petites allées, rencontrer un peintre qui utilise le trottoir comme palette, et, place du Tertre, vous mêler à tous les touristes, avant d'admirer du parvis du Sacré-Cœur, ce gros gâteau de mariage, un autre panorama de Paris; de nuit pour observer place Pigalle, la foule cosmopolite attirée par les lumières, les lieux de plaisir, les cabarets des chansonniers, les spectacles risqués. C'est le Paris dont les étrangers ont entendu parler.

Eh bien! n'êtes-vous pas à bout de souffle? Il reste encore bien des coins à visiter: le quartier des affaires, je vous le laisse; la Bourse, les grands journaux parisiens; mais il ne faut pas quitter Paris sans voir le Marais, la délicieuse, provinciale place des Vosges, et les hôtels de ce vieux quartier.

Des Halles il ne reste presque plus rien qu'un grand chantier dont on ne sait pas encore ce qu'on fera.

Montparnasse? oui; les artistes se réunissent encore à la Coupole, à la Rotonde, mais les tours modernes font de ce coin un quartier d'affaires moins accueillant qu'il ne l'était autrefois.

Faites une visite au parc Montsouris, près de la Cité Universitaire, et une autre au cimetière du Père Lachaise. Allez un matin à la rue Mouffetard, ce marché si animé et si pittoresque. Faites une croisière sur les bateaux-mouches, pour revoir sous un autre angle les quais de la Seine. Prenez un autobus sur les périphériques et constatez que Paris contient aussi des habitations modestes et pauvres. A l'est vous pourrez visiter Vincennes et son château moyen-âgeux: le bois est une réplique du bois de Boulogne, mais il est moins élégant: l'université de Paris vient d'y ouvrir les portes de bâtiments nouveaux. A St. Denis, au nord, vous visiterez la Chapelle des Rois de France qui contient leurs tombeaux, de Dagobert (eh oui, le roi de notre chanson) à Louis XVIII. Les trains de banlieue et le nouveau splendide RER sont prêts à vous emporter dans des coins célèbres autour de Paris. Versailles, St. Germain, Fontainebleau, Sceaux, Champs, Chantilly — on ne peut pas tout voir, il faut choisir. Mais déjà Paris est devenu un peu votre patrie, votre

Qu'est-ce que c'est?

«deuxième amour,» comme le dit la chanson. Votre caméra emporte les diapositives que vous serez fier de montrer à vos amis; vous avez la tête pleine de souvenirs et d'images, et vous avez laissé dans cette ville un peu de votre cœur.

Vocabulaire

à bout de souffle out of breath
amical friendly
à mon avis in my opinion
auparavant beforehand
berceau, (*m.*) cradle
bouquiniste, (*m.*) old prints, secondhand booksellers. (The books are displayed in boxes placed on the walls.)
cave, (*f.*) cellar, basement
chansonnier, (*m.*) writer of satirical songs
cloche, (*f.*) bell
colline, (*f.*) hill
diapositive, (*f.*) slide
encadrer to frame
envahir to invade
équestre on a horse
étalage, (*m.*) display
fier proud
flâner to idle
flèche, (*f.*) spire
foule, (*f.*) crowd
gratte-ciel, (*m.*) skyscraper
grimper to go up
immeuble, (*m.*) apartment house
longer to walk along

les marchands des quatre saisons les marchands qui vendent dans des petits chariots, au coin de la rue, les fruits des quatre saisons de l'année
mériter to deserve
miette, (*f.*) crumb
moineau, (*m.*) sparrow
nettoyer to clean
ombre, (*f.*) shadow
parvis, (*m.*) place at the entrance of a cathedral
platane, (*m.*) plane tree
passa *passé simple, voir p. 369*
poche, (*f.*) pocket
poupe, (*f.*) stern
proue, (*f.*) prow
quai, (*m.*) river bank
rejoindre join
réverbère, (*m.*) street light
siéger to hold its meetings
trottoir, (*m.*) sidewalk
vert-galant (*nom donné au Roi Henri IV,* the young gallant King)
Ville-Lumière, (*f.*) City of Light (un nom qu'on donne fréquemment à Paris)
vitrail, (*m.*) stained glass
vœu, (*m.*) wish
vue, (*f.*) sight

APPENDICES

Chapitres 1–5

Exercice I Donnez la forme du verbe **être, avoir** ou **aller,** ou le verbe du premier groupe.

1. être: Nous _____ féministes.
2. avoir: Elles _____ une idée extraordinaire.
3. aller: Vous _____ au cinéma.
4. former: Les communistes _____ un gouvernement.
5. organiser: Tu _____ un gouvernement.
6. regretter: Je _____ l'absence de mes amis.
7. être: Il _____ pacifiste.
8. avoir: Anne et Bernadette _____ un appartement.
9. décorer: Elles _____ la maison.
10. danser: Nous _____ dans le jardin.
11. aller: Tu _____ à la police?
12. protester: Les étudiants _____ .
13. être: Vous _____ coquettes.
14. avoir: La directrice _____ une photographie d'Alain Delon dans son bureau.
15. expliquer: Vous _____ la grammaire.
16. abandonner: Jean-Jacques et Thérèse _____ leurs enfants.
17. être: Ils _____ ridicules.
18. visiter: Le président _____ les villages.
19. adorer: Nous _____ la symphonie.
20. indiquer: J'_____ la différence.
21. cultiver: Vous ne _____ pas votre jardin.
22. consulter: Elle _____ le dictionnaire.
23. exister: Est-ce que les Martiens _____ ?
24. organiser: Nous _____ un bal de charité.
25. marcher: Ils ne _____ pas sur la lune.

Exercice II Indiquez le genre des noms avec l'article: **le, la, un, une.**

1. papier	9. anniversaire	17. expérience	25. optimisme
2. poésie	10. richesse	18. grammaire	26. accident
3. armée	11. culture	19. société	27. moteur
4. tragédie	12. régiment	20. possibilité	28. pollution
5. distance	13. télévision	21. imagination	29. moment
6. frigidaire	14. langage	22. salaire	30. solitude
7. différence	15. lecture	23. mariage	31. violette
8. pâleur	16. destinée	24. message	

Exercice III Mettez l'article défini devant le premier nom. Mettez **de, de la, de l'** ou **du, des** devant le nom de la second colonne.

$$\text{le, la, les} \qquad de + \begin{cases} \text{le} & = \textbf{du} \\ \text{la} & = \textbf{de la} \\ \text{l'} & = \textbf{de l'} \\ \text{les} & = \textbf{des} \end{cases}$$

EXEMPLE: bureau   professeur
le bureau   du professeur

1. talent   Brigitte
2. président   gouvernement américain
3. voyage   acteur
4. spectateur   comédie
5. assistant   directeur
6. idée   révolution
7. arrivée   princesse
8. importance   questions
9. production   industrie
10. bicyclette   Marie
11. géographie   continent
12. mariage   dentiste
13. directrice   journal
14. patriotisme   officiers   armée
15. salaires   enfants   Paul
16. culture   capitaliste et   communiste
17. moment   émotion
18. destinée   dynastie
19. beauté   instruction
20. question   message
21. réalisme   photographie
22. dettes   auteurs
23. révolution   consciences
24. monument   monarchie
25. poésie   mouvement

Exercice IV Mettez **un, une, le, la, du: c'est un, c'est une** ou **c'est le... de la, c'est la... du.**

1. C'est   géant
2. C'est   département   agriculture
3. C'est   peinture
4. C'est   nature   intelligence
5. C'est   autorité
6. C'est   psychologie   actrice
7. C'est   expédition difficile

8. C'est   cérémonie magnifique
9. C'est   anniversaire   dictateur
10. C'est   apparence
11. C'est   coquette
12. C'est   politesse   conversation
13. C'est   invitation

Exercice V   Après **il y a** mettez **un, une, des.** Après **dans** mettez **le, l', la, les.**

1. Il y a   télévision dans   appartement de mes parents.
2. Il y a   touristes dans   village.
3. Il y a   entrée dans   vallée.
4. Il y a   monument dans   jardin public.
5. Il y a   communistes dans   gouvernement.
6. Il y a   éléphant dans   garage!
7. Il y a   tragédies dans   histoire.
8. Il y a   division dans   population.
9. Il y a   message dans   littérature.

Exercice VI   Pluriel des noms des articles et des adjectifs.

(*a*.) Écrivez et répétez au pluriel.

1. une terre fertile
2. un jardin fantastique
3. un moment comique
4. une université riche
5. la question nécessaire
6. un général féroce
7. la composition formidable
8. le sculpteur romantique
9. un président honnête
10. l'actrice populaire
11. une éducation élémentaire
12. la liberté démocratique

(*b*.) Écrivez et répétez au singulier.

1. des usages vulgaires
2. des officiers sincères
3. des langages respectables
4. des beautés artistiques
5. des entrées ridicules
6. des bals spectaculaires
7. les spectateurs timides
8. les hôpitaux modernes
9. des visions historiques
10. les décisions justes
11. les théories durables
12. les journaux économiques

Exercice VII   Mettez la préposition: **dans, sur, à, en, au.**

1. Il y a des papiers _____ la table. 2. _____ ma maison nous avons six pièces.
3. Ils vont _____ Rome et _____ Madrid. 4. Ils arrivent _____ Italie et _____
Espagne? 5. _____ États-Unis les appartements ne sont pas économiques.
6. Vous allez _____ l'université? 7. Il y a des oiseaux _____ la forêt? 8. Vous
retournez _____ Canada ou _____ Japon? 9. Elles dansent _____ le salon.
10. Il expose ses sculptures _____ une galerie. 11. _____ Angleterre, on parle
anglais. 12. Les images sont _____ le tableau.

Exercice VIII   Mettez l'adjectif possessif.

1. Moi, j'ai _____ idées, _____ opinion, _____ convictions, _____ intelligence, _____ expériences, _____ avantage, _____ raisons.
2. Toi, tu as _____ maison, _____ frigidaire, _____ auto, _____ compte en banque, _____ situation, _____ richesse.
3. Pierre, il a _____ éducation, _____ politesse, _____ manières, _____ ironie, _____ usages, _____ expérience, _____ indépendance.
4. Marie, elle a _____ patience, _____ attitude, _____ réalisme, _____ image, _____ tolérance, _____ psychologie.
5. Nous avons, sur la terre, _____ fleurs, _____ montagnes et _____ rivières, _____ atmosphère, _____ géographie, _____ animaux et plantes, _____ industries, _____ pollutions.
6. Vous, à Berkeley, vous avez _____ université, _____ révolution, _____ accidents, _____ police, _____ contestation.
7. Les étudiants, ils ont _____ études, _____ campus, _____ problèmes, _____ difficultés, _____ distractions, _____ culture.

Exercice IX   Accordez l'adjectif avec le nom. Mettez l'adjectif à sa place.

1. intelligent: C'est une réponse.
2. délicieux: Voilà des fruits.
3. anglais: Ce sont des habitudes.
4. dernier: Écoutez la nouvelle (*news*).
5. vieux: Les dames sont dans le salon.
6. beau: La salle de bains!
7. américain: Il a une voiture.
8. ancien: La pendule est très
9. brun: Elle aime les hommes.
10. possessif: «Mon» est un adjectif _____ et toi, tu est une femme _____ .

Exercice X   Accordez l'adjectif avec le nom. Mettez l'adjectif à sa place.

1. blanc: Quelle jolie robe!
2. sec: Les abricots sont
3. gentil: Ce sont des garçons.
4. long: La route est
5. mauvais: Les programmes sont
6. nouveau/beau: Les maisons ne sont pas
7. gros: La dame est dans le fauteuil vert.
8. premier: Janvier est le _____ mois de l'année.
9. vieux: Il y a un arbre dans son jardin.
10. frais: Elle préfère les fleurs.

Exercice XI   Donnez la forme du verbe.

1. commencer: (Nous) _____ l'exercice 12.
2. avancer: Elle _____ dans l'allée.

3. fleurir: Cet arbre ne _____ pas en mai.
4. pénétrer: Vous _____ dans la chambre de ma fille.
5. précéder: Une entrée _____ le salon.
6. prononcer: (Nous) _____ distinctement.
7. réfléchir: Ils _____.
8. obéir: Mes enfants n'_____ pas.
9. répéter: Tu _____ l'exercice de phonétique.
10. pâlir: Elle regarde ma maison et elle _____.
11. exagérer: Il _____.
12. jaunir: Les feuilles _____.
13. placer: Ils _____ leur argent à la banque.

Exercice XII Traductions.

1. My name is George. 2. How are you? 3. Not bad. 4. See you tomorrow. O.k.? 5. I am not a movie star. 6. That's Catherine's purse. That's it! 7. For the love of God! 8. It's crummy. 9. Are you in a dream? 10. The students are not on the campus. 11. There are flowers on the planet? 12. I don't have a nephew. 13. Do you have relatives? 14. They cultivate their garden. 15. Cadet Rousselle has three houses. 16. First look at my house. 17. Then come in! 18. Finally, let us go to the second floor. 19. There is no third floor. 20. At my sister's house there are four bedrooms, but no swimming pool. 21. Here is her garden. 22. It is a charming little house. 23. I am going back to my mother's. 24. What day do we have? 25. What time is it? 26. How lucky! 27. What a drag! 28. On Mondays I go to the supermarket. 29. He is early. She is late. 30. Where do we have a date? 31. It's 12:30 P.M. It's 10 A.M. It's 6:15 P.M.

Chapitres 6–7

Exercice XIII Accordez l'adjectif: **ce, cet, cette, ces; quel, quelle, quels, quelles; tout, toute, tous, toutes.**

1. (ce) La dame va au marché.
2. (quel) _____ marché? _____ dame?
3. (tout) Elle achète _____ les produits chers.
4. (ce) _____ épicier a du bon café.
5. (quel) _____ boulangerie est-ce que vous préférez?
6. (tout) _____ les boulangeries sont identiques.
7. (ce) Ce n'est pas vrai. _____ boulangerie au coin de la rue est la meilleure.
8. (quel) _____ blague!
9. (ce) _____ gâteaux sont délicieux.
10. (quel) _____ gâteaux?

Exercice XIV   Répétez avec le verbe **aller.**

EXEMPLE: Je fais un bon feu.   Je **vais faire** un bon feu.

1. Vous choisissez des fruits?
2. Elle passe devant le théâtre.
3. Nous avons un bébé.
4. Tu es fatigué.
5. Ils vont en voyage.
6. Ils mangent des oranges.
7. Vous restez à la maison?
8. Les colchiques fleurissent.
9. Il fait froid.
10. Ma mère téléphone.

Exercice XV   Faites des phrases de comparaison avec le vocabulaire suggéré.

EXEMPLE: (+ gros) le chat, la souris: **Le chat est plus gros que la souris.**

1. (+ poli)   Les officiers sont _____ les beaux messieurs.
2. (− vieux)   La Tour Eiffel _____ Notre-Dame.
3. (= important)   L'histoire _____ la géographie.
4. (− facile)   La prononciation _____ la dictée.
5. (+ brun)   Marie _____ Jeanne.
6. (+ long)   Cette rue _____ la rue de la Paix.
7. (= jeune)   Ma mère n'est pas _____ votre mère.
8. (− chaud)   L'été en Alaska _____ l'été au Mexique.

Exercice XVI   Traductions.

1. I am cold. It is cold today. 2. My coffee is cold. 3. It's raining. It's windy.
4. In spring the weather is nice. 5. People do not work on May 1. 6. I adore
bread. There is bread in the kitchen. 7. He does not like bread. There is no
bread. 8. It is the song of the big bad wolf. 9. What are you doing? 10. Make
love, not war. 11. I am going to take a nap tonight. 12. All evening long she
does her homework. 13. She is standing. 14. He is as intelligent as you.
15. But you are taller than I.

Chapitres 7–8

Exercice XVII   Mettez l'article correct: **un, une, des; le, la, l', les; du, de la, de l'.**

Au marché, j'achète _____ fruits, _____ viande, _____ poulet, _____ pain,
_____ beurre, _____ bananes, _____ bière, _____ céleri, _____ pommes de
terre, _____ savon, _____ lait, _____ crème, _____ riz, _____ sel, _____
pâtes.

Pour le déjeuner en France, on mange _____ hors d'œuvre, _____ carottes,
_____ jambon, _____ viande et _____ légumes, _____ salade, _____ fromage
et _____ fruit et _____ pain bien sûr. Pour le dîner, _____ soupe, _____
omelette ou _____ pâtes, _____ fromage ou _____ yaourt et _____ dessert.

Exercice XVIII   Mettez les phrases suivantes à la forme négative.

1. Il a du courage.
2. Elle mange du pain.
3. Il y a des poissons dans la rivière.
4. J'aime le camping.
5. L'épicier a du café.
6. J'achète des oranges.
7. Il préfère le lait.
8. Nous choisissons la liberté.
9. Le boulanger vend du fromage.
10. Je choisis des légumes.
11. Les cannibales mangent des hommes.
12. Les végétariens adorent le bifteck.

Exercice XIX   (*a.*) Faites des adverbes avec les adjectifs suivants:

1. ironique
2. brave
3. tragique
4. juste
5. grave
6. magnifique
7. héroïque
8. féroce
9. rapide
10. honnête
11. ordinaire
12. obligatoire
13. historique
14. vague
15. sincère
16. solide
17. sauvage
18. géographique
19. démocratique
20. évident

(*b.*) Faites un adverbe avec l'adjectif entre parenthèses. Placez l'adverbe après le verbe ou devant l'adjectif.

1. Elle marche (lent).
2. Vous travaillez (méthodique).
3. Le professeur parle (énergique).
4. Ce musée est décoré (riche).

Chapitre 9

Exercice XX   (*a.*) Faites des phrases avec le superlatif: **le plus, le moins, la plus, la moins.**

1. C'est
   - (+) le gentil garçon
   - (−) la grosse banane
2. Ce sont
   - (+) les produits chers
   - (+) les tomates mûres
   - (−) l'histoire brève
   - (−) les mauvais gâteaux
   - (+) les vieilles habitudes
   - (+) le bon café

(*b.*) Terminez les phrases ci-dessus avec un complément choisi dans la liste suivante. Choisissez le mot convenable.

EXEMPLE: C'est le plus gentil garçon **de la classe.**

| le marché | la forêt | le jardin | l'épicerie |
| la boulangerie | son repertoire | ce pays | le monde |

Exercice XXI Mettez un adverbe de quantité: **beaucoup, un peu, assez, trop, plus, moins (de).**

1. (trop)   Il y a de la pollution dans l'atmosphère.
2. (moins)   En automne mon jardin a des fleurs.
3. (beaucoup) En France, il y a des fromages.
4. (assez)   Il a de l'argent pour aller au cinéma.
5. (un peu)   Il y a du vent.
6. (plus)   Elle est jolie.

Exercice XXII Répétez les phrases suivantes avec **beaucoup de** ou **beaucoup le, la, les.**

1. Il a de la patience.
2. Elle mange des pommes.
3. J'aime le fromage.
4. Vous achetez un bifteck.
5. L'épicier a des produits chers.
6. Nous n'aimons pas le vin.
7. Il y a du vent.
8. Les enfants font du bruit.
9. Ils ont des amis.
10. On trouve une différence.

Chapitre 10

Exercice XXIII Répétez les phrases avec un pronom objet direct ou objet indirect.

1. Il connaît les problèmes.
2. Je préfère le vin français.
3. Tu téléphones à Catherine.
4. Elle obéit à son mari.
5. Nous choisissons nos distractions.
6. Vous discutez la politique internationale.
7. Ils approuvent l'union libre.
8. Je fais la cuisine.
9. Elle vend ses vieux livres.
10. Il ne répond pas au président.
11. Vous aimez les légumes congelés?
12. Ils connaissent la musique.

Exercice XXIV Mettez le pronom tonique correct.

1. Jean-Jacques travaille pour un producteur de cinéma.
2. Elizabeth habite chez une vieille tante.
3. Je vais au cinéma avec mes cousins de Bretagne.
4. C'est un joli tableau des filles de Renoir.
5. Ils font des études avec les fils du président.
6. Il est assis à côté de (je).
7. Elle est debout devant (tu).

8. Vous vous promenez avec (votre frère).
9. Il travaille pour (vous).
10. Priez pour (je).

Exercice XXV   Mettez la forme correcte du verbe.

1. entendre: Vous _____ le bruit des autos?
2. changer: Ils _____ de maison tous les ans.
3. voyager: Nous _____ en été.
4. acheter: Vous _____ des oranges au marché?
5. appeler: Ils _____ leur chien «Oscar.»
6. jeter: Le bébé _____ sa soupe par terre.
7. vendre: Le boulanger _____ des gâteaux?
8. manger: Nous _____ beaucoup de pain.
9. descendre: Le père Noël _____ dans les cheminées.
10. attendre: Danielle et Jean Pierre _____ l'autobus.
11. prendre: Vous _____ un grog pour un rhume? Et Philippe, _____ un grog. Les Français _____ un grog.
12. mettre: Elle _____ du rouge sur son visage? Et toi _____ du vert.
13. écrire: Moi, j_____ au président? Ma sœur aussi _____ au président.
14. dire: Mes enfants _____ leurs prières le soir, et vous _____ vos prières.
15. lire: Nous ne _____ pas le journal du dimanche, mais nos amis américains le _____ .
16. voir: Vous _____ les choses que je _____ .
17. croire: Je _____ , nous _____ que la paix va exister un jour sur la terre.
18. peser: Il _____ 120 kilos. Et vous, combien est-ce que vous _____ ?
19. employer: Pour faire ce gâteau, elle _____ du beurre. Vous, vous _____ de la margarine.
20. se regarder: Elle _____ dans une glace. Et toi, tu _____ ?
21. boire: Nous _____ du vin le soir. Elle _____ du lait.
22. essayer: J'_____ de lire ce livre.
23. s'appeler: Moi, je _____ Jacques. Et vous, vous _____ comment?
24. se laver: Nous _____ le dimanche. Eux, ils _____ tous les jours!
25. manger: Nous _____ du pain. Toi, tu _____ des gâteaux.

Exercice XXVI   Mettez l'expression avec **avoir** qui convient: **avoir faim, soif, chaud, froid, peur, raison, tort, envie, l'air...**

1. Est-ce que vous écoutez? Vous avez _____ distrait.
2. Quand une voiture me dépasse à 120 km à l'heure, j'ai _____ .
3. Il fait −20° dehors, tu vas _____ .
4. Mais s'il fait +40°, alors on _____ .

5. Je bois un grand verre de bière parce que j'ai _____.

6. Avez-vous _____ de faire une balade avec moi? — Non, je préfère me reposer.

7. Ils ont arrêté de fumer. Ils _____.

8. Les gens qui s'énervent ont _____. C'est mauvais pour le cœur.

Exercice XXVII   Traductions.

1. She has red hair and blue eyes. 2. I am hungry. 3. You are thirsty. 4. They are wrong. 5. She is afraid. 6. You look tired. 7. You must not forget the tip. 8. Every morning I dress. 9. I look at them. 10. I listen to them. 11. I wait for them. 12. I look for them. 13. I ate well. I ate a lot. I ate already. I ate enough. Yesterday I ate. 14. She is twenty years old. 15. Waiter! Yes sir, what will you have? 16. What type of fish do you have? 17. How many fingers do you have? 18. I am going to the butcher's. 19. At the bakery there is good bread. 20. You must go to the market with me.

Chapitres 11–14

Exercice XXVIII   Mettez les verbes suivants au présent de la personne indiquée.

1. vouloir: Votre fiancée _____ un grand mariage et vous, vous _____ un petit mariage.

2. pouvoir: Vous _____ dormir avec le bruit mais moi, je ne _____ pas.

3. partir: Le train _____ à 4 h. Elles _____ pour le Mexique.

4. sortir: Tu _____ avec moi, ce soir. Vous _____ sans lui?

5. dormir: Il _____ sur le divan. Nous _____ par terre.

6. venir: Est-ce qu'elle _____ dîner ce soir; oui et ses parents _____ aussi.

7. ouvrir: J'_____ mon livre. _____ votre livre.

8. couvrir: Il _____ ses plantes la nuit. Et vous _____ vos plantes.

9. offrir: Tu lui _____ des fleurs. Nous lui _____ des bonbons.

10. savoir: Il ne _____ pas sa leçon. Et vous, vous ne la _____ pas non plus.

11. connaître: Il _____ mon grand-père. Vous le _____ aussi?

12. s'asseoir: Elle entre et elle _____. Les étudiants _____.

13. souffrir: Ah! comme je _____. Vous aussi, vous _____.

Exercice XXIX   Répétez les phrases de l'exercice 28 au passé composé.

Exercice XXX   Donnez l'imparfait des verbes suivants.

1. nous choisissons	6. je suis	11. tu lis
2. vous continuez	7. nous avons	12. vous dites
3. ils dorment	8. ils vont	13. il brille
4. elle voyage	9. je fais	14. elle chante
5. tu avances	10. vous étudiez	15. j'ai

Exercice XXXI   Donnez le passé composé des verbes suivants — positif, puis négatif.

1. je parle	9. elle fait	17. vous skiez
2. tu rougis	10. nous montons	18. ils appellent
3. il entend	11. vous descendez	19. je me regarde
4. nous sommes	12. ils achètent	20. tu te laves
5. vous avez	13. je dors	21. elle se lave
6. ils vont	14. tu restes	22. nous nous habillons
7. je sors	15. elle tombe	23. vous vous dépêchez
8. tu dis	16. nous arrivons	24. ils se téléphonent

Exercice XXXII   (*a*.) Donnez le présent, l'imparfait négatif, le passé composé positif et le passé composé négatif des verbes suivants.

1. je   se lever
2. elle   se maquiller
3. il   se raser
4. vous   se reposer
5. nous   s'habiller
6. ils   s'ennuyer

(*b*.) Donnez l'impératif positif et l'impératif négatif des verbes suivants.

1. tu   se dépêcher
2. vous   s'amuser
3. nous   se fâcher

Exercice XXXIII   L'accord du participe passé.

EXEMPLE: J'ai mangé la pomme. La pomme, je l'ai **mangée.**

Mettez les phrases suivantes au passé composé. Accordez le participe passé, si c'est nécessaire.

1. Votre température, vous la prenez, oui ou non?
2. Et ta composition, tu la fais?
3. Cette histoire «drôle,» je ne la comprends pas.
4. La vérité, il la dit, c'est vrai.
5. Vous pouvez toujours me poser des questions. La leçon? Je ne l'apprends pas.
6. La clé de l'appartement, où est-ce que je la mets?
7. Dans la classe de français nous apprenons mille choses fascinantes.

Exercice XXXIV   Voici une petite histoire d'amour. Écrivez-la au passé composé.

Un jour Georges et Joséphine se rencontrent à une soirée; ils se regardent, ils se trouvent sympathiques. Bientôt, ils s'embrassent; le lendemain ils se fiancent et trois jours plus tard ils se marient! Ils s'installent dans un joli petit appartement.

Au début ils s'entendent plutôt bien: ils s'amusent ensemble, ils se disputent plusieurs fois, ils se mettent en colère. Alors un jour, ils se séparent. Ils ne se parlent plus, ils ne se voient plus, ils ne se téléphonent plus. Mais tout est bien qui finit bien!* Un jour ils se réconcilient.

Exercice XXXV   Mettez le relatif correct: **qui** (sujet) ou **que** (objet direct).

1. Vous achetez pour vos enfants des vêtements _____ sont trop grands.
2. Les enfants _____ grandissent vite coûtent cher.
3. Le spécialiste _____ je vais voir me donne des médicaments _____ me font dormir.
4. C'est le médecin _____ je vous ai recommandé.
5. Oui, c'est lui _____ a guéri la sœur de la belle mère de Josette.
6. La jeune fille _____ il aime a les yeux bleus.
7. J'ai habité dans un pays _____ a des plages immenses.
8. C'est le soleil _____ je regrette surtout.
9. Il y a une grande partie du monde _____ n'a pas assez à manger.
10. C'est un problème important _____ il faut résoudre (*solve*).

Exercice XXXVI   Répétez les phrases; changez le premier verbe. Attention à la préposition.

(*a.*) Est-ce que tu veux venir me voir ce soir?

Elle ne peut pas...   Je vous invite...
Il oubliera...   Ils refusent...

(*b.*) Essayez de téléphoner au docteur.

J'ai bien envie...   Il faut...
Ils ont réussi...   Nous décidons...
Vous avez peur...

Exercice XXXVII   Mettez les pronoms-adverbes **en, y** ou le pronom tonique **à lui, à elle.**

1. Tu prends de l'aspirine?
2. Je pense à mes voyages.
3. Elle a trop de fièvre.
4. Vous achetez un kilo d'oranges.
5. Elles ont fait beaucoup d'exercices.
6. Est-ce que vous pensez à vos amis?
7. Nous avons écrit trois lettres.
8. Ne buvez pas de cette eau.
9. Vous voulez un verre de bière?
10. Pensez à votre travail.
11. Cette auto est à votre mère?
12. Je m'adresse aux étudiants.
13. Vous avez douze enfants!
14. Ne rêvez pas à des choses impossibles.
15. Tu as rapporté assez de souvenirs.

*Laissez cette phrase au présent. C'est un proverbe.

Exercice XXXVIII   Mettez les verbes entre parenthèses au temps qui convient: imparfait, passé composé.

Mon grand-père (être) un homme terriblement capricieux. Surtout, il (aimer) beaucoup terroriser ma grand-mère. Un jour, mon père et mon oncle (venir) le voir pour le dîner. C' (être) le printemps et la table (être) mise près de la fenêtre ouverte: il (faire) beau et le jardin (être) plein de fleurs. Ma grand-mère (apporter) le premier plat. C' (être) des œufs à la coque (*soft boiled eggs*). Mon grand-père (regarder) son assiette, (lever) la tête et (dire), «Qu'est-ce que c'est que ça? Des œufs à la coque? Mais ce sont des manières bourgeoises de manger des œufs à la coque!» (mon grand-père (être) un homme du peuple, un boulanger). Alors il (prendre) son assiette et (jeter) l'œuf à la coque par la fenêtre. Mon père et mon oncle n' (être) plus des petits garçons. Ils (se regarder) et ils (décider) de donner une leçon à mon grand-père. Ils (attraper) toutes les choses qui (être) sur la table, et ils les (jeter) par la fenêtre. Mon grand-père (ouvrir) des yeux tout grands: il (être) bien surpris. Il (dire): «Qu'est-ce que vous faites?» Alors mon oncle (répondre): «Ah! nous (penser) que tu (vouloir) dîner dehors, parce qu'il (faire) si beau, alors nous (mettre) le couvert dans le jardin.»

Ils (rire)* tous les trois, et mon grand-père (s'excuser). Mais ma grand-mère (être) furieuse: deux de ses assiettes et trois verres (être) cassés!

Exercice XXXIX   Traductions.

1. What am I going to wear today? 2. She wears her blue dress on Sundays. 3. The baker is dressed in white. 4. What is your pullover made of? 5. He visits his cousins every year. 6. We are going to visit the cathedral. 7. They leave at 5:15. They left at 5:15. 8. We leave the United States in June. They left the United States in May. 9. Last night I left my books at my friend's place. 10. He drives fast. 11. We are driving to L.A. 12. She sat in the most comfortable armchair. 13. We are not standing, we are sitting on chairs. 14. He came back from France Friday. 15. I went to the flower market. 16. What is the matter with you? 17. I have a headache. 18. I know Paris. I know this man. I know that you are sick. 19. That is strange. That means... 20. I need a grog.

Chapitres 15–20

Exercice XL   Donnez la forme correcte des verbes: présent, imparfait, futur et passé composé.

1. recevoir: Vous _____ le journal.
2. cueillir: Tu _____ des fleurs.
3. devoir: Elle _____ cent francs.
4. vivre: Nous _____ aux U.S.A.
5. suivre: La femme _____ son mari.

*Le passé composé est: **j'ai ri.**

6. battre: Ils _____ leurs enfants.

7. rire: Vous _____.

8. naître: Le bébé _____ le 14 juin. ⎫

9. mourir: Son grand-père _____. ⎬ (*pas à l'imparfait, s'il vous plaît*)

10. paraître: Tu _____ fatiqué.

11. se taire: Il _____.

12. se tuer: Il _____.

13. plaire: Ça me _____.

14. pleuvoir: Il _____.

15. s'enfuir: Vous _____.

Exercice XLI   Donnez le futur de:

1. je vais
2. nous savons
3. tu fais
4. il envoie
5. je veux

6. tu as
7. nous sommes
8. ils voient
9. je peux
10. tu viens

Exercice XLII   Mettez le pronom possessif ou le pronom démonstratif.

1. Mes sœurs et vos sœurs ont le même âge.
2. Mes sœurs et les sœurs de Jacques ont le même âge.
3. Achetez vos billets et mes billets aussi.
4. Achetez vos billets et les billets de Georgette aussi.
5. Le mariage de Jules et mon mariage ont été célébrés le même jour.
6. Mon mariage était plus réussi que le mariage de Jules.
7. La pollution aux U.S.A. est moins sévère que notre pollution en France.
8. La pollution qui affecte la respiration, est-elle plus grave que la pollution qui affecte les yeux?

Exercice XLIII   Mettez le pronom personnel qui convient.

1. Il nous montre ses photos de vacances.
2. Il nous montre des photos de son enfance.
3. Il leur montre ses photos.
4. Il leur montre des photos.
5. Vous pensez à votre enfance?
6. Non, je pense à ma fiancée.
7. Je prête mon auto à Joséphine.
8. Je ne prête pas mon auto à Joséphine.
9. Prête ton auto à Joséphine.
10. Les marchands me vendent des cartes postales.
11. Il vous envoie une lettre.
12. Ils envoient leurs enfants en Angleterre.

Exercice XLIV   Mettez le pronom interrogatif qui convient.

1. _____ a pris la Bastille?
2. Avec _____ est-ce que les Parisiens ont tué le roi Louis XVI?
3. _____ vous voyez du haut de la Tour Eiffel? Tout Paris.
4. _____ parlent les députés à l'Assemblée Nationale? Des problèmes du gouvernement.
5. _____ dites-vous?
6. _____ est arrivé le 14 Juillet 1789?
7. Pour _____ est-ce que le gouvernement fait des lois? Pour les citoyens.
8. _____ pollue l'atmosphère? La fumée des usines.

Exercice XLV   Répétez les phrases au passif.

1. Les nouvelles lois libèrent les femmes.
2. L'explosion a blessé trois ouvriers.
3. Les députés voteront cette loi.
4. Le ministre conseillait le président.
5. Toutes les voitures embouteillent la rue.
6. Des jeunes filles ont cueilli les fleurs de lavande.

Exercice XLVI   Répétez à la forme négative.

1. Tout le monde vous aime.
2. Elle comprend tout.
3. Il est toujours absent le vendredi.
4. Tu as déjà fini.
5. Ils ont des complexes.
6. J'ai vu quelqu'un dans le placard.
7. Il fume encore.
8. Quelque chose vous ennuie?

Exercice XLVII   Mettez le pronom relatif qui convient.

1. Les problèmes _____ je parle sont la pollution, le chômage, la surpopulation.
2. Le pays _____ il pense n'est pas sur la carte.
3. Le président a donné le stylo avec _____ il a signé la déclaration des droits.
4. Voilà le régime _____ il a besoin.
5. La chaise sur _____ il était assis s'est cassée et il est tombé.
6. C'est le professeur _____ parle.
7. La symphonie _____ il a écrite va être jouée par l'orchestre de l'ORTF.
8. Les étudiants _____ dorment en classe seront punis.

Exercice XLVIII   Traductions.

1. He is a doctor. He is a good doctor.   2. The more he drinks, the more he sleeps.   3. I am afraid because we have an exam.   4. I am afraid because of the exam.   5. Remember I am waiting for you.   6. We were supposed to go out, but we could not.   7. It must be nice in Hawaii.   8. He left ten minutes ago.   9. I have been working on this book for a year.   10. Paul just bought a new car.

11. Is it working? 12. She brushes her hair. 13. He only eats vegetables. 14. I have three dollars left. 15. There are six exercises left. 16. We are forbidden to smoke. 17. You make me laugh. 18. This news makes me sick. 19. It seems they are going to get married. 20. You look tired. 21. The baby will be born in three months. 22. She finished her homework in ten minutes. 23. Before going out, she takes her umbrella. 24. After going out, she sees it is raining. 25. She is somebody important in the government. 26. You bought something nice for me. 27. I miss you. 28. You missed a good program. 29. He lacks will power **(volonté).** 30. You should read this book. 31. You should have read the book before seeing the movie. 32. Nobody loves me. Nothing pleases me. 33. It rained; that did not please me. 34. I heard they found life on Mars. 35. I heard about this discovery. 36. This book is about love. 37. Even though she is hungry, she does not eat. (three ways) 38. I want you to do the dishes. 39. She is happy that we came. 40. It is not being done. 41. It's obvious. (it can be seen)

Chapitre 2: Au clair de la lune

Au clair de la lune,	Au clair de la lune,
Pierrot répondit:	On n'y voit qu'un peu:
«Je n'ai pas de plume,	On cherche la plume,
Je suis dans mon lit.	On cherche le feu.
Va chez la voisine,	En cherchant de la sorte
Je crois qu'elle y est,	Je ne sais ce qu'on trouva,
Car dans sa cuisine	Mais je sais que la porte
On bat le briquet.»	Sur eux se ferma.

battre le briquet   to strike a light

répondit, trouva, se ferma   passés simples: le sens est **a répondu, a trouvé, s'est fermée**

Chapitre 5: Voici le mois de mai

2. Le fils du roi s'en va, (*bis*)
   S'en va les ramassant.
   S'en va les ramassant,
   Si jolies, mignonnes,
   S'en va les ramassant...
   Si mignonnement.
3. Il en ramassa tant
   Qu'il en remplit ses gants.

4. Il les porte à sa mie,
   Pour lui faire un présent.
5. Tenez, tenez, dit-il,
   Tenez, voici des gants.
6. Vous ne les mettrez guère,
   Que quatre fois par an.
7. A Pâques, à la Toussaint,
   A Noël, à la Saint-Jean.

s'en va les ramassant   = **s'en va et les ramasse en même temps**
                               (*at the same time*)

il ramassa   passé simple: **il a ramassé**

il remplit   passé simple: **il a rempli**

sa mie, ma mie   contraction de **sa amie** = **s'amie**; **ma amie** = **m'amie** = **son amie,
   mon amie**

mettrez   futur de **mettre**

Chapitre 6: Colchiques dans les prés

   Châtaignes dans les bois, se fendent, se fendent
   Châtaignes dans les bois se fendent sous les pas.
   La feuille d'automne...
3. Nuages dans le ciel s'étirent, s'étirent
   Nuages dans le ciel s'étirent comme une aile.
   La feuille d'automne...
4. Et ce chant dans mon cœur murmure, murmure
   Et ce chant dans mon cœur appelle le bonheur.
   La feuille d'automne...

châtaigne, (*f.*) chestnut	**s'étirer** to stretch
se fendre to split	**cœur,** (*m.*) heart
un bois = **une forêt**	**murmurer** to whisper
pas, (*m.*) step	**bonheur,** (*m.*) happiness

Chapitre 9: Chevaliers de la Table Ronde

2. S'il est bon, s'il est agréable (*bis*)
   J'en boirai jusqu'à mon plaisir.
   J'en boirai, oui, oui, oui...
3. Si je meurs, je veux qu'on m'enterre
   Dans la cave où y a du bon vin.
   Dans la cave, oui, oui, oui...
4. Les deux pieds contre la muraille
   Et la tête sous le robinet.
   Et la tête, oui, oui, oui...
5. Et les quatre plus grands ivrognes
   Porteront les quatr'coins du drap.
   Porteront, oui, oui, oui...
6. Pour donner le discours d'usage
   On prendra le bistrot du coin.
   On prendra, oui, oui, oui...
7. Sur ma tombe je veux qu'on inscrive
   «Ici gît le roi des buveurs.»
   Ici gît, oui, oui, oui...

boirai   futur de **boire**
je meurs   verbe **mourir**
enterrer   = mettre dans la terre, quand on est mort
la muraille   = le mur de la cave
robinet, (*m.*)   faucet of the barrel
drap, (*m.*)   mourning sheet
bistrot, (*m.*)   local pub
inscrive   subj. d'**inscrire** (cf. **inscription**)
Ici gît   "Here lays..." (as inscribed on a stone)
le buveur = **un ivrogne** (a drunk)

Chapitre 12: A la claire fontaine

2. A l'ombre d'un beau chêne
   Je me suis fait sécher;
   Sur la plus haute branche
   Le rossignol chantait.
3. Chante, rossignol, chante,
   Toi qui as le cœur gai,
   Tu as le cœur à rire,
   Moi je l'ai à pleurer!
4. C'est pour mon ami Pierre
   Qui ne veut plus m'aimer,
   Pour un bouton de rose
   Que je lui refusai.
5. Je voudrais que la rose
   Fût encore au rosier
   Et que mon ami Pierre
   Fût encore à m'aimer.

chêne, (*m.*)   oak
sécher   to dry
rossignol, (*m.*)   nightingale

je refusai   passé simple: **j'ai refusé**
fût   subjonctif imparfait d'**être**: **soit**
rosier, (*m.*)   rosebush

Chapitre 18: Brave marin

2. S'en va trouver dame l'hôtesse, *(bis)*
   Tout doux
   «Qu'on apporte ici du vin blanc,
   Que le marin boive en passant,
   Tout doux!»
3. Brave marin se mit à boire *(bis)*
   Tout doux
   Se mit à boire et à chanter,
   La belle se mit à pleurer
   Tout doux!
4. «Ah! qu'avez-vous, dame l'hôtesse?
   Tout doux.
   Regrettez-vous votre vin blanc,
   Que le marin boit en passant
   Tout doux!»
5. «C'est pas mon vin que je
   regrette
   Tout doux.
   Mais c'est la mort de mon
   mari,
   Monsieur, vous ressemblez à
   lui
   Tout doux!»
6. «Ah! dites-moi, dame
   l'hôtesse,
   Tout doux.
   Vous aviez de lui trois
   enfants,
   En voilà quatre z'à présent,
   Tout doux!»
7. «J'ai tant reçu de tristes
   lettres,
   Tout doux.
   Qu'il était mort et enterré,
   Que je me suis remariée
   Tout doux!»
8. Brave marin vida son verre
   Tout doux
   Sans remercier, tout en
   pleurant
   S'en retourna t'au régiment
   Tout doux!

qu'on apporte let's bring
que le marin boive let the sailor drink (**Apporte and boive** *are subjunctive. They*
   stand for a third person singular imperative.)
se mit passé simple: **s'est mis**
vous ressemblez à lui modern: **vous lui ressemblez** you look like him
quatre z'à présent *the* **z** *indicates a popular but incorrect liaison and also supplies*
   the missing syllable

Chapitre 19: Le roi a fait battre tambour

2. «Marquis, dis-moi, la connais-tu
   (bis)
   Qui est cett' joli' dame?»
   Le marquis lui a répondu:
   «Sire roi, c'est ma femme.»
3. «Marquis, tu es plus heureux
   qu'moi,
   D'avoir femme si belle,
   Si tu voulais me l'accorder
   Je me chargerais d'elle.»

4. «Sir, si vous n'étiez pas le roi,
   J'en tirerais vengeance,
   Mais puisque vous êtes le roi,
   A votre obéissance.»

5. «Marquis, ne te fâche donc pas,
   T'auras ta récompense,
   Je te ferai dans mes armées
   Beau maréchal de France.»

6. «Adieu, ma mie, adieu, mon cœur,
   Adieu mon espérance!
   Puisqu'il te faut servir le roi,
   Séparons-nous d'ensemble.»

7. La reine a fait faire un bouquet,
   De belles fleurs de lyse,
   Et la senteur de ce bouquet
   A fait mourir marquise.

accorder *ici:* **donner**
se charger de   to take care of
tirer vengeance   to get revenge

récompense, (*f.*)   reward
senteur, (*f.*)   fragrance

Chapitre 20: Passant par Paris

2. Un de mes amis (*bis par le chœur*)
   Me dit à l'oreille
   Jean, prends garde à toi
   L'on courtis' ta belle.
   Bon, Bon, Bon.
   Le bon vin m'endort, etc.

3. ... Courtis' qui voudra,
   Je me fie en elle.

4. ... J'ai eu de son cœur
   La fleur la plus belle.

5. ... Dans un beau lit blanc,
   Gréé de dentelles.

6. ... J'ai eu trois garçons,
   Tous trois captaines.

7. ... L'un est à Bordeaux,
   L'autre à La Rochelle.

8. ... L'plus jeune à Paris
   Courtisant les belles.

9. ... Et l'père est ici
   Qui hal' la ficelle.

prends garde   = **fais attention**
courtiser   = **faire la cour à**
se fier (à)   to trust
gréé (*for a ship:* rigged) here the bed is compared to a ship
dentelles, (*pl.*)   laces
hal' la ficelle   pulling the rope (of a ship)

C'est un temps qu'on emploie seulement pour écrire. On le rencontre dans des romans et dans des récits historiques. Il a la même valeur que le passé composé.

EXEMPLE: *Vous lisez dans un livre d'histoire, dans un roman:*   *Vous expliquez à une personne:*

Napoléon Bonaparte naquit en Corse.	Napoléon Bonaparte est né en Corse.
Il fit des études et fut général à 26 ans.	Il a fait des études et a été général à 26 ans.
Il gagna beaucoup de batailles.	Il a gagné beaucoup de batailles.
Il devint empereur et conquit beaucoup de pays.	Il est devenu empereur et a conquis beaucoup de pays.
Il fut vaincu par une coalition.	Il a été vaincu par une coalition.
On l'envoya en exil à Ste. Hélène où il mourut.	On l'a envoyé en exil à Ste. Hélène où il est mort.

Les formes:

Pour les verbes du 1ᵉʳ groupe, on a un **a** à toutes les personnes (sauf la 3ème personne du pluriel).

parler	**aller**
je parlai	j'allai
tu parlas	tu allas
il parla*	il alla*
nous parlâmes	nous allâmes
vous parlâtes	vous allâtes
ils parl**èrent***	ils all**èrent***

Remarquez l'orthographe de ces deux verbes en **-ger** et en **-cer**.

manger	**placer**
je man**geai**	je pla**çai**
tu man**geas**	tu pla**ças**
il man**gea**	il pla**ça**
nous man**geâmes**	nous pla**çâmes**
vous man**geâtes**	vous pla**çates**
ils man**gèrent**	ils pla**cèrent**

Verbes du 2ème groupe:

Il y a un **i** à toutes les personnes.

finir	
je finis**	nous finîmes
tu finis**	vous finîtes
il finit**	ils finirent

---

*Ces deux personnes sont les plus employées.
**C'est comme le présent.

Verbes du 3ème groupe:

Certains verbes ont un **i**.
Certains verbes ont un **u**.

Verbes au passé simple en **i**:

l'infinitif	*le passé simple*	*le passé composé*
attendre	j'attend**is**	j'**ai attendu**
descendre	je descend**is**	je **suis descendu**
dire	je d**is**	j'**ai dit**
entendre	j'entend**is**	j'**ai entendu**
faire	je f**îs**	j'**ai fait**
mettre	je m**is**	j'**ai mis**
partir	je part**is**	je **suis parti**
perdre	je perd**is**	j'**ai perdu**
prendre	je pr**is**	j'**ai pris**
répondre	je répond**is**	j'**ai répondu**
sortir	je sort**is**	je **suis sorti**
vendre	je vend**is**	j'**ai vendu**
voir	je v**is**	j'**ai vu**

Verbes au passé simple en **u**:

l'infinitif	*le passé simple*	*le passé composé*
boire	je b**us**	j'**ai bu**
connaître	je conn**us**	j'**ai connu**
croire	je cr**us**	j'**ai cru**
il faut	il fall**ut**	**il a fallu**
lire	je l**us**	j'**ai lu**
pouvoir	je p**us**	j'**ai pu**
savoir	je s**us**	j'**ai su**
recevoir	je re**çus**	j'**ai reçu**
vouloir	je voul**us**	j'**ai voulu**
avoir	j'**eus**	j'**ai eu**
être	je f**us**	j'**ai été**

Il y a deux verbes spéciaux (et leurs composés) en **in**:

venir: je v**in**s, tu v**in**s, il v**in**t
nous v**în**mes, vous v**în**tes, ils v**in**rent
(ils sont venus)

tenir: je t**in**s, tu t**in**s, il t**in**t
nous t**în**mes, vous t**în**tes, ils t**in**rent
(ils ont tenu)

1. Verbe: **avoir**

INDICATIF

Présent

j' ai
tu as
il a
nous avons
vous avez
ils ont

Passé Composé

j' ai eu
tu as eu
il a eu
nous avons eu
vous avez eu
ils ont eu

Imparfait

j' avais
tu avais
il avait
nous avions
vous aviez
ils avaient

Plus-que-parfait

j' avais eu
tu avais eu
il avait eu
nous avions eu
vous aviez eu
ils avaient eu

Futur

j' aurai
tu auras
il aura
nous aurons
vous aurez
ils auront

Futur Antérieur

j' aurai eu
tu auras eu
il aura eu
nous aurons eu
vous aurez eu
ils auront eu

CONDITIONNEL

Présent

j' aurais
tu aurais
il aurait
nous aurions
vous auriez
ils auraient

Passé

j' aurais eu
tu aurais eu
il aurait eu
nous aurions eu
vous auriez eu
ils auraient eu

SUBJONCTIF

Présent

que j' aie
que tu aies
qu' il ait
que nous ayons
que vous ayez
qu' ils aient

Passé

que j' aie eu
que tu aies eu
qu' il ait eu
que nous ayons eu
que vous ayez eu
qu' ils aient eu

IMPÉRATIF

aie, ayons, ayez

INFINITIF

Présent   *Passé*
avoir   avoir eu

GÉRONDIF

en ayant

PASSÉ SIMPLE

j' eus   nous eûmes
tu eus   vous eûtes
il eut   ils eurent

2. Verbe: **être**

INDICATIF

Présent

je suis
tu es
il est
nous sommes
vous êtes
ils sont

Passé Composé

j' ai été
tu as été
il a été
nous avons été
vous avez été
ils ont été

Imparfait

j' étais
tu étais
il était
nous étions
vous étiez
ils étaient

Plus-que-parfait

j'   avais   été
tu   avais   été
il   avait   été
nous avions été
vous aviez été
ils   avaient été

Futur

je   serai
tu   seras
il   sera
nous serons
vous serez
ils   seront

Futur Antérieur

j'   aurai   été
tu   auras   été
il   aura   été
nous aurons été
vous aurez été
ils   auraient été

CONDITIONNEL

Présent

je   serais
tu   serais
il   serait
nous serions
vous seriez
ils   seraient

Passé

j'   aurais   été
tu   aurais   été
il   aurait   été
nous aurions été
vous auriez été
ils   auraient été

SUBJONCTIF

Présent

que je   sois
que tu   sois
qu' il   soit
que nous soyons
que vous soyez
qu' ils   soient

Passé

que j'   aie   été
que tu   aies   été
qu' il   ait   été
que nous ayons été
que vous ayez été
qu' ils   aient été

IMPÉRATIF

sois, soyons, soyez

INFINITIF

Présent   *Passé*
être   avoir été

GÉRONDIF

en étant

PASSÉ SIMPLE

je fus   nous fûmes
tu fus   vous fûtes
il fut   ils   furent

3. Verbe: **chanter** (1er groupe)

INDICATIF

Présent

je   chante
tu   chantes
il   chante
nous chantons
vous chantez
ils   chantent

Passé Composé

j'   ai   chanté
tu   as   chanté
il   a   chanté
nous avons chanté
vous avez chanté
ils   ont   chanté

Imparfait

je   chantais
tu   chantais
il   chantait
nous chantions
vous chantiez
ils   chantaient

Plus-que-parfait

j'   avais   chanté
tu   avais   chanté
il   avait   chanté
nous avions chanté
vous aviez chanté
ils   avaient chanté

Futur

je   chanterai
tu   chanteras
il   chantera
nous chanterons
vous chanterez
ils   chanteront

Futur Antérieur

j'   aurai   chanté
tu   auras   chanté
il   aura   chanté
nous aurons chanté
vous aurez chanté
ils   auront chanté

CONDITIONNEL

Présent

je   chanterais
tu   chanterais
il   chanterait
nous chanterions
vous chanteriez
ils   chanteraient

Passé

j'   aurais   chanté
tu   aurais   chanté
il   aurait   chanté
nous aurions chanté
vous auriez chanté
ils   auraient chanté

SUBJONCTIF

Présent		*Passé*		
que je	chante	que j'	aie	chanté
que tu	chantes	que tu	aies	chanté
qu' il	chante	qu' il	ait	chanté
que nous	chantions	que nous	ayons	chanté
que vous	chantiez	que vous	ayez	chanté
qu' ils	chantent	qu' ils	aient	chanté

IMPÉRATIF	INFINITIF
chante, chantons, chantez	*Présent* *Passé*
	chanter avoir chanté

GÉRONDIF   PASSÉ SIMPLE

en chantant

je chantai	nous chantâmes
tu chantas	vous chantâtes
il chanta	ils chantèrent

4. Verbe: **finir** (2ème groupe)

INDICATIF

Présent		*Passé Composé*			*Imparfait*	
je	finis	j'	ai	fini	je	finissais
tu	finis	tu	as	fini	tu	finissais
il	finit	il	a	fini	il	finissait
nous	finissons	nous	avons	fini	nous	finissions
vous	finissez	vous	avez	fini	vous	finissiez
ils	finissent	ils	ont	fini	ils	finissaient

Plus-que-parfait		*Futur*		*Futur Antérieur*		
j'	avais fini	je	finirai	j'	aurai	fini
tu	avais fini	tu	finiras	tu	auras	fini
il	avait fini	il	finira	il	aura	fini
nous	avions fini	nous	finirons	nous	aurons	fini
vous	aviez fini	vous	finirez	vous	aurez	fini
ils	avaient fini	ils	finiront	ils	auront	fini

CONDITIONNEL   SUBJONCTIF

Présent		*Passé*			*Présent*		*Passé*		
je	finirais	j'	aurais	fini	que je	finisse	que j'	aie	fini
tu	finirais	tu	aurais	fini	que tu	finisses	que tu	aies	fini
il	finirait	il	aurait	fini	qu' il	finisse	qu' il	ait	fini
nous	finirions	nous	aurions	fini	que nous	finissions	que nous	ayons	fini
vous	finiriez	vous	auriez	fmi	que vous	finissiez	que vous	ayez	fini
ils	finiraient	ils	auraient	fini	qu' ils	finissent	qu' ils	aient	fini

<table>
<tr><td>IMPÉRATIF</td><td colspan="2">INFINITIF</td><td>GÉRONDIF</td></tr>
</table>

IMPÉRATIF	INFINITIF		GÉRONDIF
finis, finissons, finissez	*Présent*	*Passé*	en finissant
	finir	avoir fini	

PASSÉ SIMPLE

je finis	noùs finîmes
tu finis	vous finîtes
il finit	ils finirent

5. Verbe: **attendre** (3ème groupe)

INDICATIF

Présent

j'	attends
tu	attends
il	attend
nous	attendons
vous	attendez
ils	attendent

Passé Composé

j'	ai	attendu
tu	as	attendu
il	a	attendu
nous	avons	attendu
vous	avez	attendu
ils	ont	attendu

Imparfait

j'	attendais
tu	attendais
il	attendait
nous	attendions
vous	attendiez
ils	attendaient

Plus-que-parfait

j'	avais	attendu
tu	avais	attendu
il	avait	attendu
nous	avions	attendu
vous	aviez	attendu
ils	avaient	attendu

Futur

j'	attendrai
tu	attendras
il	attendra
nous	attendrons
vous	attendrez
ils	attendront

Futur Antérieur

j'	aurai	attendu
tu	auras	attendu
il	aura	attendu
nous	aurons	attendu
vous	aurez	attendu
ils	auront	attendu

CONDITIONNEL

Présent

j'	attendrais
tu	attendrais
il	attendrait
nous	attendrions
vous	attendriez
ils	attendraient

Passé

j'	aurais	attendu
tu	aurais	attendu
il	aurait	attendu
nous	aurions	attendu
vous	auriez	attendu
ils	auraient	attendu

SUBJONCTIF

Présent

que j'	attende
que tu	attendes
qu' il	attende
que nous	attendions
que vous	attendiez
qu' ils	attendent

Passé

que j'	aie	attendu
que tu	aies	attendu
qu' il	ait	attendu
que nous	ayons	attendu
que vous	ayez	attendu
qu' ils	aient	attendu

IMPÉRATIF	INFINITIF		GÉRONDIF
attends, attendons, attendez	*Présent*	*Passé*	en attendant
	attendre	avoir attendu	

PASSÉ SIMPLE

j' attendis	nous attendîmes
tu attendis	vous attendîtes
il attendit	ils attendirent

6. Le verbe pronominal: **se rappeler**

INDICATIF

Présent

je me rappelle
tu te rappelles
il se rappelle
nous nous rappelons
vous vous rappelez
ils se rappellent

Passé Composé

je me suis rappelé
tu t' es rappelé
il s' est rappelé
nous nous sommes rappelés
vous vous êtes rappelés
ils se sont rappelés

Imparfait

je me rappelais
tu te rappelais
il se rappelait
nous nous rappelions
vous vous rappeliez
ils se rappelaient

Plus-que-parfait

je m' étais rappelé
tu t' étais rappelé
ils s' était rappelé
nous nous étions rappelés
vous vous étiez rappelés
ils s' étaient rappelés

Futur

je me rappellerai
tu te rappelleras
il se rappellera
nous nous rappellerons
vous vous rappellerez
ils se rappelleront

Futur Antérieur

je me serai rappelé
tu te seras rappelé
il se sera rappelé
nous nous serons rappelés
vous vous serez rappelés
ils se seront rappelés

CONDITIONNEL

Présent

je me rappellerais
tu te rappellerais
il se rappellerait
nous nous rappellerions
vous vous rappelleriez
ils se rappelleraient

Passé

je me serais rappelé
tu te serais rappelé
il se serait rappelé
nous nous serions rappelés
vous vous seriez rappelés
ils se seraient rappelés

SUBJONCTIF

Présent

que je me rappelle
que tu te rappelles
qu' il se rappelles
que nous nous rappelions
que vous vous rappeliez
qu' ils se rappellent

Passé

que je me sois rappelé
que tu te sois rappelé
qu' il se soit rappelé
que nous nous soyons rappelés
que vous vous soyez rappelés
qu' ils se soient rappelés

IMPÉRATIF

rappelle-toi, rappelons-nous
rappelez-vous

INFINITIF

Présent	*Passé*
se rappeler	s'être rappelé

GÉRONDIF

en se rappelant

PASSÉ SIMPLE

je	me	rappelai	nous	nous	rappelâmes
tu	te	rappelas	vous	vous	rappelâtes
il	se	rappela	ils	se	rappelèrent

7. Conjugaison passive

INDICATIF

Présent			*Passé Composé*			*Imparfait*		
je	suis	aimé	j'	ai	été aimé	j'	étais	aimé
tu	es	aimé	tu	as	été aimé	tu	étais	aimé
il	est	aimé	il	a	été aimé	il	était	aimé
nous	sommes	aimés	nous	avons	été aimés	nous	étions	aimés
vous	êtes	aimés	vous	avez	été aimés	vous	étiez	aimés
ils	sont	aimés	ils	ont	été aimés	ils	étaient	aimés

Plus-que-parfait			*Futur*			*Futur Antérieur*		
j'	avais	été aimé	je	serai	aimé	j'	aurai	été aimé
tu	avais	été aimé	tu	seras	aimé	tu	auras	été aimé
il	avait	été aimé	il	sera	aimé	il	aura	été aimé
nous	avions	été aimés	nous	serons	aimés	nous	aurons	été aimés
vous	aviez	été aimés	vous	serez	aimés	vous	aurez	été aimés
ils	avaient	été aimés	ils	seront	aimés	ils	auront	été aimés

CONDITIONNEL

Présent			*Passé*		
je	serais	aimé	j'	aurais	été aimé
tu	serais	aimé	tu	aurais	été aimé
il	serait	aimé	il	aurait	été aimé
nous	serions	aimés	nous	aurions	été aimés
vous	seriez	aimés	vous	auriez	été aimés
ils	seraient	aimés	ils	auraient	été aimés

SUBJONCTIF

Présent			*Passé*		
que je	sois	aimé	que j'	aie	été aimé
que tu	sois	aimé	que tu	aies	été aimé
qu' il	soit	aimé	qu' il	ait	été aimé
que nous	soyons	aimés	que nous	ayons	été aimés
que vous	soyez	aimés	que vous	ayez	été aimés
qu' ils	soient	aimés	qu' ils	aient	été aimés

IMPÉRATIF	INFINITIF		GÉRONDIF
sois aimé, soyons aimés,	*Présent*	*Passé*	en étant aimé
soyez aimés	être aimé	avoir été aimé	

PASSÉ SIMPLE

je fus aimé	nous fûmes aimés
tu fus aimé	vous fûtes aimés
il fut aimé	ils furent aimés

8. Verbe: **aller**

INDICATIF

Présent	*Passé Composé*	*Imparfait*
je vais	je suis allé	j' allais
tu vas	tu es allé	tu allais
il va	il est allé	il allait
nous allons	nous sommes allés	nous allions
vous allez	vous êtes allés	vous alliez
ils vont	ils sont allés	ils allaient

Plus-que-parfait	*Futur*	*Futur Antérieur*
j' étais allé	j' irai	je serai allé
tu étais allé	tu iras	tu seras allé
il était allé	il ira	il sera allé
nous étions allés	nous irons	nous serons allés
vous étiez allés	vous irez	vous serez allés
ils étaient allés	ils iront	ils seront allés

CONDITIONNEL

Présent	*Passé*
j' irais	je serais allé
tu irais	tu serais allé
il irait	il serait allé
nous irions	nous serions allés
vous iriez	vous seriez allés
ils iraient	ils seraient allés

SUBJONCTIF

Présent	*Passé*
que j' aille	que je sois allé
que tu ailles	que tu sois allé
qu' il aille	qu' il soit allé
que nous allions	que nous soyons allés
que vous alliez	que vous soyez allés
qu' ils aillent	qu' ils soient allés

IMPÉRATIF	INFINITIF		GÉRONDIF
va, allons, allez	*Présent*	*Passé*	en allant
	aller	être allé	

PASSÉ SIMPLE

j' allai	nous allâmes
tu allas	vous allâtes
il alla	ils allèrent

This chart shows how, for the majority of French verbs, some tenses are related.

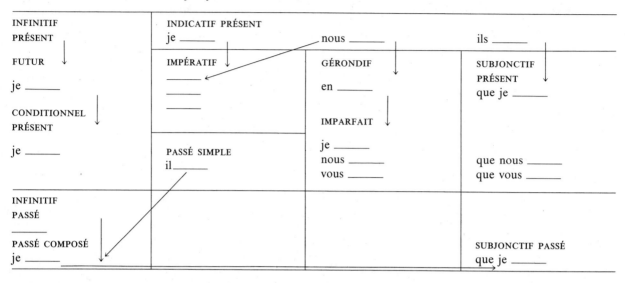

The verbs that follow have their main tenses listed on the above pattern.

I. Verbes réguliers*

acheter	j'achète	nous achetons	ils achètent
j'achèterai	achète		que j'achète
	achetons	en achetant	
j'achèterais	achetez		
		j'achetais	
	il acheta	nous achetions	que nous achetions
		vous achetiez	que vous achetiez
avoir acheté			
j'ai acheté			que j'aie acheté

envoyer	j'envoie	nous envoyons	ils envoient
j'enverrai	envoie		que j'envoie
	envoyons	en envoyant	
j'enverrais	envoyez		
		j'envoyais	
	il envoya	nous envoyions	que nous envoyions
		vous envoyiez	que vous envoyiez
avoir envoyé			
j'ai envoyé			que j'aie envoyé

*Regular verbs which present orthographical changes or accent problems.

jeter	je jette	nous jetons	ils jettent
je jetterai	jette	en jetant	que je jette
	jetons		
je jetterais	jetez		
	il jeta	je jetais	que nous jetions
		nous jetions	que vous jetiez
		vous jetiez	
avoir jeté			
j'ai jeté			que j'aie jeté
manger (et tous les verbes en **-ger**)	je mange	nous mangeons	ils mangent
je mangerai	mange	en mangeant	que je mange
	mangeons		
je mangerais	mangez		
	il mangea	je mangeais	que nous mangions
		nous mangions	que vous mangiez
		vous mangiez	
avoir mangé			
j'ai mangé			que j'aie mangé
nettoyer (et tous les verbes en **-oyer, -ayer, -uyer**)	je nettoie	nous nettoyons	ils nettoient
je nettoierai	nettoie	en nettoyant	que je nettoie
	nettoyons		
je nettoierais	nettoyez		
	il nettoya	je nettoyais	que nous nettoyions
		nous nettoyions	que vous nettoyiez
		vous nettoyiez	
avoir nettoyé			
j'ai nettoyé			que j'aie nettoyé
placer (et tous les verbes en **-cer**)	je place	nous plaçons	ils placent
je placerai	place	en plaçant	que je place
	plaçons		
je placerais	placez		
	il plaça	je plaçais	que nous placions
		nous placions	que vous placiez
		vous placiez	
avoir placé			
j'ai placé			que j'aie placé

II. Verbes irréguliers

---

apercevoir (et **recevoir, décevoir**)		nous apercevons j'aperçois	ils aperçoivent
j'apercevrai j'apercevrais	aperçois apercevons apercevez	en apercevant	que j'aperçoive
	il aperçut	j'apercevais nous apercevions vous aperceviez	que nous apercevions que vous aperceviez
avoir aperçu j'ai aperçu			que j'aie aperçu
s'asseoir	je m'assieds	nous nous asseyons	ils s'asseyent
je m'assoirai je m'assoirais	assieds-toi asseyons-nous asseyez-vous	en s'asseyant	que je m'asseye
		je m'asseyais nous nous asseyions vous vous asseyiez	que nous nous asseyions que vous vous asseyiez
s'être assis je me suis assis	il s'assit		que je me sois assis
battre	je bats	nous battons	ils battent
je battrai je battrais	bats battons battez	en battant	que je batte
	il battit	je battais nous battions vous battiez	que nous battions que vous battiez
avoir battu j'ai battu			que j'aie battu
boire	je bois	nous buvons	ils boivent
je boirai je boirais	bois buvons buvez	en buvant	que je boive
	il but	je buvais nous buvions vous buviez	que nous buvions que vous buviez
avoir bu j'ai bu			que j'aie bu

conduire	je conduis	nous conduisons	ils conduisent
je conduirai	conduis conduisons conduisez	en conduisant	que je conduise
je conduirais	il conduisit	je conduisais nous conduisions vous conduisiez	que nous conduisions que vous conduisiez
avoir conduit j'ai conduit			que j'aie conduit

connaître (et **paraître, disparaître**)	je connais	nous connaissons	ils connaissent
je connaîtrai	connais connaissons connaissez	en connaissant	que je connaisse
	il connut	je connaissais nous connaissions vous connaissiez	que nous connaissions que vous connaissiez
avoir connu j'ai connu			que j'aie connu

courir	je cours	nous courons	ils courent
je courrai	cours courons courez	en courant	que je coure
je courrais	il courut	je courais nous courions vous couriez	que nous courions que vous couriez
avoir couru j'ai couru			que j'aie couru

croire	je crois	nous croyons	ils croient
je croirai	crois croyons croyez	en croyant	que je croie
je croirais	il crut	je croyais nous croyions vous croyiez	que nous croyions que vous croyiez
avoir cru j'ai cru			que j'aie cru

cueillir	je cueille	nous cueillons	ils cueillent
je cueillerai	cueille cueillons	en cueillant	que je cueille
je cueillerais	cueillez		
	il cueillit	je cueillais nous cueillions vous cueilliez	que nous cueillions que vous cueilliez
avoir cueilli j'ai cueilli			que j'aie cueilli

dire	je dis	nous disons	ils disent
je dirai	dis disons	en disant	que je dise
je dirais	dites		
	il dit	je disais nous disions vous disiez	que nous disions que vous disiez
avoir dit j'ai dit			que j'aie dit

devoir	je dois	nous devons	ils doivent
je devrai	(inusité)	en devant	que je doive
je devrais			
	il dut	je devais nous devions vous deviez	que nous devions que vous deviez
avoir dû j'ai dû			que j'aie dû

dormir	je dors	nous dormons	ils dorment
je dormirai	dors dormons	en dormant	que je dorme
je dormirais	dormez		
	il dormit	je dormais nous dormions vous dormiez	que nous dormions que vous dormiez
avoir dormi j'ai dormi			que j'aie dormi

écrire	j'écris	nous écrivons	ils écrivent
j'écrirai	écris écrivons	en écrivant	que j'écrive
j'écrirais	écrivez		
	il écrivit	j'écrivais nous écrivions vous écriviez	que nous écrivions que vous écriviez
avoir écrit j'ai écrit			que j'aie écrit

faire	je fais	nous faisons	ils font
je ferai	fais faisons	en faisant	que je fasse
je ferais	faites		
	il fit	je faisais nous faisions vous faisiez	que nous fassions que vous fassiez
avoir fait j'ai fait			que j'aie fait

falloir	il faut		
il faudra			qu'il faille
il faudrait		il fallait	
	il fallut		
avoir fallu il a fallu			qu'il ait fallu

fuir	je fuis	nous fuyons	ils fuient
je fuirai	fuis fuyons	en fuyant	que je fuie
je fuirais	fuyez		
	il fuit	je fuiyais nous fuiyions vous fuiyiez	que nous fuiyions que vous fuiyiez
avoir fui j'ai fui			que j'aie fui

lire	je lis	nous lisons	ils lisent
je lirai	lis	en lisant	que je lise
je lirais	lisons		
	lisez		
		je lisais	
	il lut	nous lisions	que nous lisions
		vous lisiez	que vous lisiez
avoir lu			
j'ai lu			que j'aie lu

mettre	je mets	nous mettons	ils mettent
je mettrai	mets	en mettant	que je mette
je mettrais	mettons		
	mettez		
		je mettais	
	il mit	nous mettions	que nous mettions
		vous mettiez	que vous mettiez
avoir mis			
j'ai mis			que j'aie mis

mourir	je meurs	nous mourons	ils meurent
je mourrai	meurs	en mourant	que je meure
je mourrais	mourons		
	mourez		
		je mourais	
	il mourut	nous mourions	que nous mourions
		vous mouriez	que vous mouriez
être mort			
je suis mort			que je sois mort

naître	je nais	nous naissons	ils naissent
je naîtrai	nais	en naissant	que je naisse
je naîtrais	naissons		
	naissez		
		je naissais	
	il naquit	nous naissions	que nous naissions
		vous naissiez	que vous naissiez
être né			
je suis né			que je sois né

ouvrir	j'ouvre	nous ouvrons	ils ouvrent
j'ouvrirai	ouvre ouvrons	en ouvrant	que j'ouvre
j'ouvrirais	ouvrez		
	il ouvrit	j'ouvrais nous ouvrions vous ouvriez	que nous ouvrions que vous ouvriez
avoir ouvert j'ai ouvert			que j'aie ouvert
partir	je pars	nous partons	ils partent
je partirai	pars partons	en partant	que je parte
je partirais	partez		
	il partit	je partais nous partions vous partiez	que nous partions que vous partiez
être parti je suis parti			que je sois parti
peindre	je peins	nous peignons	ils peignent
je peindrai	peins peignons	en peignant	que je peigne
je peindrais	peignez		
	il peignit	je peignais nous peignions vous peigniez	que nous peignions que vous peigniez
avoir peint j'ai peint			que j'aie peint
plaire	je plais	nous plaisons	ils plaisent
je plairai	plais plaisons	en plaisant	que je plaise
je plairais	plaisez		
	il plut	je plaisais nous plaisions vous plaisiez	que nous plaisions que vous plaisiez
avoir plu j'ai plu			que j'aie plu

pleuvoir	il pleut		
il pleuvra			qu'il pleuve
il pleuvrait		il pleuvait	
	il plut		
avoir plu il a plu			qu'il ait plu

pouvoir	je peux	nous pouvons	ils peuvent
je pourrai		en pouvant	que je puisse
je pourrais			
	il put	je pouvais nous pouvions vous pouviez	que nous puissions que vous puissiez
avoir pu j'ai pu			que j'aie pu

prendre	je prends	nous prenons	ils prennent
je prendrai	prends prenons	en prenant	que je prenne
je prendrais	prenez		
	il prit	je prenais nous prenions vous preniez	que nous prenions que vous preniez
avoir pris j'ai pris			que j'aie pris

rire	je ris	nous rions	ils rient
je rirai	ris rions	en riant	que je rie
je rirais	riez		
	il rit	je riais nous riions vous riiez	que nous riions que vous riiez
avoir ri j'ai ri			que j'aie ri

savoir	je sais	nous savons	ils savent
je saurai	sache sachons	en sachant	que je sache
je saurais	sachez		
	il sut	je savais nous savions vous saviez	que nous sachions que vous sachiez
avoir su j'ai su			que j'aie su

sentir	je sens	nour sentons	ils sentent
je sentirai	sens sentons	en sentant	que je sente
je sentirais	sentez		
	il sentit	je sentais nous sentions vous sentiez	que nous sentions que vous sentiez
avoir senti j'ai senti			que j'aie senti

sortir	je sors	nous sortons	ils sortent
je sortirai	sors sortons	en sortant	que je sorte
je sortirais	sortez		
	il sortit	je sortais nous sortions vous sortiez	que nous sortions que vous sortiez
être sorti je suis sorti			que je sois sorti

suivre	je suis	nous suivons	ils suivent
je suivrai	suis suivons	en suivant	que je suive
je suivrais	suivez		
	il suivit	je suivais nous suivions vous suiviez	que nous suivions que vous suiviez
avoir suivi j'ai suivi			que j'aie suivi

tenir	je tiens	nous tenons	ils tiennent
je tiendrai	tiens	en tenant	que je tienne
je tiendrais	tenons tenez		
	il tint	je tenais nous tenions vous teniez	que nous tenions que vous teniez
avoir tenu j'ai tenu			que j'aie tenu

valoir	il vaut		
il vaudra			qu'il vaille
il vaudrait		il valait	
	il valut		
avoir valu il a valu			qu'il ait valu

venir	je viens	nous venons	ils viennent
je viendrai	viens	en venant	que je vienne
je viendrais	venons venez		
	il vint	je venais nous venions vous veniez	que nous venions que vous veniez
être venu je suis venu			que je sois venu

vivre	je vis	nous vivons	ils vivent
je vivrai	vis	en vivant	que je vive
je vivrais	vivons vivez		
	il vécut	je vivais nous vivions vous viviez	que nous vivions que vous viviez
avoir vécu j'ai vécu			que j'aie vécu

voir	je vois	nous voyons	ils voient
je verrai	vois voyons	en voyant	que je voie
je verrais	voyez		
	il vit	je voyais nous voyions vous voyiez	que nous voyions que vous voyiez
avoir vu j'ai vu			que j'aie vu

vouloir	je veux	nous voulons	ils veulent
je voudrai	veuille veuillons	en voulant	que je veuille
je voudrais	veuillez		
	il voulut	je voulais nous voulions vous vouliez	que nous voulions que vous vouliez
avoir voulu j'ai voulu			que j'aie voulu

DICTIONNAIRE

abord: d' ____ at first
abordable reasonable (price)
accord: d' ____ agreed; **être d'** ____ to agree
un **achat** purchase
acheter to buy
un **accrochage** collision
une **action** share of stock
une **addition** bill
adieu farewell, good-bye (hello, in some parts of France)
adroit skillful
une **affaire** affair; bargain
un **agent de police** policeman
agir: il s'agit de it is a question of; it is about
agréable agreeable, pleasant
une **aide** aid, help
aider to help, to aid
une **aile** wing
aimer to love; ____ **mieux** to prefer
ainsi thus, so, that way
un **air: en l'** ____ up
une **aise** ease; **être à l'** ____ to be "well-off"
ajouter to add
aliéné crazy, mad
une **alimentation** food; un **magasin d'** ____ grocery store
aller to go; **s'en** ____ to go away
allumer to light
une **allumette** match
alors then
une **alouette** lark
un **amant** lover
une **âme** soul
aménagé set up
amener to bring
un **ami** friend
un **amour** love
amoureux de in love with; **les amoureux** the lovers
s' **amuser** to have fun
un **an** a year; **le nouvel** ____ New Year
ancien, ancienne ancient, old, former

un **âne** donkey
un **ange** angel
une **année** year
un **anniversaire** birthday
août August
apercevoir to see, to perceive
un **appareil (photo)** camera
appeler to call; **s'** ____ to be named
apporter to bring
apprendre to learn
après after
après-midi (*m.* or *f.*) afternoon
un **arbre** tree
un **argent** money; silver
arranger to fix
s' **arranger** to manage
arrêter to arrest, to stop
arrière: en ____ behind
arriver to arrive; to happen
arroser to water
un **asile** asylum
s' **asseoir** to sit down
assez enough
une **assiette** plate
un **atelier** workshop
attacher to tie; to fasten
attendre to wait
attirer to attract
attraper to catch
augmenter to increase
aujourd'hui today
au revoir good-bye
aussi too
autant as much
une **auto** car
auto-stop hitchhiking; **faire de l'** ____ to hitchhike
une **autoroute** freeway
autour: ____ **de** around
autre other
autrefois formerly
autrement otherwise
autre part elsewhere
avant before
un **avare** miser, greedy person
avare (*adj.*) greedy
avarice (*f.*) greed, greediness

avec with
un **avenir** future
un **avion** plane
un **avis** advice; **à mon** ____ in my opinion
un **avocat** a lawyer
avoir to have
un **avortement** abortion

un **baccalauréat** bachelor's degree
une **bagnole** (*slang*) car
une **bague** ring
se **baigner** to bathe, to swim
un **bain** bath
un **baiser** kiss
une **baisse** fall
baisser to lower
un **bal** dance
une **balade** walk
un **balai** broom
balayer to sweep
un **balayeur** street sweeper
une **balle** ball; bullet
un **ballon** (foot)ball
banal trite
un **banc** bench
une **banlieue** suburb
une **banque** bank
un **banquier** banker
une **barbe** beard; **quelle** ____ what a drag
un **bas** stocking
bas, basse (*adj.*) low
bas: en ____ downstairs
une **bataille** battle
un **bateau** boat
un **bâtiment** building
bâtir to build
un **bâton** a stick
battre to beat; **se** ____ to fight
beau beautiful; **il fait** ____ the weather is nice; **avoir** ____ to do in vain
beaucoup a lot; ____ **de** much, many
un **besoin** need; **avoir** ____ **de** to need
bête (*adj.*) stupid
une **bête** animal
une **bêtise** silly thing, wrong thing

un **beurre** butter
une **bibliothèque** library
une **bicyclette** bicycle
bien well
bientôt soon; **à** ____ see you soon
la **bière** beer
un **bigoudi** hair curler
une **bijouterie** jewelry store
un **billet** ticket
une **biscotte** zwieback
un **bistrot** local pub
blanc, blanche white
une **blanchisserie** laundromat
blesser to wound
une **blessure** a wound
un **bobo** little sore
un **bœuf** ox, beef
boire to drink
le **bois** wood
une **boîte** box; **les boîtes de nuit** nightclubs
bon good
un **bonbon** candy
bonjour! good day, good morning
bon marché cheap
bondé jammed
une **bonne** maid
un **bord** edge; **le** ____ **de la mer** seashore
une **bouche** mouth
un **boucher** butcher
une **boucherie** butcher shop
un **boudin** blood sausage
bouffer to guzzle, to wolf (food)
bouger to move
une **bouillabaisse** fish soup
bouillir to boil
un **boulanger** baker; ____**ère** baker's wife
une **boulangerie** bakery
Bourse (*f.*) Stock Exchange; Wall Street
une **bourse d'étudiant** scholarship
bousculer to knock down
un **bout** end, tip; **au** ____ **de** at the end of
une **bouteille** bottle
un **bouton** button, bud
un **bras** arm
brave brave, courageous

un **break**   station wagon
briller   to shine
un **brin**   bit; twig
une **brosse**   brush; **la** _____ **à dents**
toothbrush
un **brouillard**   fog
un **bruit**   noise
une **brume**   fog, mist
brun, brune   brown
brunir   to turn brown, to tan
une **bruyère**   heather
un **bureau**   office; writing desk

ça   that
un **cabinet**   office, study; **les** _____ **s**
restroom
cacher   to hide
cachette: en _____   in secret
un **caddie**   cart in a store
un **cafard**   cockroach; **avoir le** _____   to
have the blues
un **camion**   truck
une **campagne**   countryside
un **canard**   duck
un **caoutchouc**   rubber
une **caravane**   trailer
la **carrière**   career
une **carte**   map
casser   to break
une **casserole**   pot
un **cauchemar**   nightmare
une **ceinture**   belt
celle, celle-ci (_f._)   this one
celles, celles-ci (_f._)   these ones
un **cent**   hundred
une **centaine**   around one hundred
chacun, chacune   each one
un **chagrin**   grief
un **chahut**   rough housing
une **chaîne**   chain, assembly line
une **chaise**   chair
un **châlet**   mountain cabin
une **chambre**   bedroom
un **champ**   field
une **chance**   luck; **avoir de la** _____   to
be lucky
une **chandelle**   candle
une **chanson**   song
chanter   to sing

une **chanteuse**   singer
un **chapeau**   hat
chaque (_adj._)   each
chasse (_f._)   hunting
un **chat**   cat
un **château**   castle
chaud   hot, warm; **il fait** _____   the
weather is hot; **avoir** _____   to be hot
un **chauffard**   bad driver
une **chaussette**   sock
une **chaussure**   shoe
une **cheminée**   fireplace, chimney
une **chemise**   shirt
cher, chère   dear, expensive
chercher   to look for
un **cheval**   horse
un **chevalier**   knight
chevaline (la boucherie)   horsemeat
butchershop
les **cheveux**   hair; **un cheveu**   one hair
un **chevron**   rafter
chez   at the house of
chic   elegant
un **chien**   dog
une **chienne**   bitch
des **chiffons** (_m._)   rags
chimie (_f._)   chemistry
la **Chine**   China
un **Chinois**   Chinese
choisir   to choose
un **choix**   choice
un **chômage**   unemployment
un **chômeur**   unemployed person
une **chose**   thing
ciel (_m._)   sky
un **cil**   eyelash
un **cinéma**   movie theater, cinema,
"movies"
une **circulation**   traffic
un **citron**   lemon
une **citronnade**   lemonade
clair(e)   clear; **au** _____ **de la lune**
in the moonlight
un **clochard**   tramp, hobo
un **cochon**   pig
un **cœur**   heart; **avoir mal au** _____   to
have a stomach ache
(se) **coiffer**   to brush one's hair
un **coiffeur**   hairdresser, barber
un **coin**   corner, place

une **colchique** colchicum (fall crocus-like flower)
colère (*f.*) anger; **être en** _____ to be angry
combien de how much, how many
comme as, how
comment how, what?
une **commode** chest of drawers; (*adj.*) practical
comprendre to understand
un **comptoir** counter
concevoir to conceive
concierge (*m.* ou *f.*) house or apartment manager
un **concours** competitive exam
conduire to drive
une **conduite d'eau** water pipe
une **conférence** lecture
un **congé payé** paid holiday
connaître to know
un **conseil** advice
construire to construct, to build
un **conte** short story; _____ **de fées** fairy tale
contre against
convenable correct
une **convention collective** collective bargaining
une **copie** paper
un **coq** rooster
coquin naughty
une **corde** rope
un **cordonnier** shoemaker
un **corps** body
corriger to correct
une **côte** hill; coast
un **côté** side; **à** _____ near; **à** _____ **de** next to
une **côtelette** rib
un **cou** neck
un **coucher** bedtime
se **coucher** to go to bed
coudre sew
coulant permissive
couler to flow
un **coup** blow; **un** _____ **de téléphone** phone call; _____ **de pompe** sudden feeling of tiredness; **tout à** _____ suddenly
couper to cut

courant current, fluent
courir to run
un **cours** course
les **courses** races, horse races, errands
court short
un **coussin** cushion, pillow
un **couteau** knife
coûter to cost
une **coutume** custom
couture (*f.*) sewing
une **couturière** seamstress; **couturier** (*m.*) designer
un **couvercle** lid
un **couvert** knife-fork-spoon
une **couverture** bed cover
couvrir to cover
cracher to spit
une **cravate** tie
un **crayon** pencil
une **crème** cream
une **crémerie** dairy store
un **crémier** dairy store keeper
un **cri** cry, shout
crier to shout
croire to believe; **cru** believed; raw
les **croûlants** (*familiar*) old people
croûler to fall apart
cueillir to pick
une **cuillère** spoon
un **cuir** leather
cuire to cook
une **cuisine** kitchen
une **cuisinière** stove, cook (*f.*)
une **culotte** tight pants, panties
un **cultivateur** farmer

une **dame** lady
dans in
un **débouché** opportunity
debout standing up
se **débrouiller** to manage, to muddle through
un **début** beginning; **au** _____ in the beginning
décevoir to deceive
un **déchet** waste (garbage)
un **découragement** discouragement
découvrir to discover

un **dédale** maze
dedans inside
un **défaut** shortcoming
défendre to forbid
déguster to enjoy
dehors outside
déjà already
un **déjeuner** lunch; **un petit** _____
breakfast
déjeuner to lunch
demain tomorrow
demander to ask
se **demander** to wonder
déménager to move
une **demeure** house
demeurer to stay; to live
demi half
démolir to demolish
une **dent** tooth
un **départ** departure
dépenser to spend
dépensier (_m._ ou _f._) spender
depuis since; _____ **que** since
déranger to bother
dernier last
dérouler to unroll
derrière (_adv._ et _prép._) behind; —
(_nom m._)
descendre to go down
se **déshabiller** to undress
un **dessin** drawing
dessiner to draw
dessous under; **au-**_____, **au** _____
de underneath
dessus above; **au-**_____, **au** _____
de on top of
deux two
deuxième second
devant (_adv._ et _prép._) in front
devenir to become
devoir to owe; to have to
un **devoir** duty
une **dictée** dictation
Dieu (_m._) God
dimanche (_m._) Sunday
dîner to have dinner
un **dîner** dinner, supper
dire to say
diriger to direct; **se** _____ to direct
oneself

un **discours** speech
discuter to argue
disparaître to disappear
un **disque** record
dix ten
une **dizaine** around ten
un **djebel** African mountain
un **doigt** finger
dommage: c'est _____ too bad!
donc then, therefore
donner to give
dormir to sleep
un **dos** back
doubler to pass (in a car)
une **douche** shower
doux, douce sweet, soft
douze twelve
une **douzaine** a dozen
un **drapeau** flag
une **drogue** drug, remedy
une **droguerie** variety or hardware store
un **droguiste** variety or hardware store
keeper
droit (_adj._) right; **les droits** tuition
dur hard
durer to last

eau (_f._) water
un **éboueur** garbage collector
un **écart** difference
une **écharpe** scarf
un **éclair** lightning
éclairer to give light to
une **école** school
économe thrifty
l' **économie** (_f._) economy
les **économies** savings
économique economic
les **économiquement faibles** underprivileged
économiser to save
écouter to listen
écrire to write
un **écrivain** writer
un **écu** gold coin
effacer to erase
égal equal
une **église** church
égratigner to scratch

élève (*m.* ou *f.*) student, pupil
élever to raise; **bien élevé** well-mannered; **mal élevé** ill-mannered
un **embouteillage** bottleneck, traffic jam
embrasser to kiss
emmener to take (someone to a place)
empêcher to prevent
un **emploi** use; job
employer to employ, to use
empoisonner to poison
emporter to take (something) along
emprunter to borrow
un **enchaînement** linking of two sounds
encore again
s' **endormir** to go to sleep
un **endroit** place; **à l'**____ right side on
s' **énerver** to become nervous, irritated
une **enfance** childhood
l' **enfant** (*m.* ou *f.*) child; **un** ____ **arriéré** retarded child
enfin finally, at last, in short
engager to hire
enlever to take off
un **ennui** boredom, worry, problem
s' **ennuyer** to get bored
ennuyeux boring, bothersome
enregistrer to check (luggage)
enseignement (*m.*) teaching profession
enseigner to teach
ensemble together
un **ensemble** a suit; **un grand** ____ big housing development
ensuite then, next
entendre to hear
entier whole
entourer to surround
entre between
entretenir to keep up
envers: à l'____ wrong side out or backwards
une **envie** envy; **avoir** ____ **de** to feel like
environ about
les **environs** surroundings

envoyer to send
épais thick
une **épaule** shoulder
une **épicerie** grocery store
un **épicier** grocer
épouser to marry
épuiser to exhaust
une **équipe** team
un **escalier** stairway
un **escargot** snail
une **esclave** slave
un **escroc** swindler
espagnol (*adj.*) Spanish
Espagnol(e) Spaniard
espérer to hope
un **esprit** spirit, wit, mood
essayer to try
une **essence** gasoline
essuyer to wipe
un **estomac** stomach
un **étage** floor
une **étagère** shelf
un **étain** tin
un **état** state, condition
un **été** summer
une **étoile** star
étonnant surprising
étonner to surprise
étrange strange
un **étranger** stranger, foreigner; **à l'**____ abroad
une **étrangère** stranger, foreigner
être to be
un **être** a being
étroit narrow
une **étude** study
un **étudiant, une étudiante** student
étudier to study
évident obvious
éviter to avoid
exaltant exciting, thrilling
exprimer to express

fâché sorry, angry
se **fâcher** to get mad
une **façon** way; **de toute** ____ anyway
un **facteur** mailman
faim (*f.*) hunger; **avoir** ____ to be hungry

faire to do, to make; **tout à fait** entirely

falloir: il faut must

la **famine** hunger

fauché broke

une **faute** mistake

un **fauteuil** armchair

une **femme** woman, wife; **la _____ au foyer** housewife; **une _____ de ménage** charwoman, cleaning lady

une **fenêtre** window

fer (*m.*) iron

une **ferme** farm

fermer to close

un **fermier** farmer

ferraille (*f.*) metal, junk

une **fête** holiday

un **feu** fire or light (for lighting a cigarette)

une **feuille** leaf; **_____ de papier** sheet of paper

février February

fier, fière proud

une **fièvre** fever

une **figure** face

un **fil** thread; **_____ de fer** barbed wire

un **filet** net

une **fille** girl; daughter

un **fils** son

une **fin** end

finir to finish

une **fleur** flower

fleurir to blossom

un **flic** cop

flotter to float

une **foi** faith

un **foie** liver

une **fois** time

un **fond** bottom

un **fonctionnaire** civil servant

fondre to melt

une **forêt** forest

forfaitaire (*adj.*) package deal

formidable great, wonderful

fort strong

fou, folle crazy

foudre (*f.*) lightning

foudroyant thundering

une **foule** crowd

une **fourchette** fork

une **fourrure** fur

frais, fraîche fresh

franc, franche frank

un **franc** franc

frapper to knock; to hit

un **frère** brother

un **frigidaire** refrigerator

frisé curly

froid cold; **avoir _____** to be cold; **il fait _____** the weather is cold

un **fromage** cheese

un **front** forehead; front

une **frontière** border

un **fruit** fruit

fuir to flee

une **fumée** smoke

fumer to smoke

une **fusée** rocket

un **fusil** shotgun

gagner to win

les **gains** (*m.*) earnings

une **galette** round-shaped, flat pastry

un **gant** glove

un **garçon** boy

garder to keep

un **gardien dans un parc** ranger

une **gare** station

un **gâteau** cake, pastry

gauche left; **à _____, à _____ de** on, to the left

un **géant** giant

un **gendarme** highway patrolman

gêner to bother

un **génie** genius

un **genou** knee

un **genre** gender

les **gens** (*m. pl.*) people

gentil nice

une **gestion** management

une **glace** mirror; ice, ice cream

un **glaçon** ice cube

une **gorge** throat

un **gouffre** gap

goût (*m.*) taste

un **goûter** snack

goûter to taste

une **goutte** drop

grâce à thanks to

grandir to grow up
une **grand-mère** grandmother
un **grand-père** grandfather
les **grands-parents** grand-parents
une **grève** strike
une **grille** gate
une **grippe** flu
gris grey
gros fat
grossir to put on weight
guère: ne...guère not much
guérir to cure
une **guerre** war
guetter to watch; to threaten
un **guichet** booth, window

habiller to dress
un **habit** formal suit
habiter to live
une **habitude** habit; **d'**____ usually
s' **habituer à** to get used to
une **hache** hatchet
haché ground (meat)
haïr to hate
haut high
une **herbe** grass
un **héritage** inheritance
hériter to inherit the fortune of
one's parents
une **héroïne** heroine
un **héroïsme** heroism
un **héros** hero
une **heure** hour
heureusement happily
heureux, heureuse happy
hier yesterday
une **hirondelle** swallow
une **histoire** story
histoire (*f.*) history
un **hiver** winter; **en plein** ____ in the
middle of winter
un **homme** man
une **honte** shame; **avoir** ____ to be
ashamed
une **huile** oil
une **huître** oyster
humanité (*f.*) mankind
une **humeur** mood; **être de bonne** ____
to be in a good mood; **être de**

mauvaise ____ to be in a bad mood
humide humid

ici here
ignorer to not know, to be ignorant
of
une **île** island
il y a there is, there are
une **image** picture
un **immeuble** apartment house
un **imper** raincoat
imperméable waterproof
un **impôt** tax
inconnu unknown
infirmier, infirmière nurse
ingénieux skillful
inonder to flood
inquiet worried
s' **inquiéter** to worry
une **inscription** registration; **les droits**
d'____ tuition
installer: s'installer to settle down
interdire to prohibit
inutile useless
un **invité** guest
ivre drunk
un **ivrogne** drunk

jaloux, jalouse jealous
jamais: (ne) jamais never
une **jambe** leg
un **jambon** ham
janvier January
Japon (*m.*) Japan
un **jardin** garden
jardiner to garden
jaune yellow
jaunir to turn yellow
jeter to throw
un **jeu** game
jeudi Thursday
jeune young; **un** ____ **homme**
young man; **une** ____ **fille** young
woman; **les jeunes gens** young
people or *pl.* of **jeune homme**
un **jeûne** fast
jeunesse (*f.*) youth
joli pretty

une **joue** cheek

jouer (de, à) to play, to gamble

un **jouet** toy

un **jour** day; **tous les jours** every day

un **journal** newspaper

journaliste (*m.* ou *f.*) reporter

une **journée** day

joyeux joyous

un **juge** judge

juger to judge

juif, juive Jew, Jewish

juillet July

juin June

une **jupe** skirt

un **jus** juice

jusqu'à: ____ **ce que** until

là there; ____**-bas** over there

laid ugly

laideur (*f.*) ugliness

une **laine** wool

laïque non-religious

laisser to let, to allow

lait (*m.*) milk

une **lame** blade

large wide; **au** ____ in the wide open sea

une **larme** tear

laver to wash; **se** ____ to wash oneself

une **lecture** reading

léger light

un **légume** vegetable

lent slow

une **lessive** laundry, washing of clothes

lever to raise; **se** ____ to get up

une **lèvre** lip

une **liaison** linking

un **libraire** bookseller

une **librairie** bookstore

un **lieu** place; **avoir** ____ to take place; **au** ____ **de** instead of

une **ligne** line

lire to read

un **lit** bed

un **litre** liter

une **livre** pound

un **livre** book

une **loi** law

loin far; ____ **de** far from

un **loisir** leisure

longtemps long, a long time

louer to rent

un **loup** wolf; **le** ____ **garou** the big bad wolf

lourd heavy

un **loyer** rent

une **lumière** light

lundi Monday

une **lune** moon

lunettes (*f. pl.*) eye glasses

lutter to fight

un **lyeée** high school

un **lycéen, une lycéenne** high school boy, girl

une **machine:** ____ **à écrire** typewriter; ____ **à laver** washing machine; ____ **à sous** slot machine

un **magasin** store

mai May

maigre thin

maigrir to lose weight

un **maillot de bain** swimsuit

une **main** hand

maintenant now

une **mairie** city hall

mais but

une **maison** house; ____ **de jeux** gambling house

un **maître** master

une **maîtresse** mistress

mal bad; **avoir** ____ **à** to hurt; **un** ____ evil

malade sick

une **maladie** sickness

un **malheur** unhappiness

malheureux unhappy

une **maman** mother

une **manche** sleeve

la **Manche** Channel

manger to eat; **faire** ____ to feed

manquer to miss, to lack

un **manteau** overcoat

se **maquiller** to put make-up on

un **marché** market; **bon** ____ cheap

marcher to walk; to work

mardi Tuesday

une **marée** tide
un **mari** husband
un **mariage** wedding
se **marier** to marry
Maroc (*m.*) Morocco
mars March
un **matin** morning
mauvais bad; **il fait** ___ the weather is bad
un **mécanicien** mechanic
méchant mean
un **médecin** physician
la **médecine** art of medicine
un **médicament** medicine, drug
meilleur better
mêler to mix
même same, even; **moi** ___ myself; **lui** ___ himself
le **ménage** housecleaning; **faire le** ___ to clean house; **la femme de** ___ charwoman; **les ordures ménagères** garbage
un **mensonge** lie
mentir to lie
une **mer** sea
merci thank you
mercredi Wednesday
une **mère** mother
mériter to deserve
merveilleux wonderful
un **métier** trade, job
un **métro** subway
mettre to put, to put on; **se** ___ **à** to begin
un **meuble** piece of furniture
un **meunier** miller
Mexique (*m.*) Mexico
midi noon
Midi (*m.*) south of France
mieux better; **tant** ___ so much the better
mijoter to cook slowly, to simmer
milieu (*m.*) social sphere; **au** ___ in the middle of
mille thousand
un **milliard** billion
un **millier de** about a thousand
un **million** million
un **millionnaire** millionaire
mince slender

la **mine** complexion; **faire la** ___ to make a face
minuit midnight
misère (*f.*) poverty, destitution
moche crummy, ugly
moins less; **au** ___ at least; **moins...moins** the less . . . the less
un **mois** month
une **moitié** half
monde (*m.*) world
une **monnaie** change
monsieur Sir! mister
monter to go up
une **montre** watch
montrer to point at, to show
se **moquer de** to make fun of
un **morceau** a piece
mordre to bite
mort(e) dead
une **mort** death
un **mot** word or a note; **les gros mots** swear words
un **motard** cop on a motorcycle
une **motocyclette** motorcycle
mou, molle soft
une **mouche** fly
mouillé wet
un **moulin** windmill
mourir to die
un **moustique** mosquito
un **mouton** sheep, lamb
un **moyen** way, means
moyen average
muet mute
un **mur** wall
mûr ripe

nager to swim
naître to be born
une **nappe** tablecloth
natal native
un **naufrage** wreck
neige (*f.*) snow; **il neige** it snows
nettoyer to clean
neuf nine; brand new
neuvième ninth
un **neveu** nephew
un **nez** nose
ni...ni neither . . . nor

noir black; **un** ＿ black man
nommer to give the name of
non plus neither
nord (*m.*) north
une **note** (school) mark
nouveau, nouvel (*m.*), **nouvelle** new
une **nouvelle** piece of news
un **nuage** cloud
une **nuit** night
nulle part nowhere
un **numéro** number

obligatoire compulsory
obliger to force
obtenir to obtain
une **occasion** opportunity
occuper to occupy
s' **occuper de** to take care of
un **œil** eye (*pl.* **yeux**)
un **œuf** egg
un **oiseau** bird
une **ombre** shade, shadow
onze eleven
or (*m.*) gold
un **orage** storm
une **oreille** ear
un **os** bone
oser to dare
ôter to take off
ou or
où where
oublier to forget
ouest (*m.*) west
oui yes
un **ouragan** hurricane
un **ours** bear
un **outil** tool
ouvert(e) open
un **ouvrier** laborer
ouvrir to open
oxyde de carbone (*m.*) carbon
monoxide

un **pain** bread
paix (*f.*) peace
un **palais** palace
pâlir to turn pale
une **pancarte** sign, poster

un **panier** basket
une **panne** breakdown
un **pantalon** trousers, pants
un **papillon** butterfly
Pâques Easter
un **parapluie** umbrella
un **parcmètre** parking meter
pareil similar
un **parent** parent; relative; **les parents**
(*pl.*)
paresseux lazy
parier to bet
un **parking** parking lot
parler to speak
une **partie** part; party
partir to leave for
partout everywhere
un **pas de porte** doorstep
un **passant** a passer-by
passé gone, faded; ＿ (*m.*) past
une **pâte** paste, dough
le **pâté** meat pie
la **pâtée** dog or cat food
un **patois** local language, dialect
une **patte** paw
pauvre poor
la **pauvreté** poverty
payer to pay; ＿ **comptant** to
pay cash
un **pays** country
un **paysage** landscape
peau (*f.*) skin
pêcher to fish
peindre to paint
une **peine** sorrow
une **pelouse** lawn
pendant during
une **pendule** clock
penser à to think of
la **Pentecôte** Pentecost
un **percepteur** tax collector
perdre to lose
un **père** father
un **permis de conduire** driver's license
une **perruche** parakeet
peser to weigh
petit small, short
peu little; **un** ＿ a little
une **peur** fear; **avoir** ＿ to be afraid
peut-être maybe

une **phrase**   sentence
une **pièce**   coin; room; play
un **pied**   foot
un **pilule**   a pill
   pincer   to pinch
une **piscine**   swimming pool
un **placard**   cupboard; closet
une **place**   place; seat; square
   placer   to place
une **plage**   beach
 se **plaindre**   to complain
   plaire   to please
   plaisanter   to kid, to joke
une **plaisanterie**   joke
un **plaisir**   pleasure
un **plat**   dish
un **plateau**   tray; plateau
   plein   full
   pleurer   to cry
   pleuvoir   to rain
   plonger   to dive
   pluie (*f.*)   rain
une **plume**   feather or pen (old style)
   plumer   to pluck
   plus   more; **plus...plus**   the more . . .
   the more
   plusieurs   several
un **pneu**   tire
une **poche**   pocket
un **poids**   weight
un **poil**   hair
un **poing**   fist
une **poire**   pear
un **poisson**   fish
une **poissonnerie**   fish market
un **poissonnier**   fish monger
une **poitrine**   chest; breast
une **pomme**   apple; **une** ____ **de terre**
   potato
un **pompier**   fireman
un **pont**   bridge
une **popote**   *familiar* for cooking; (*adj.*)
   "bourgeois," stay-at-home type
une **porte**   door
un **portefeuille**   wallet
   poser   to put; ____ **une question**   to
   ask a question
un **pot**   pot, jar
une **poterie**   pottery
une **poubelle**   garbage pail; **faire la**
   ____ collect things in garbage

un **pouce**   thumb
une **poule**   hen
un **pouls**   pulse
une **poupée**   doll
un **pourboire**   tip
un **pourcentage**   percentage
   pourquoi   why
   pourtant   however, yet
   pousser   to push; to grow
une **poutre**   beam
   pouvoir   to be able to
un **pré**   meadow
   prendre   to take, to catch
   près   near
   pressé: être ____   to be in a hurry
un **prêt à porter**   ready-to-wear
   prêter   to lend
   prévoyant   prudent
   printemps (*m.*)   spring
un **procès verbal**   citation
   prochain   next
un **produit**   product
   profiter   to take advantage of
   profond   deep
 se **promener**   to take a walk
   propos: à ____ **de**   speaking of
   propre   clean
   puisque   since
   punir   to punish

   quand   when
   quant à   as for
un **quart**   quarter
un **quartier**   district of town
   quelque chose   something
   quelquefois   sometimes
   quelqu'un   somebody
une **querelle**   quarrel
une **queue**   tail; **faire la** ____   to stand
   in line
   quitter   to quit
   quoi   what

une **racine**   root
   raconter   to relate, to tell
un **radical**   stem
une **raison**   reason; **avoir** ____   to be
   right
   ramasser   to pick up

un **rang** rank, row

se **rappeler** to remember

ras: en avoir _____ **l'bol** to have it up to here, to be fed up with the whole thing

se **raser** to shave; to be bored

un **raton** (_slang_) North African

une **ratonnade** beating up of North Africans

un **rayon** ray; aisle; shelf

rebutant unattractive

recevoir to receive; _____ **un diplôme final** to graduate

un **récit** narration

une **réclamation** complaint; **faire une** _____ to complain

un **reçu** note; receipt

redouté feared

réfléchir to think over

regarder to look at

une **règle** rule

une **reine** queen

remarquer to notice

rembourser to reimburse

remercier to thank

remuer to move, to stir

rencontrer to meet; to come across

rendre to give back

un **renseignement** information

une **rente** yearly income

rentrer to come back

réparer to repair

un **repas** meal

répondre to respond, to answer

un **représentant de commerce** salesman

résoudre to solve

respirer to breathe

ressembler à to look alike

ressentir to feel

un **reste** rest

rester to remain; **il reste** there remains, there is (something) left

un **retard** delay; **en** _____ late

retenir to reserve

retourner to go back

une **retraite** retirement; **prendre sa** _____ to retire

réussir to succeed

un **rêve** dream

(se) **réveiller** to wake up

revenir to come back

un **revenu** income

un **rez-de-chaussée** first floor

un **rhume** cold

riche rich, wealthy

une **richesse** wealth

une **ride** wrinkle

rien nothing

rire to laugh

riz (_m._) rice

une **rizière** rice paddy

un **roi** king

un **roman** novel; _____ **policier** detective story

ronfler to snore

un **rosbif** roast beef

rougir to blush

rouler to roll

une **route** route, road

roux, rousse red (hair)

une **rue** street

sable (_m._) sand

un **sac** bag, purse

saisir to seize

une **saison** season

un **salaud** pig

sale dirty

se **salir** to make oneself dirty

une **salle à manger** dining room

une **salle de bain** bathroom

un **salon** living room

Salut! Hi!

samedi Saturday

sang (_m._) blood

sans without

une **santé** health; **à votre** _____ to your health, cheers!

sauter to jump; **faire** _____ explode

sauvage savage, wild

(se) **sauver** to run away

savoir to know

scolaire: année _____ school year

un **secteur privé** private enterprise

un **sentiment** feeling

sentir to feel

une **serveuse** waitress

une **serviette** napkin; briefcase; towel

servir to serve; _____ **à** to be used for + _inf._; _____ **de** to be used as + _noun_ se **servir** to help oneself; ____ **de** to use

seul alone

un **siècle** century

une **sieste** nap; **faire** ____ to take a nap

un **sirop** syrup

ski (*m.*) skiing; **le** ____ **de fond** cross-country skiing

skier to ski

une **sœur** sister

une **soie** silk

soif (*f.*) thirst; **avoir** ____ to be thirsty

soigner to take care of

un **soin** care

un **soir** evening

une **soirée** evening party

soleil (*m.*) sun

sommeil (*m.*) sleep; **avoir** ____ to be sleepy

sonner to ring

sortir to go out

sot stupid

un **sou** penny

un **souci** worry

soucieux worried

souffrir to suffer

sourd deaf

sourire to smile; ____ (*nom m.*) smile

une **souris** mouse

sous under

souvent often

sucre (*m.*) sugar

sud (*m.*) south

Suisse (*f.*) Switzerland

suivant following

suivre to follow

une **surboum** teenager party

surgelé frozen

surmené overworked

surtout overall; especially

sympathique nice, likeable

tabac (*m.*) tobacco

un **tableau** painting; board

une **tache** stain

une **taille** waist; size

(se) **taire** to keep quiet

une **tante** aunt

une **tartine** slice of bread

une **tasse** cup

un **taudis** slum house

tellement...que so much . . . that

un **tempérament** nature, disposition

la **tempête** storm

temps (*m.*) weather; time; tense

terre (*f.*) earth

une **tête** head

tiercé (*m.*) betting on horses

un **timbre** stamp

un **tissage** weaving

tisser to weave

un **titre** title

une **toile** canvas

toilette (*f.*) cleaning up (for person); **faire sa** ____ to clean up; **les toilettes** restroom

un **toit** roof

tomber to fall

un **ton** tone

tonnant thundering

tonnerre (*m.*) thunder

tordu twisted

tort (*m.*): **avoir** ____ to be wrong

tôt early

toujours always

une **tour** tower

tourbillonner to whirl; **tomber en tourbillonnant** to spiral down

tourner to turn

tousser to cough

tout everything

tout le monde everybody

une **toux** cough

traduire to translate

train: être en ____ **de** to be doing something

traîner to lie about

une **traite** bill

transpirer to perspire

un **travail** work, job

traverser to cross

un **tremblement de terre** earthquake

tricher to cheat

tricoter to knit

tromper to deceive; **se** ____ to be mistaken

trop too much; **être de** ____ to be unwanted

un **trou** hole

troué   with holes
un **troupeau**   flock, herd
trouver   to find
une **truite**   trout
un **tube**   famous song
tuer   to kill
un **type**   type; kind guy

une **urne**   ballot box
une **usine**   factory
utile   useful

les **vacances** (*f. pl.*)   vacation
une **vache**   cow
vaisselle (*f.*)   dishes; **faire la** _____
to wash the dishes
une **valise**   valise, suitcase
varier   to vary
un **veau**   calf, veal
une **vedette**   movie star
une **vendeuse**   seller
vendre   to sell
vendredi   Friday
venir   to come; _____ **de**   to have just
vent (*m.*)   wind; **il fait du** _____   it
is windy
un **ventre**   abdomen, stomach, belly
un **verre**   glass
vert   green
un **veston**   jacket
un **vêtement**   clothing
une **viande**   meat
vide   empty
vider   to empty

vie (*f.*)   life
un **vieillard**   old man
vieille, vieux, vieil   old; **mon vieux**
old chap
vilain   ugly
une **ville**   city, town; **en** _____   in town,
to town
un **vin**   wine
une **virgule**   comma
un **visage**   face
vite   quickly
une **vitrine**   store window
vivre   to live
voici   here is
voilà   there is; that is all
voir   to see
un **voisin**   neighbor
une **voiture**   car
une **voix**   voice
un **volant**   steering wheel
voler   steal
un **voleur**   robber
vouloir   to want; _____ **dire**   to mean
un **voyage**   trip; **faire un** _____   to take
a trip
voyager   to take a trip
un **voyageur**   passenger
une **voyelle**   vowel
un **voyou**   hoodlum
vrai(e)   true
vraiment   truly

un **yaourt**   yogurt
les **yeux** (*pl.*)   eyes (*sing.* œil)

3 4 5 6 7 8 9 10

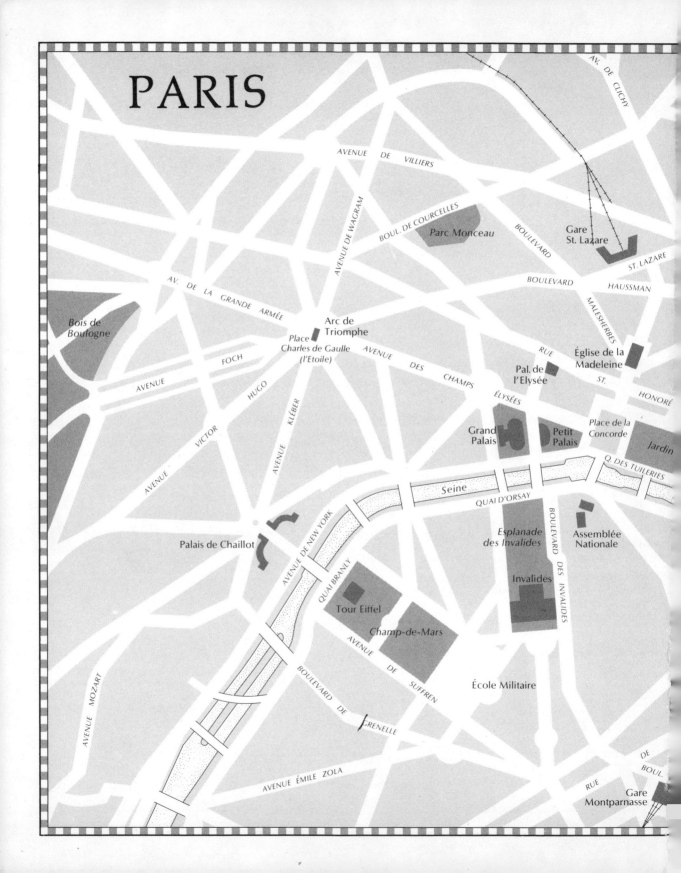